VISUAL QUICKSTART GUIDE

DREAMWEAVER 1.2

FOR WINDOWS AND MACINTOSH

J. Tarin Towers

Visual QuickStart Guide

Dreamweaver for Windows and Macintosh

J. Tarin Towers

Peachpit Press
1249 Eighth Street
Berkeley, CA 94710
(510) 524-2178
(510) 524-2221 (fax)

Find us on the World Wide Web at: http://www.peachpit.com

Visit this book's Web site at: http://www.peachpit.com/vqs/dreamweaver/

Published by Peachpit Press in association with Macromedia Press. Peachpit Press is a division of Addison Wesley Longman Publishing Company.

Editor: Corbin Collins
Copy editor: Vivian Perry
Production coordinators: Kate Reber, Amy Changar
Production: David Van Ness
Cover design: The Visual Group

Figures 1 and 2 in Chapter 5 are from Christian Cosas's home page at http://www.beanbagcentral.com/ccosas/.

Figures 1 through 4 in Chapter 13 are by Amy Franceschini for the Future Farmers Web site at http://www.futurefarmers.com/.

Figure 2 in Chapter 15 is of the "Slap a Spice Girl" Shockwave movie on the urban75 Web site at http://www.urban75.com/. The game was written by Paul Maguire/urban75 and all other artwork on the site is by Mike Slocombe.

ISBN: 0-201-35339-3

0 9 8 7 6 5 4

Printed and bound in the United States of America

Printed on recycled paper

Dedication

To Sean Porter, for the pitchfork.

Acknowledgements

I'd like to thank everyone who helped me with this book: Corbin Collins at Peachpit, for his persistence and encouragement; Vivian Perry, freelance copyeditor to the stars, for her keen eye and great sense of humor; David Van Ness for his clever layout skills, Kate Reber and Amy Changar for their patience and exactitude; technical editor Paul LaFarge, for watching for missteps on the tightrope; Karen Tucker, Beth Davis, and Jon Brovitz at Macromedia for getting me all the stuff I needed to write the book; Christian Cosas, Amy Franceschini, and Mike Slocombe, for lending me their art; Christian Crumlish, Chuck Green, N.C. Hanger, William R. Stanek, Bill Weinman, and countless other folks on the Studio B mailing list, a bottomless source of information; Derek Powazek, for the use of his Mac; Brenda Kienan, for getting me started; Sean Porter, Brian Matheson, and Mark Walsh, for learning me some of the technical ropes; and 9x9 Industries, for the tripod malaria.

TABLE OF CONTENTS

INTRODUCTION

Welcome to the *Dreamweaver 1.2 for Windows and Macintosh: Visual QuickStart Guide*! Dreamweaver is exciting software: it's simple to use and it's one of the very best WYSIWYG (What You See Is What You Get) editing tools to ever come down the pike.

Dreamweaver isn't just another visual HTML tool. It does do what all the best editors do: creates tables, edits frames, and switches easily from page view to HTML view.

But Dreamweaver goes way beyond the other editors to allow you to create Dynamic HTML (DHTML) gadgets and pages. Dreamweaver fully supports Cascading Style Sheets (CSS-1) as well as layers and JavaScript behaviors. It even includes its own DHTML animation tool: the Timelines inspector.

No matter what your level of Web experience, you can use Dreamweaver and this book. I'm assuming you've used some sort of page creation tool before, even if it's just a text editor. You should use this book if you're:

- An absolute beginner who wants an editor that writes great HTML.
- A graphic designer who's used to using document editors like Director, PageMaker, or Photoshop, but who isn't as proficient with HTML.
- An HTML expert who likes to hand code but wants automation of simple tasks.
- Frightened of Dynamic HTML.
- Someone who needs to learn Dreamweaver quickly.

QuickStart Conventions

If you've read a previous Visual QuickStart Guide, you know that this book is made up of two main components: numbered lists that take you step by step through the things you want learn, and illustrations that show you what the heck I'm talking about.

I explain what needs to be explained, but I don't pontificate about the acceleration of information technology or wax dramatic about proprietary tags.

✔ Tips

- In every chapter, you'll find tips like these that point out something extra-handy.
- Code in the book is set off in `code font`.
- Sometimes you can find extra tidbits of info in the figure captions, too.

Browsers Beware

I use sidebars to point out "extra" information about specific features, including HTML tricks that aren't directly supported by Dreamweaver.

This sidebar is about browser wars. I've made every effort to be fair to both the powerhouse browsers, Netscape Navigator (which I usually call Navigator, or just NN) and Microsoft Internet Explorer (called MSIE, or sometimes Explorer). I also point out differences important differences between them, which are most apparent when talking about 4.0 browsers.

What's in this Book

Here's a quick rundown of what I cover in this book.

Dreamweaver Basics

In the first two chapters I introduce you to the Dreamweaver interface. If you never want to look at any HTML when you use Dreamweaver, you don't have to; on the other hand, if you want to learn HTML, there's no better way than by creating a page and looking at the code you just made.

Web Page Basics

Chapters 3 and 4 talk about text and all the things you can do with it, and Chapter 5 describes linking in more detail than you thought possible. Chapter 6 gets you on your way with images—and Appendix A, on the Web site for this book, describes how to make client side image maps with the image map editor.

Tables, Frames, and Forms

Chapters 7–9 are what most folks consider the "intermediate" range in HTML—7 is tables, 8 is frames, and 9 is forms, all of which are much easier to construct in Dreamweaver than by hand.

Dynamic HTML

Then we get to the Dynamic part of the book. The components of DHTML are covered in Chapters 10-13. Chapter 10 covers Cascading Style Sheets. In Chapter 11, you'll learn about layers and all that goes with them, including absolute positioning. Chapter 12 covers Behaviors, a Chinese food menu way of putting together JavaScript actions—just choose one from column A and one from column B. And Chapter 13 discusses Timelines, Dreamweaver's DHTML animation tool.

Site Management

Chapter 14 discusses two ways of automating common tasks in Dreamweaver, Libraries and custom objects. Libraries are a site management tool, whereas you use custom objects to modify Dreamweaver's Insert functions. In Chapter 15, you'll learn everything you need to know about putting plug-ins and other multimedia content on your site. Appendix A on the companion Web site describes how to make your Web pages work and look the way you want them to in all kinds of browsers. And Chapter 16 is all about site management with Dreamweaver's Sites window, a full-fledged FTP client.

But Wait, There's More on the Web Site!

The companion Web site for this book contains lots and lots of links to developers' pages, handy shareware tools, and example sites, and because the page is on the Web, you don't have to type in a bunch of URLs. You'll also find online appendixes covering the image map editor, roundtrip HTML, and browser compatibility. I also include my own sample pages, including some DHTML I made just for this book. (You can only see the DHTML stuff if you're using a 4.0 or later browser, but the site is open to everyone, and I made it all using Dreamweaver, naturally.)

Visit http://www.peachpit.com/vqs/dreamweaver/ and let me know what you think of the book and the Web site by emailing dreamweaver@tarin.com.

Special to Mac Users

I wrote this book on a PC. I want to admit that up front. I love Macs, but my old Powerbook doesn't have a CD-ROM drive or Internet access. I repeatedly checked out the program on the Mac, as did my technical editor. The differences are negligible, as you can see in **Figures 1** and **2**.

There are some basic platform differences that will cause the screen shots to look slightly different. Windows windows (ha ha) have a menu bar affixed to each and every window, whereas the Mac menu bar is always at the top of the screen, and it changes based on the program you choose from the Application menu (the one in the upper right of the Mac screen, next to the clock).

Windows windows close by clicking on the close box on the upper right, whereas close boxes on the Mac are on the upper left. Occasionally, buttons will have different names. For instance, in some dialog boxes, the button says Browse in Windows and Choose on the Mac. They're always close enough.

HTML is HTML

Like the song, HTML remains the same, whether you construct it on a Mac or PC. Even better, Dreamweaver's Roundtrip HTML feature ensures that HTML you create outside the program will retain its formatting—although obvious errors, like unclosed tags, will be fixed.

The PC version of Dreamweaver comes with HomeSite, and the Mac version comes with BBEdit. You can set up either program to work with any HTML editor you like, however. See Appendix B, on the companion Web site for this book, to find out how to set up these editors and how Dreamweaver will treat your HTML.

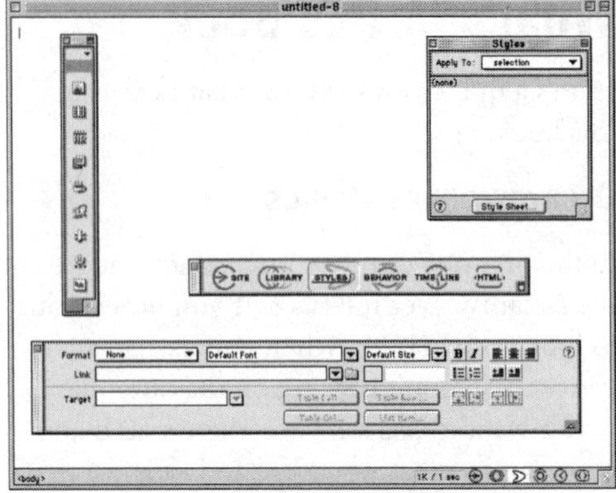

Figure 1 Dreamweaver's Document window and some of its floating windows, as seen on the Mac.

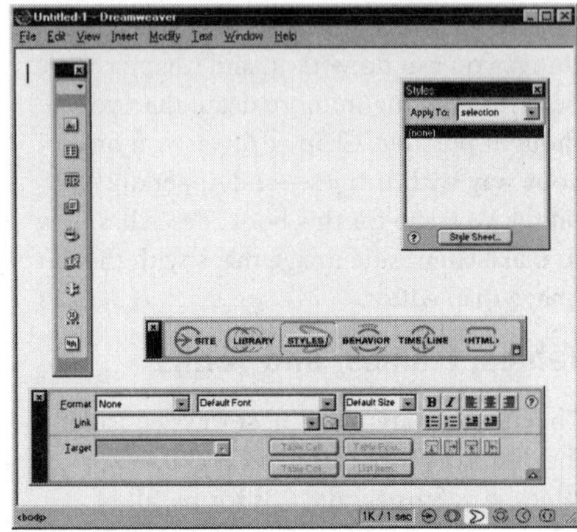

Figure 2 Dreamweaver's Document window and some of its floating windows, as seen on Windows. Not many differences other than the title bar and menu bar.

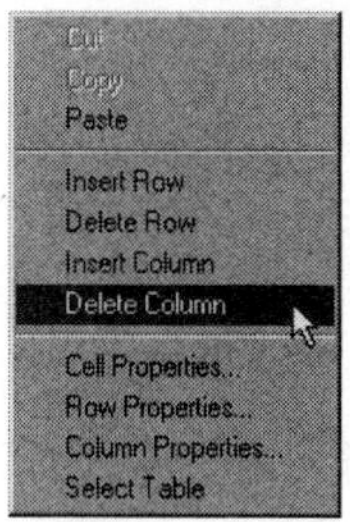

Figure 3 If you're a Windows user, right-click on an object to pop up a contextual menu. If you're a Mac user, just click on the object and hold down the mouse button. The pop-up menu will appear in a second or two.

Keyboard conventions

When I refer to key commands, I put the Windows command first and the Mac command in parentheses, like this:

Press Ctrl+L (Command+L)

I use this format for some other differences, too, like system fonts:

The source code uses the Courier New (Courier) font face.

Mouse conventions

Some Mac mouses have more than one button, and some don't. For that matter, some folks don't really use mice at all, they have those touchpad and stylus thingies. That said, I do refer to right-clicking an awful lot. On a Windows machine, when you click the right rather than the left mouse button, a contextual pop-up menu appears (**Figure 3**).

To make this window appear by using a one-button mouse, just point and click and hold down the mouse button for a couple seconds.

And now ... on to the book!

1

GETTING STARTED

When you start Dreamweaver (**Figure 1**) for the first time, you'll see a main window, called the *Document window*, and several floating windows, called either *palettes* or *inspectors*.

The main components of Dreamweaver that I'll introduce in this chapter are the Document window, the HTML inspector, the Properties inspector, the Launcher, and the Object palette.

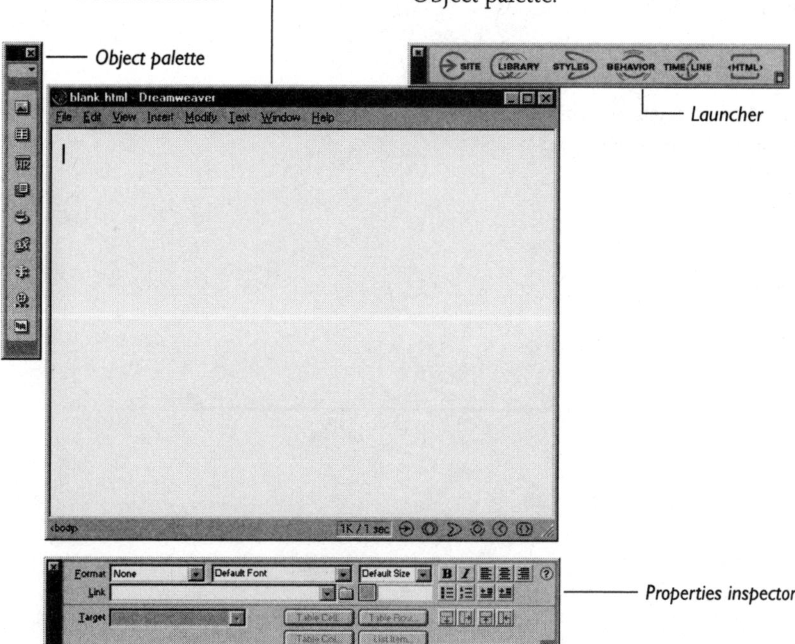

Figure 1 Here's the Dreamweaver work environment, complete with the floating windows you'll see on startup.

Starting Dreamweaver

When you start Dreamweaver, a new, blank document will appear in the Document window (**Figure 1**).

To start Dreamweaver (Windows):

1. Click on the Start menu button to pop up a list of options.
2. From the Start menu, choose Programs > Macromedia Dreamweaver > Dreamweaver.

To start Dreamweaver (Mac):

1. Locate the Dreamweaver shortcut.
2. Double-click on it (single-click if the icon is in the Launcher).

✔ Tip

- Unless you specified a custom location for the program, the pathname should follow the predictable conventions.

  Windows: `C:\Program Files\Macromedia\Dreamweaver\Dreamweaver.exe`

  Macintosh: `file:\\\Macromedia\Dreamweaver\Dreamweaver`

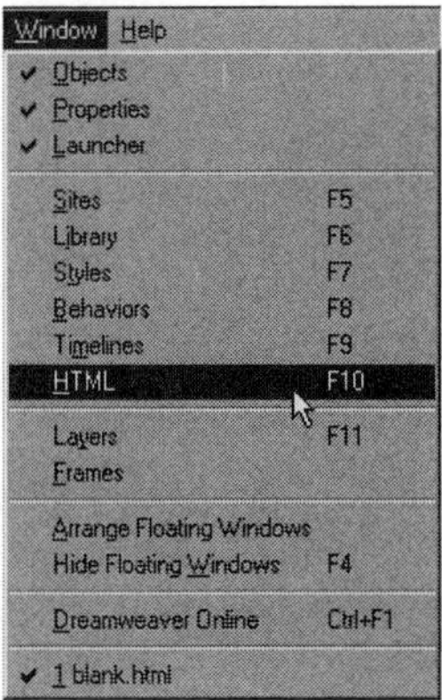

Figure 2 You can open any of Dreamweaver's windows, palettes, and inspectors from the Document window's Window menu.

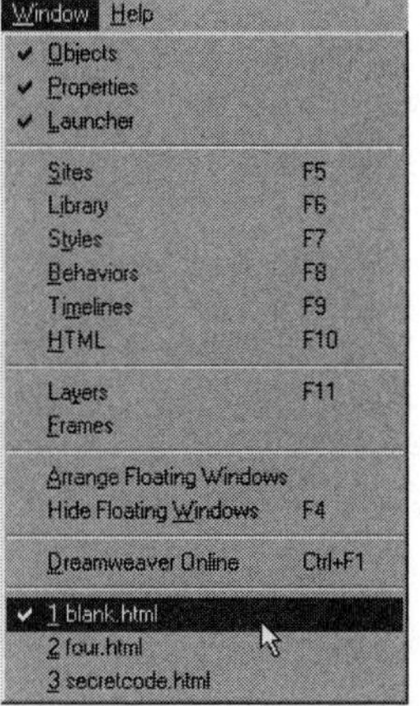

Figure 3 When you're working with multiple documents, each will appear in its own Document window. Each of these windows will be accessible from the Window menu.

Dreamweaver Terminology

The various components that comprise Dreamweaver are called windows, palettes, and inspectors. Although all these items are available from the Window menu (**Figure 2**), they are not all called windows.

A *window*, in Dreamweaver, is a standalone window that will show up on the Windows 95 status bar (the Chooser menu on the Macintosh). The Document window is one example of a window, and the Sites window is another.

You can have multiple document windows open; the filename for each will appear at the bottom of the Window menu (**Figure 3**).

The miniature, floating windows that are used to adjust particular sets of properties are called either inspectors or palettes. These are similar to the palettes and inspectors you may have used in other multimedia creation programs, such as Photoshop, PageMaker, or Director.

In general, an inspector changes appearance based on the current selection, whereas a palette controls elements, such as styles or library items, that are available to the entire current site.

You can control your workspace by moving any of these windows, or by closing them to get rid of them altogether.

✔ Tip

- To view or hide any window, palette, or inspector, select its name from the Window menu.

To close any window:

1. Just click on the X in the upper-right corner (Windows). On a Mac, click on the close box in the upper-left corner.

✔ Tips

- Dreamweaver will remember the window positions you set when you exit the program. When you start Dreamweaver again, your window preferences will remain the way they were when you last exited.
- To move the floating windows back to their original, default positions, select Window > Arrange Floating Windows from the Document window menu bar.
- To hide all the floating windows at once, select Window > Hide Floating Windows from the Document window menu bar, or press F4.

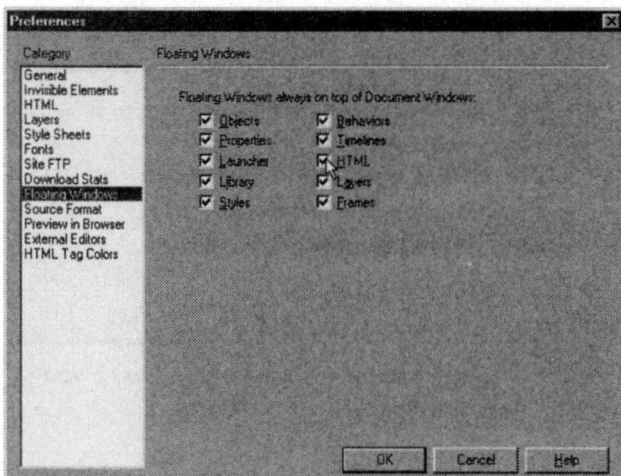

Figure 4 The floating windows panel of the Preferences dialog box lets you disable the "always on top" feature of any of Dreamweaver's floating windows.

To change floating window preferences:

1. From the Document window menu bar, select Edit > Preferences. The Preferences dialog box will appear.
2. In the Category box at the left of the window, click on Floating windows. The Floating windows panel of the dialog box will come to the front (**Figure 4**).
3. This panel of the dialog box includes a checkbox for every floating window that's a part of Dreamweaver. Each window will always appear layered over the Document window (and the Sites window), unless you uncheck its checkbox here.

   To neutralize a window's floating superpower, click on its checkbox to remove the checkmark.
4. When you're done, click on OK to close the Preferences dialog box and return to the Dreamweaver window.

The Document Window

The Document window (shown on the next page in **Figure 6**) is the main center of activity in Dreamweaver. Since Dreamweaver is a WYSIWYG HTML tool, the Document window approximates what you'll see in a Web browser window.

The *title bar* displays the filename, not the title, of the current Web page.

All the menu commands available to Dreamweaver take place on the Document window *menu bar*.

The *body* of the HTML document is displayed in the main viewing area of the Document window. The *status bar* indicates three things about the current document:

- The tag selector displays all the HTML tags that apply to the current selection.
- The download area displays the total size, in K (kilobytes), of the current page, and the amount of time it would take to download over a 28.8 Kbps modem.
- The Launcher bar includes the same buttons as the Launcher, which is discussed later in this chapter in the section called *The Launcher*.

To hide the status bar:

1. From the Document window menu bar, select View > Hide Status bar.

The status bar will disappear (**Figure 5**).

✔ Tip

- You can resize the Document window as you would any other window: by clicking on the lower-right corner and dragging to make the window larger or smaller. I show the Document window in many different sizes throughout this book, depending on the kind of content I'm discussing at the time.

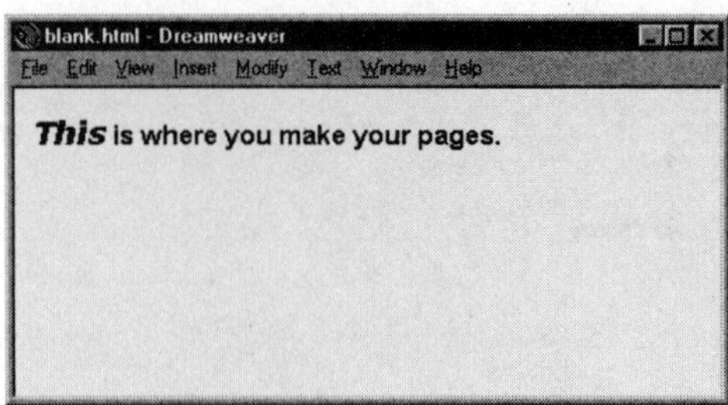

Figure 5 You can make the status bar go away if you want more screen space.

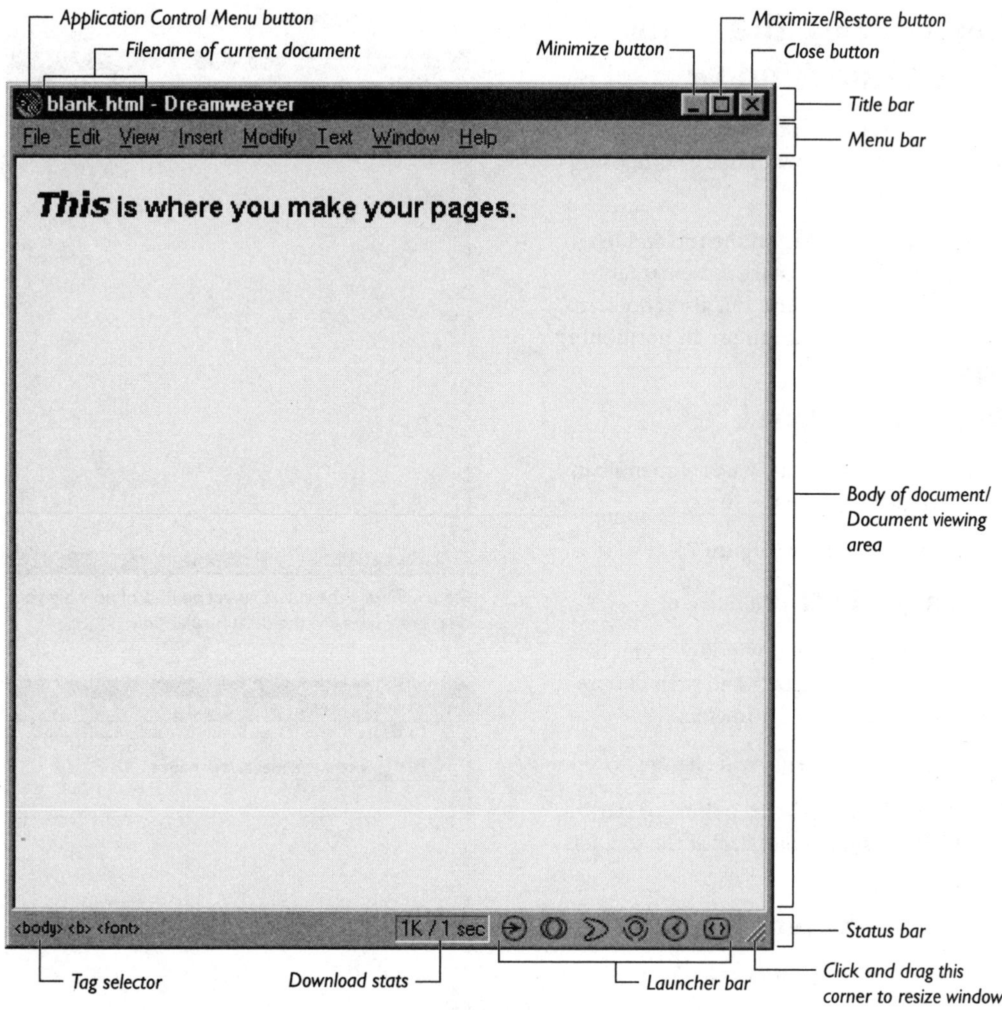

Figure 6 The Document window is where you compose your pages.

Customizing the Document Window

You can turn on and off several options in the Document window to make composing pages easier.

You can display a ruler on the top and left sides of the screen to make incremental measurements easier. You can also choose to display a grid that you can use in positioning objects.

To view the Rulers:

1. From the Document window menu bar, select View > Rulers > Show.

The rulers will appear (**Figure 7**).

To change Ruler units:

1. From the Document window menu bar, select View > Rulers > and then choose Pixels, Inches, or Centimeters.

The ruler measurements will change.

By default, the rulers' zero points, or starting point for measurements, start at the top, left corner.

To change the zero point:

1. View the rulers, if you haven't already.
2. Click on the zero point (**Figure 8**), and drag it into the window. When the point is where you want it to be, let go of the mouse button.

Now, when you look at the rulers, the measurements will reflect the new zero point. If you change your mind, you can reset the zero point so that the zeros are at the top-left corner of the viewing area.

To reset the zero point:

1. From the Document window menu bar, select View > Rulers > Reset Origin.

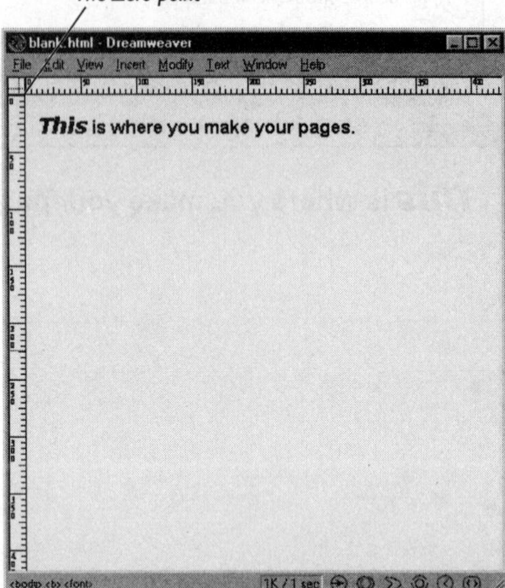

Figure 7 View the rulers to get an idea of how big your ideas are. Pixels are the default ruler unit.

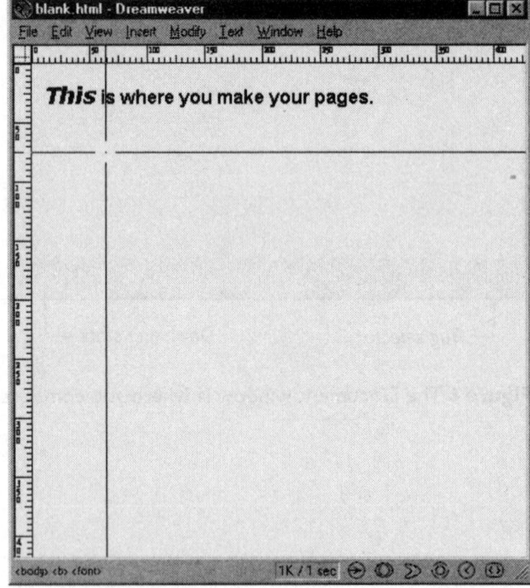

Figure 8 Click on the zero point and drag it to a new location to change the ruler origins.

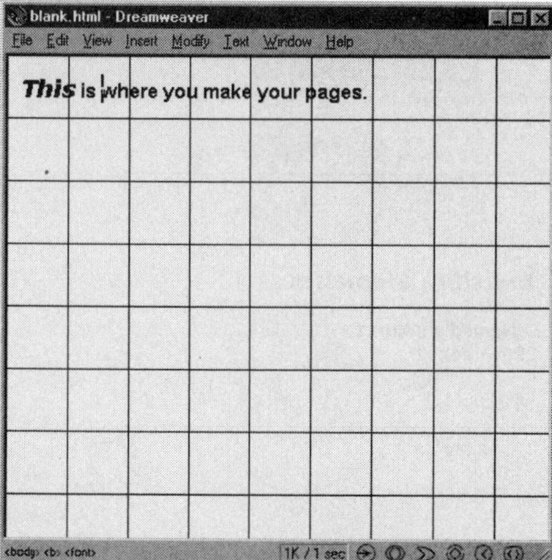

Figure 9 To get even more precise measurements, turn on the grid.

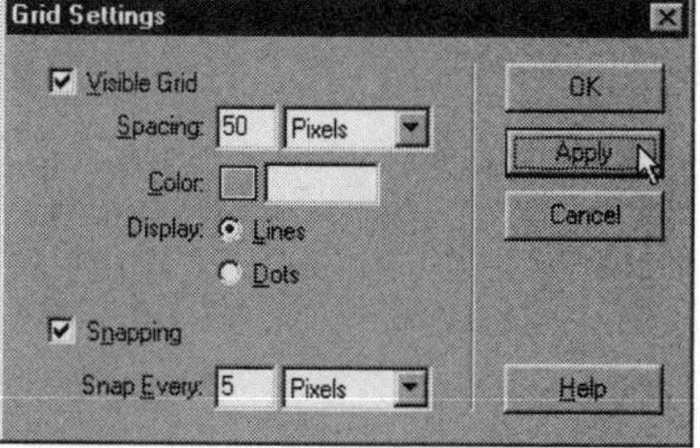

Figure 10 Control the grid by changing the Grid settings.

✔ Tip

- Rulers and grids are most useful for positioning Layers, discussed in Chapter 11.

To view the grid:

1. From the Document window menu bar, select View > Grid > Show.

The grid will appear (**Figure 9**). You can make items that are affected by absolute positioning snap to the grid lines, if you want.

To turn on the "snapping" option:

1. Show the grid, if necessary.
2. From the Document window menu bar, select View > Grid > Snap to.

Now items that you drag in the Document window will snap to the grid.

To change grid settings:

1. From the Document window menu bar, select View > Grid > Settings. The Grid Settings dialog box will appear (**Figure 10**).
2. The Visible Grid checkbox is the same as Show Grid, and the Snapping checkbox is the same setting as Snap to Grid.
3. To change the spacing of the grid lines, type a number in the Spacing text box, and choose a unit from the Spacing drop-down menu: Pixels, Inches, or Centimeters.
4. To change the color of the grid lines, click on the Color button, and the Color palette will appear. Click on a color to choose it.
5. To display dotted rather than solid lines, click on the Dots radio button.
6. To change the snapping settings, type a number in the Snap Every text box, and then choose a unit from the drop-down menu: Pixels, Inches, or Centimeters.
7. To view your changes before you return to the Document window, click on Apply.
8. To accept the changes, click on OK. The Grid Settings dialog box will close, and you'll return to the Document window.

Invisible Elements

Dreamweaver's Document window approximates what you'd see in a Web browser window; it tries to replicate the way a browser would interpret HTML.

One exception to this is invisible elements. These elements would not be visible to a Web browser, but you may have occasion to display them in order to select or move them.

To view invisible elements:

1. From the Document window menu bar, select View > Invisible Elements.

Any invisible elements on the current page will show up in the form of little icons (**Figure 11**).

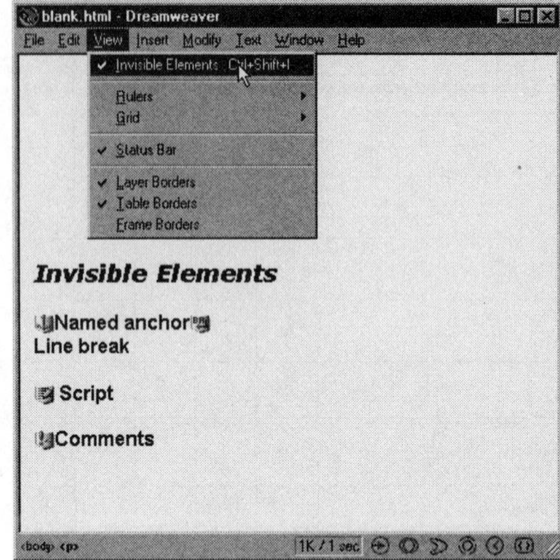

Figure 11 When you view invisible elements, you'll see all kinds of little icons that weren't visible before.

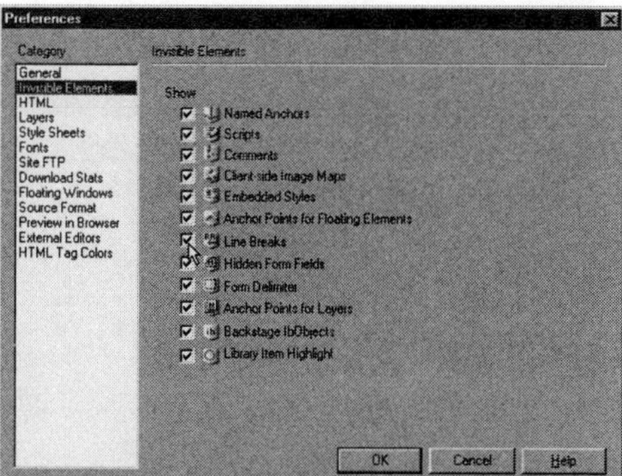

Figure 12 You can choose not to view certain invisible elements when you want to see some, but not all, of them.

To change invisible element preferences:

1. From the Document window menu bar, select Edit > Preferences. The Preferences dialog box will appear.
2. In the Category box at the left of the Preferences dialog box, click on Invisible Elements. The Invisible Elements panel of the dialog box will appear (**Figure 12**).
3. The Invisible Elements panel of the dialog box displays all the different kinds of invisible elements that will become visible when you select View > Invisible Elements.

   Each kind of invisible element has a corresponding checkbox. Line breaks are deselected by default.
4. To deselect any element, click on its checkbox to remove the checkmark.

   To select any element without a checkmark, click on its checkbox to place a checkmark there.
5. When you're finished, click on OK to close the Preferences dialog box.

✔ Tips

- Each of these invisible elements is discussed in the chapter that covers the topic to which it's related.
- **Figure 12** is also a handy reference for what the symbols stand for.

The HTML Inspector

The HTML inspector (**Figure 13**) shows the HTML code for the current page. Dreamweaver always adds the code shown in **Figure 13** to a new Web page.

To view the HTML inspector:

1. From the Document window menu bar, select Window > HTML

   or

   Click on the HTML button on the Launcher

   or

   Press F10.

In any case, the HTML inspector will appear. If you change windows to view a different document, the HTML inspector will update to show the code of the current page.

To close the HTML inspector:

1. Click on the HTML button on the Launcher

   or

   Press F10.

The HTML inspector will close, returning you to the Document window. (Don't press Ctrl+W—as I do by reflex to close a window—because Dreamweaver will close the Document window as well.)

Any changes you make to the code in the HTML inspector will be shown in the Document window when you close the HTML inspector, and any changes you make in the Document window will be automatically updated in the HTML inspector.

✔ Tips

- Select the Wrap checkbox to make the text wrap within the window.
- Line numbers are indicated at the top right.

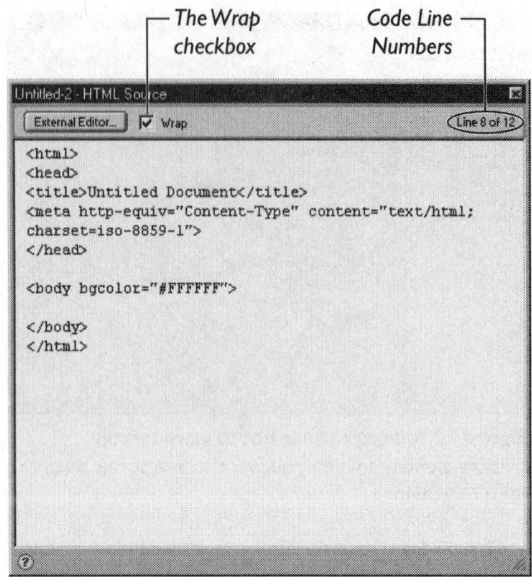

Figure 13 The HTML inspector allows you to view and edit code for the pages in the Document window.

Colorful Code

Dreamweaver 1.2 color-codes the tags in the HTML inspector. By default, regular code is blue, table tags are green, and content is brown. You can set almost limitless color options for the HTML inspector. View the Preferences for Dreamweaver by pressing Ctrl+U (Command+U), and then click on HTML Tag Colors to view that panel of the dialog box. I discuss setting these options in more detail in Appendix B, on the Web site for this book.

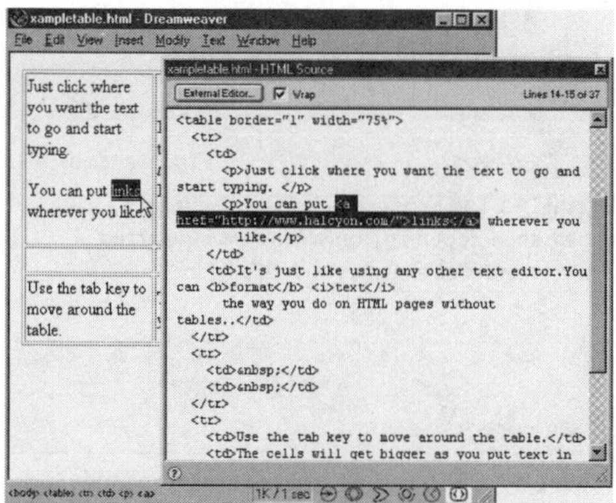

Figure 14 The Document window and the HTML inspector offer parallel selection: highlight code in one window, and it will also be selected in the other.

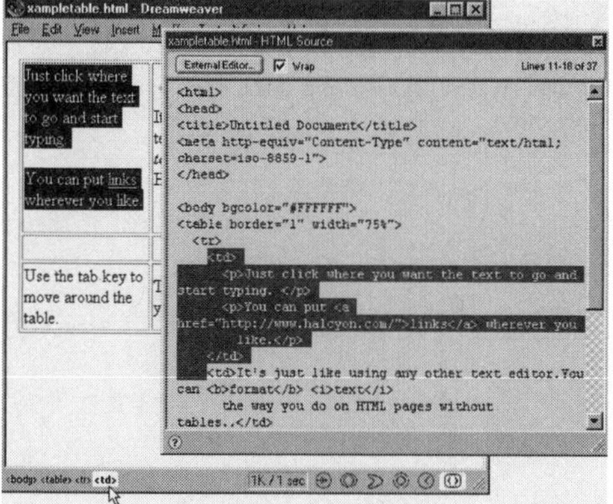

Figure 15 Click on one of the tags in the tag selector in the Document window's status bar to select the tag and everything it encloses.

Selecting Objects

Selecting objects in the Document window is similar to selecting them in any other program:

- To select a word, double-click on it.
- To select a line of text, highlight it with your mouse, or press Shift+Arrow to select a few characters at a time.
- To select an image, click on it.
- To select a table, right-click on it (hold down the mouse button on the Macintosh), and from the pop-up menu that appears, choose Select Table.

When an item is selected, you can cut, copy, delete, or paste over it. You can also modify it with the Properties inspector, as described later in this chapter.

If you select an item in the Document window and then open the HTML inspector, the item will remain selected in the HTML inspector, which is really handy for finding things in particular table cells or on pages with a lot of content (**Figure 14**).

Similarly, if you select some code in the HTML inspector and then return to the Document window, the objects you selected will appear highlighted in the Document window.

To select code:

1. To select all the code and content that appears between a particular set of tags, first click on a word or image on the proper area of the page.
2. Click on the appropriate tag in the tag selector that appears in the Document window's status bar (**Figure 15**).

For instance, to select an entire paragraph, you can click on a word within the paragraph and then click on the <p> tag on the tag selector. This makes selecting links <a>, tables <table>, and the entire body of a page <body> easier.

The Properties Inspector

The Properties inspector is a handy tool that changes appearance depending on which object is currently selected.

To display the Properties inspector:

1. From the Document window menu bar, select Modify > Selection Properties. The Properties inspector will appear (**Figure 16**).
2. To display the entire Properties inspector, click on the expander arrow in the bottom-right corner of the Properties inspector (**Figure 17**).

If no object is selected, the Properties inspector will display text properties (**Figure 18**).

To modify object properties:

1. Select the object you wish to modify.
2. Display the Properties inspector, if necessary.
3. Based on your choices: click on formatting buttons, make menu selections from the drop-down menus, type numbers or names in the text boxes, and select checkboxes or radio buttons.
4. Some of your choices will be applied immediately; to make sure properties are applied to the selection, click on the Apply button (shown in Figure 16).

✔ Tips

- All Properties selections except text have an Apply button.
- You can also display the Properties inspector by double-clicking on some objects.

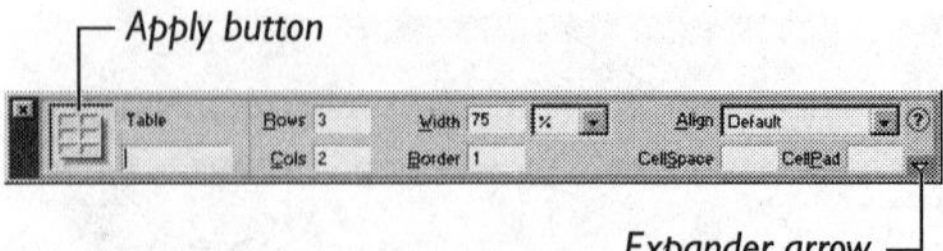

Figure 16 The Properties inspector changes appearance depending on what item is selected. Table properties are shown in this figure.

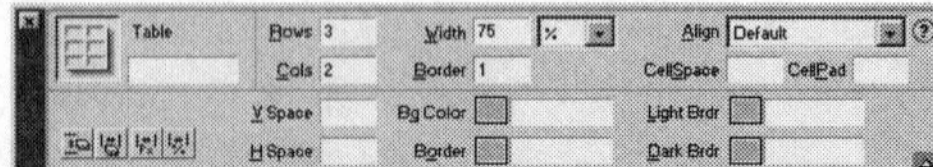

Figure 17 Click on the expander arrow, and the Properties inspector will expand to show more options.

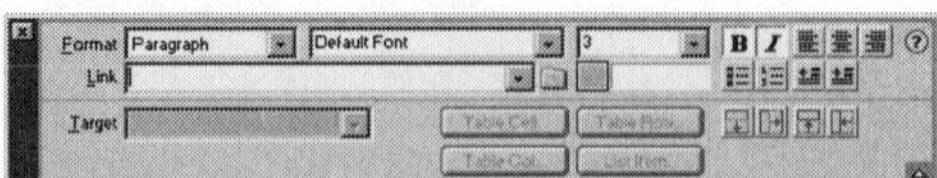

Figure 18 Text properties are the ones you'll see most often.

Direction button

Figure 19 Click on one of the Launcher buttons to pop open the associated window.

The Launcher

The Launcher (**Figure 19**) provides an easy, one-click way to open some auxiliary windows in Dreamweaver. Click on the Launcher button, and the window will open. Click on the same button, and the window will close.

You can't minimize the auxiliary windows and palettes in Dreamweaver, but you can pop them open and closed easily with the Launcher.

Site

The Site button opens the Site window, which you can use to make a local site on your hard drive that's parallel to the directory structure of the site on your Web server. Using the Site window is discussed in Chapter 16.

Library

Click on the Library button to view the Library palette. The Library is a collection of HTML elements that can be shared from page to page. Using the Library is discussed in Chapter 14.

Styles

The Styles button opens the Styles palette, which keeps track of any custom style sheets you add to the current page. Style sheets are explained in Chapter 10.

Behavior

The Behaviors button opens the Behaviors inspector, which is used to set up JavaScript actions and test their compatibility with different generations of browsers. I discuss behaviors in Chapter 12.

Timeline

Timeline opens the Timelines inspector, which controls a sequence of events in Dynamic HTML. More in Chapter 13.

HTML

Clicking on the HTML button opens the HTML inspector, which was discussed earlier in this chapter. We'll be using the HTML inspector throughout this book.

✔ Launcher Tips

- Click on the Direction button to change the orientation of the Launcher (**Figure 20**).
- If you close the Launcher and wish to open it again, select Window > Launcher from the Document window menu bar.
- Even when the Launcher window is closed, a mini version of the Launcher will be visible in the bottom-right corner of the Document window (**Figure 21**).
- When a Dreamweaver window is open, its Launcher button will look like it's "pushed in" (**Figure 20**).
- In the Launcher bar in the Document window status bar, any open windows will be "lit up" (**Figure 21**).
- If you don't want the Launcher to appear in the status bar for some reason, you can change this in the Preferences. From the Document window menu bar, select Edit > Preferences. The Preferences dialog box will appear. In the Category box at the left of the window, select General. In the General panel of the list box, locate the checkbox marked *Show Launcher in Status Bar.* Deselect this option to make the launcher go away from the status bar. You can always reselect it later.

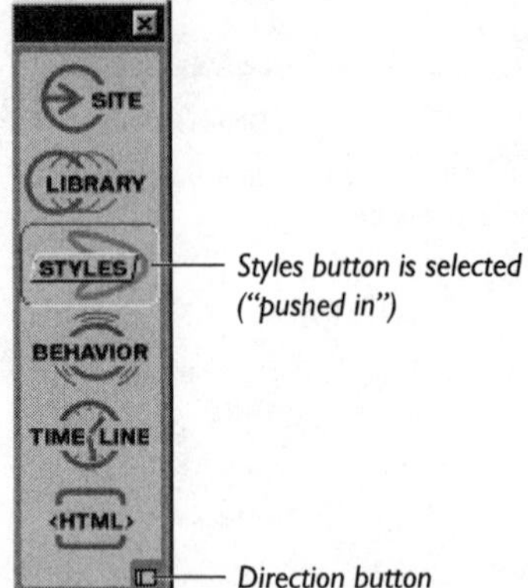

Figure 20 Click on the Direction button to make the Launcher change orientation (horizontal or vertical). Note how the Styles button is selected in this example.

Figure 21 There's a launcher bar at the bottom of the Document window. The Styles button is selected in this example.

Figure 22 Click on a button in the Object palette to insert the associated object. When you mouse over the Object palette, a tool tip will appear to remind you what each button does.

Figure 23 Click on the menu arrow to pop up a menu of panels.

The Object Palette

The Object palette (**Figure 22**) offers shortcut buttons for placing common items on pages in the Document window.

To view or hide the Object palette:

1. From the Document window menu bar, select Window > Objects. The Object palette will appear.

The Object palette consists of three panels: Common, Forms, and Invisibles.

To change Object palette panels:

1. Click on the menu arrow at the top of the Object palette. A pop-up menu will appear (**Figure 23**).

   From the pop-up menu, choose Common, Forms, or Invisibles.

The Object palette will display the panel you chose.

To insert an object:

1. With the both the current page and the Object palette in view, click on the icon for the object you wish to insert.
2. If Dreamweaver needs more information to insert the object, a dialog box will appear.
3. Fill out the dialog box, if necessary, and then click on OK.

The Object will appear in the Dreamweaver window.

To select and modify an object:

1. You can select most objects by highlighting them or double-clicking on them.
2. When an object is selected, the Properties inspector will display its properties.
3. Refer to the chapter in which the object is discussed for information about object properties (see the chapter references that follow).

Dreamweaver Objects

All the objects available to the Object palette are also available from the Insert menu (**Figure 24**).

The *Common elements,* as seen earlier in **Figure 23**, include (from top to bottom):

- Images (Chapters 2 and 5)
- Tables (Chapter 7)
- Horizontal Rules (Chapter 4)
- Layers (Chapter 11)
- Applets (Chapter 15)
- ActiveX Controls (Chapter 15)
- Plug-ins (Chapter 15)
- Flash Movies (Chapter 15)
- Shockwave Director Elements (Chapter 15)

The *Invisible elements* (**Figure 25**) are:

- Named Anchors (Chapter 6)
- Comments (Chapter 3)
- Scripts (Chapter 12)
- Line Breaks (Chapters 2 and 4)

The *Form elements* (**Figure 26**) are discussed in Chapter 9. They are:

- Form Border
- Text Field
- Form Button
- Checkbox
- Radio Button
- List or Menu

✔ Tip

■ You can create custom objects and even add panels to the Object palette. See Chapter 14 to find out how.

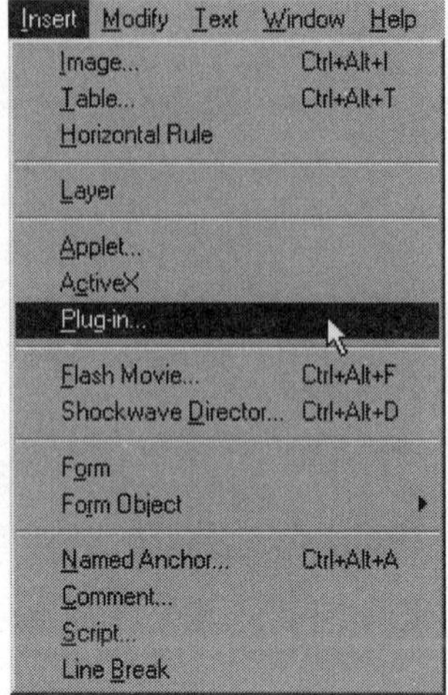

Figure 24 Objects available from the insert menu

Figure 25 Invisible elements

Figure 26 Form elements

Figure 27 The Dreamweaver help files open in your default browser.

Getting Help

Macromedia offers several forms of help for Dreamweaver users, including the *Using Dreamweaver* manual; the Dreamweaver help files; the Dreamweaver Online support page; Dreamweaver newsgroups; and a variety of examples and tutorials.

To open Dreamweaver help:

1. From the Document window menu bar, select Help > Dreamweaver Help Topics (or press F1).
2. Your default browser will open and load the Dreamweaver help files (**Figure 27**).
3. To get a list of all topics covered by the help files, click on Index.

   To read topic headings by subject, click on Contents, and then click on one of the subject headings. The contents will expand to show subheadings, and the help descriptions will appear in the right-hand frame.

✔ Tips

- Wherever you see a ?, click on it to get help about what you're seeing.
- Click on Guided Tour of Dreamweaver to play an animation of common Dreamweaver tasks.
- Click on Show Me to watch a demo.

To read Dreamweaver's support page:

1. Connect to the Internet as you normally do.
2. From the Document window menu bar, select Window > Dreamweaver Online. Your default browser will open the Dreamweaver support page (**Figure 28**).

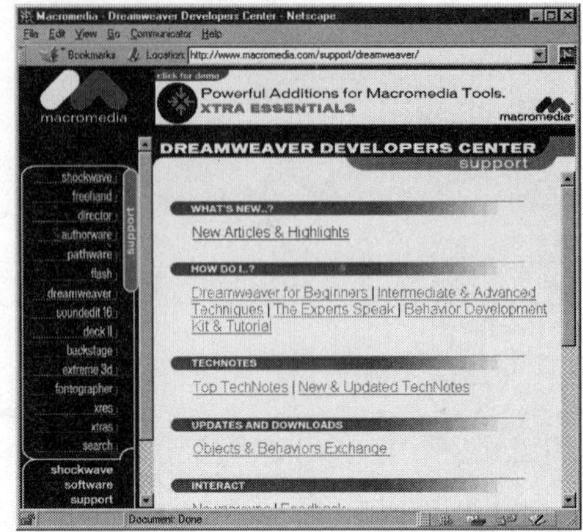

Figure 28 Macromedia's online support pages are updated frequently.

✔ Tip

- Dreamweaver's support page is at http://www.macromedia.com/support/dreamweaver/

To read the Dreamweaver discussion groups:

1. In your Web browser, on the Dreamweaver Online Support page, click on the Newsgroups link

   or

   Open the following URL:

   http://www.macromedia.com/support/dreamweaver/interact/newsgroups/
2. Click on the link to the newsgroup you want to read. The URL is a news: URL, and your newsreader client, if you have one, will open automatically.

To open a template or example:

1. From the Dreamweaver menu bar, select Help > Open Template or Open Example. Either way, the Open File dialog box will appear.
2. Select a file that looks interesting or helpful.
3. Click on Open.

The file you have selected will appear in the Document window.

✔ Tip

- To reuse the tricks in the template or example, select File > Save As from the menu bar and then modify the file.

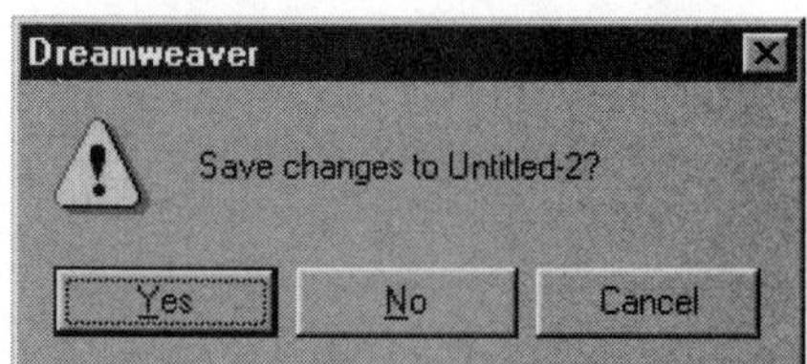

Figure 29 You'll be prompted to save any changes when you exit Dreamweaver.

Exiting Dreamweaver

When you exit Dreamweaver, you will be prompted to save any unsaved changes to pages that are open in the Document window. For more details on saving, see *Saving Your Work*, in Chapter 2.

To exit the program:

1. From the Document window menu bar, choose File > Exit.
2. You'll be prompted to save work in Document windows containing unsaved changes. Click on Yes to save the changes or No to close the pages without saving.
3. All open windows will close, one by one.

✔ Tip

- You can also exit Dreamweaver by closing all open Document and Site windows one at a time.

2

BASIC WEB PAGES

In the last chapter, we got acquainted with the Dreamweaver interface. This chapter looks more closely at the Document window. (Most of the material in this chapter will be a review for people who have used nearly any document creation software at all.) We'll also introduce some very basic starting points for making Web pages in the Document window.

In this chapter, we'll perform the following simple tasks:

- Open a page
- Create a new page
- Put some stuff on it
- Save your work
- Adjust the page properties
- Preview the page in a browser
- Print the page from the browser
- Save a copy of the file
- Close the file
- Open a Dreamweaver template
- Create a new template

Opening an HTML File

If you have previously created HTML files you want to update with Dreamweaver, you can open then with no fear of Dreamweaver replacing your code with proprietary (and arbitrary) corrections.

Of course, sooner or later you'll also want to open files you create with Dreamweaver.

To open a file:

1. From the Document window menu bar, select File > Open. The Open dialog box will appear (**Figure 1**).
2. If the file extension is not `.htm` or `.html` (you open a `.cgi` or `.asp` file, for instance), select All Types from the Files of Type list box.
3. Browse through the files and folders on your computer until you find the file you want to open.
4. Select the file by clicking on its icon. The filename will appear in the File Name list box.
5. Click on Open. The file will appear in a new Document window.

✔ Tips

- You can open the last four files you viewed with Dreamweaver by selecting them from the File menu (**Figure 2**).
- The book's Web site covers Roundtrip HTML, which affects how Dreamweaver treats HTML files created in other programs.

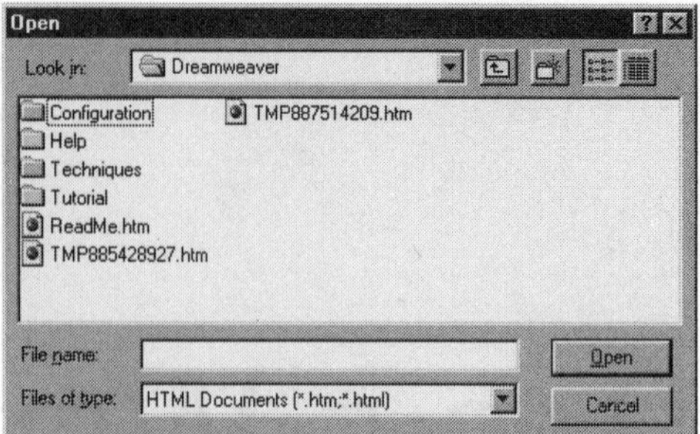

Figure 1 Use the Open dialog box to select a file on your computer to open in the Document window. By default, the Open dialog box looks in the Dreamweaver folder first unless you have a Site window open (see Chapter 18).

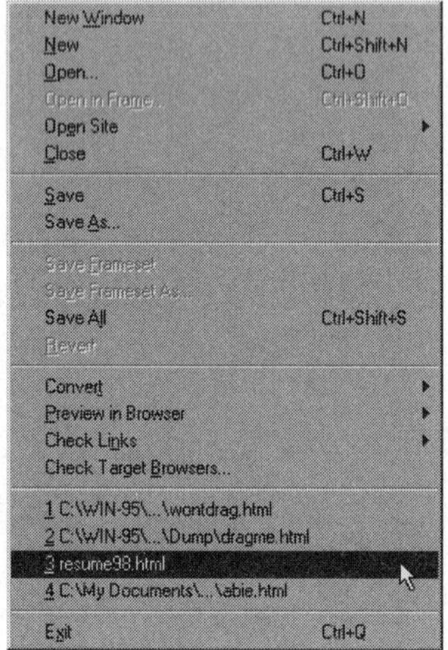

Figure 2 Open the last four files you've edited in Dreamweaver by selecting their names from the file menu.

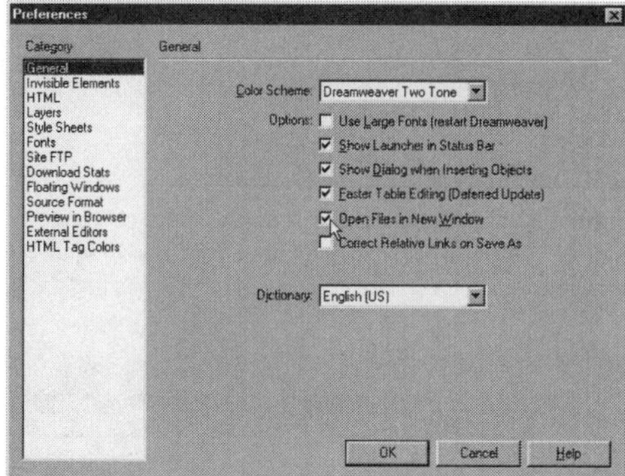

Figure 3 If you only want one Document window open at a time, you can change Dreamweaver's preferences. This is a good solution for computers without much built-in memory.

Text from Other Sources

When you paste text from another program, such as an e-mail or word-processing program, it will lose all its formatting, including paragraph breaks.

One way to keep this from happening is to use a word-processing program to save the text as HTML. Many word processors, including Microsoft Word, Nisus Writer, and Corel WordPerfect, include HTML conversion extensions (try File > Save as HTML, or consult the program's help files).

While these programs write atrocious HTML in some cases, they're just fine for coding paragraph and line breaks.

Another good shortcut is Microsoft Excel's Save as HTML feature, which saves spreadsheets as not-too-terrible HTML tables.

When you open a file in Dreamweaver, a new document window will open that contains the selected file. If you'd rather have Dreamweaver reuse the same window, you can change the window preferences.

To change the Open prefs (Windows only):

1. From the Document window menu bar, select Edit > Preferences. The Preferences dialog box will appear.
2. In the Category box at the left of the dialog box, click on General. The General panel will move to the front.
3. Identify the checkbox marked *Open Files in New Window*. To turn this option off, deselect it.
4. Click on OK to close the dialog box and return to the Dreamweaver window.

✔ Tip

- If you change your preferences to have only one Document window open, it will only contain one document (unlike some other programs which use the same window to hold multiple documents). You may notice some strange behavior in the Window menu, which may reference documents that are not only *not* open but that do not *exist*.

✔ Definition

- A *file* is a chunk of related data stored by computer media—programs are also files. A *document*, loosely speaking, is a computer file created by a text editor or a word processor. An *HTML document* or *HTML file*, then, is a document that is written in the Hypertext Markup Language. A *Web page* (referred to as just a page in this book) is an HTML file that's intended for consumption on the Web. A *Web site* is a collection of Web pages, generally located on the same server.

Creating a New Page

You can create a new file at any time while you're using Dreamweaver. You can open the file in the Document window you're currently using or in a new Document window.

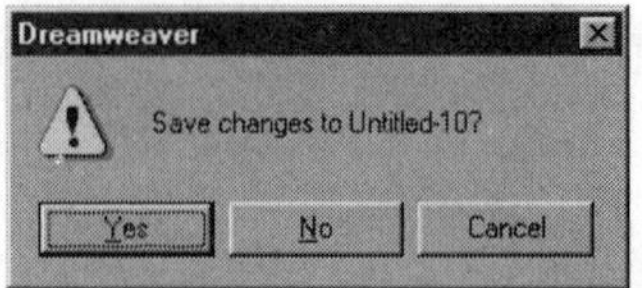

Figure 4 When you create a new file in the current window, Dreamweaver may prompt you to save your changes.

To create a file in the current window (Windows):

1. From the Document window menu bar, select File > New.
2. If you have already saved the current page, a new blank document will appear in the Document window.

   or

   If the current file has changes that have not yet been saved, you will be prompted to save your work (**Figure 4**).
3. To save your changes, click on Yes.
   - If you have previously saved and named the file, Dreamweaver will save the changes and create a new, blank document in the current window.
   - If you have not yet saved your page, the Save As dialog box will appear. Type a file name for the page in the File Name list box, and click on Save to close the Save As dialog box. A new, blank file will appear in the Document window.

   To close the page without saving the changes, click on No. A new, blank file will appear in the Document window.

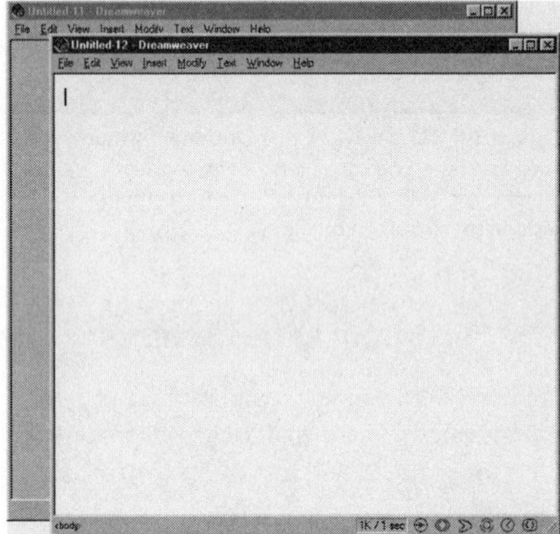

Figure 5 You can open a new window, or several, and work on several documents simultaneously.

To create a new file in a new window:

1. From the Document window menu bar, select File > New Window. A new, blank Document window will appear (**Figure 5**).

✔ Tip

- You can have as many documents open as your memory allotment will allow.

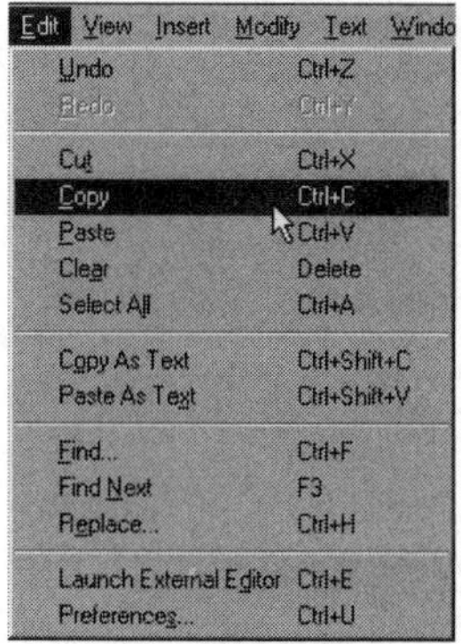

Figure 6 Dreamweaver's Edit menu.

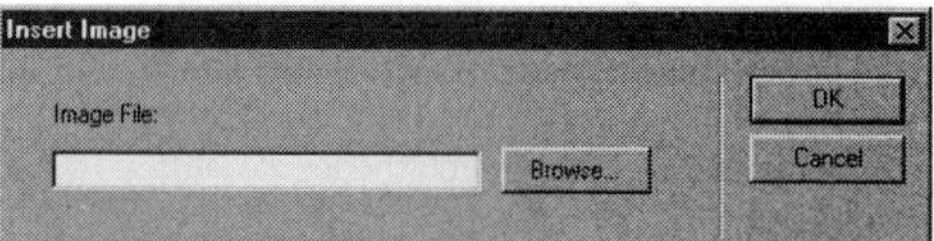

Figure 7 In the Insert Image dialog box, click on Browse to select an image from your hard drive. Dreamweaver likes it if you save your page first.

Creating Content

When you open Dreamweaver, the Document window creates a new, blank page. You can start from this tabula rasa to create your own Web page.

To place text:

1. Just start typing!
2. Press Enter (Return) to make a paragraph break, or press Shift+Enter (Shift+Return) to make a line break.

Dreamweaver acts like a text editor for most text functions, which are available from the Edit menu (**Figure 6**). For more about formatting text in Dreamweaver, see Chapters 3 and 4.

To place an image:

1. Click to place the insertion point where you want the image to appear.
2. From the Document window menu bar, select Insert > Image. The Insert Image dialog box will appear (**Figure 7**).
3. Type the location of the image in the Image Location text box.

   or

   Click on Browse. The Select File dialog box will appear. Browse through the files and folders on your computer until you locate the image file. When you've selected the image, click on Open. The Select File dialog box will close, and the image location will appear in the Insert Image text box.
4. When the image location is in the Insert Image dialog box, click on OK. The image will appear on the page.

To find out more about images and image properties, see Chapter 5.

To make a link:

1. Highlight the object (text or image) that you want to make into a link.
2. View the Properties inspector, if necessary, by selecting Modify > Selection Properties from the Document window menu bar.
3. In the Link text box, type the URL of the link.
4. Press Enter (Return), and the object will become linked (**Figure 8**).

For more about links, see Chapter 6.

To make a table:

1. Click to place the insertion point where you want your table to appear.
2. From the Document window menu bar, select Insert > Table. The Insert Table dialog box will appear (**Figure 9**).
3. Verify the number of columns and rows you want to appear in your table.
4. Click on OK. The Insert Table dialog box will close, and the table will appear on your page.

To find out how to format tables, see Chapter 7.

✔ Tip

- Many of the different kinds of content you can insert into a Web page are available from the Document window's Insert menu (**Figure 10**). There is a list of what kind of media is covered in which chapter in Chapter 1.

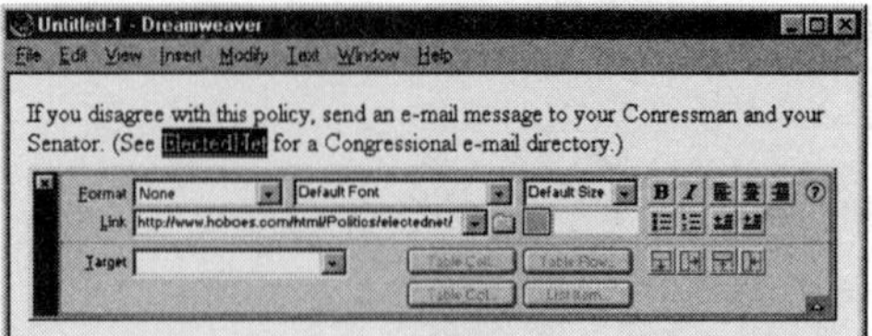

Figure 8 To make a link, highlight the text to be linked and then type or paste the URL in the Properties inspector's Link text box.

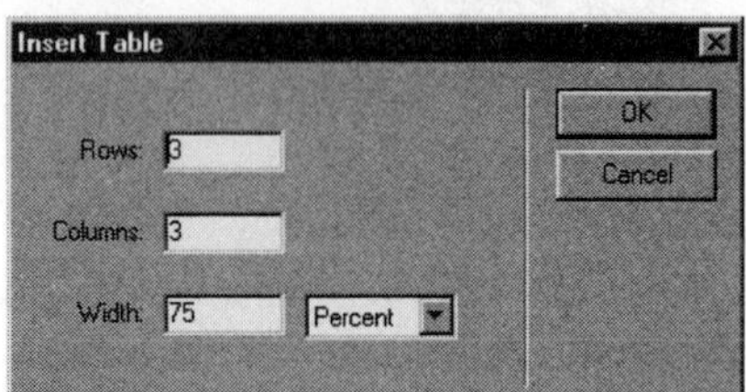

Figure 9 Select Insert > Table from the Document window menu bar to pop open the Insert Table dialog box.

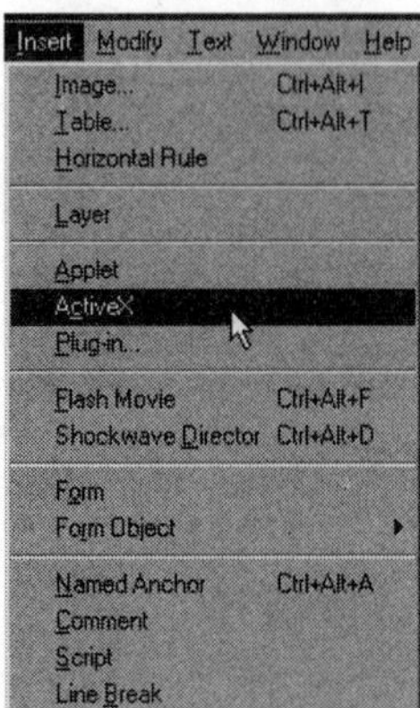

Figure 10 Many other objects you can put on your pages are available from the Insert menu.

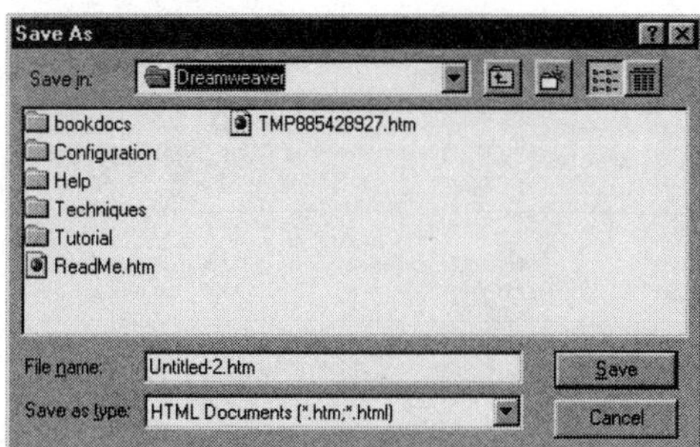

Figure 11 Type a filename for your Web page in the File Name text box, then click on Save to save it.

Saving Your Work

If you're creating more than just an afternoon's entertainment, you'll want to save the work you do and the Web pages you make.

To save the current page:

1. From the Document window menu bar, select File > Save, or press Ctrl+S (Command+S). The Save As dialog box will appear (**Figure 11**).
2. Make sure the Save In list box indicates the proper location in which to save the file. If not, browse through the folders on your computer until you find the one in which you want to save your work.
3. Type a name for your file in the File Name text box. The name cannot include any spaces, but you can use underscores (as in `main_page.html`).
4. Click on Save. The Save As dialog box will close, and you'll return to the Document window.

✔ Tip

- By default, PCs will save HTML files with the `.htm` extension, and Macs will save them with the `.html` extension. If you want to use a different extension, type the entire filename in the File Name text box. I prefer the `.html` extension, so I type out entire filenames, such as `dork.html`, on my PC.

To save all open files:

1. From the Document window menu bar, select File > Save All.
2. All the named files that have been changed since the last time you saved will be saved now.
3. A Save As dialog box will appear for all open files that have not been named and saved.

SAVING YOUR WORK

Page Properties

Page properties are elements that apply to an entire page, rather than to just an object on the page. Visual properties include the page's title, a background color or image, and the text and link colors. Other page properties include the document encoding and the site root, if any.

To view page properties:

1. From the Document window menu bar, select Modify > Page Properties. The Page Properties dialog box will appear (**Figure 12**).

To change the document title:

1. Open the Page Properties dialog box.
2. In the Title text box, type the title of your page.
3. Click on OK to close the Page Properties dialog box, or leave the dialog box open to modify other properties.

✔ Tips

- Most of the page properties are stored in the document's **<head>** tag, rather than the **<body>** tag, which is where the content goes.
- Unlike some other page creation tools, Dreamweaver doesn't prompt you to give your pages a title—in fact, it titles all your pages "Untitled Document" until you change the Page Properties.
- The title you give your page will be displayed in the Web browser's title bar (**Figure 13**).
- Choose a good title for your page, something more descriptive than "My Home Page." Many search engines use the words in the page title to index pages.

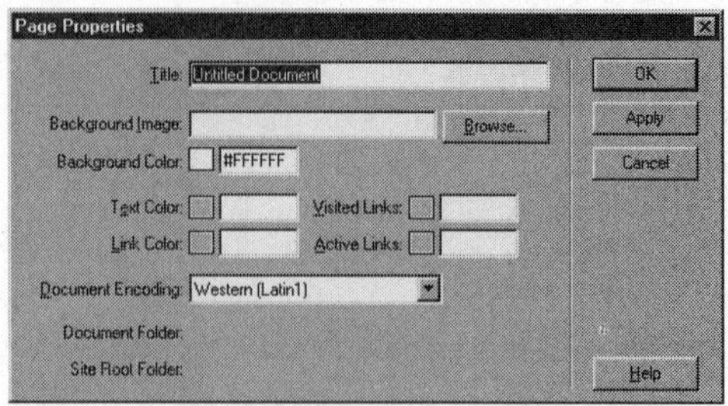

Figure 12 The Page Properties dialog box allows you to set options that apply to an entire page.

Figure 13 The title you choose for your Web page will be displayed in the Web browser's title bar.

Browser-safe Colors

You may have heard something about browser-safe color schemes. There are 216 colors that Netscape and Microsoft browsers on both Windows and Macintosh platforms use, and these colors are called "browser safe." The colors in the browser safe area all contain a 00, 33, 66, 99, CC, or FF pair in their hex code.

The Colors palette that you'll see when you click on any color selection button (**Figure 14**), in a dialog box or in the Properties inspector, is comprised of these browser-safe colors. If you're planning your page around browser-safe colors, the colors palette is a good place to start.

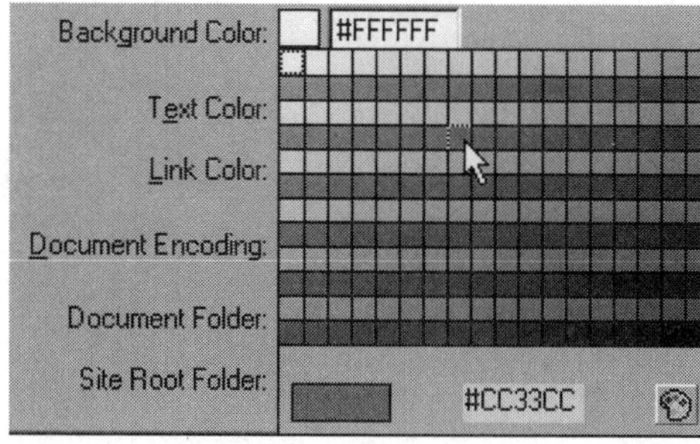

Figure 14 Click on the Background Color button and the Colors palette will appear—then just click on a color to select it.

Colors and Web Pages

In Web pages, each color you can use is represented by a *hex code*, a six-digit number that represents a particular color.

There are many different color selections you can make for your Web pages, including background color, text color, link color, active link color, and visited link color. You can also choose colors for text selections, table backgrounds, table borders, frame borders, and layers.

This isn't even counting any colors that appear in images you add to your pages.

In general, it's a good idea to keep a fixed color scheme in mind while planning your pages. It's an even better idea to plan text and background colors with readability in mind; if you clash yellow text with an orange background, it may look striking, but no one will stick around to read a page that gives them a headache.

Modifying the Page Background

By default, Dreamweaver will set the background color of your page as plain white. You can choose a different background color, or use a background image instead.

To set the background color:

1. Open the Page Properties dialog box.
2. In the Background Color text box, type the hex code for the color you wish to use.

   or

   Click on the Background Color button. The Colors palette will appear (**Figure 14**). Click on a color to select it.

   or

   In the Colors palette, click on the Color button: . The Color dialog box will appear (**Figure 15**).

To use the Colors dialog box:

1. You can choose one of the preselected colors by clicking on it.

   or

   You can choose a custom color by first clicking on one of the Custom Colors boxes at the left of the dialog box.
2. In the Colors dialog box, click on a hue (color) in the large colors box, and then click on a shade (lighter or darker) in the narrow panel to the right of that. The combination of your clicks will be displayed in the Color|Solid box.
3. To select this color, click on the Add to Custom Colors button. Your color will appear in the box you selected in Step 1.
4. Click on OK to close the Colors dialog box. The hex code for the color you chose will appear in the Background Color text box.

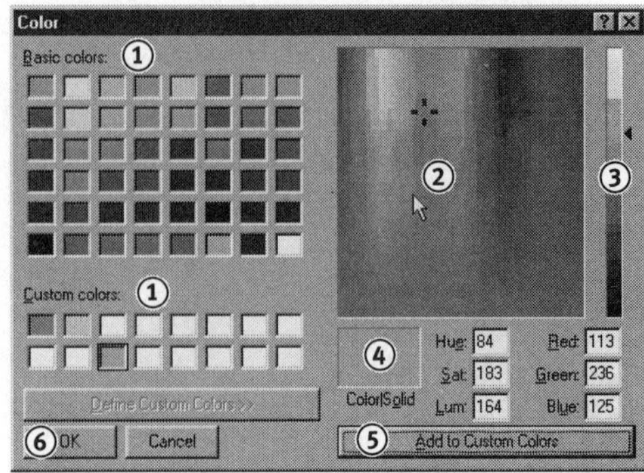

Figure 15 The Color dialog box. (1) Select a predefined color, or select an empty Custom Colors box. (2) Select a hue and (3) a shade. (4) Click on the Color|Solid box and (5) click on Add to Custom Colors. (6) Click on OK.

MODIFYING THE PAGE BACKGROUND

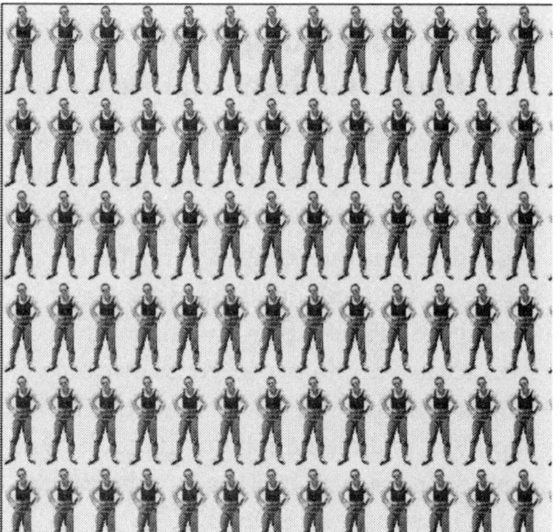

Figure 16 A tiled background image. The image repeats from left to right and then down the page.

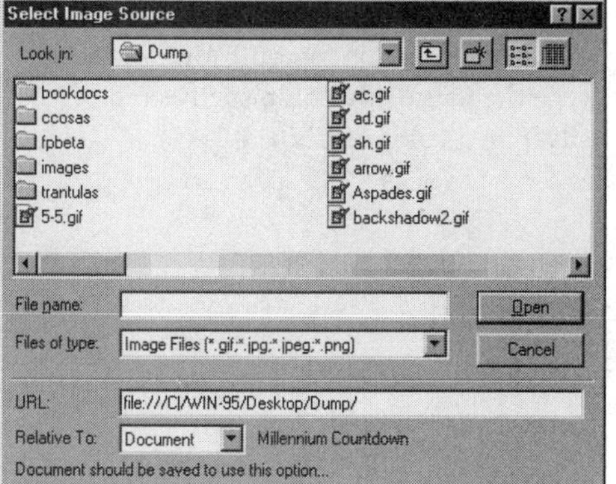

Figure 17 The Select Image Source dialog box, like an Open dialog box, lets you browse through your computer's files to select an image.

Background images are supported by most browsers created after Netscape Navigator 2. A background image can consist of one large image, but more frequently, it's a smaller image that the browser window *tiles* so that it repeats in a contiguous pattern across and down the browser window (**Figure 16**).

To set a background image:

1. Open the Page Properties dialog box by selecting Modify > Page Properties from the Document window menu bar.
2. In the Page Properties dialog box, type the pathname of the image you wish to use.

   or

   Click on the Browse button. The Select Image Source dialog box will appear (**Figure 17**). This is similar to the Open dialog box.
3. Browse through the files and folders on your computer until you find the GIF or JPEG image you want to use. Click on the file icon so that the image's pathname appears in the Path Name text box.
4. Click on Open to close the Select Image Source dialog box and return to the Page Properties dialog box, where you'll see the pathname of the image in the Background Image text box.
5. Click on OK to close the Page Properties dialog box and return to the Document window, where your image will appear as the page background.

✔ Tip

- You can set both a background image and a background color. The image will override the color in most cases, and the color will show up in browsers that support background colors but not background images.

Setting the Text Colors

By default, the text color of a Web page is black; obviously, you'll want to use a different color for pages with darker backgrounds. You can also set colors for the links on your pages. Be sure to use colors that will be legible on the background color or image you're using.

To set the text colors:

1. Open the Page Properties dialog box.
2. In the Text text box, type (or paste) the hex code for the color you wish to use.

   or

   Click on the Background Color button. The Colors palette will appear (as shown back in **Figure 14**). Click on a color to select it.

   or

   In the Colors palette, click on the Color button. The Colors dialog box will appear (as shown back in **Figure 15**). Follow the instructions in the section called *Modifying the Page Background*, and then click on OK.
3. Repeat steps 1 and 2 for the link colors, if you wish.
4. Click on OK to close the Page Properties dialog box, where your new text color will be visible.

✔ Tips

- More details about what link colors are and how they work are available in Chapter 6.
- You can find out how to make selected portions of text a different color in Chapters 3 and 10.

Converting Other Color Numbers into Hex

Colors are definable by a three-number sequence of hue, saturation and luminosity, or by another three-number sequence: the red-green-blue, or RGB, ratio. There are boxes for these numbers in the Color dialog box (**Figure 14**). You can get the RGB sequence of a particular color from an image editor, like Photoshop or Paint Shop Pro, and then duplicate the color by typing the correct numbers into the right boxes in the Colors dialog box. Then, of course, you should jot down that hex code for further reference. (You can copy RGB numbers into an image editor, too, if you want to duplicate a background color in an image for some reason.) You can also type the name of a color, such as red or silver, in a color text box.

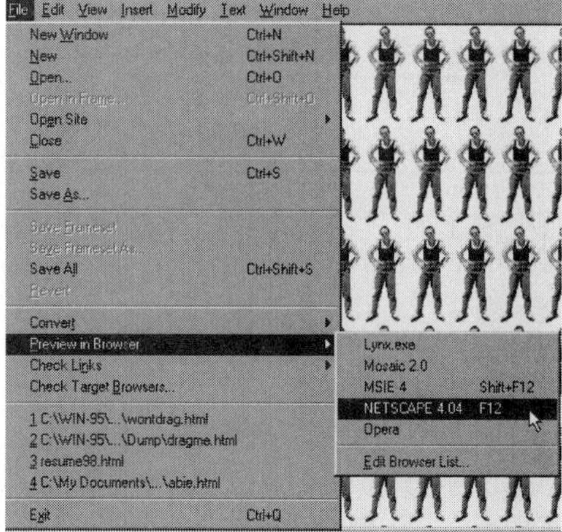

Figure 18 Select File > Preview in Browser and then select a browser. Find out how to add browsers to your list in Chapter 15.

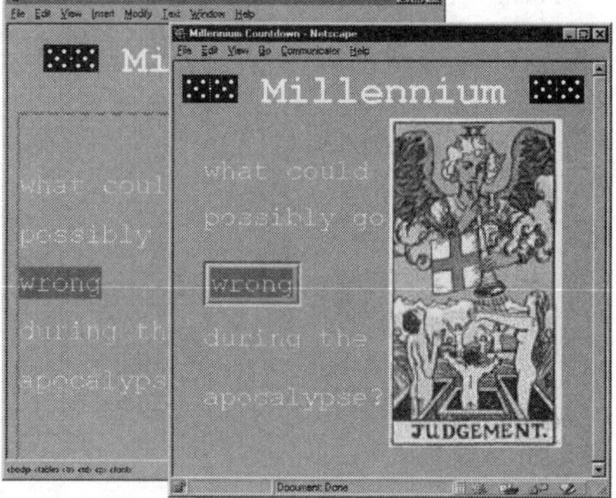

Figure 19 Preview your page in a browser, no matter what stage of the design process you've reached, to find out what it really looks like.

Previewing in a Browser

While Dreamweaver is pretty much WYSIWYG, there are some tags it doesn't support. Additionally, Dreamweaver's representation of HTML is a kind of fusion of Navigator and MSIE. To find out how your page looks in a particular browser, you need to actually use that browser to view your page.

To view your page in a browser:

1. With the page you want to preview in the Document window, select File > Preview in Browser > Browser Name from the menu bar (**Figure 18**), or press F12.
2. If the browser isn't open yet, Dreamweaver will launch it and load the current page (**Figure 19**).
3. If the browser is already open, Dreamweaver will load the current page into the last window you used in that browser.
4. To make changes, return to the Document window by using the Taskbar (the Applications menu).

✔ Tips

- Dreamweaver creates a temp file that it uses as the browser preview file. Pressing Reload or Refresh in the browser window will not show the most current version of the file. Instead, you'll need to repeat the steps for previewing.
- For more details on previewing, and to find out how to add and remove browsers from the preview list, refer to the book's Web site.
- You can also use the browser itself to open a saved file on your hard drive. Choose File > Open Page from the browser's menu bar.

Printing from the Browser Window

Dreamweaver's Document window does not include a Print command. You can, however, print a file after you preview it in the browser window.

To print a file:

1. Preview the file in the browser window as described in the previous section.
2. From the Web browser's menu bar, select File > Print. The Print dialog box will appear.
3. Verify the number of copies, the destination printer, and the pages to print in the Print dialog box.
4. Click on OK. The browser will send the document to the printer.

You can return to Dreamweaver by using the Windows Taskbar (the Applications menu on a Mac).

✔ Tip

- To adjust the destination printer and the paper size, select File > Page Setup from the browser's menu bar.
- Netscape Navigator includes a Print Preview command (**Figure 20**) that displays the pages as they'll look on paper (pages are printed without background colors or images). Print Preview also offers more printing options, including the ability to see how much of the page fits on an 8.5x11-inch piece of paper. To view the print preview, select File > Print Preview from Navigator's menu bar.
- Navigator also offers a File > Print Frame command for printing individual frames.

Figure 20 Navigator's Print Preview feature lets you see what you're getting before you send it to the printer. Good thing, because white text won't print on white paper (this is the same page we saw in **Figure 19**).

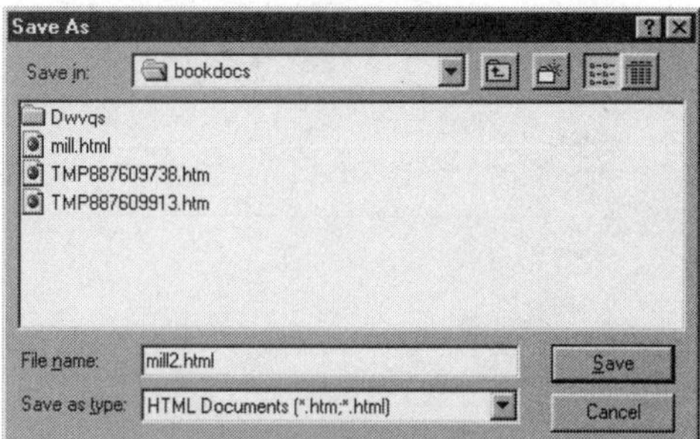

Figure 21 You use the same Save As dialog box to save a copy of a file as you do to save it in the first place. In this figure, we're saving the file `mill.html` as `mill2.html`, so we'll have two versions of the same file.

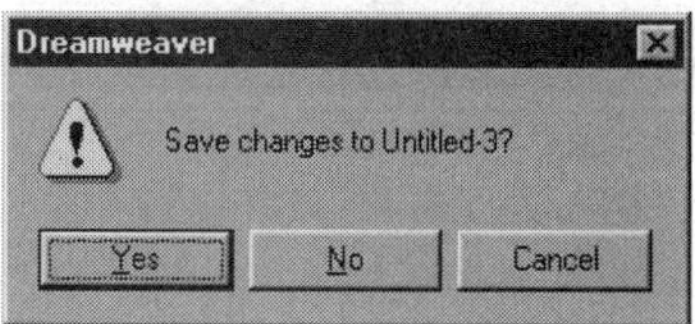

Figure 22 To close a file (such as a template or example) without saving the changes, click on No when this dialog box appears.

Saving a Copy of a File

If you want to use a page as a template for another, similar page, you can save a copy of the page with a different filename. Guidelines for using Dreamweaver templates and creating custom templates are in the *Using Templates* section of this chapter.

To save a copy of a page:

1. Open the page in the Document window, if it's not there already.
2. From the Document window menu bar, select File > Save As. The Save As dialog box will appear (**Figure 21**).
3. Type a filename for the new page in the File Name text box.
4. Click on Save. The Save As dialog box will close and return you to the Document window.

The Document window will now display the copy of the file, as indicated by the filename in the Document window's title bar.

To close a page:

1. Click on the close box, or select File > Close from the Document window menu bar.

Occasionally, you may open a page, make a few changes, and realize that something has gone horribly wrong. Or you may be fooling around with a document you have no intention of saving. In those instances, you can close without saving the changes.

To close without saving:

1. From the Document window menu bar, select File > Close. A dialog box will appear asking you if you want to save your changes (**Figure 22**).
2. Click on No. The dialog box will close, and a new, blank document will appear in the Document window.

Using Templates

Dreamweaver includes several templates with common design issues all worked out. The templates that include tables and frames might be especially helpful for beginners.

To open a Dreamweaver template:

1. From the Document window menu bar, select Help > Open Templates. The Open Template dialog box will appear, with the Templates folder selected (**Figure 23**).
2. Choose one of the templates from the files list box.
3. To keep yourself from making changes to the template, place a checkmark in the Read Only check box.
4. Click on Open to view the template.

The template will open in the Document window (**Figure 24**).

To modify a Dreamweaver template:

1. Open a template without marking it as read-only (see step 3, above).
2. Make any desired changes to the template.
3. Save the template, with the same name, in the Dreamweaver templates folder.

The next time you open the template, you'll see your changes.

✔ Tip

- The pathname for the Templates folder should be as follows:

  Windows: C:\Program Files\Macromedia\ Dreamweaver\Configuration\Templates

  Macintosh: file:\\\Hard Drive Name\ Dreamweaver\Configuration\Templates

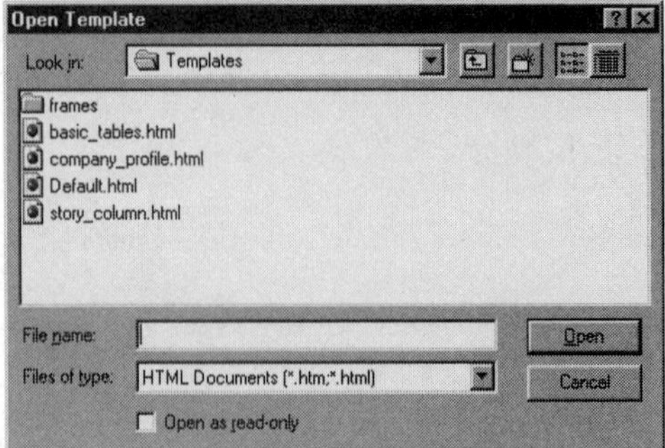

Figure 23 Select Help > Open Templates, and the Open Template dialog box will appear with the Templates folder selected.

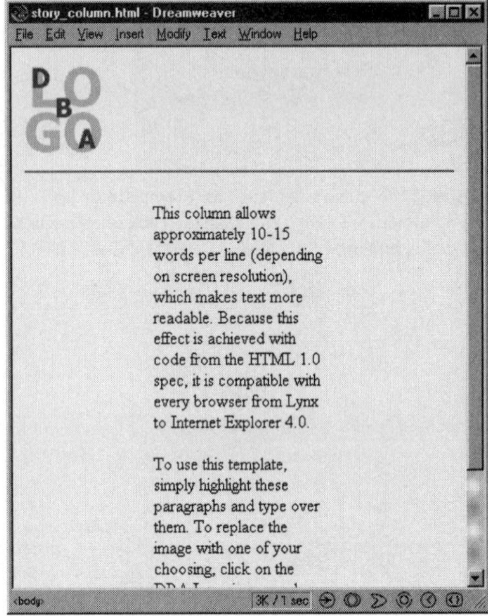

Figure 24 This Dreamweaver template, story_column.html, offers a simple layout that you can duplicate by saving a copy of the file.

Creating Templates

The default Dreamweaver template is the blank page that appears when you open a new document window. This file is called Default.htm (Default.html on the Mac). You can modify the code for this template, putting in META tags and changing the page properties. You can also change the entire page, so that when you're working on a big project, a template for that project opens automatically.

✔ Tip

- You may want to save a copy of the default template elsewhere on your hard drive, in case you want to restore it to its original, blank form later on.

To modify the default template:

1. Open the default template by following the steps in *To open a Dreamweaver template* and selecting Default.htm as the file to open. Be sure not to mark the template as read-only.
2. Make the desired changes to the template, in either the Document window or the HTML inspector.
3. Save the template, with the same name, in the Templates folder.

After these changes, every time you create a new document, it will include the modifications you made.

To create a Dreamweaver template:

1. Create a Web page that includes all the features you want on your template.
2. Save the file in the Dreamweaver Templates folder.

Now, when you open the templates folder, your template will be there with the pre-made Dreamweaver templates. You can set the new file to read-only, if you like.

3

Working with Text

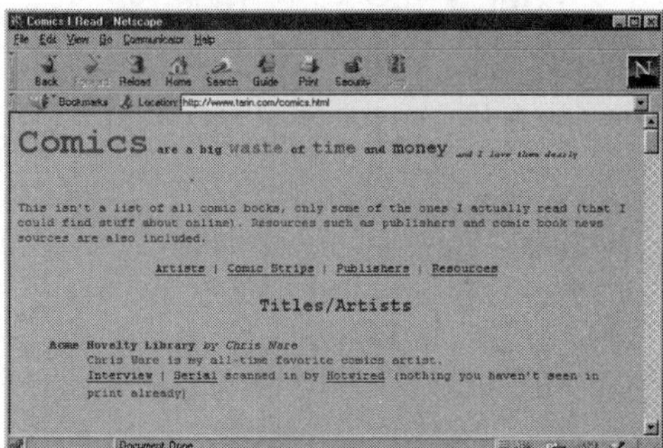

Figure 1 You can use different sizes, colors, and text styles on a single Web page, or even in a single paragraph.

What's Where

This chapter covers font sizes, font faces, text styles, font colors, comments, finding and replacing text, and checking your spelling.

In Chapter 4 you'll find information on paragraphs versus line breaks, headings, preformatted text, numbered lists, bulleted lists, definition lists, paragraph alignment, divisions, indent and outdent, nonbreaking spaces, special characters, and horizontal rules.

Text comes in all shapes, sizes, and colors—or at least it can do so on Web pages (**Figure 1**). In this chapter, we'll go over the very basic ways of working with text for very beginners. We'll find out how to accomplish rudimentary typographical changes: font size, font face, and font color, as well as various text styles. You can also add invisible text remarks, called *comments*, as annotations to your documents. And we'll also see how you can use Dreamweaver's word-processing tools, such as find-and-replace and spell check.

There's a lot more you can do with text, of course. All the basics of laying out blocks of text, called paragraphs, are covered in Chapter 4.

And, of course, all the endless variety of text manipulations you can accomplish with cascading style sheets are explored in Chapter 10.

Placing Text

There are several ways to put text on your pages with Dreamweaver (**Figure 2**).

To put text on your page:

1. Just start typing in the Document window!

   or

   Select some text from another program or window, copy the text to the clipboard (usually by pressing Ctrl+C (Command+C)), return to the Dreamweaver window, and paste it there by pressing Ctrl+V (Command+C).

   or

   Convert a text file or word-processed document to HTML, as described in Chapter 2, and then open it with Dreamweaver.

Once you have text on your Web page, you can treat it like you do in any other text editor. You can highlight the text and then copy, cut, delete, or paste over it. Use these commands:

- Copy Ctrl+C (Command+C)
- Cut Ctrl+X (Command+X)
- Paste Ctrl+V (Command+V)
- Clear Delete/Backspace

✔ Tips

- If you copy text from another source and paste it into the Document window, it will not retain any formatting you've given it—including paragraph breaks. See Chapter 4 for information on using preformatted text.
- If you want to copy some formatted text, but not the formatting, select the text, and then choose Edit > Copy as Text from the Document window menu bar.
- To paste text you've copied without any formatting, choose Edit > Paste as Text from the Document window menu bar.

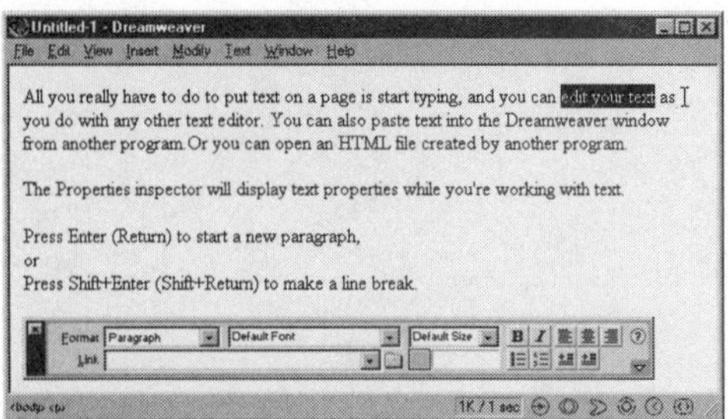

Figure 2 You can use the Dreamweaver document window to type and edit text as you do with any other text editor.

Mom, What's Deprecated?

Custom style sheets are so nifty that they're making obsolescent a lot of the physical font manipulations people have been so happy about for a while—most of the stuff in this chapter. The <font> tag, for instance, is going to die quietly, along with its attributes—a process called *deprecation* (meaning the tags are being phased out of the HTML standard).

On the other hand, this won't be a quick or easy death. Tons of people still use Navigator and Explorer 2–4 and all the browsers that have been revamped in the same time period that support the <font> tag. And people who use versions of Navigator earlier than 4, and versions of Explorer earlier than 3, can't see all the wonderful things that style sheets can do.

If you want to design for a wide audience, you need to be able to use these *deprecated* tags for the older generation browsers, and find out how to get along without them in the newest incarnations. While the deprecated tags will eventually be phased out, they won't die until no one on earth is surfing with an out-of-date browser: not a likely prospect, unless the earth loses all electrical power tomorrow.

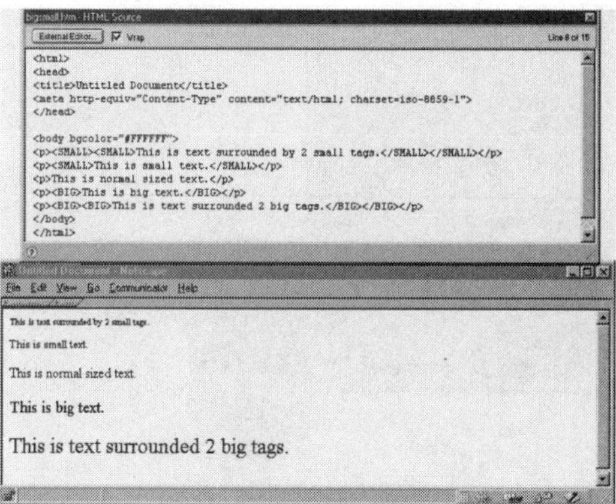

Figure 3 The big and small tags can be used for relative size changes.

Language Encoding

Not everyone makes Web pages in the English language, and Dreamweaver 1.2 addresses that. Western encoding is what most European languages use, and you can also set the encoding as Japanese, Traditional Chinese, Simplified Chinese, or Korean. To do this, open the Preferences dialog box by pressing Ctrl+U (Command+U), and then click on Fonts to bring that panel to the front of the dialog box. Choose your encoding from the Encoding list box.

While you're there, you can select which screen font faces and sizes to use in Dreamweaver for the proportional and fixed fonts. (Those terms are discussed in full in the sidebar called *I Shot the Serif*, later in this chapter).

Changing Font Size

There are several ways to indicate font size in HTML. Using style sheets (see Chapter 10), you can set a font size in points, like you do in word-processing and page-layout programs.

Without style sheets, however, you set font sizes relative to a base size. This base size is not something you can fix exactly, because every user has the option of customizing the basic font size in their browser software to whatever size they choose. The font sizes that you set will be relative to this basic font size, which is generally 12 or 14 points.

There are two separate scales you can use to determine size: the "absolute" 1–7 scale (which is still relative to the user's preferences) and the relative-to-base-font scale. Some folks also prefer using the very relative <big> and <small> tags.

Figure 3 demonstrates the use of the <big> and <small> tags. Nesting these tags isn't a directly supported HTML convention, but it works in most browsers that support the tags. See the sidebar *Not-So-Basic Basic HTML* later in this chapter to find out how to use these and other non-Dreamweaver-supported tags.

To use the absolute scale:

1. Select the text whose size you want to change.
2. From the Document window menu bar, choose Text > Size > and then choose a number between 1 and 7 (**Figure 4**).

   or

   In the Properties inspector, click on the Font Size drop-down menu, and choose a number between 1 and 7 (**Figure 5**).

In either case, the size of your text will change (**Figure 6**).

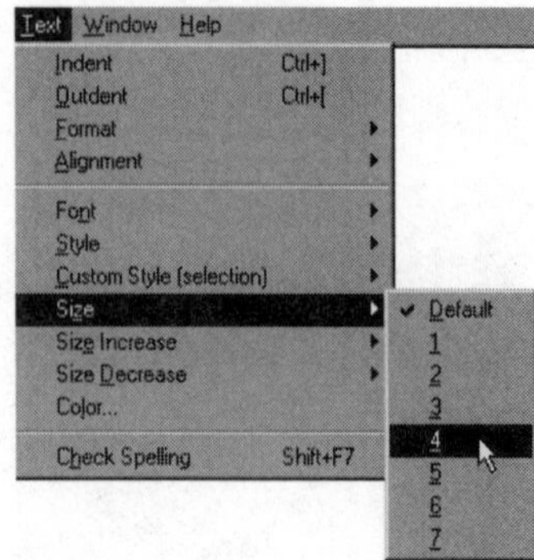

Figure 4 To adjust text size on the "absolute scale," select Text > Size > N from the Document window menu bar.

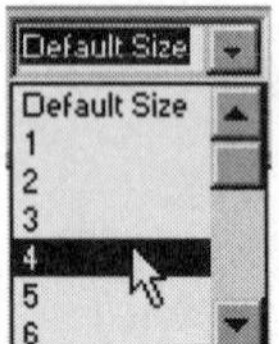

Figure 5 You can also choose a text size from the Properties inspector's Font Size drop-down menu.

1234567

The default size is 3.

Figure 6 The absolute scale of text starts with size 1 as the smallest available size and moves up to a maximum font size of 7.

✔ Tips

- If you choose size 3, you likely won't see any change in size, because size 3 is the default font size unless you specify otherwise.
- If you change font size and then change your mind, select the offending text, and then select Default Size from the Text > Size menu or the Property inspector's Font size text box.
- To change the size of all the text on a page, select Edit > Select All from the Document window menu bar. Then follow the steps described earlier. Or, you can change the base font size, as described on the next page.

You can set a base font size other than 3 for your page, in which case all differing font sizes will be set relative to this new size.

To set the base font size:

1. Open the HTML window for your page by selecting Window > HTML from the Document window menu bar (or by pressing F10).
2. At the top of the document, locate the <body> tag.
3. Directly after the <body> tag, but before any other text, type the following line of code:

   <basefont size=n>where n is a number between 1 and 7. Your code would look something like this:

   ```
   <body>
   <basefont size=4>
   ```

   although there may be other stuff inside the <body> tag.
4. Press Ctrl+S (Command+S) to save the changes to the code.
5. Close the HTML inspector by pressing F10.

Since Dreamweaver doesn't directly support the basefont tag, you won't see any changes in the Dreamweaver window. However, any relative size changes you make will be based on the basefont number you specified, rather than on the default basefont size of 3. (You didn't go to all that trouble to set a basefont of 3, did you?)

You can use relative font sizes whether or not you change the basefont size. The effects of relative font sizes are displayed in **Figure 7**.

To use relative font sizes:

1. Select the text whose size you want to adjust.
2. To increase font size, select Text > Size Increase from the menu bar, and then choose a number from +1 to +7 (**Figure 8**)

   or

   On the Properties inspector, choose a number from +1 to +7 from the Font Size drop-down menu (shown earlier in **Figure 5**).
3. To decrease font size, select Text > Size Decrease from the menu bar, and then choose a number from –1 to –7 (**Figure 9**)

   or

   On the Properties inspector, choose a number from –1 to –7 from the Font Size drop-down menu (shown earlier in **Figure 5**).

You'll see the size change immediately, but the actual size relative to the basefont size you've set won't show up properly until you preview the page in a browser.

✔ Tip

- As there are only seven gradations of font size, in total, the actual deportment of the font will vary depending on the basefont size. In other words, if your basefont size is 5, and you set the size increase to +7, the font will not get any bigger than size 7 (**Figure 7**).

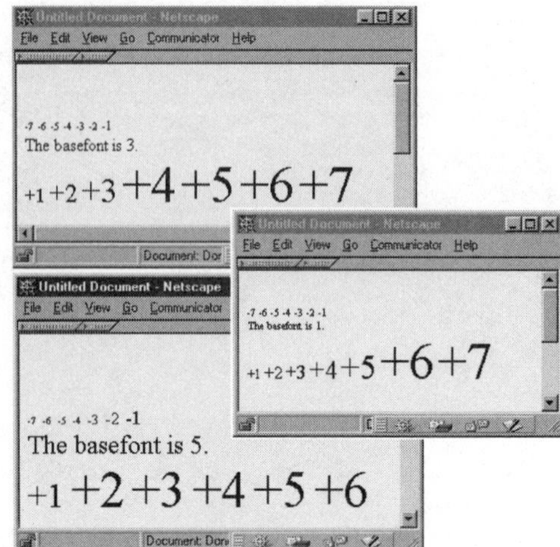

Figure 7 Relative sizes display differently based on the basefont size. In these three examples, the basefont is 3, 1, and 5 (moving clockwise). Notice how none of the examples exceeds the maximum absolute size of 7 or the minimum absolute size of 1 (**Figure 6**).

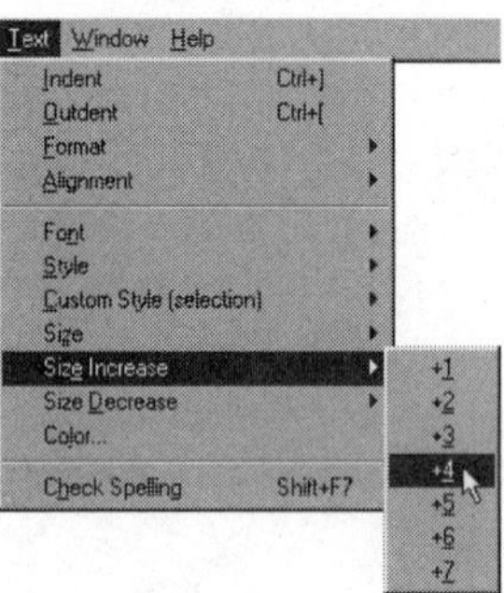

Figure 8 To increase relative font size, select Text > Size Increase > N.

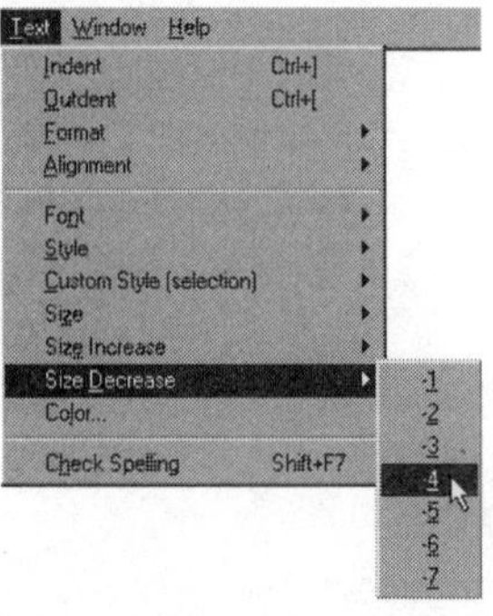

Figure 9 To decrease relative font size, select Text > Size Decrease.

Figure 10 In many browsers, the <strong> tag displays as bold and the <em> tag displays as italic. In Lynx, a text-only browser, all four tags are given the same emphasis. Other browsers may interpret the <strong> and <em> tags differently.

Using Text Styles

You're probably used to using text styles, such as **bold**, *italic*, and underline, in your word-processing program or page-layout tool. You can use these styles in HTML, too, to add emphasis or visual contrast to pieces of text.

✔ Attention!

- Text styles are not the same as style sheets. Text styles are one of the few font attributes that have not been deprecated, because there's more call to make them available to single words and not groups of layout elements. Style sheets, as explained in Chapter 10, offer even more text attributes than regular text styles, but not all browsers have style-sheet-processing capabilities.

There are two kinds of styles in HTML: physical and logical. *Physical styles* tell the text exactly how to look, while *logical styles* suggest an attribute and let the browser decide how to interpret it. For example, <b> (bold) is a physical style. On the other hand, <strong> (strong emphasis) is a logical style. While most graphical browsers display the <strong> tag as boldfaced text, other software may treat it differently. Text-to-speech browsers, for instance, may read <strong> text with verbal emphasis.

Figure 10 contrasts the bold and strong tags, as well as the italic and emphasis tags.

To make text boldface:

1. In the Document window, select the text you'd like to make boldface.
2. In the Properties inspector, click on the Bold **B** button. The text will become boldface.

To italicize text:

1. In the Document window, select the text you'd like to make italic.
2. In the Properties inspector, click on the Italic *I* button. The text will become italic.

To underline text:

1. In the Document window, select the text you'd like to appear underlined.
2. From the Document window menu bar, select Text > Style > Underline. The text will become underlined.

✔ Tips

- If you prefer menu commands to the Properties inspector, you can select Bold and Italic from the Text > Style menu instead.
- The key commands for bold and italic are Ctrl+B (Command+B) and Ctrl+I (Command+I), respectively.
- To remove a text style, reapply it.

Not-So-Basic Basic HTML

Dreamweaver is a good program for most uses, but there are many tags it doesn't directly support, and among them are a lot of text tags. If there is a tag you want to use that Dreamweaver doesn't make available to you directly, it's simple to make the changes directly to the HTML.

1. In the Document window, select the text to which you want to apply the tag.
2. From the Document window menu bar, select Window > HTML. The HTML window will appear, and the text you selected will be highlighted here.
3. Before the word or phrase (with no spaces between the word and the tag), type the tag, including angle brackets.
4. After the word (with no spaces between the word and the tag), type the closing tag, including angle brackets.

For instance, you'd apply the <big> tag with this code:

```
<big>This is a big phrase!</big>
```

When you close the HTML inspector, your changes appear in the Document window.

Physical Text Styles

Other physical styles are demonstrated in **Table 3.1**. Strikethrough and teletype are supported by Dreamweaver, and you can apply them by using the Text > Style menu.

Table 3.1

Physical Text Styles

STYLE	APPEARANCE	CODE EXAMPLE
Strikethrough	~~strikes out text~~	<strike>strikes out text</strike>
Superscript	$E=MC^2$	E=MC²
Subscript	H_2O	H₂O
Typewriter or teletype	`old fashioned` monospace font	<tt>old fashioned</tt>

Style Name	Tag	Uses
Emphasis	<em>	indicates importance
Strong Emphasis	<strong>	indicates strong importance
`Code`	<code>	programming code and scientific equations
Variable	<var>	in tutorials, marks placeholders for user-defined text
`Sample`	<samp>	samples of code output
`Keyboard`	<kbd>	in tutorials, indicates text the user should input
Citation	<cite>	a citation or reference
Definition	<dfn>	marks the first use of a keyword in educational texts

Figure 11 This figure illustrates how the logical text styles supported by Dreamweaver are displayed in most browsers. There are many other such styles, these are merely some of the most common. To mark up text with any of these styles, select Text > Style > N from the Dreamweaver menu bar.

Logical Text Styles

The logical styles that Dreamweaver supports are shown in **Figure 11** as displayed by most browsers. If you have a special concern as to how they're used in other browsers, you'll need to load the page into that browser.

To use a logical style:

1. In the Document window, select the text whose style you'd like to change.
2. From the Document window menu bar, select Text > Style > and then choose an item from the list. The text will change appearance to reflect your choice.

✔ Tip

- To use a style that's not supported, refer to the sidebar on page 48 called *Not-So-Basic Basic HTML.*

Changing Font Face

Unless you specify a font face, any text on your pages will appear in the user's browser window in their browser's default font face. Most users probably have Times New Roman (Times) as their default proportional font, although some may have changed it.

When specifying font faces in HTML, keep in mind that, for the time being, not every user has every font installed—far from it. Additionally, fonts that come from the same typeface family can be named several different things (such as Arial, Helvetica, and Univers), particularly on different platforms (Times New Roman, Times, New York).

Luckily, when you're specifying font faces in HTML, you can offer several choices. The browser will check to see if the first suggested font is installed, and then the second, and so on. If none of the recommended display fonts are available, the text will be displayed in the user's default browser font—not the end of the world.

Dreamweaver offers several preset font combinations, shown in **Figure 12**. You can also define your own font combinations.

Arial, Helvetica, sans serif

Times New Roman, Times, serif

Courier New, Courier, mono

Georgia, Times New Roman, Times, serif

Verdana, Arial, Helvetica, sans serif

Figure 12 These are the preset font combinations available in Dreamweaver. You can include any number of fonts in a font combination; the browser will try each one in turn, from left to right. Serif, Sans Serif, and Mono are not fonts, but types of fonts. See the sidebar "I Shot the Serif," later in this chapter.

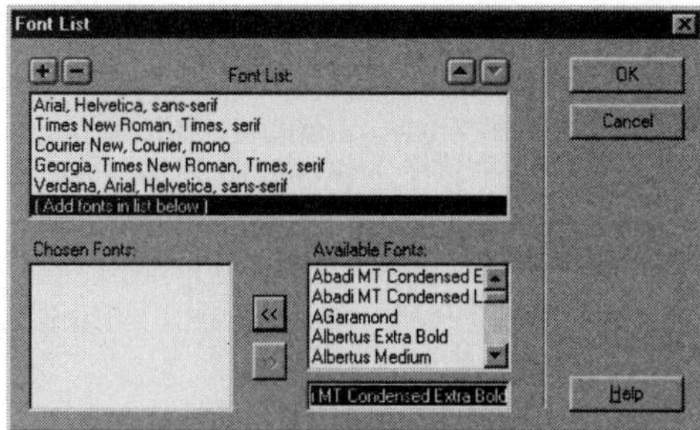

Figure 13 The Font List dialog box lets you define font combinations using any font on your computer.

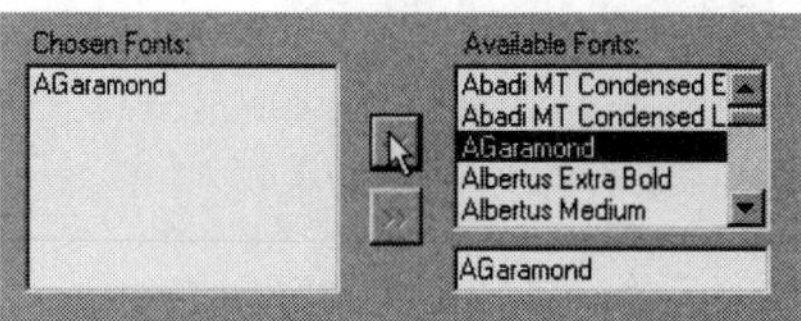

Figure 14 Select the font from the Available Fonts list box, then click on the left arrow button to move it to the Chosen Fonts list box.

To define a font combination:

1. From the Document window menu bar, select Text > Font > Edit Font List.

   or

   In the Properties inspector, choose Edit Font List from the Font Face drop-down menu.

   In either case, the Font List dialog box will appear (**Figure 13**).
2. Dreamweaver's existing font combinations will appear in the Font List text box. All system fonts installed on your computer appear in the Available Fonts list box.
3. Locate your first-choice font in the Available Fonts list box and click on it.
4. Click on the left arrow button «, and the font's name will appear in the Chosen Fonts list box (**Figure 14**).
5. Repeat steps 3 and 4 for all the font faces you want to appear in this particular font combination.
6. To remove a font you chose, click on the right arrow button. »
7. When you've chosen the right combination of fonts, click on the + button to add the font combination to the Font List list box.
8. When you're all done, click on OK to close the dialog box and return to the Document window. Your new font combination will be available in the Text > Font menu and in the Properties inspector's Font Face drop-down list.

✔ Tips

- There's no preview available in the Font List dialog box, and Dreamweaver doesn't allow you to display an individual font without adding it to the Font List. Therefore, it's advisable to choose your font faces in another program so that you know what you're getting.
- You can change the order in which the font combinations appear in the list. Open the Edit Font List dialog box, and in the Font List list box, click on a font combination you'd like to move up or down in the list of fonts. Then click on the Up or Down arrow buttons. When you're done, click on OK to close the Font List dialog box.

I Shot the Serif

Serifs are those curly things some fonts use at the ends of strokes in letters. They have their origins in ancient times when stonecutters had to make a terminating stroke in a letter in order to remove the chisel from the stone.

A *sans serif* font, then, is a font without any serifs. As illustrated in **Figure 12**, sans serif fonts, such as Arial and Verdana, have a different look than serif fonts.

Mono refers to a *monospace* font, which is the same as a fixed-width font. In a *fixed-width font*, each letter occupies the same amount of space. Most e-mail and Telnet programs use monospace fonts.

A *proportional font* is a font that's designed so that each letter, or character, takes up only as much space as it needs. Letter combinations such as fi and *th* fit together, rather than standing apart.

Proportional fonts are used for body text on most Web pages, while fixed-width fonts are used for the text typed into forms, as well as the font for several text styles, such as teletype, code, and citation. Preformatted text, as described in Chapter 4, also employs a fixed-width font.

Courier New (Courier), used in **Figure 12**, is the most popular fixed-width font. Some browsers, however, allow their users to change their proportional and fixed-width fonts so that the choices don't necessarily correspond to their character.

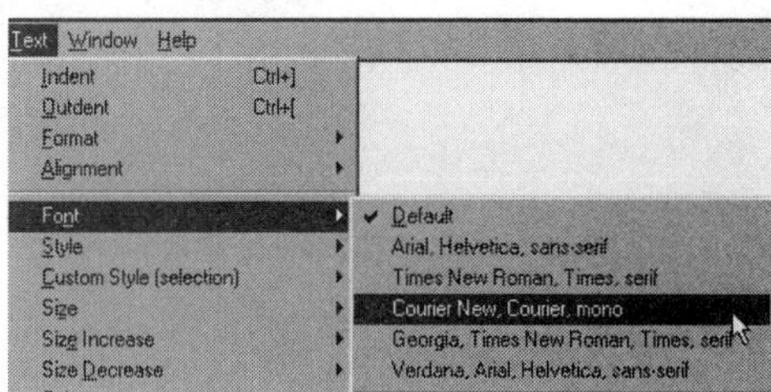

Figure 15 From the Document window menu bar, select Text > Font> and then choose a font combination from the menu bar. Any font combinations you added with the Font List dialog box will appear in this menu.

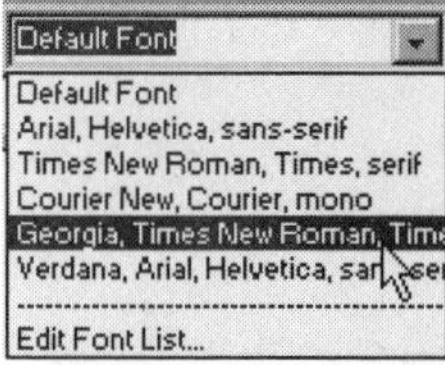

Figure 16 You can choose a font combination from the Properties inspector's Font Face drop-down menu.

Basefont Face

You can set the basefont for a page, too, by adding the FACE attribute to the <basefont> tag. Follow the instructions in the section called *Setting a Basefont*, and to the basefont tag, add the attribute FACE ="Name". Your code will look something like this:

```
<basefont size=4 face="Arial">
```

To set the face for a page:

1. With the document open in the browser window, select Edit > Select All from the Document window menu bar.
2. From the Document window menu bar, select Text > Font > and then choose a font group from the list (**Figure 15**).

   or

   In the Properties inspector, choose a font face group from the Font Face drop-down menu (**Figure 16**).

All the text on the page will change to the first installed font face on the list, unless it's formatted using a tag, such as <code>.

✔ Tip

- To remove any font face specifications, select the text whose font face you've changed, and then change the font face settings to Default Font, using either the Text > Font menu or the Properties inspector.

To set the face for selected text:

1. With the document open in the browser window, highlight the text whose font you wish to change.
2. From the Document window menu bar, select Text > Font > and then choose a font group from the list (**Figure 15**).

   or

   In the Properties inspector, choose a font face group from the Font Face drop-down menu (**Figure 16**).

The selected text will change to the first installed font face on the list.

Specifying Fonts You Don't Own

Font combinations such as Times New Roman, Times are meant to cover two names for the same font on the PC and Mac platforms. Unfortunately, you can't do this for other fonts with the Font List dialog box. (You can add the serif and sans-serif attributes by selecting them from the font list.)

To specify a font that you don't have installed, you need to add the name of the font to the code. You can begin by adding the fonts you do have installed to the Edit Font dialog box, if you wish.

1. Select the text whose font face combination you wish to adjust.
2. From the Document window menu bar, select Window > HTML. The HTML window will appear, with the selected text highlighted.
3. If the text already has the <font> tag applied, you simply need to edit the list of faces. You can also type the entire font tag by hand.

   For instance, to specify two versions of the Bookman font, the code would be:

   `<font face="Bookman Old Style, Bookman">`

   To also include a third choice, and the serif specification, the code would be:

   `<font face="Bookman Old Style, Bookman, Times New Roman, serif">`
4. When you're done, close the HTML window. The first listed font that you have installed will be displayed in the Document window.

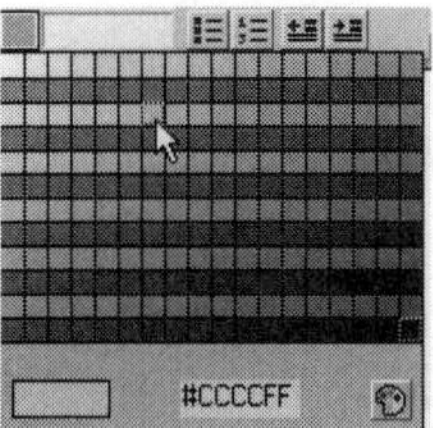

Figure 17 Click on the font color button, and then select a color by clicking on a color choice in the Colors palette.

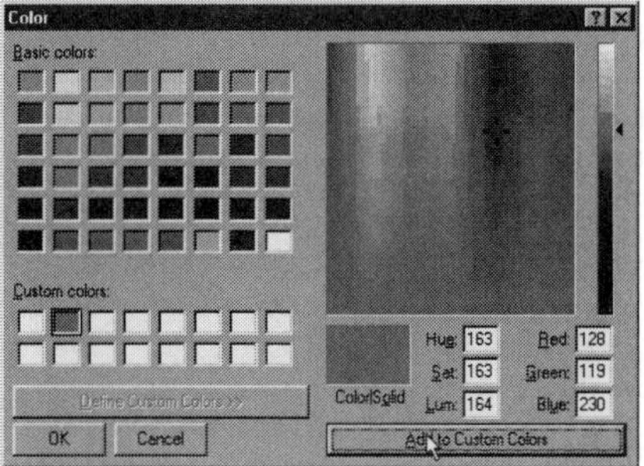

Figure 18 The Color dialog box offers a wider range of color choices.

Color Recycling

Hex codes are defined in Chapter 2; in short, it's sufficient to say they have six (hex) digits.

To use the same color on another piece of text:

1. Select the hex code (including the # sign) from the Properties inspector's Color text box and copy it to the clipboard by pressing Ctrl+C (Command+C).
2. Select the next piece of text whose color you want to change.
3. Paste the hex code into the Properties inspector's Color text box, by pressing Ctrl+V (Command+V).
4. Press Enter (Return), and your text will change to that other color.

Changing Font Color

You learned how to set the text color for an entire page in Chapter 2. You can also set a different font color for specific pieces of text.

To change font color:

1. With your page open in the Document window, select the text whose color you want to change.
2. In the Properties inspector, type (or paste) the hex code for the color in the Color text box and press Enter (Return).

   or

   Click on the Color button beside the Color text box. The Colors palette will appear (**Figure 17**). Click on a color to select it.

   or

   Click on the Colors button in the Colors palette. The Color dialog box will appear (**Figure 18**). Click on a hue and shade to choose a color, and click on OK to close the Color dialog box and return to the Page Properties dialog box. (For more details on using the Color dialog box, refer to Chapter 2.)

No matter the method you use, the color of the text will change to reflect your choice.

✔ Tips

- To remove a font color you've set, select the text in question and then delete the hex code from the Font Color text box.
- To jump directly to the Color dialog box, select Text > Color from the Document window menu bar.

Comments

Comments are notes you want to leave for yourself in the code that won't show up in the browser window.

You might want to add a reminder of when you created the file, when you last updated it, or who made the last revision. You can also use comments to demarcate sections of a document, such as where a table begins and ends, or what part of the document constitutes the footer and copyright notice.

Comments look like this:

<--! You can't see me -->

To add a comment:

1. In the Document window, click to place the insertion point in the area where you want the comment to appear.
2. From the Document window menu bar, select Insert > Comment.

   or

   On the Object palette (Invisibles panel), click on the Comment button.
3. The Comment dialog box will appear (**Figure 19**).
4. Type the text you want to include in the comment in the Comment text box.
5. Click on OK to close the dialog box.

If you have invisible element viewing turned on, you'll see the comment icon: .

Otherwise, you can look at the code in the HTML inspector to see your comment.

✔ Tip

- You can adjust the comments later on by selecting the Comments icon and viewing the Properties inspector (**Figure 20**).

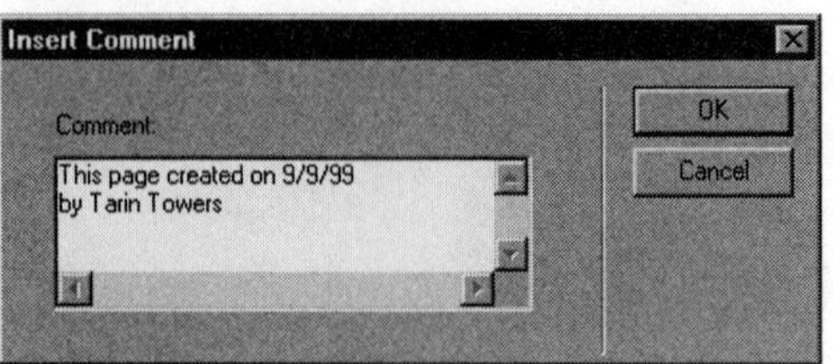

Figure 19 Type the hidden comments you want to place in the code in the Comment text box.

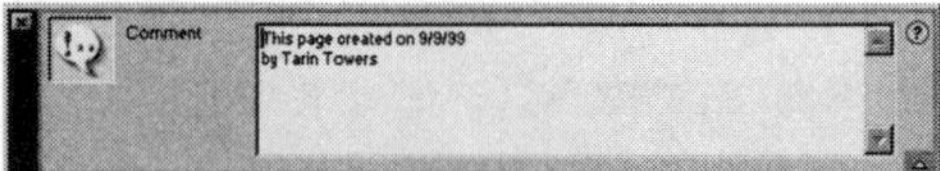

Figure 20 If you select the Comments icon, you can view or revise your comments in the Properties inspector.

Figure 21 Type the text you want to find in the Find text box.

Find and Replace

Dreamweaver can search your document and locate a particular piece of text. It can also replace one text string with another.

To find a piece of text:

1. With the current page open in the Document window, select Edit > Find from the Document window menu bar, or press Ctrl+F (Command+F). The Find dialog box will appear (**Figure 21**).
2. Type what you're looking for in the Find what text box. This can be a whole word, a phrase, or part of a word.
3. If you want to look for a particular case pattern (upper or lower), place a checkmark in the Match Case checkbox.
4. Click on Find Next. If Dreamweaver finds what you're looking for, it will highlight the text in question on the current page (although you may have to move the Find dialog box to see it).
5. Now you can close the Find dialog box by clicking on Cancel.

✔ Tips

- If Dreamweaver doesn't find the text in question, a dialog box will appear telling you the search item was not found.
- To find the same item again (even on a different page), select Edit > Find Next from the Document window menu bar.
- You can also use the Find command in the HTML inspector.

To replace one piece of text with another:

1. From the Document window menu bar, select Edit > Replace, or press Ctrl+H (Command+H). The Replace dialog box will appear (**Figure 22**).
2. Type the text you want to destroy in the Find What text box.
3. Type the text you want to replace it with in the Replace With text box.
4. If you want to restrict the search to a specific case pattern (upper or lower), place a checkmark in the Match case checkbox.
5. To supervise the search, click on Find Next, and when Dreamweaver finds an instance of the Find text string, it will highlight it in the document window. Then, you can click on Replace to supplant it with the text in the Replace text box.

   or

   To have Dreamweaver automatically replace all Find what text with the Replace with text, click on Replace all. A dialog box will appear informing you how many replacements were made.
6. When you're all done, click on Cancel to return to the Document window.

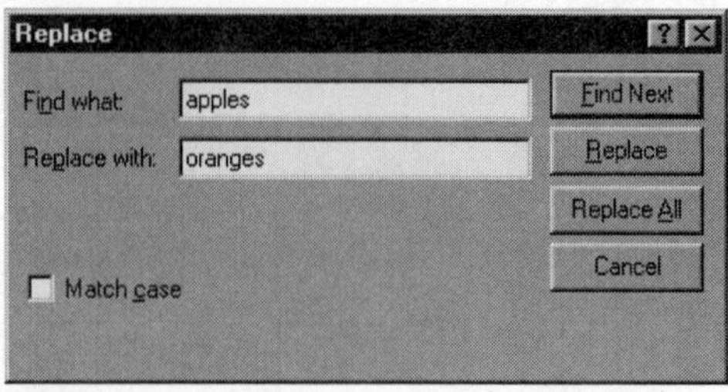

Figure 22 Type the text you want to find in the Find text box, and the text you want to replace it with in the Replace text box.

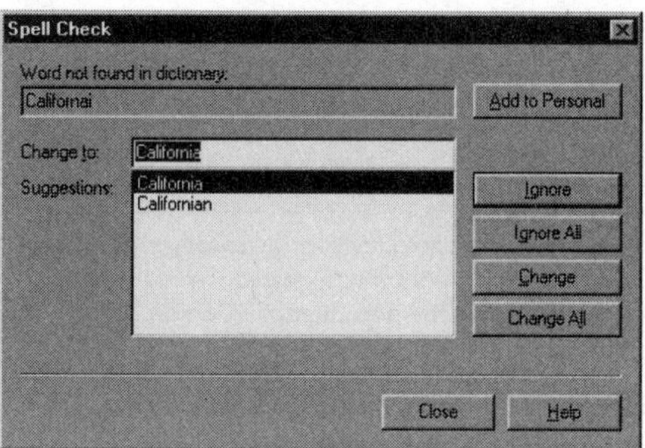

Figure 23 The Spell Check dialog box allows you to ignore the unrecognized word, add it to your personal dictionary, or change it by typing it into the Change to text box or selecting a word from the Suggestions list box.

Checking Your Spelling

The nice thing about using a WYSIWYG editor to do HTML is that you can check the spelling on your pages without the spell checker constantly asking you to validate tags or URLs. You can check the spelling of an individual selection or an entire page.

To check the spelling of a page:

1. With the page in question open in the Dreamweaver window, click to place the insertion point at the beginning of the page (or the place at which you'd like to begin the spell check).
2. From the Document window menu bar, select Text > Check Spelling, or press Shift+F7. The Spell Check dialog box will appear (**Figure 23**).
3. When Dreamweaver finds the first questionable word, that word will appear in the Word Not Found in Dictionary text box. You have several options here:
   - If the word is spelled correctly, click on Ignore.
   - If the word is spelled correctly, and you think it might appear more than once on your page, click on Ignore All.
   - If the word is misspelled, and the correct spelling appears in the Suggestions list box, click on the correct word, and then click on Change.
   - If you think the word may be misspelled more than once, click on the correct word in the Suggestions list box, and then click on Change All.
   - You can also manually correct the word by typing the correction in the Change to text box and then clicking on Change.

   Make this choice for each word the spell check questions.

(continued)

4. When the spell check reaches the end of the page, Dreamweaver may ask you if you want to check the beginning of the document (**Figure 24**). It's usually a good idea to click on Yes.

5. When the spell check is complete (including cases where there are no spelling errors), a dialog box will appear telling you so (**Figure 25**). It will also report the number of "errors." These errors include words not in the dictionary that you chose to ignore, such as an unusual proper name like Ronkowski or Gravity7. Click on OK to close this dialog box and return to the Document window.

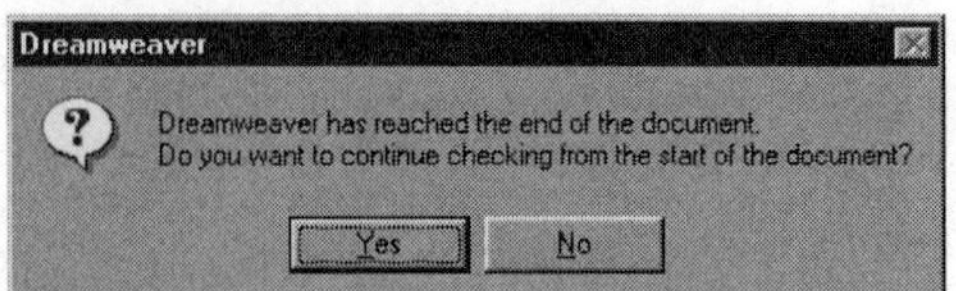

Figure 24 If you are checking the spelling of a selection, click on No. If you started the spell check partway through the document, click on Yes.

Figure 25 When the spell check is complete, you'll be told how many errors were found.

✔ Tips

- If a word is spelled correctly but is not in the dictionary, and you'd like to add this word to the custom dictionary, click on Add to Personal. The word will be added to your personal dictionary, and future spell checks will not question this word. Keep in mind, though, that you may also have to add variations on the word, such as plurals (*gorrillafishes*) or possessives (*Dorkface's*).

- To spellcheck a single word or phrase, highlight the text in question, and then start the spell check as described in Step 1. If you want to skip the rest of the page, when the dialog box appears asking you if you want to check the rest of the document (shown back in **Figure 24**), click on No, and the spell check will go away.

PARAGRAPHS AND LAYOUT

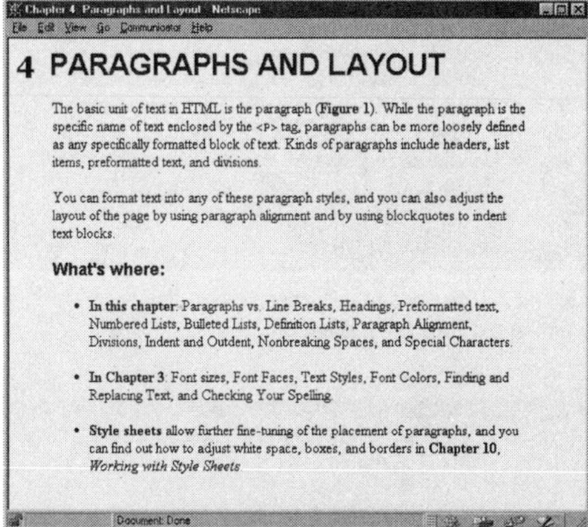

Figure 1 Look familiar? I converted this page into HTML by applying paragraph breaks, two kinds of headings, blockquotes, and a bulleted list. We also used the Arial font face for the headings, and applied the bold and <tt> styles in a few places, as described in Chapter 3. If we wanted to replicate the exact layout of this page we would have used tables, which are covered in Chapter 7.

The basic unit of text in HTML is the paragraph (**Figure 1**). While the paragraph is the specific name of text enclosed by the **<p>** tag, paragraphs can be more loosely defined as any specifically formatted block of text. Paragraph types include headers, list items, preformatted text, and divisions.

You can format text into any of these paragraph styles, and you can adjust the layout of the page by using paragraph alignment and by using blockquotes to indent text blocks. You can also divide a page with ruled lines called horizontal rules.

What's Where

In this chapter you'll find information about paragraphs versus line breaks, headings, preformatted text, numbered lists, bulleted lists, definition lists, paragraph alignment, divisions, indent and outdent, nonbreaking spaces, special characters, and horizontal rules.

Chapter 3 covers font sizes, font faces, text styles, font colors, comments, finding and replacing text, and checking your spelling.

Style sheets allow further fine-tuning of the placement of paragraphs, and you can find out how to adjust white space, boxes, and borders in Chapter 10.

Paragraphs versus Line Breaks

Your elementary school English teacher probably told you that a paragraph contains a minimum of three sentences, and that longer paragraphs include a topic sentence. In HTML, the paragraph is simply a unit of text. Each paragraph is separated from other paragraphs by a blank line. **Figure 2** shows a page that consists of four paragraphs.

To make a paragraph:

1. In the Document window, type the text in the first paragraph. The text will wrap automatically.
2. At the end of the paragraph, press Enter (Return).

The line will be broken, and a line of blank space will be inserted between the paragraph and the insertion point (**Figure 3**).

✔ Tip

- You can also place the insertion point within an existing block of text and press Enter (Return) to insert a paragraph break.

If you want to break the line without inserting a line of blank space, you can use a line break.

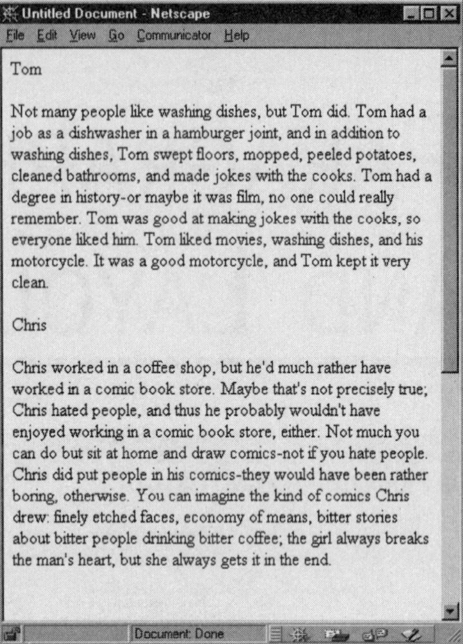

Figure 2 There are four paragraphs on this page: The single-word lines are paragraphs, too.

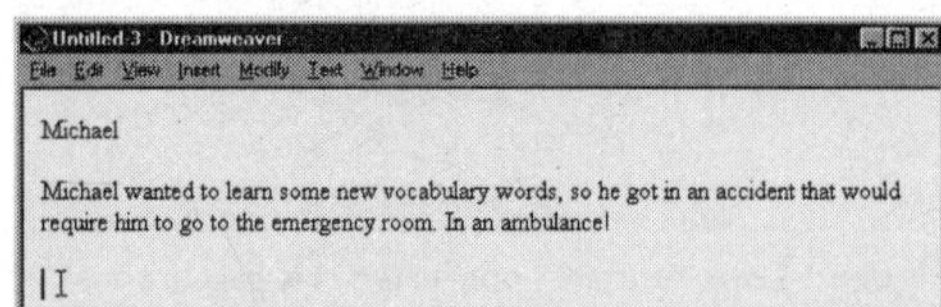

Figure 3 The text will wrap in the Document window—and in the browser window, as well—until you insert a paragraph break. When you press Enter (Return), the insertion point skips a line of blank space and then starts a new paragraph. Technically, there are three paragraphs on this page.

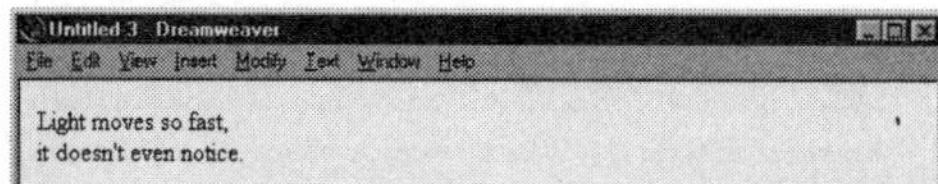

Figure 4 The only way to break a line without adding white space, as you would in a poem, is to use a line break rather than a paragraph break. Press Shift+Enter (Shift+Return).

What's My Line Break?

The tag for a line break is <br>. The <br> tag is one of those tags that doesn't need to be closed.

To make a line break:

1. In the Document window, type the text in the first paragraph. The text will wrap automatically.
2. At the end of the line you want to break, press Shift+Enter (Shift+Return).

The line will break, and the insertion point will begin at the next line (**Figure 4**).

✔ Tip

- You can achieve the same effect by selecting Insert > Line Break from the Document window menu bar.

Paragraph Properties

The tag for a paragraph is <p>. Technically, the <p> tag doesn't need a closing tag. However, if you surround a paragraph with <p> and </p> tags, as Dreamweaver does, that encloses the paragraph in the paragraph format.

Until the introduction of style sheets, this wasn't an issue anyone worried about; however, style sheets allow you to change the properties of an enclosed tag, and defining the <p> tag's properties only does any good if you close your paragraphs with the </p> tag.

Div and Span

There are two other kinds of text blocks that you might run across: <div> and <span>. The <div> tag stands for division, and it's used to mark blocks of text that (generally) span more than one paragraph. You can't end the division within a paragraph, because the </div> closing tag automatically breaks the paragraph. The <span> tag, on the other hand, can be used to mark up an area of text within a single block of text, such as within a paragraph or blockquote.

These two tags are mostly used in conjunction with style sheets, but I'm pointing them out here because of their properties of breaking paragraphs (or not). In the section of this chapter called *Text Alignment*, we'll look more closely at the alignment properties of the <div> and <span> tags.

Break Properties

The break tag has a CLEAR attribute that can be used when combining text and floating elements, particularly floating images aligned at the left or right margin. Image alignment properties are discussed in Chapter 5. If you see code like this: <br clear=left>, it refers to the combination of text and images and how the text flows around the image. In addition to LEFT, other CLEAR attributes are ALL, RIGHT, and NONE (**Figure 5**).

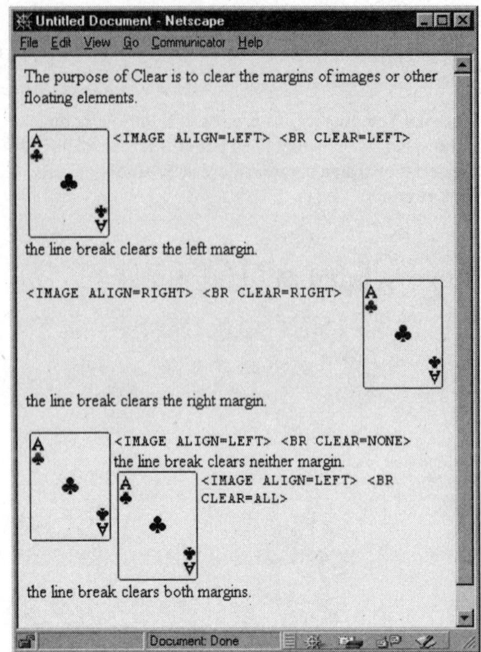

Figure 5 The CLEAR attribute of the break tag is demonstrated here in four possible permutations. The most obvious actions of the CLEAR attribute are visible when working with images aligned to the left or right margin. It takes a bit of experimentation to figure out exactly what's what. Refer to Chapter 5 for more on image alignment.

Heading 1

Heading 2

Heading 3

Heading 4

Normal Text

Heading 5

Heading 6

Figure 6 There are six levels of headings, from 1 (largest) to 6 (smallest). Heading 4 is the same size as the default font size.

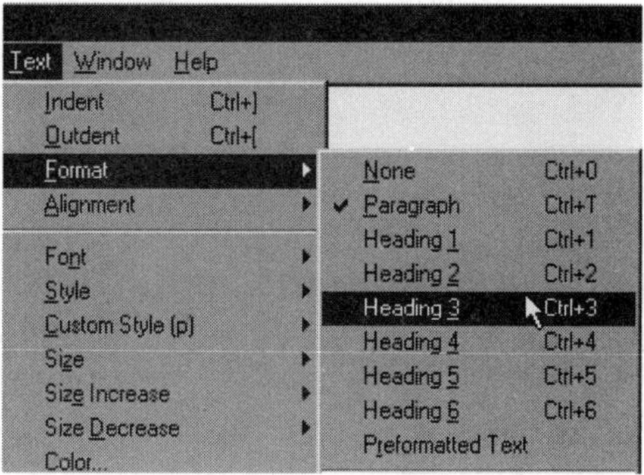

Figure 7 Choose a heading size, from 1 to 6, from the Text > Format menu.

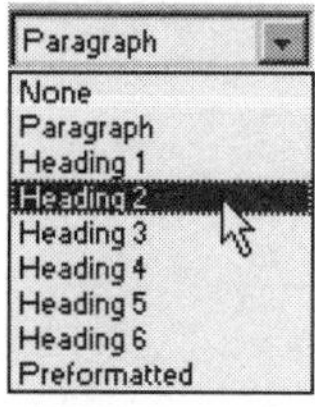

Figure 8 You can also set headings using the Properties inspector's Format drop-down menu.

Headings

Think of headings (also called headers) as being the same as headlines in a newspaper. They're larger than the body text of an article and are generally boldfaced. There is always a paragraph break between a heading and the text that follows.

There are six sizes, or levels, of headings (**Figure 6**). Heading 1 is the largest, and Heading 6 is often smaller than the text on a page.

To format a heading:

1. Click within the line of text you want to make into a heading.
2. From the Document window menu bar, select Text > Format > and from the menu that appears (**Figure 7**), select a heading (size 1–6).

   or

   On the Properties inspector, select a heading (size 1–6) from the Format drop-down menu (**Figure 8**).

The text will become a heading: that is, there will likely be a size change; the text will become boldface; and a blank line will be inserted after the heading.

Preformatted Text

In general, when you paste text into the Document window, it doesn't retain any of its formatting. This includes line breaks, paragraph breaks, spacing, tabs, text-formatted tables, and the like.

If you have formatted text in another program and you wish it to retain its shape, you can place it into HTML as preformatted text. None of the other conventions of HTML will govern this text; for instance, in HTML, only one typed space will be displayed, even if you type 50 in a row. In preformatted text, any shaping of the text done with spaces or line breaks will be preserved.

Figure 9 shows a piece of ASCII art preserved with preformatted text, and **Figure 10** shows the same characters without the preformatted text format applied.

It's generally easier to set up the preformatted style before you paste in the text.

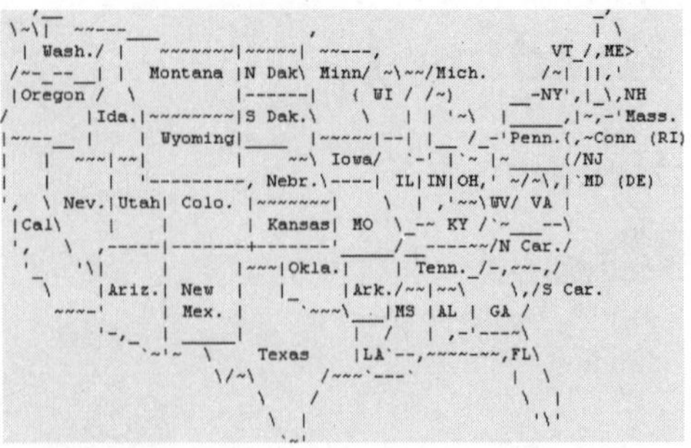

Figure 9 Someone worked very hard formatting this map of the United States in a text editor. (Pictures made with plain text are called ASCII art.)

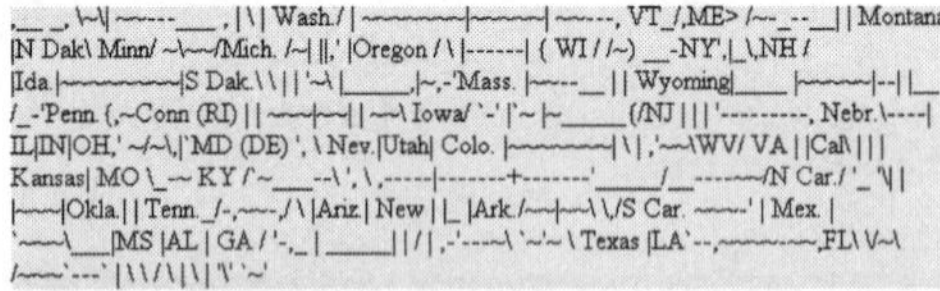

Figure 10 If you don't preserve the preformatted text, it looks like a jumble of characters.

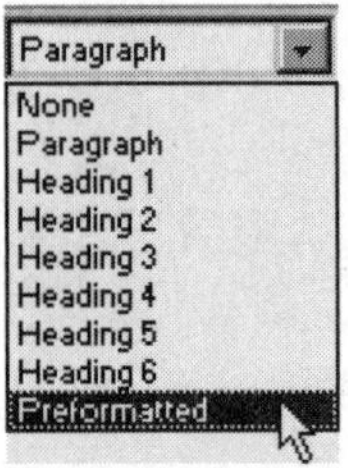

Figure 11 Select Preformatted text from the Properties inspector's Format drop-down menu.

Preformatted Face

By default, the font used in preformatted text is the default monospace font, generally Courier or Courier New. The reason for this, as explained in Chapter 3, is that each character in a monospace font is the same width, which means that you can more easily control formatting of ASCII art or poetry (**Figure 12**).

You can change the font face, however, in addition to designating it as preformatted. Follow the steps in Chapter 3, in the section called *Changing Font Face*, to change the face of the preformatted text. Or you can refer to Chapter 10 to find out how to change the attributes of the <PRE> tag.

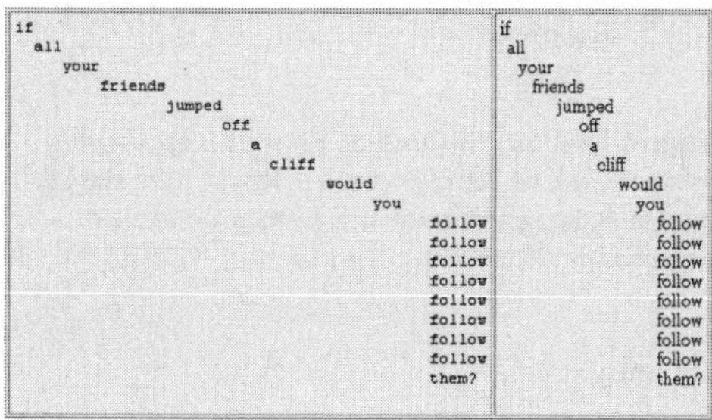

Figure 12 If you apply a non-monospace font to preformatted text, you'll get a different effect, because each character (including spaces) is not the same width.

To place preformatted text:

1. In the Document window, click to place the insertion point where you want the preformatted text to begin.
2. From the Document window menu bar, select Text > Format > Preformatted Text.

   or

   On the Properties inspector, select Preformatted Text from the Format drop-down menu (as seen previously in **Figure 11**).
3. Now you can paste in the text from the other program whose formatting you wish to retain.

✔ Tip

- You can also apply the Preformatted style to text already on a page, or type the work directly into Dreamweaver, although you may get better results using a text editor.

Formatting Lists

Dreamweaver directly supports two kinds of lists: numbered lists, also called *ordered lists;* and Bulleted lists, also called *unordered lists.* There is an additional kind of list called a definition list that is partially supported by Dreamweaver.

To make a numbered list:

1. In the Dreamweaver window, type (or paste) the items you'd like to make into a numbered list, *omitting the numbers* (**Figure 13**).
2. Select the list items.
3. From the Document window menu bar, select Text > Format > Ordered List.

   or

   On the Properties inspector, click on the Ordered List button.

The list will become numbered (**Figure 14**).

To add an item to a numbered list:

1. To add an item to the end of a list, click to place the insertion point at the end of the last numbered line, and press Enter (Return). A new number will appear at the end of the list.
2. To add an item to the middle of the list, click to place the insertion point at the end of one of the lines, and press Enter (Return). A new number will appear in the middle of the list (**Figure 15**).

To remove an item from a numbered list:

1. Select the item to be removed, and press Delete (Backspace).
2. Press Delete (Backspace) again, and the numbered line will be removed.

The list will renumber itself to reflect any additions or subtractions from the list.

Morning

wake up

feed the cat

make coffee

eat breakfast

brush teeth

shower

Figure 13 Type the items you want to make into a list.

Morning

1. wake up
2. feed the cat
3. make coffee
4. eat breakfast
5. brush teeth
6. shower

Figure 14 After the Ordered list style is applied, the list items will be numbered and indented from the left margin. A paragraph break is automatically applied before and after the list.

Morning

1. wake up
2. feed the cat
3. make coffee
4.
5. eat breakfast
6. brush teeth
7. shower

Figure 15 If you add or remove items from the list, it will automatically renumber itself.

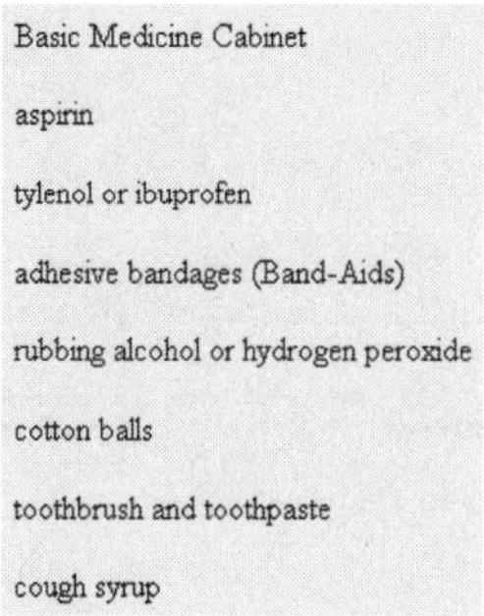

Basic Medicine Cabinet

aspirin

tylenol or ibuprofen

adhesive bandages (Band-Aids)

rubbing alcohol or hydrogen peroxide

cotton balls

toothbrush and toothpaste

cough syrup

Figure 16 Type the items you want to appear in the list, one to a line.

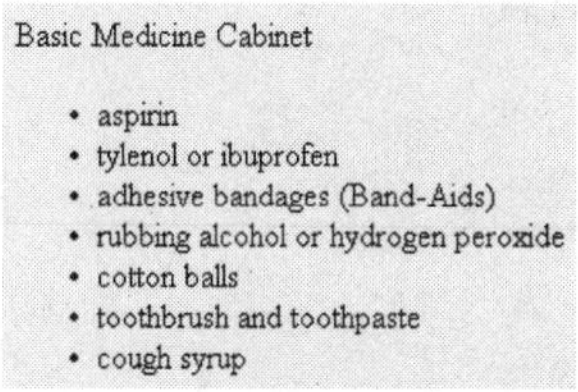

Basic Medicine Cabinet

- aspirin
- tylenol or ibuprofen
- adhesive bandages (Band-Aids)
- rubbing alcohol or hydrogen peroxide
- cotton balls
- toothbrush and toothpaste
- cough syrup

Figure 17 After you select the unordered list format, the list items will be single spaced and indented, and bullets will be added.

Images as Bullets

You may have seen a page that appears to use small images as bullets (**Figure 18**). This is not, in fact a bulleted list. Each image is placed on a line (you can copy and paste them with Dreamweaver), and then the lines can be optionally indented. (See the section in this chapter called *Indent and Outdent*).

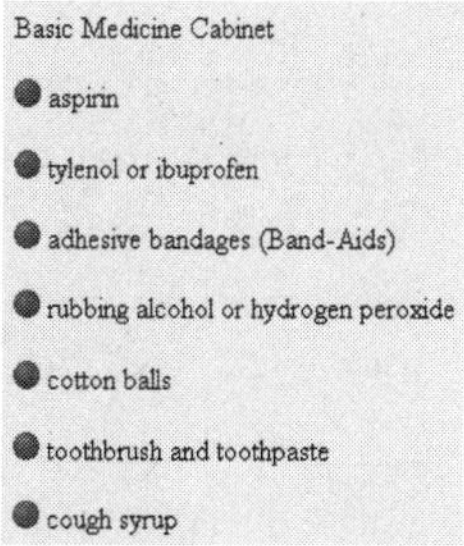

Basic Medicine Cabinet

● aspirin

● tylenol or ibuprofen

● adhesive bandages (Band-Aids)

● rubbing alcohol or hydrogen peroxide

● cotton balls

● toothbrush and toothpaste

● cough syrup

Figure 18 You can use tiny images on each line instead of making a bulleted list.

To make a bulleted list:

1. In the Dreamweaver window, type (or paste) the items you'd like to make into a bulleted list, *omitting any asterisks or other bullet placeholders* (**Figure 16**).
2. Select the list items.
3. From the Document window menu bar, select Text > Format > Unordered List.

   or

   On the Properties inspector, click on the Unordered List button.

The list will become bulleted and indented (**Figure 17**).

✔ List Tips

- To convert a list back to paragraph style, reapply the style (select it from the menu bar or deselect the list button on the Properties inspector).
- Lists can only be bulleted or numbered, not both (thank goodness). To convert a list from bulleted to numbered (or vice versa), select the list and then apply the other list format.
- If some extraneous text before or after the list gets added to the list, select the offending line of text and click on the corresponding list button to deselect it.
- By default, a paragraph break will be inserted both before and after the list. Press Enter (Return) twice to end the list.
- The items in the list will be single-spaced by default. To add a line of blank space between the list items, press Enter+Return (Shift+Return) *twice* after each list item.
- Other list options are available using style sheets; see Chapter 10.

A third kind of list, called a definition list, is also supported by Dreamweaver, albeit not very elegantly. In a definition list, there are two kinds of list items: a definition term <dt>, and a definition <dd>.

As you'd find in a glossary, the definition is indented under the definition term (**Figure 21**). The items in a definition list don't have to be definitions; you can use it anywhere where you want this sort of formatting.

To make a definition list:

1. Type the definition terms and the definitions in the Document window (**Figure 20**). Place each term and definition on a separate line, and omit any indentations.
2. Select the list items.
3. From the Document window menu bar, select Text > Format > Definition List (**Figure 21**).

The list will be formatted so that every other item is a term and a definition (**Figure 19**).

✔ Tips

- If you're having trouble getting Dreamweaver to format the list properly, try selecting it in the HTML inspector. Make sure you select all opening and closing tags (including <p> and <p> tags).
- If you want to format the definition list yourself, surround each definition term with <dt>and</dt>, and every definition with <dd>and</dd>.
- You can include more than one definition per definition term.
- This is an alternative way to indent blocks of text, because they are indented only from the left margin, not from both margins (as opposed to blockquotes).

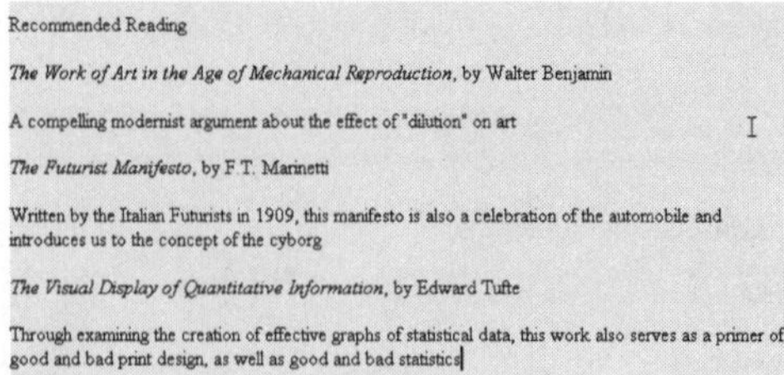

Recommended Reading

The Work of Art in the Age of Mechanical Reproduction, by Walter Benjamin

A compelling modernist argument about the effect of "dilution" on art

The Futurist Manifesto, by F.T. Marinetti

Written by the Italian Futurists in 1909, this manifesto is also a celebration of the automobile and introduces us to the concept of the cyborg

The Visual Display of Quantitative Information, by Edward Tufte

Through examining the creation of effective graphs of statistical data, this work also serves as a primer of good and bad print design, as well as good and bad statistics

Figure 19 Type the terms and definitions, one to a line, in the Document window.

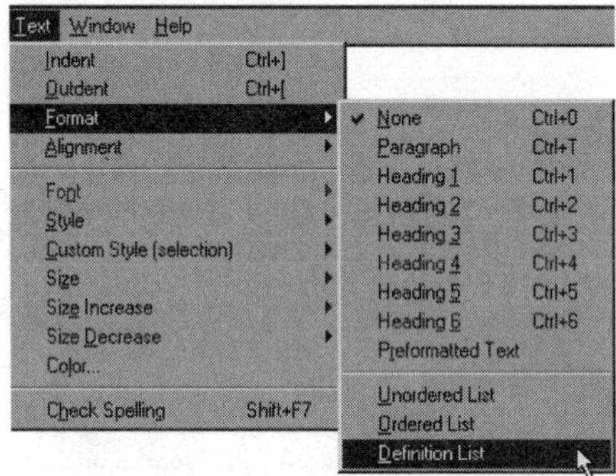

Figure 20 From the Document window menu bar, select Text > Format > Definition List.

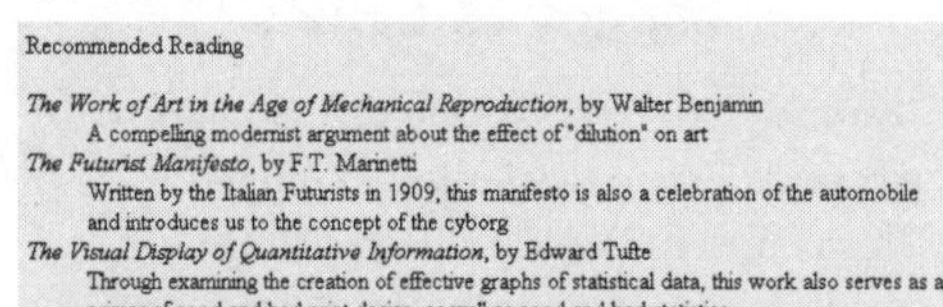

Recommended Reading

The Work of Art in the Age of Mechanical Reproduction, by Walter Benjamin
    A compelling modernist argument about the effect of "dilution" on art
The Futurist Manifesto, by F.T. Marinetti
    Written by the Italian Futurists in 1909, this manifesto is also a celebration of the automobile and introduces us to the concept of the cyborg
The Visual Display of Quantitative Information, by Edward Tufte
    Through examining the creation of effective graphs of statistical data, this work also serves as a primer of good and bad print design, as well as good and bad statistics

Figure 21 The list will be formatted so that every other item is a term or a definition. You can add other formatting and line breaks later.

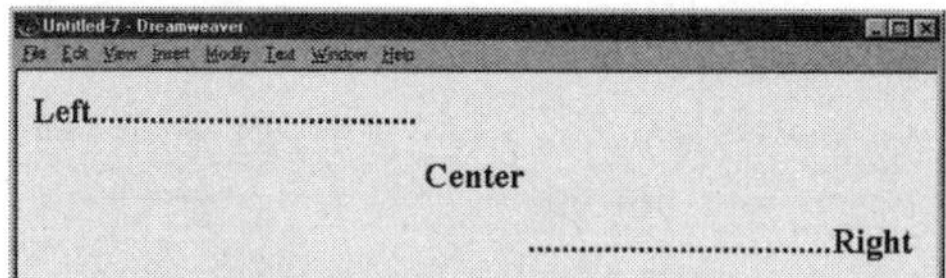

Figure 22 You can align text to the left margin, the center of the page, or the right margin.

Terms of Alignment

Depending on what kind of text you're aligning—and how much—Dreamweaver may use different code. All default (unspecified) alignment is to the left margin.

The <center> tag can be used to center any element between the opening tag and the closing </center> tag.

Headers can be aligned by using the align attribute within the <Hn> tag. For instance: <H2 align=center>.

A similar attribute exists for paragraphs, although it's being deprecated (removed from the HTML standard). You may, however, see this in use: <p align=right> The align attribute will end with the closing </p> tag.

For more than one line of text, Dreamweaver tends to use the <div> tag to define all the text with a non-left alignment. For instance: <div align=center>centered text</div>

As we mentioned earlier in the chapter, the </div> tag creates a paragraph break. Centering applies to an entire division or paragraph; this includes line breaks within the <p> or <div>.

To align part of a paragraph or division, you can use the <span> tag to surround a few lines of text within a <p> or <div>:

```
<span align=right
one line<br></span>
```

Text Alignment

As is the case with word-processing programs, you can align part or all of a page of text with the left margin, the right margin, or the center of the page (**Figure 22**).

To change the alignment of text:

1. Select the text whose alignment you wish to change. This can be a single paragraph, a heading, a list, or an entire page.
2. From the Document window menu bar, select Text > Alignment > and then Left, Right, or Center.

   or

   On the Properties inspector, click on the Left, Right, or Center alignment button.

The text will become aligned according to the option you selected.

✔ Tip

- When you're working with images, or with tables, there are more than three alignment options available. Refer to Chapter 5 or to Chapter 7 for more on these alignment options.

Indenting Text

There are no tabs in regular HTML; the kind of five-space paragraph indent used in other types of publishing is generally replaced by setting off each paragraph by a line of white space.

You can, however, indent an entire block of text. One way to accomplish this is by using Definition Lists (see the *Formatting Lists* section in this chapter). Or use the <blockquote> tag, which is what Dreamweaver does.

To indent a block of text:

1. In the Dreamweaver window, click within the paragraph you wish to indent; to select more than one paragraph, highlight the text you want to indent (**Figure 23**).
2. From the Document window menu bar, select Text > Indent.

   or

   On the Properties inspector, click on the Indent button.

Either way, the text will become indented (**Figure 24**).

✔ Tips

- You can repeat Step 2 for multiple indent levels (**Figure 25**).
- <blockquote> indents text from both margins; to indent text from one margin only, use a definition list (see the section called *Formatting Lists* in this chapter).
- You can also create an artificial indent by using nonbreaking spaces (see *The Nonbreaking Space*, in this chapter).
- Tables are another way to create margins. See Chapter 7.
- Paragraph indents are available in style sheets; see Chapter 10.

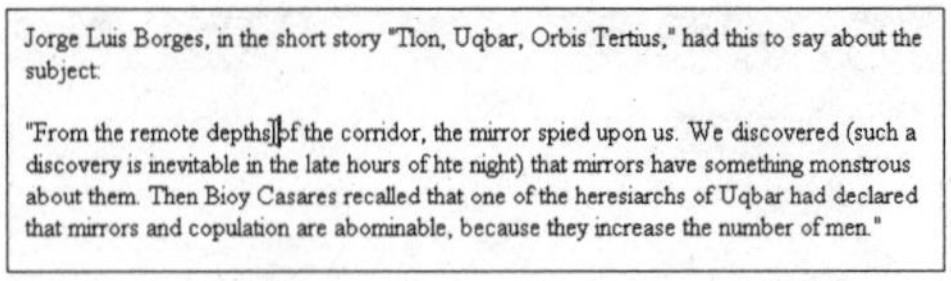

Jorge Luis Borges, in the short story "Tlon, Uqbar, Orbis Tertius," had this to say about the subject:

"From the remote depths of the corridor, the mirror spied upon us. We discovered (such a discovery is inevitable in the late hours of hte night) that mirrors have something monstrous about them. Then Bioy Casares recalled that one of the heresiarchs of Uqbar had declared that mirrors and copulation are abominable, because they increase the number of men."

Figure 23 Click within the paragraph you want to indent.

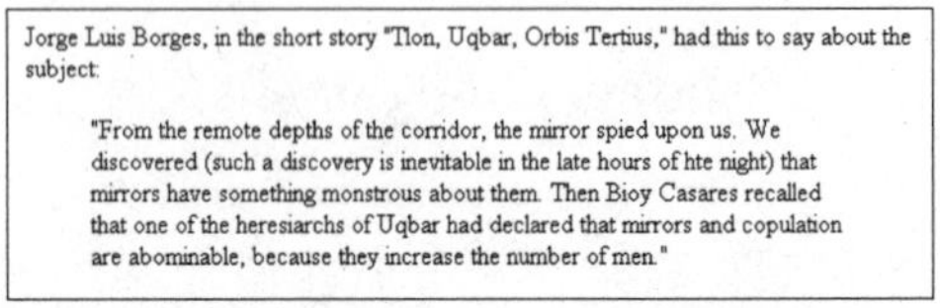

Jorge Luis Borges, in the short story "Tlon, Uqbar, Orbis Tertius," had this to say about the subject:

> "From the remote depths of the corridor, the mirror spied upon us. We discovered (such a discovery is inevitable in the late hours of hte night) that mirrors have something monstrous about them. Then Bioy Casares recalled that one of the heresiarchs of Uqbar had declared that mirrors and copulation are abominable, because they increase the number of men."

Figure 24 Dreamweaver indents text by applying the <blockquote> format.

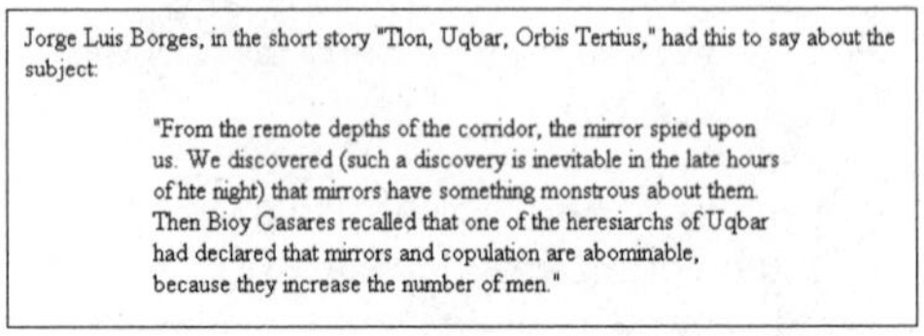

Jorge Luis Borges, in the short story "Tlon, Uqbar, Orbis Tertius," had this to say about the subject:

> > "From the remote depths of the corridor, the mirror spied upon us. We discovered (such a discovery is inevitable in the late hours of hte night) that mirrors have something monstrous about them. Then Bioy Casares recalled that one of the heresiarchs of Uqbar had declared that mirrors and copulation are abominable, because they increase the number of men."

Figure 25 You can indent the paragraph more than one level; by doing so here, it becomes more apparent that blockquotes are indented from both margins.

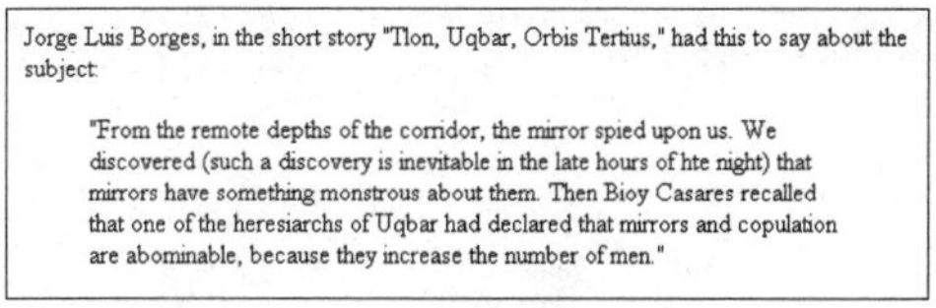

Jorge Luis Borges, in the short story "Tlon, Uqbar, Orbis Tertius," had this to say about the subject:

> "From the remote depths of the corridor, the mirror spied upon us. We discovered (such a discovery is inevitable in the late hours of hte night) that mirrors have something monstrous about them. Then Bioy Casares recalled that one of the heresiarchs of Uqbar had declared that mirrors and copulation are abominable, because they increase the number of men."

Figure 26 You can remove a level of indent by clicking on the outdent button. This often works for removing list formatting, too.

Outdenting?

Here's a completely useless side note. The word *indent* derives from the Latin *in-* (in) + *dent* (tooth), meaning to bite into (in Middle English, the word *endenten* meant "to notch"). The text, then, bites its way into the page. Since you can't "unchew" something, this explains why "outdenting" isn't a conventional layout term.

If you decide to change your mind, you can remove one or more indent levels. Dreamweaver calls this "outdenting."

To remove a level of indent:

1. In the Dreamweaver window, click within the paragraph from which you wish to remove a level of indent; to select more than one paragraph, highlight the text.
2. From the Document window menu bar, select Text > Outdent.

   or

   On the Properties inspector, click on the Outdent button.

Either way, one level of indent will be removed (**Figure 26**).

✔ Tip

- You can repeat step 2 until the text is at the margin, if you like.

The Nonbreaking Space

In HTML, while spaces count as characters, they're shady ones. Only one simple spacebar-typed space will display in an HTML browser, even if you type 50 of them. There is an entity, however, called the *nonbreaking space*. This is part of a family of special characters that you can't type easily with ASCII text; each character is represented by a *control code* or *escape sequence*.

Dreamweaver automatically puts nonbreaking spaces in the code where it thinks you need them; for instance, when you need more than one line of blank space, the nonbreaking space is used as an entity. Paragraphs can't be empty, and you also can't line up <p> tags to create multiple paragraph breaks (they are also ignored).

Figure 27 shows a page and its code; while most of the page appears to be blank, it requires some behind-the-scenes code to work.

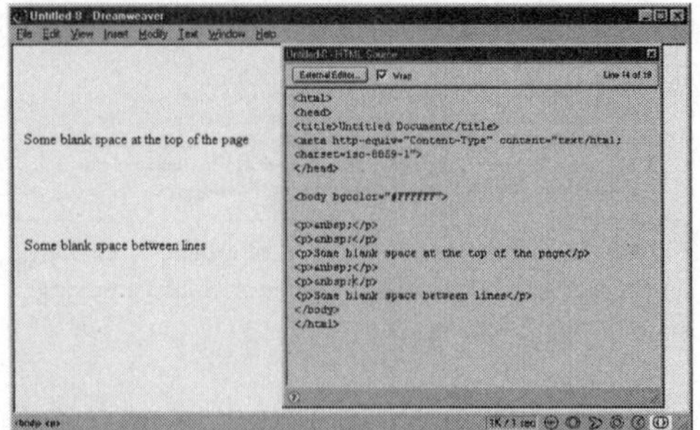

Figure 27 As the code for this page indicates, the nonbreaking space is a useful placeholder.

To insert a nonbreaking space:

1. In the Document window, click to place the insertion point at the place in the code where you want to insert a non-breaking space.
2. View the HTML window by selecting Window > HTML from the Document window menu bar.
3. Type the following characters:
4. When you close the HTML window, Dreamweaver will automatically convert the escape sequence into its visual equivalent, an ordinary-looking space.

If you take a look at the code, you'll see that the   sequence is still there where you put it.

✔ Tip

- A keyboard shortcut for inserting a non-breaking space: Shift+Ctrl+spacebar (Shift+Command+spacebar)

Special Characters in HTML

There are a variety of special characters in HTML that you may want to use on your pages (see **Table 4.1**). Dreamweaver does not have any direct support for inserting these characters, but if you type the escape sequence for any of these characters in the HTML window, Dreamweaver will print the character instead of the sequence.

Table 4.1

Commonly Used Special Characters in HTML

The Character	The Code
&	&
©	©
®	®
<	<
>	>
– (n-dash)	
¿	¿
¡	¡
é	é
è	è
ü	ü
ñ	ñ
ç	ç

Horizontal Rules

A horizontal rule is a line that goes across the page horizontally and provides an explicit rather than implied division between parts of a document (**Figure 28**). Some people swear by them; others think they're the scourge of HTML, but I'm going to show you how to make one, regardless.

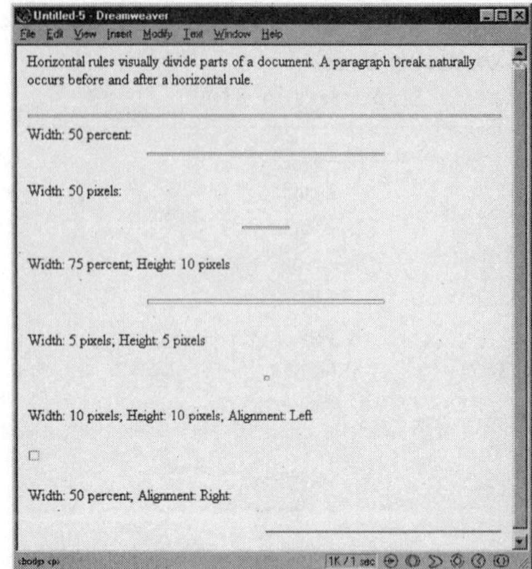

Figure 28 Horizontal rules can come in many different shapes and sizes; the first horizontal rule in this figure has the default attributes of 100 percent width, center alignment, and 3-D shading.

To insert a horizontal rule:

1. Click to place the insertion point where you want the ruled line to appear.
2. From the Document window menu bar, select Insert > Horizontal Rule.

A ruled line will appear, the width of the page, a paragraph break before and after it.

To change the rule:

1. Select the horizontal rule, if necessary, by double-clicking it.
2. Display the Properties inspector, if necessary, by choosing Modify > Selection Properties. The Properties inspector will display Horizontal Rule Properties (**Figure 29**).
3. To name the Horizontal rule, type a lowercase word in the HR text box.
4. To adjust the width, type a number, in either pixels or percent of window, in the W text box. Then, choose the unit of measure from the W drop-down menu.
5. To adjust the height, type a number (in pixels) in the H text box.
6. To adjust the alignment, choose Left, Center, or Right from the Align drop-down menu.
7. To remove the 3-D shading (also called the beveling), deselect the Shading checkbox.
8. Click on the Apply button to apply the changes to the horizontal rule.

Figure 29 You can change the appearance of a horizontal rule with the Properties inspector.

WORKING WITH IMAGES

Figure 1 The splash page for Christian Cosas's personal home page uses a simple image against a plain background. Both the image and the text link point to the site's table of contents, shown in **Figure 2**.

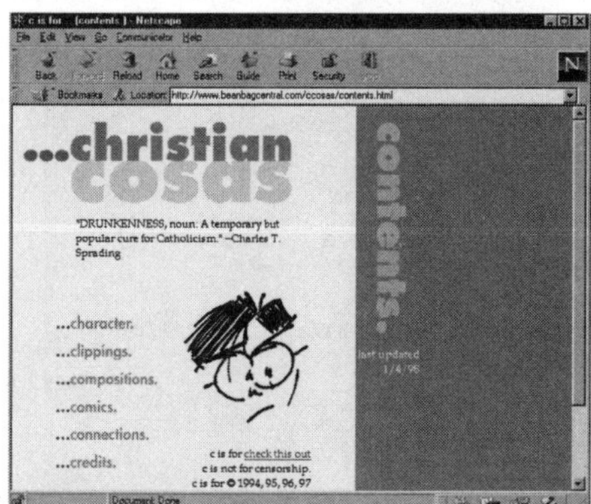

Figure 2 The home page, or table of contents page, for Christian's site includes linked images—the words along the left side of the page are all images. Since Christian's site is partly a showcase for his artwork, the contents page includes an example so you know where you're headed. With 11 images on the page including the background, the whole page weighs in at only 27K.

Chances are, if Mosaic hadn't introduced the prospect of inline image viewing in its Web browser in 1994, the Web still wouldn't be a big deal. Other Internet tools, such as WAIS and gopher, don't match the Web in popularity—not because the systems themselves aren't as versatile, but because the browsing software doesn't support inline media other than text.

Used to be, if you found an image online, you had to download it, get offline, and then open the image in a viewing program. That all seems like ancient history these days.

When used well, images can add not just visual interest but information and versatility to a Web page. **Figures 1** and **2** show Christian Cosas's site, which makes excellent use of images.

✔ Tips

- To find out about using background images, refer to Chapter 2.
- For instructions on making an image map, see Appendix A.

Placing an Image

There are several ways to place images with Dreamweaver.

To place an image:

1. With the desired page open in the Document window, click at the place on the page where you'd like the image to appear.
2. From the Document window menu bar, select Insert > Image (**Figure 3**).

   or

   Click on the Image button in the Object palette (**Figure 4**).

   or

   Press Ctrl+Alt+I (Command+Option+I).

   Regardless of the method, the Insert Image dialog box will appear (**Figure 5**).
3. If you know the location of the image on the Web or on your computer, type it in the Image File text box.

   or

   Click on Browse. The Select File dialog box will appear (**Figure 6**). Browse through the files and folders on your computer until you find the image file. Click on the image file's icon, so that its name appears in the File Name text box. Click on Open to close the Browse dialog box, and the Insert Image dialog box will reappear, with the location of your image in the text box.
4. Click on OK to close the Insert Image dialog box. The image will appear at the insertion point in the Document window.

✔ Tip

- If you haven't yet saved your page, a dialog box will appear telling you about file pathnames. Click on OK to close this dialog box. I'll talk more about pathnames later in Chapters 6 and 16.

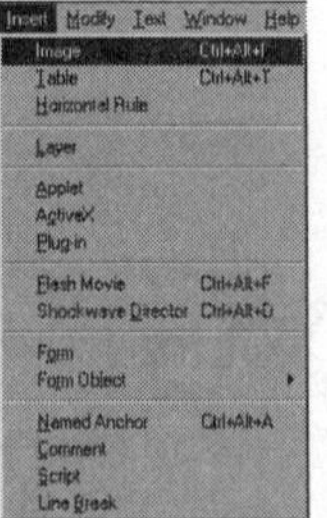

Figure 3 Select Insert > Image from the Document window menu bar.

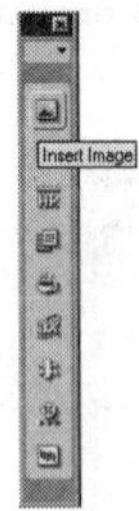

Figure 4 Click on the Image button in the Object palette.

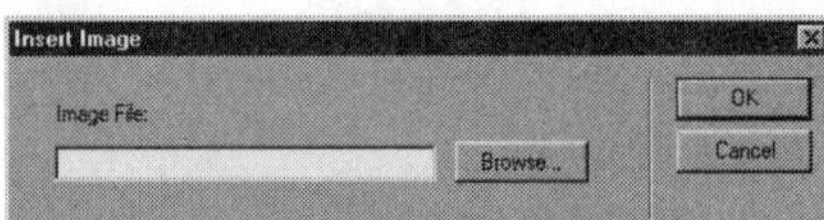

Figure 5 Type the image location in the Insert Image dialog box, or click on the Browse button to locate the image file on your computer.

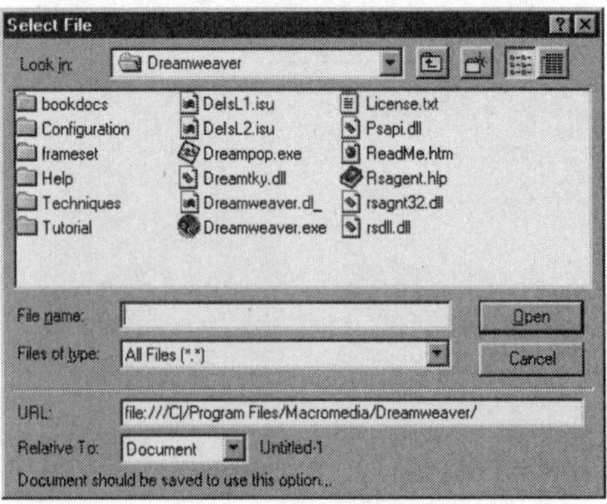

Figure 6 The Select File dialog box is similar to the familiar Open dialog box. Browse through the files and folders on your computer until you find the file you're looking for.

Definitions

A *splash page* (**Figure 1**) is what you call an opening screen that leads in to the rest of a site. Not essential, the splash page should be simple, load quickly, and show you what the point of a site is. A *home page*, on the other hand (**Figure 2**), generally serves as a table of contents for the main sections of a site.

Selecting an Image

When you first insert an image with Dreamweaver, it'll look muddy and gray—do not adjust your set (see Figures 10 and 15 to see what I mean). Dreamweaver selects images when they're first placed in the Document window.

To select/deselect an image:

1. To select an image, just click on it. (Dragging the cursor over an image highlights it, but it doesn't select it for the purposes of the Properties inspector.)
2. To deselect an image, click on any other part of the Document window.
3. To select multiple images, hold down the Shift key while you click on each image.

✔ Tips

- When an image is selected, you can copy, cut, delete, or paste over it, just as you do with text in a word processor. All of these commands are available from the Document window's Edit menu.
- Double-click on an image to make the Properties inspector appear.

The Properties Inspector

As with most HTML entities in Dreamweaver, the Properties inspector displays properties specific to images when an image is selected.

To use the Properties inspector:

1. Display the Properties inspector, if necessary, by selecting Modify > Selection Properties from the Document window menu bar.
2. Select the image whose properties you'd like to investigate. The Properties inspector will display properties for that image with a thumbnail of the image as the Apply button, which will appear as a thumbnail of the image (**Figure 7**).
3. To display all the image properties that the inspector has to offer, click on the expander arrow in the bottom-right corner of the inspector (**Figure 8**).

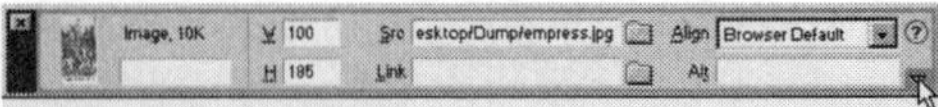

Figure 7 When an image is selected, the Properties inspector will display the image properties. A thumbnail of the image will appear as the Apply button.

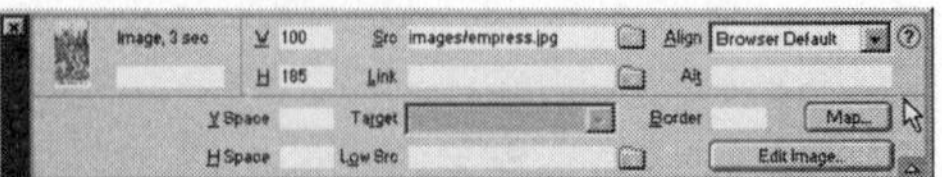

Figure 8 Click on the Expander arrow in the bottom right corner of the Properties inspector (look at the pointer in **Figure 7**) to display the full set of Image properties.

Image Editor Integration

If you want to edit an image while you're working with it in Dreamweaver, it's a snap. Dreamweaver 1.2 has full image editor integration, and you can set Dreamweaver to work with your favorite editor, whether it's Paint Shop Pro, Fireworks, or Photoshop.

To select an image editor, open the Preferences dialog box by pressing Ctrl+U (Command+U). Click on External Editors to bring that panel to the front of the dialog box. Click on Browse, and use the Select External Editor for Images dialog box to locate the program file for the image editor (on Windows, it will end in **.exe**). Click on Open to select the file, and OK to close the Preferences dialog box.

When you want to edit an image, just select it in the Document window and then click on Edit in the expanded Properties inspector (shown in **Figure 8**). The image will be updated when you return to Dreamweaver.

How Do You Say CHEEZ?

Like a lot of computer lingo, there's some question as to the pronunciation of image file names. While *no one* says *gee-eye-eff*, people can't agree on whether it's pronounced *gif*, like gift, or Jiff, like the peanut butter. (I personally prefer the *gif*(t) pronunciation.) The other terms are easier. JPEG is pronounced *jay-peg*, like a hyphenated name. And PNG is pronounced *ping*, as in pong.

Image Formats

Most Web browsers display two image formats: CompuServe GIF (known as simply GIF) and JPEG (also called JPG). Dreamweaver also supports an image format that is newly supported by generation 4 Web browsers: PNG.

If you've got digitized images that you want to use in your pages, but they're in a format other than GIF or JPEG, you need to use an image editing program to convert them to one of these formats before you can put them on the Web. (Generally, you can do this by selecting File > Save As from the image editor's menu bar.)

JPEG & GIF: What's the Diff?

The JPEG format was designed for digitized color photographs. JPEGs can support millions of colors, and they're best used when that's what you need. JPEGs are what's called a "lossy" format: the more you compress them, the more information they lose (information in the sense of number of colors, which can lead to decreases in sharpness of the image).

The GIF format was invented by CompuServe so that folks on their online service could exchange graphics quickly and easily. GIFs support up to 256 colors (any 256, not a predetermined set). GIFs are the best choice for most nonphotographic images, as well as black-and-white or grayscale photographs and graphics.

Image Properties

Once the image is on the page, there are several properties you can adjust. These include appearance properties (dimensions and border), layout properties (alignment, Vspace, and Hspace), and page loading properties (alt tags and low source).

You can also provide a name for your images. This name doesn't show up on screen, but it can be useful if you're planning on working directly with the code, and it's essential for using images in Javascript or VBscript code.

To name an image:

1. Select the image by clicking on it.
2. In the Properties inspector, type a name for your image (all lowercase, no spaces or funky characters) in the Image text box (**Figure 9**).
3. Press Enter (Return) or click on the Apply button.

The image will now be named in the code.

Figure 9 Name your image by typing a name in the Image text box and clicking on the Apply button.

PNG Pong

PNG is a new image format developed by some designers who were frustrated by the limitations of the GIF format and the lossiness of JPEG. Additionally, the GIF format is owned by CompuServe, who requires software that produces GIFs to license the GIF patent.

The PNG development group would like PNG eventually to replace the GIF as a patent-free, lossless image format with dozens of new features. But right now, only a handful of browsers can display it at all. Explorer 4 can view PNG images, and versions of Navigator later than 4.1 should be able to display it. Additionally, users of Navigator 2 or later can download a plug-in to enable PNG viewing. You can find out all about PNG at http://www.cdrom.com/pub/png/.

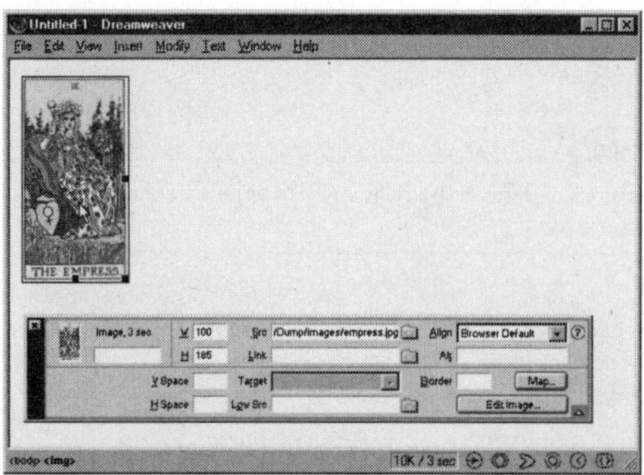

Figure 10 Select the image to display image properties in the Properties inspector.

Border 5

Figure 11 Type a number, in pixels, in the Border text box.

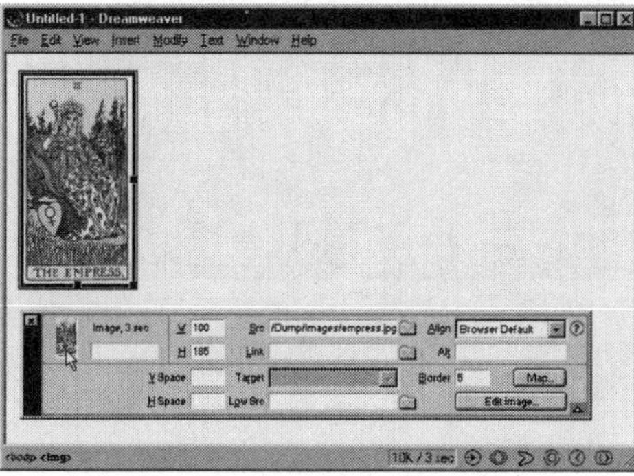

Figure 12 Click on the Apply button, and the border will appear around the image. I used a 5-pixel border here.

Appearance Properties

In Dreamweaver, the default for displaying images is to display them without any border, but you can add a border if you'd like.

To add an image border:

1. Select the image to which you'd like to add a border (**Figure 10**). The Properties inspector will display the image properties.
2. If necessary, expand the Properties inspector by clicking on the Expander arrow in the lower-right corner.
3. In the Properties inspector, type a number in pixels in the Border text box (**Figure 11**).
4. Press Enter (Return), or click on the Apply button. The border will be displayed around the image in the Document window (**Figure 12**).

The default border color is black, unless you link the image, in which case the image border will take on the link color (see Chapter 6).

✔ Tip

- Animated GIFs in the GIF89a format will display in Dreamweaver. For information about creating animated GIFs, see the book's Web site.

Transparent GIFs

All GIFs are rectangular, but some are more rectangular than others. You can use an image editing program to create a GIF89 or GIF89a, which support transparency and interlacing (see the section called *Image Size*). Everything that's a certain color in the image will disappear. The trick to making this work to your advantage on a Web page is making the transparency color the same color as your page's background (or vice versa). For obvious reasons, the easiest colors to match are white and black. (To find out how to match the page's background color to an image's RGB color, see Chapter 2.)

When you first place an image with Dreamweaver, it will have the original dimensions it was given when it was created. It's easy to reassign a new height and width to an image to make it fit into the layout of your page. However, Dreamweaver does not have automatic image scaling capabilities.

To change image dimensions:

1. Select the image you'd like to resize. The Properties inspector will display the Image dimensions in pixels in the W(idth) and H(eight) text boxes.
2. In either text box, you can type a new measurement in any of the following units: pixels, centimeters (cm), inches (in), millimeters (mm), picas (pc), or points (pt).

   For instance, to change the image width to 2 inches, you'd type **2in** (no space between measurement and unit) in the W text box (**Figure 13**).
3. Press Enter (Return), or click on the Apply button. The Properties inspector will convert your measurements to pixels, if necessary, and the new measurement will be displayed in boldface in the text box (**Figure 14**).

The Document window will display the image's new measurement(s) (**Figure 15**).

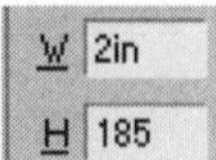

Figure 13 Type the new measurement in the W or H text box.

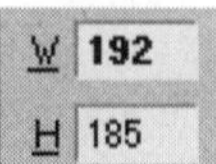

Figure 14 When the original image dimensions have been changed, the new measurements are displayed in boldface.

Figure 15 After I changed the width to 2 inches (and after Dreamweaver converted it to 192 pixels), the image appeared as shown.

✔ Tips

- To return the image to its original dimensions, click on the text box label (the letter W or H).
- If the browser knows the image dimensions when it loads the page, the page will finish loading faster, because the browser will draw a space of the right size for the image.
- Changing an image's dimensions with Dreamweaver does not change the file size of the image.

Drag to Resize

Images used to *be* a drag to resize using Dreamweaver, because it wouldn't automatically scale an image based on the values you typed in the Properties inspector. Now you *can* drag to resize an image, using the three selection handles shown in **Figures 10** and **12**, and Dreamweaver will enter the new H and W values in the Properties inspector. To constrain the image to its original scale, hold down the Shift key while you drag.

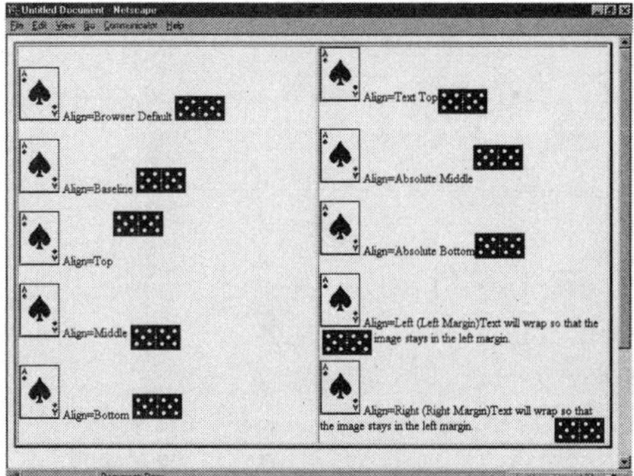

Figure 16 Here you can see the various alignment options demonstrated. Each option was applied to the domino figure. Depending on the option, the domino is either aligned with the largest object in the same paragraph (the ace) or with the text.

Layout Properties

Image alignment is slightly more complicated than text alignment. There are 10 options for image alignment; those options are detailed in the sidebar on this page and demonstrated in **Figure 16**.

To adjust image alignment:

1. Select the image whose alignment you want to adjust.
2. In the Properties inspector, click on the Alignment drop-down box and select one of the alignment options displayed in **Figure 16**.

As soon as you select an item from the menu, the image will move to reflect your choice. Some options visibly differ from others only when combined with other objects.

✔ Tip

- To align an image with the center of the page, select the image and select Modify > Alignment > Center from the Document window menu bar.

Notes on Alignment Options

- The Browser Default alignment is usually *Baseline*.
- The Baseline option aligns the bottom of the image with the baseline of the text or the nearest object. A text baseline is the imaginary line the text sits on; descenders are the little lines that go below the baseline, as in j or *g*.
- The Bottom option aligns the image's bottom with the bottom of the largest nearby object, and Top aligns the top of the image with the top of the object.
- Middle aligns the middle of the image with the text baseline.
- Text Top aligns the top of the image with the top of the tallest character in the nearest line of text.
- Absolute Bottom aligns the bottom of the image with the lowest descender in the nearest line of text (the letter *g*, in **Figure 16**).
- Absolute Middle aligns the middle of the image with the middle of the text.
- The Left and Right options align the image with the respective margin, wrapping the nearby text so that the image stays at the margin.

An image can bump right up against text or other images, as seen in **Figure 17**. (By default, Dreamweaver places a space between each image.) If you want your image to have some breathing room, you can put some invisible space around the image. Vspace is vertical space, above and below the image. Hspace is horizontal space, to the left and right of the image.

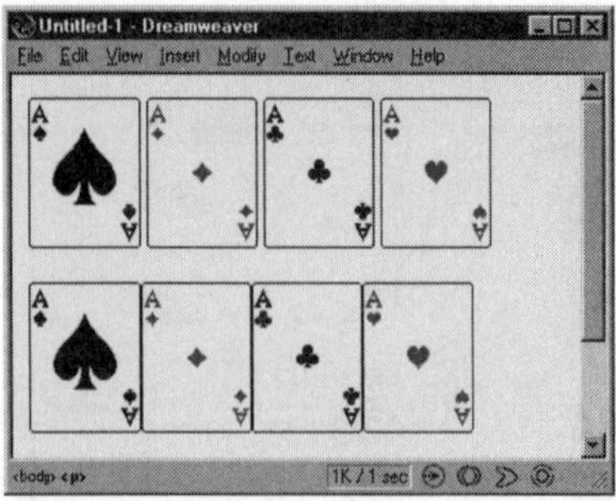

Figure 17 By default, Dreamweaver places a space between each image placed in a row. In the second row of images, I removed the spaces to place the images even closer together.

To adjust Vspace & Hspace:

1. Click on the image to which you want to add some space.
2. In the Properties inspector, type a number, in pixels, in the Vspace or Hspace text box (**Figure 18**).
3. Press Enter (Return) or click on the Apply button. You'll see the rectangle of highlighting around the image increase in size (**Figure 19**).

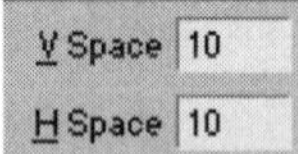

Figure 18 In the Vspace and/or Hspace text box, type the amount of space, in pixels, that you want to surround your image.

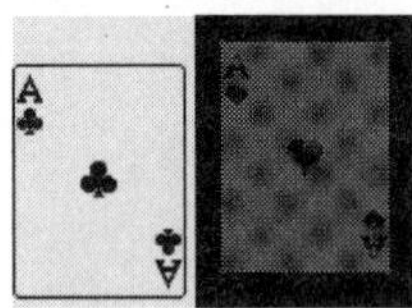

Figure 19 I added 10 pixels of both Vspace and Hspace to the image on the right.

Most likely, you'll want to experiment with the amount of Vspace and Hspace you need on your pages. In **Figure 20**, the image at the center has 10 pixels of Vspace and Hspace surrounding it.

Figure 20 The center image, the ace of hearts, has 10 pixels of Vspace and Hspace surrounding it. Notice how the Vspace affects the entire paragraph (or row): the images above and below the ace of hearts are the same distance from the entire row, even though only one of the images has Vspace added to it.

Figure 21 Type the alternate text description, or *alt text*, in the Alt text box. Unlike a regular HTML entity, the Alt tag can be in plain English with capital and lowercase letters, spaces, and punctuation; and it can be much longer than the tiny box on the Properties inspector.

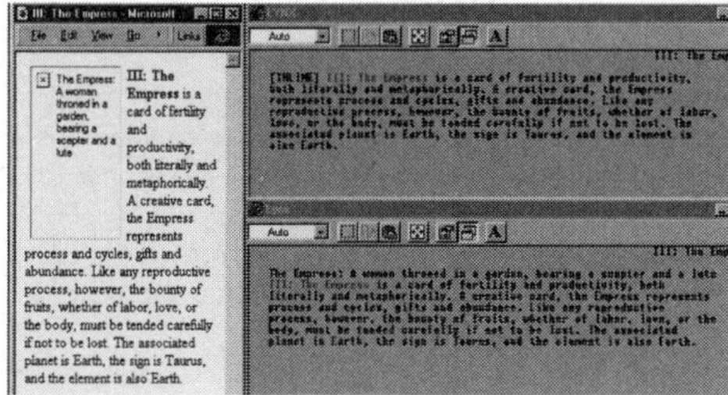

Figure 22 In the browser window at left, IE4 has auto-image loading turned off. Instead of simply seeing the broken image icon, the user sees the text description, and can decide whether to load the image. At right are two windows from Lynx, the most popular text-only browser. The upper window shows a version of the page without an Alt tag—all you see is the word [INLINE] to indicate an image. The other Lynx window displays the Alt tag instead.

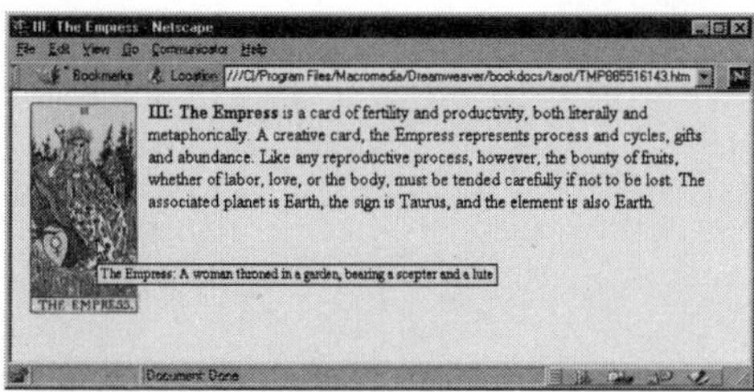

Figure 23 Alt tags come in handy even when browsing with images: when you mouse over the image in Navigator 4, you can read the Alt tag.

Page Loading Properties

Not everyone who surfs the Web does so with image capabilities. Some users who have graphical browsers turn image auto-loading off, while others browse with a text-only browser. The only way these users will know the content of your images is if you provide a text alternative, called an Alt tag.

To use an image Alt tag:

1. Select the image for which you want to provide an Alt tag.
2. In the Properties inspector, type a description in the Alt text box (**Figure 21**).
3. Press Enter (Return), or click on the Apply button.

Users who view your page without image-viewing capability will be able to read the text description to find out whether they want to view or download the image (**Figure 22**).

✔ Tips

- Users of many graphical browsers will see the alt text displayed as a tool tip when they mouse over the image (**Figure 23**).

Beyond the Alt Tag

If you're using an image map (see Appendix A), a button bar, or some other navigational tool that relies on images as links, make sure you supply a text equivalent so that users who aren't loading images can still browse your site. Appendix C on the Web site discusses making a plain-text version of your site and other ways to accommodate users who don't or can't see images when browsing the Web.

If your image is larger than 30K, it will take more than a few seconds to load. One option to take the pain out of waiting for this image to load is to provide a *low-source,* or *low-res,* image that will load more quickly. The low-res image will be replaced by the regular image once it finishes loading. **Figure 24** demonstrates this effect.

To use a low-source image:

1. Use your image editor to create a smaller, faster-loading image, such as a black-and-white or grayscale version of the image.
2. Select the image for which you created the low source version.
3. In the Properties inspector's Low Source text box (**Figure 25**), type the location of the image, and press Enter (Return).

   or

   Click on the Browse icon, and use the Select Image Source dialog box to browse through the files and folders on your computer. When you locate the image, click on its name, and then click on Open to close the dialog box and return to the Dreamweaver window.

Your selection will not be visible in the Document window, but you can see the effect if you preview the page in your browser.

✔ Tip

- When you upload your page to the Web server, be sure to send both versions of the image with the page.

Figure 24 The image on the right, which is the image I want to use on my page, is a 21K full-color JPEG. The image on the left, which took me about 10 seconds to make in a paint program, is a 1K black and white GIF. The low-source image will load immediately while the browser downloads the larger image. That way, no one has to feel like they're waiting.

Figure 25 Type the location of the image in the Low Src text box, or click on the Browse icon to open the Select Image Source dialog box.

Image Size

When you look at image properties in the Properties inspector, one thing you'll see is the image's size. This is a handy shortcut—otherwise, you'd have to use your operating system's file management system to see the file size of the image.

Why do you want to know the file size of your images? Because the smaller your image is—in kilobytes (K), not screen size—the faster it will load. Nothing kills interest in a Web site faster than a horrendous download time, and each image on your page increases that time, so it's wise to keep image size low.

What can you do to make images load faster?

- Always specify the dimensions of your image. Browsers will read this information and draw a space for the image, so that the rest of the page can load while it's waiting for the image data to come through.
- Provide a low-res version of the image. (See the section called *To use a low-source image.*)
- Use fewer colors. There are few good reasons to use millions of colors in run-of-the-mill graphics.
- Use GIFs for everything but color photographs and extremely high-color graphics.
- Provide thumbnails. If you're putting art or photographs on the Web, and you really need to use million-color JPEGs, put each large image on a separate page, and provide links to them through tiny, linked images (image linking is described in Chapter 4).
- Use interlaced GIFs. This image format will load in chunks. Once all the chunks are loaded, the image will come together.

6

WORKING WITH LINKS AND URLs

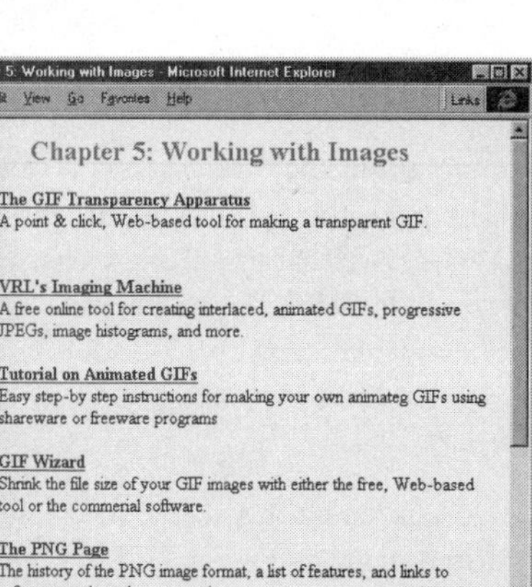

Figure 1 This page uses images, a background image, tables, and style sheets, but the real content is in the links. Even if I added background music, Shockwave files, frames, and a flaming logo, the links would still be the meat here.

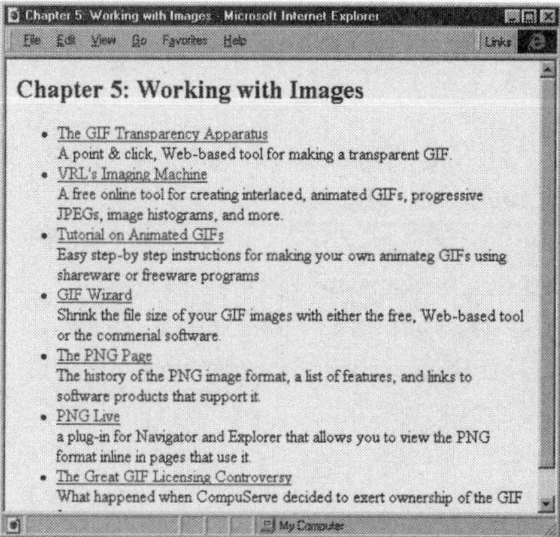

Figure 2 This is the same page as shown in **Figure 1**, with all the extras removed. The content remains the same—you can get there from here without anything but links.

One could easily argue that links, more than fancy typographical or image capabilities, make the Web the Web (**Figures 1** and **2**). While the bells and whistles of the showier pages are what impress the easily impressed and cause the browser market to boom, the fact is that the most important element in the Hypertext Transfer Protocol—that *http* at the beginning of Web URLs—is the word *hypertext*. The transfer protocol part had been around in different forms, from FTP (File Transfer Protocol) to e-mail to Veronica and Archie, for years before the Web was much more than a concept.

The combination of clickable links to documents anywhere on the Internet and the ability to display inline images is what made the first graphical Web browser, Mosaic, overshadow other hypertext efforts like gopher and WAIS.

With regular old HTML, you can link your pages to other documents within your own site or anywhere in the world. I say *documents* because you can link to images, multimedia files, and downloadable programs as well as other Web pages. You can make text or images into links, as well as linking on text entities that are part of headings, lists, tables, and frames.

Since making links is so impossibly easy with Dreamweaver, this chapter also explores some of the details of how to use links effectively and what makes up a URL.

✔ Definitions

- A *link* is a pointer from one page to another. The page that contains the link that you click on is called the *referring page*, and the destination of the click is called the *target* of the link (although there are some other definitions of target, too). The code for a link looks like this: `<A HREF="file.html">` linked text `</a>`. A stands for *anchor*, the original name for a link. HREF means Hypertext Reference.

Pathnames and Images

Site-root-relative names are particularly useful for using images. You can create an images directory at a solid location on your site, and make all the image pathnames relative to /images. Then, if you move the page that contains the image, the browser will still locate the proper directory. See Chapter 5 for more about placing images.

Auto Link Checking

It's a big pain in the butt when you finish up a Web page chock full of external links, only to discover that half the sites have ceased to exist. With Dreamweaver 1.2, you can automatically check both internal and external links for a single page or an entire site.

1. If you haven't already, save the current page.
2. Connect to the Internet as you normally do.
3. From the Document window menu bar, select File > Check Links > This Document or File > Check Links > Entire Site. A Link Checker dialog box will appear.

After the Link Checker tests all your links, it will tell you which, if any, are broken; how many external links are present; and whether there are any orphaned files. Double-click an entry to open the villainous link, and then make any necessary changes in the Properties inspector.

Different Links for Different Things

Except in those cases where you're using a relative link to a document in the same site as the referring page, you always need to specify the protocol type for the link. Even though some browsers can locate sites that lack the http:// when typed into the browser's navigation bar, most browsers won't recognize links without a protocol type being specified. Besides http, there are several other kinds of protocols you may use; mailto and ftp are the two most common after http.

gopher://	Gopher hypertext index
shttp://	Secure hypertext transfer protocol, used by secure commerce servers supporting the protocol.
ftp://	File Transfer Protocol
mailto:	An Internet e-mail address; launches a mail composition window in some browsers
news:	A Usenet or other network news resource group or discussion group; often launches a newsgroup browser
telnet:	Remote access to a Telnet server; often launches a Telnet client
wais://	Wide Area Internet Search

Absolute vs. Relative Links

Before you start putting links on your Web pages, you should be aware of the different kinds of pathnames you can use to link to another document on the Internet. There are four different kinds of pathnames you can use:

- **Absolute pathnames** point to a location on the Internet outside the site where the current page is located. In the pathname http://www.tarin.com/BayArea/baynav.html, the document baynav.html is located within the BayArea/ directory, which is within the root site www.tarin.com/. The URL http://www.tarin.com/ is another example of an absolute pathname, as is http://www.tarin.com/fridge.html.
- **Document-relative pathnames** point from the current document to another document within the same directory. If the documents baynav.html and bayweather.html are within the same directory (BayArea/), you can link from one to another by using the filenames alone as the full URL. The browser looks within the current directory to locate the document.
- **Site-root-relative pathnames** point from the current document to another document that's within the same site, but that is located in a different directory relative to the root of the site. For instance, a link from baynav.html to /fridge.html is a site-root-relative pathname.
- **Named anchors** link to a point within a page; either from point to point on a single page, or from one page to a specific location on another page. See the section called *Using Named Anchors* later in this chapter.

Making Links

Making links with Dreamweaver is easier than eating pie. You don't even have to remember any keystrokes or use any dialog boxes—just use the ever-handy Properties inspector to put your links in there.

To make text links:

1. With your page open in the Document window, highlight the text you want to make into a link (**Figure 3**).
2. If necessary, display the Properties inspector (**Figure 3**) by selecting Modify > Selection Properties from the Document window menu bar.
3. In the Link text box, type (or paste) the location of the document to which you want to link (**Figure 4**).
4. Press Enter (Return).

Your text will now be linked, as indicated by underlining and a change of color of the text you selected (**Figure 5**).

✔ Tips

- To unlink, delink, or remove a link, highlight the text or image that's currently linked. Then, in the Properties inspector, highlight the URL in the Link text box, and delete it. Press Enter (Return), and poof! No more link.
- The Link text box is also a drop-menu. Click on it to choose from a list of recently used links.

Figure 3 Highlight the text you want to make into a link.

Figure 4 In the Properties inspector's Link text box, type or paste the URL of the document you're linking to.

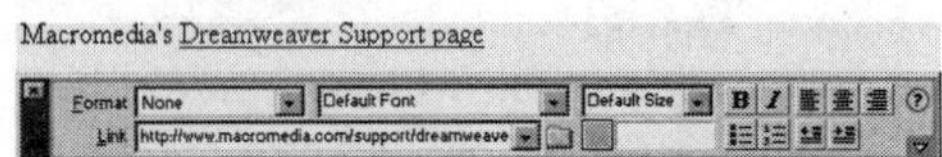

Figure 5 Press Enter (Return), and the text you selected will become a link.

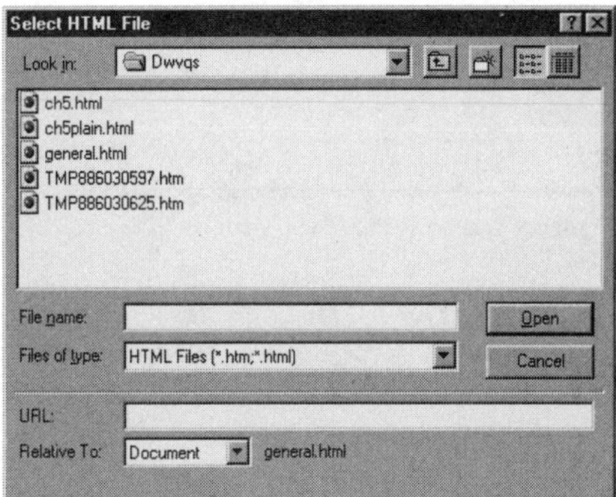

Figure 6 The Select HTML File dialog box functions like the Open dialog boxes you're used to by now.

Figure 7 From the pull-down menu, select either Document, to make the link relative to the current page, or Site Root, to make the link relative to a central location on your Web site.

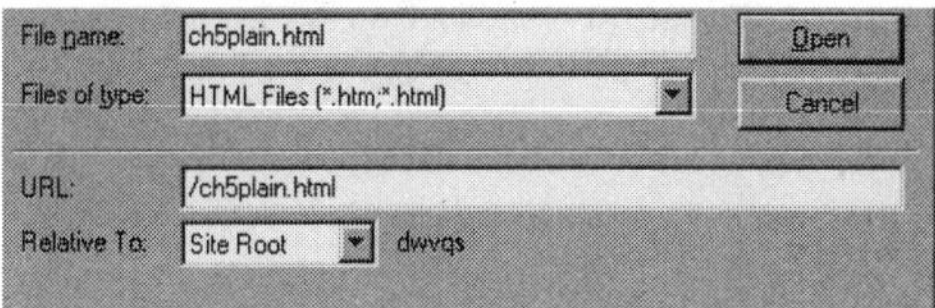

Figure 8 When you're all done, you should see a filename in the File Name text box and the path to that file in the URL text box.

Auto-Fixing Relative Links

If you want Dreamweaver to fix relative links automatically when you perform a Save As (i.e., save the file to a new location), you can set this option in the Preferences. Press Ctrl+U (Command+U) to view the Preferences dialog box, and click on General to bring that panel to the front. Select the *Correct Relative Links on Save As* checkbox, and then click on OK to close the Preferences dialog box.

Making Relative Links

An easy way to have Dreamweaver make relative links is to create a local site on your hard drive (explained in Chapter 16).

To make a relative link:

1. Save the page you're working on by selecting File > Save from the Document window menu bar. If this is the first time you're saving the page, the Save As dialog box will appear. Make sure you're saving the file in the directory (folder) of your choice, and type a filename in the File name text box. Click on Save to close the Save As dialog box and save the file.
2. Select the text you want to make into a link (as shown back in **Figure 3**).
3. In the Properties inspector, click on the Browse button. The Select HTML File dialog box will appear (**Figure 6**).
4. From the Relative To pull-down menu, select either Document or Site Root (**Figure 7**). If the two files are not in the same folder, choose Site Root.
5. Browse through the files and folders on your computer until you locate the document to which you want to link. Click on the file's icon so that its name shows up in the File Name text box. The URL text box will display the link path (**Figure 8**).
6. Click on Open to choose the file. The Select HTML File dialog box will close, returning you to the Document window. You'll see your link underlined and the path displayed in the Properties inspector.

✔ Tip

- If you know the filename of the document you want to link to, and you're creating a document-relative path, you can simply type the filename of the page in Properties inspector's Link text box.

To make image links:

1. With your page open in the Document window, select the image you want to make into a link by clicking on it (**Figure 9**).
2. If necessary, display the Properties inspector by selecting Modify > Selection Properties from the Document window menu bar.
3. In the Link text box, type (or paste) the location of the document to which you want to link (as shown back in **Figure 4**).
4. Press Enter (Return), or click on the Apply button.

Your image will now have a link-colored border around it (**Figure 10**).

✔ Tip

- To make a relative link, follow the steps on the preceding page in the section called *Making Relative Links*. Make sure you click on the Link browse button, instead of the similar button next to the Image Src text box.

To turn off that border:

1. Select the image by clicking on it.
2. If necessary, expand the Properties inspector by clicking on the expander arrow in the lower-right corner.
3. In the Properties inspector, type the number 0 in the Border text box.
4. Press Enter (Return), or click on the Apply button. The border will disappear, but your image will still be a functional link (**Figure 11**).

✔ Tip

- You can also make the border larger or smaller by typing a number other than 0 in the border text box.

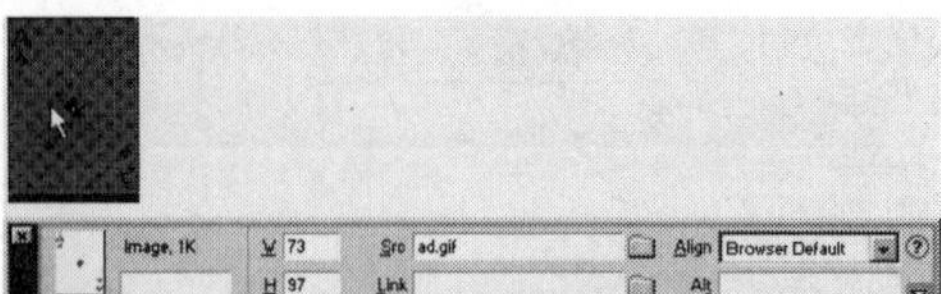

Figure 9 Select the image you want to make into a link.

Figure 10 After you specify the link destination in the Properties inspector, a border will appear around the image to indicate its *link-ness.*

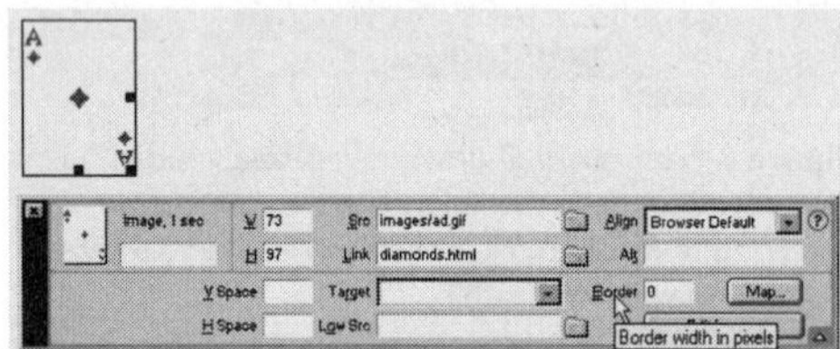

Figure 11 To get rid of the image's link border, specify a border width of zero in the Properties inspector.

What's in a URL?

Your typical Web URL might look like this: http://www.peachpit.com/,

but then again, it might look like this:

http://www.macromedia.com/support/dreamweaver/whatsnew/

or like this: http://husky.northern-hs.ga.k12.md.us/.

What's all that stuff mean, anyway?

The http: is the name of the protocol, which in the case of a Web site, is the Hypertext Transfer Protocol. (See the sidebar *Different Links for Different Things* for a description of each kind.)

The slashes (and those are forward slashes, *not* backslashes) indicate something else.

Everything between the first two slashes and the next slash is called the *domain name.*

The www, or whatever the first "word" in a URL following the slashes is, is the name of the Web server. Most folks these days use www because it's easy to remember.

The .com or .gov is called the *top-level domain,* which is administrated by InterNIC.

In the three-part URLs you see most often, such as www.peachpit.com, or thomas.loc.gov, the word between the www. and the .com is commonly called the domain name, and is called the *second level domain* by administrators and the InterNIC. It's the part you buy, if you want to register, say, macromedia.com.

In the third example above, there is a several-level hierarchy to the domain name. If you read the URL from back to front, the .us is the US domain used by state governments and such. The .md is the Maryland subdomain, the .k12 is the educational subdomain of Maryland, and the .garrett is the county subdomain of the educational system. The .northern-hs is the individual high school, and husky is the name of the Web server itself.

In the second example, the domain name itself is uncomplicated, and the rest of the URL, support/dreamweaver/whatsnew/, indicates three levels of directories within the Web server—which after all is just a computer like any other. Think of it like subfolders on your computer: C:\Program Files\Macromedia\Dreamweaver, for instance.

If the URL ends in a filename, as in http://www.tarin.com/fridge.html, that means that the fridge.html is the document itself that you're requesting. If the URL ends in a slash, it means that you're getting the *default file* for that directory. In most cases, http://www.dhtmlzone.com/index.html and http://www.dhtmlzone.com/ are the same file.

Using Named Anchors

A named anchor consists of two parts: a named entity at a point on an HTML page, and a link to that anchor. While regular old links point to an entire document, named anchors link to part of a document. Very long documents should be broken into separate pages, but there can be cases where you want a clickable table of contents (or something similar) that will direct visitors to an area of a page instead of the top of it. You can also place a link to take users from the bottom of a page to the top.

First, you need to name the part of the page you want to link to. You can name a piece of text, an image, or a headline, for instance.

To name an entity:

1. With the page on which you want to insert a named anchor open in the Document window, click to place the insertion point at the place where you want the anchor, or highlight an entity to name (such as a piece of text or an image).
2. From the Document window menu bar, select Insert > Named Anchor. The Insert Named Anchor dialog box will appear (**Figure 12**).
3. Type a name for your anchor in the Anchor Name text box. This name should be a single lowercase word or number.
4. Click on OK to close the Insert Named Anchor dialog box and return to the Document window.

A dialog box may appear that tells you what I'm about to tell you right now: You won't see any visible evidence of your anchor unless invisible element viewing is turned on.

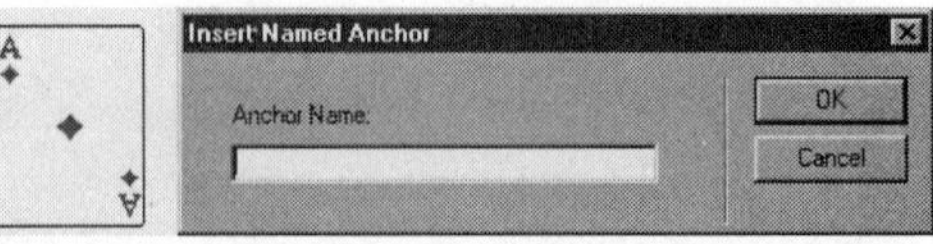

Figure 12 Name your anchor with the Insert Named Anchor dialog box. We'd rather name an anchor at this location "aced" than "ace_of_diamonds."

Common Top-Level Domains

.com	Commercial entity
.edu	Educational entity
.gov	U.S. Government
.mil	U.S. Military
.net	Network provider
.org	Nonprofit organization
.au	Australia
.ca	Canada
.ch	Switzerland
.cn	China
.de	Germany
.dk	Denmark
.es	Spain
.fi	Finland
.fr	France
.ie	Ireland
.in	India
.it	Italy
.jp	Japan
.kr	South Korea
.mx	Mexico
.my	Malaysia
.nl	Netherlands
.nz	New Zealand
.se	Sweden
.sg	Singapore
.tw	Taiwan
.uk	United Kingdom
.us	United States
.za	South Africa

Figure 13 The little blip next to the image is the Anchor icon (it has a little anchor on it). You can view or hide these invisible element icons as needed by selecting View > Invisible Elements from the Document window menu bar.

Figure 14 Click on an invisible element icon, and its properties are displayed in the Properties inspector.

To view invisible elements:

1. From the Document window menu bar, select View > Invisible Elements.
2. Any invisible elements on your pages will appear, in the form of icons (**Figure 13**). To figure out what an invisible element is or does, double-click on its icon, and the Properties inspector will display properties for that element (**Figure 14**).

Linking to Named Anchors

1. In the Document window, select the text or image you want to use as a link.
2. In the Properties inspector, type the pound sign (#) in the Link text box.
3. With no space between the pound sign and the name of the anchor, type the anchor name in the Link text box. For instance, if your anchor name is <code>top</code>, you'd type <code>#top</code> in the Link text box..
4. Press Enter (Return), and your text or image will become linked to the named anchor.

✔ Tips

- To link to an anchor on the same page, the link text box only needs to include the # and the name of the link, as in #fred.
- To link to an anchor on a page in the same directory, the link would be something like people.html#fred.
- To link to an anchor on a page elsewhere on the Web, the link would be something like http://www.homer.com/donuts.html#mmm.

Aiming Targets

A *target* is an attribute of links that tells the link *where* to open the link in question. The main use of targets is in frames-based sites, which use targets to determine in which frame a link will open. This aspect of targets is thoroughly explained in Chapter 8. There are two kinds of targets that you might want to use in non-frames pages, however.

- target=_blank makes the link open in a new, blank browser window.
- target=_top makes the link replace the content of the current window

The other kinds of targets apply only to frames. If you're making a page that you plan on using in a frames-based site, refer to Chapter 8, which also includes instructions on how to set a base target for an entire page. To set a target in the current page, follow these steps:

1. Create a link as explained in the section called *Making Links*, earlier in this chapter.
2. If necessary, expand the Properties inspector by clicking on the expander arrow in the lower-right corner.
3. From the Target pull-down menu, choose _blank or _top (**Figure 15**).

If you choose _top, the link will open in the same window as the current page. Choosing _blank will make a brand-new browser window open and load the target of the link.

✔ Tip

- Some HTML editors automatically insert the target="" attribute into the code. This is harmless; it simply reiterates that the link will open in the default or base target location. You can also remove this code with impunity in the HTML editor window.

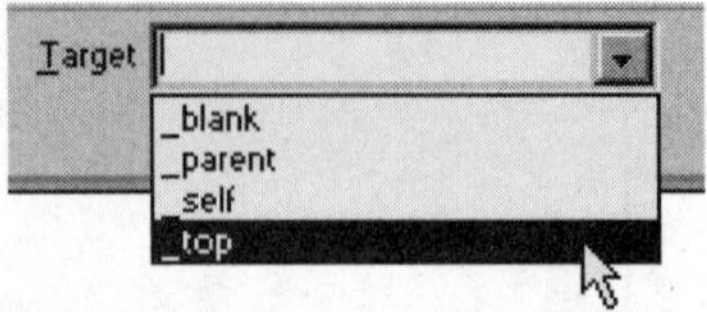

Figure 15 Choose an option from the Target-pull-down menu.

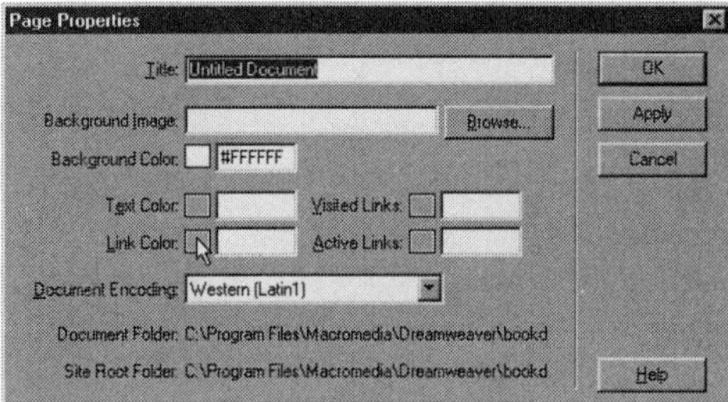

Figure 16 You can modify Link, Alink, and Vlink colors with the Page Properties dialog box.

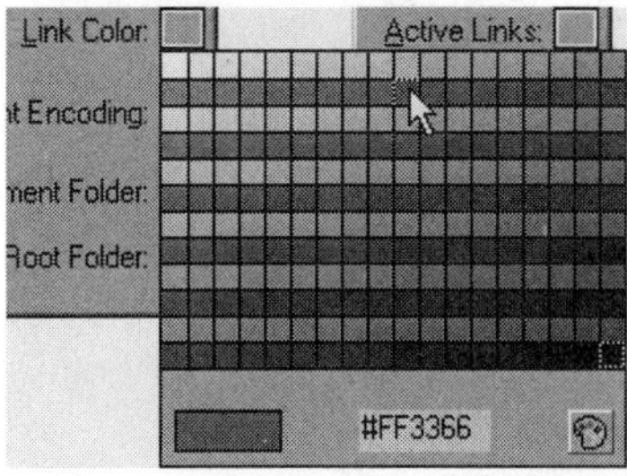

Figure 17 Click on the color button, and when the Colors palette appears, click on a color to select it.

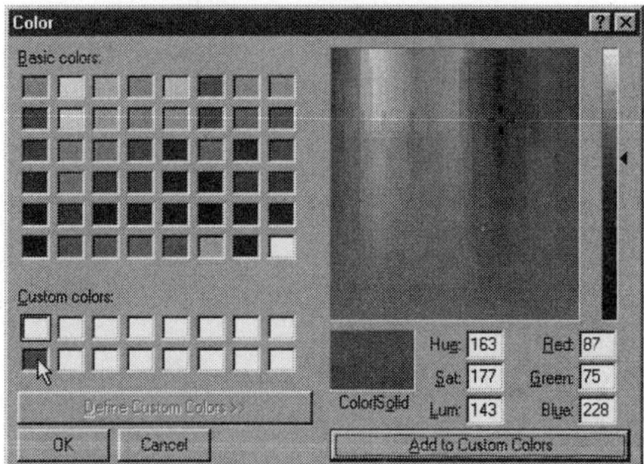

Figure 18 To use the Color dialog box, first choose a hue by clicking in the big color box. Then choose a shade by clicking in the narrow box at the right. When you have the color you want, click on it in the Color|Solid box, and then click on Add to Custom Colors. Click on the little color box in the Custom Colors area that contains your color, and then click on OK to choose the color and close the Color dialog box.

Changing Link Colors

Link colors are part of what's known as *page properties*—the set of options that are applied to an entire page, rather than to an object on that page. The other page properties are covered in Chapter 2.

To change the link colors of a given page:

1. With the page open in the Document window, select Modify > Page Properties from the menu bar. The Page Properties dialog box will appear (**Figure 16**).
2. The text boxes marked Link Color, Visited Links, and Active Links control those colors for the current page. Type (or paste) the hex code for the desired color in the appropriate text box.

   or

   Click on the Color button beside the appropriate text box. The Colors palette will appear (**Figure 17**). Click on a color to select it.

   or

   Click on the Colors button in the Colors palette. The Color dialog box will appear (**Figure 18**). Click on a hue and shade to choose a color, and click on OK to close the Colors dialog box and return to the Page Properties dialog box. (For more details on using the Color dialog box, refer to Chapter 2.)
3. In any case, when the hex code for the chosen color appears in the Page Properties dialog box, you can click on OK to close the dialog box and return to the Dreamweaver window, or you can modify the other link color options. The Link color will be the only immediately apparent change.

CHANGING LINK COLORS

Smart Linking Strategies

Links exist so visitors will click on them. While there's no right way to make a link, keep these tips in mind so that your links will make people want to click.

- Link on a meaningful word or phrase that gives the user some idea of where they're headed.

  Right: Visit our renewable energy resource page to find out more.

  Wrong: Click here to find out more about renewable energy.

- When you link to something other than an HTML page, such as a sound or multimedia file, warn the user what's coming, and how big the file is.

  Right: Combustion (AU File, 153K)

  Wrong: My Friend Larry (This is wrong if it points to a 500K MIDI file with no warning.)

- If you're linking words within a sentence, stop the link before the punctuation, and don't underline spaces unnecessarily.

  Right: I grew up in Texas, Michigan, and Sri Lanka.

  Wrong: The best red wines come from France, Italy, Germany, and California, in that order.

- Making links into *non sequiturs* (such as the word cheese pointing to a Kung Fu movie site) can work well for irreverent sites, but isn't as effective when you want someone to visit a particular page on purpose.

- If you rely on images, particularly on button bars or image maps, as navigational tools, be sure to provide text equivalents of the same links.

- Come up with house rules about link length and structure, and stick to them.

Link, Alink, and Vlink

There are three kinds of link colors: Link, Alink (Active Link), and Vlink (Visited Link). The link color is what users see when they haven't yet visited the target of the link. The Alink color is what they see while they're in the act of clicking on a link, and the Vlink color is the color the link assumes when the user has already visited the target page. (The last several days, weeks, or months of visits are recorded in the browser's History file, which is how the browser knows which links to assign the Vlink color.) If you don't choose colors for these options, the browser default colors will be used instead. In most cases, make sure that you have two different colors for Link and Vlink, so that users can tell what parts of your site they've already visited.

7

Working with Tables

Club Luxe February Schedule		
Date & Time	Band Name	Booking Contact
02/12 9 p.m.	Inspired	Karen
02/13 10 p.m.	Long Walk Home	Karen
02/14 8:30 p.m.	Poetry Night	Leonard
02/16 10 p.m.	The Hangnails	LuAnn
02/17 9 p.m.	Little Lost Dog	Karen
02/18 9 p.m.	Bonewart	LuAnn
02/20 TBA	Rumpled Stilt Walker	Karen
02/21 8:30 p.m.	Poetry Night	Leonard
02/23 9 p.m.	Cardboard Milk Truck	LuAnn
02/25 10 p.m.	Alonzo & the Rats	Karen
02/26 9 p.m.	Lesson Plan	Karen
02/27 10 p.m.	Karaoke From Mars	Karen
02/28 9 p.m.	Poetry Night	Leonard

Figure 1 HTML tables can be used to create all kinds of data tables.

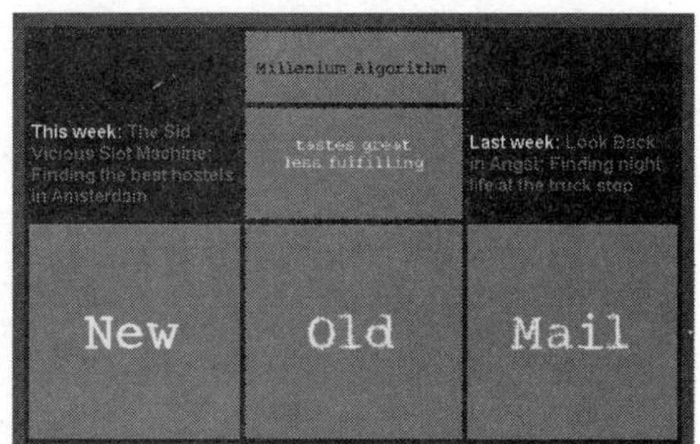

Figure 2 With a little imagination, you can use tables to replicate nearly any layout you can make with page layout programs such as Quark or PageMaker.

Table functionality was added to HTML to simplify presenting tabular data, such as scientific reports. While tables are still great for making, well, *tables* (**Figure 1**), clever designers quickly realized that tables could be used to vastly improve design options (**Figure 2**).

Like the mailboxes that line the wall at the post office, each individual cubbyhole, called a *cell*, holds discrete information that doesn't ooze over into the other boxes. As you can see in **Figure 3** on the next page, tables are divided into *rows*, which cross the table horizontally, and *columns*, which span the table vertically.

Hand-coding a table is tiresome at best. In fact, tables are probably the most convenient feature of most WYSIWYG Web page creation programs, although many of them code them rather sloppily—not so with Dreamweaver.

Setting Up Tables

Creating a table is a three-part process, although the second and third steps often take place simultaneously.

1. First, you insert the table onto your page.
2. Then, you modify the properties of the table and its cells.
3. Finally, you insert content, such as text and images, into the table.

✔ Tips

- You can plan your table beforehand, if you know how many cells you want; or you can make it up as you go along, and add cells, rows, and columns as needed.
- While virtually every current Web browser handles tables correctly, many older browsers, and most nongraphic browsers, don't. See Appendix A on the Web site, for tips on working with different kinds of browsers.
- With Dreamweaver 1.2, you can automatically convert tables to layers. From the document window menu bar, select Convert > Tables to Layers. See Chapter 11 for more on tables and Appendix C, on the Web site, for more on converting pages.

Figure 3 This table consists of three columns and five rows. The center column only consists of two cells, the larger of which was created by merging three cells together.

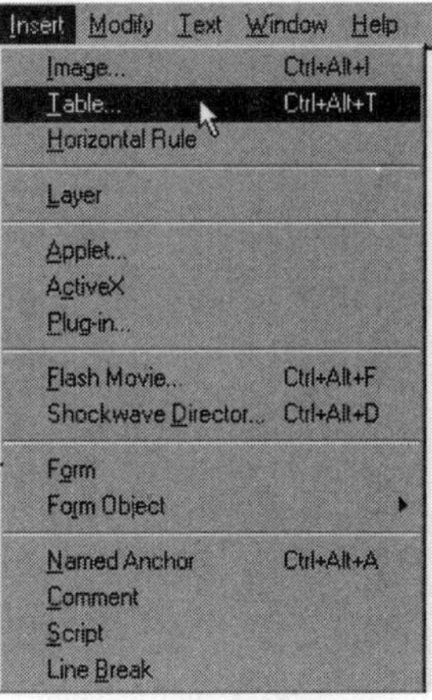

Figure 4 Choose Table from the Insert menu.

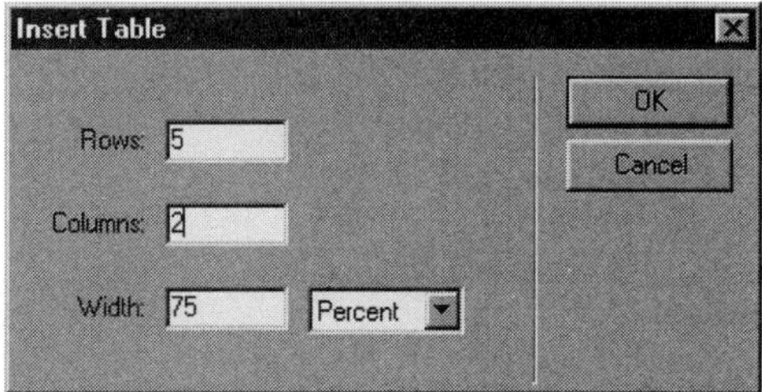

Figure 5 Click on the Table button on the Insert Table dialog box.

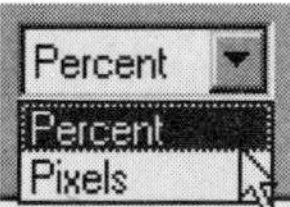

Figure 6 Click on the Width drop-down menu to make the width unit either pixels or percent of the browser window.

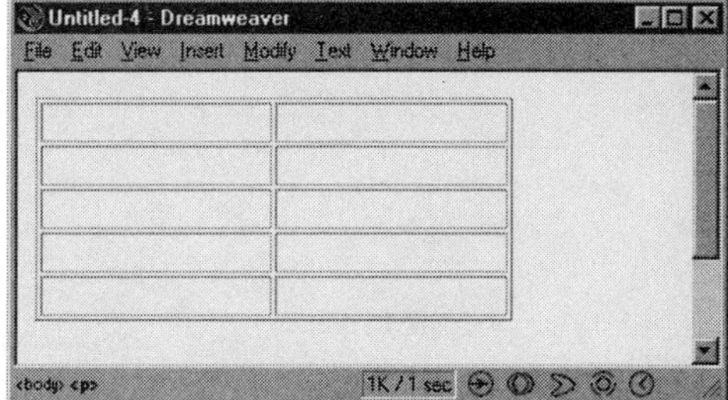

Figure 7 I inserted a new table with five rows and two columns.

To insert a table:

1. Click on your page to place the insertion point at the place on your Web page where you'd like the table to appear.
2. You can insert a table in one of two ways:
   - From the Document Window menu bar, select Insert > Table (Figure 4).

   or

   - Click on the Table button on the Object palette: .

   Either way, the Insert Table dialog box will appear (**Figure 5**).
3. In the Rows text box, type the number of rows you want in your table.
4. In the Columns text box, type the number of columns you want your table to have.
5. Choose a width for your table.
   - You can choose to have your table occupy a certain percentage of the page.

   or

   - You can choose the number of pixels your table will occupy.

   Type a number, either pixels or percent, in the Width text box.
6. Click on the Width drop-down menu to choose either pixels or percent (**Figure 6**).
7. Click on OK to close the Insert Table dialog box. Your new table will appear (**Figure 7**).

✔ Tip

- Even if you specify an exact width in pixels, your table may resize itself—it will stretch to fit the content you put in it. If you set a percentage width, the table will resize based on the size of the user's browser window.

Adding Content to a Table

Now that you've got your table right where you want it, you need to put stuff in it.

To add text to a table:

1. To add text to your table, just click in the cell where you want your text to go, and start typing and formatting (**Figure 8**).

Adding images to a table is just like adding images to any other part of a page.

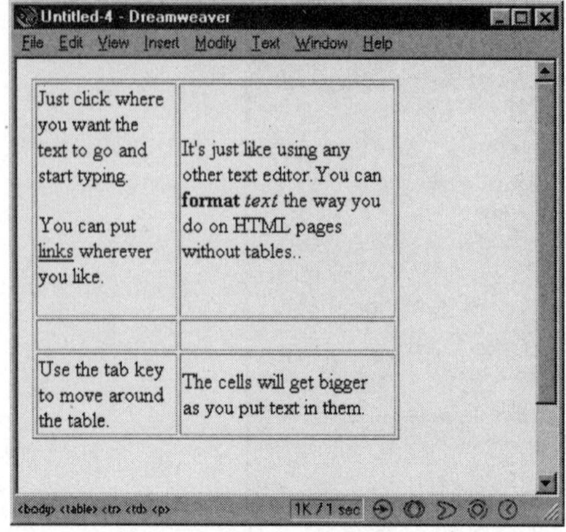

Figure 8 You can type and format text in a table just as you would text on a blank page.

To add images to a table:

1. Click to place the insertion point in the table cell where you want the image to appear.
2. From the Document window menu bar, select Insert > Image. The Insert Image dialog box will appear.
3. Type the location of your image in the Image File text box.

   or

   Click on Browse to open the Select Image File dialog box and choose an image from your computer. Then click on Open to select the image file.
4. When the image path appears in the Image File text box, click on OK to close the Insert Image dialog box. The image will appear in the table.

For more detailed instructions on working with images, refer to Chapter 5.

✔ Tips

- You can move from cell to cell in a table by pressing the tab key. Shift + Tab moves the cursor backwards.
- You can drag images and text into table cells from elsewhere on the page. Highlight the text or image, and then click on it and drag it into its new home.

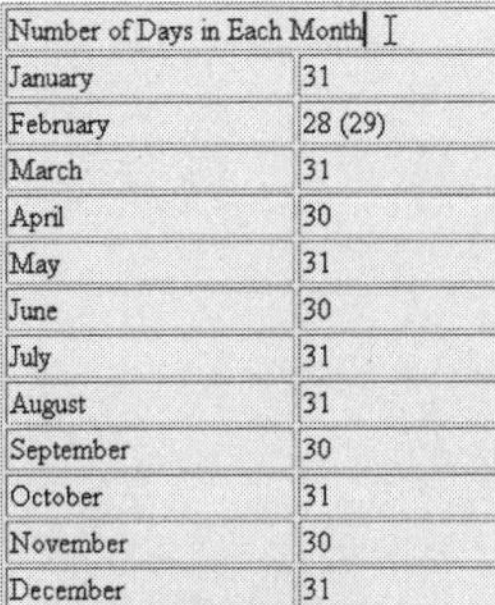

Number of Days in Each Month	
January	31
February	28 (29)
March	31
April	30
May	31
June	30
July	31
August	31
September	30
October	31
November	30
December	31

Figure 9 Click to place the insertion point in your future table header cell.

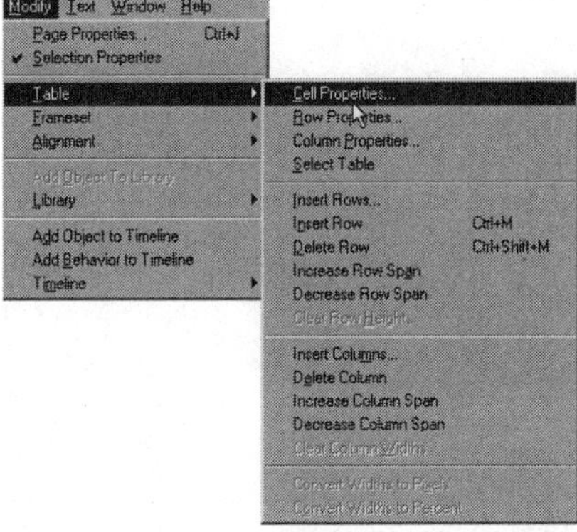

Figure 10 From the Modify menu, choose Table and then Cell Properties.

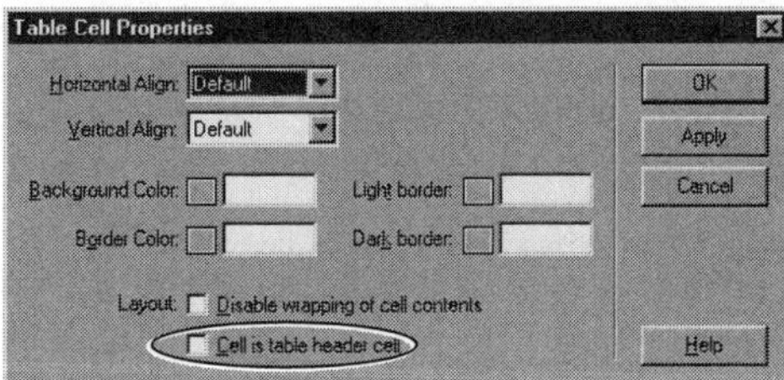

Figure 11 The Cell Properties dialog box lets you modify individual table cells.

Number of Days in Each Month	
January	31
February	28 (29)
March	31
April	30
May	31
June	30
July	31
August	31
September	30
October	31
November	30
December	31

Figure 12 The text in the new table header cell is now boldfaced and centered in the cell.

A header cell can be used to indicate the purpose of your table. In most browsers, table header cells appear with the text in them in boldface and centered in the cell.

To use a header cell:

1. Click in the cell (usually at the top of the table) that you'd like to designate as the header cell (**Figure 9**).
2. From the Document window's menu bar, select Modify > Table > Cell Properties (**Figure 10**). The Table Cell Properties dialog box will appear (**Figure 11**).
3. In the Cell Properties dialog box, click on the checkbox marked *Cell is table header cell*.
4. Click on OK to close the Cell Properties dialog box. You'll see the text in that cell centered and boldfaced. (**Figure 12**).

✔ Tips

- The appearance of table header cells may vary slightly from browser to browser, but the concept is the same: they stand out from the rest of the table.
- You can make an entire row or column of cells into table header cells. Just follow the steps for using a header cell on this page, and substitute Row Properties or Column Properties for Cell Properties.

Usually text on a Web page, just like text in a word processor, wraps to fit inside the margins. Text in table cells usually wraps to fit the width of the cell. If you turn off text wrapping, the cell will expand to fit the text.

To use the no-wrap option:

1. Right-click on some space within the column, row, or cell to which you want to apply the no-wrap option.
2. From the pop-up menu that appears, select Column, Row, or Cell Properties (**Figure 13**). The appropriate dialog box will appear (**Figure 14**).
3. To apply the no-wrap option, place a checkmark in the checkbox labeled *Cells in column (row) do not wrap* or *Disable wrapping of cell contents.*
4. Click on OK to close the dialog box.

If there is already text in any of the cells to which the no-wrap option is applied, they may expand to fit the text within them (**Figure 15**).

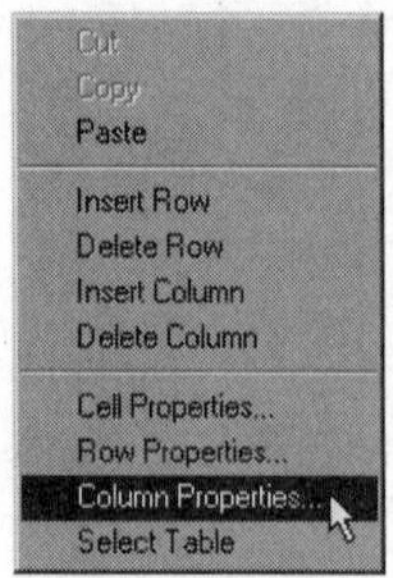

Figure 13 From the pop-up menu, choose Column, Row, or Cell Properties, depending on what entity you want to work with.

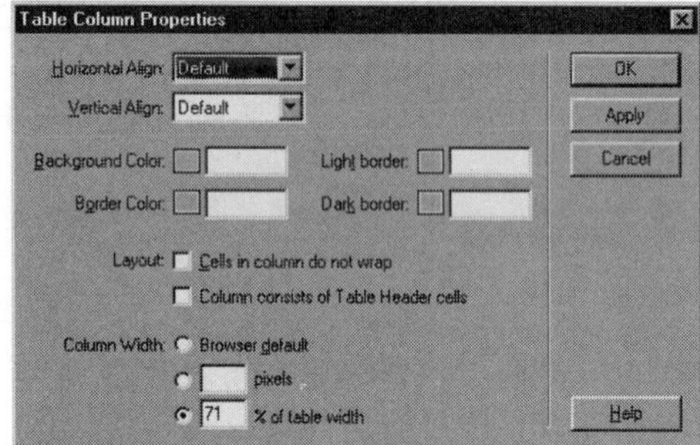

Figure 14 In the appropriate dialog box, Column Properties in this case, find the checkbox that has to do with wrapping cell contents.

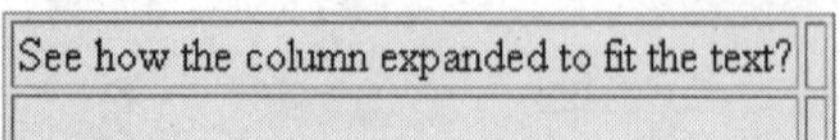

See how the column expanded to fit the text?

Figure 15 The cell expanded to fit the text that was suddenly no longer wrapped to fit the column.

Stupid No-Wrap Tricks

To break a line in non-wrapped text, you can press Enter (Return) to start a new paragraph, or Shift+Enter (Shift+Return) to insert a line break.

If you change the cell's contents so that there is extra blank space in the cell that's not being used, you can clear the column widths to close up the empty space. See the section called *To Clear Column Widths* to find out how.

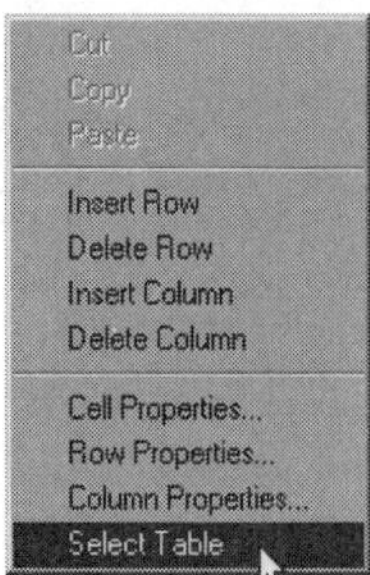

Figure 16 You can also right-click on the table and select Select Table from the pop-up menu.

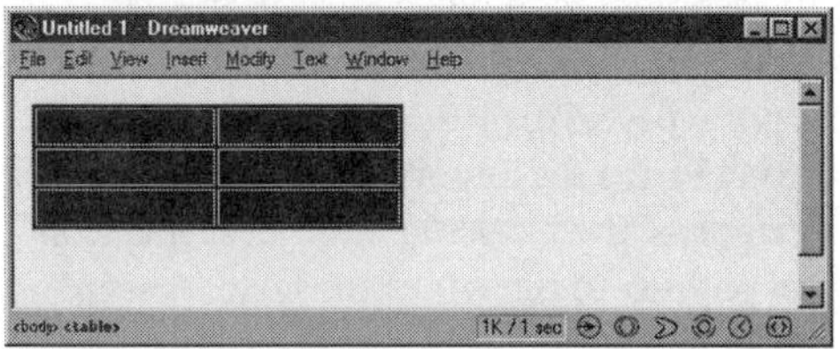

Figure 17 The entire table will appear selected. Any colors in the table, including black and white, will appear reversed. We set a dark border color for this table so that the borders would show up in the image.

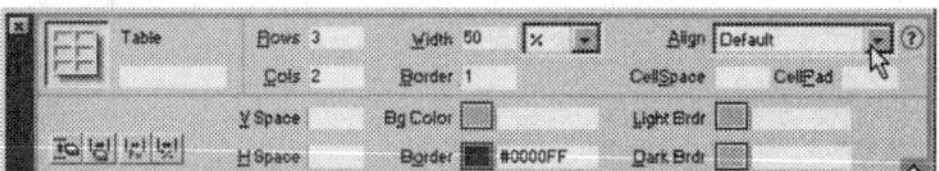

Figure 18 When the table is selected, the Properties inspector displays Table properties.

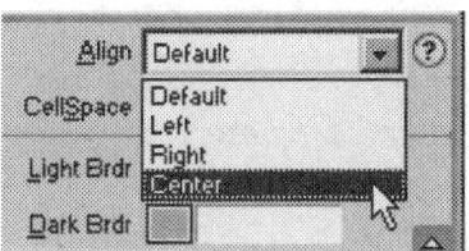

Figure 19 Use the Align drop-down menu to choose the alignment setting. Choosing Center does not actually center the table on the page.

You may want to select an entire table in order to move it or copy it to another page. You can click and drag to highlight a table, but you can accidentally drag table borders that way. Here's a foolproof way to do it.

To select a table:

1. Click on the area of the table that you want to select.
2. From the Document window menu bar, select Modify > Table > Select Table

   or

   Right-click on the table, and from the pop-up menu that appears, select Select Table (**Figure 16**).

Either way, your table will appear highlighted (**Figure 17**), and you can copy, cut, drag, or delete it.

✔ Tip

- Selecting a table makes the Properties inspector display the table's properties automatically. This is the only way to display table properties.

To set table alignment:

1. Display the Properties inspector, if necessary, by selecting Window > Properties from the Document window. Select the entire table, as seen in **Figure 17**. The Properties inspector will display Table properties (**Figure 18**).
2. In the Table Properties inspector, click on the Align drop-down menu, and select Default, Left, or Right (**Figure 19**).
3. To choose center alignment, from the Document window menu bar, select Text > Align > Center (a quirk of Dreamweaver.)

Your table will change alignment (hopefully for the forces of good).

Changing Table Size and Layout

You can adjust the appearance of your table by adjusting the number of elements in the table: by adding and removing columns and rows. You can also split or merge existing elements to adjust the layout.

There are several ways to add cells to a table. One quick way to change the dimensions of your table is by using the Table Properties inspector.

To change the number of cells:

1. Select the entire table to display Table properties in the Properties inspector, as seen previously in **Figure 18**.
2. To change the number of rows, type a new number in the Rows text box.
3. To adjust the number of columns, type a number in the Columns text box and press the apply button (**Figure 20**).

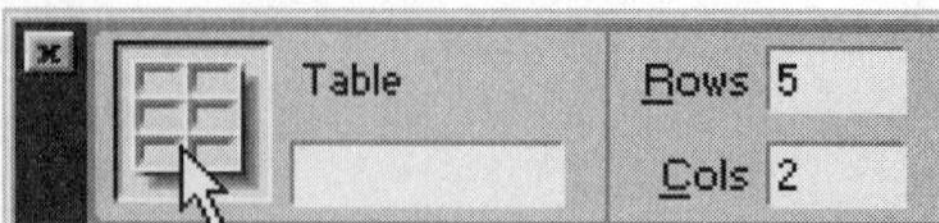

Figure 20 Type a new number in the rows and columns text boxes, and then click on the Apply button to add the new items.

Terms of Alignment

If you align a table to the right, a small placeholder icon will appear in the left margin to mark the beginning of the table on the page. This icon may disappear if you change the alignment back to left. You can place the insertion point near this icon to put text to the left of the table, as seen in **Figure 21**.

- To center a table on the page, select it and, from the Document window menu bar, select Text > Alignment > Center.
- Choosing the default setting will make the table follow the default browser settings.

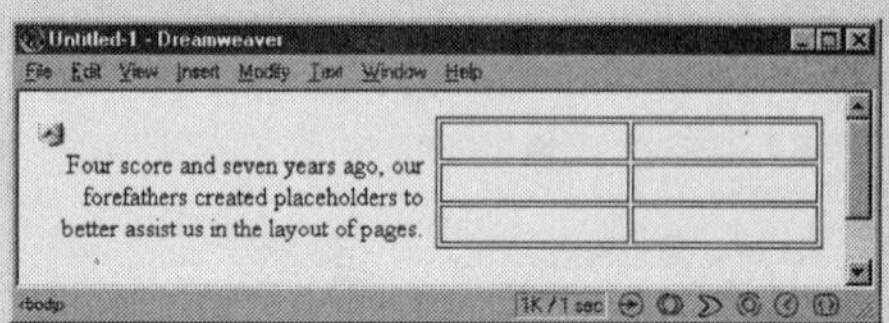

Figure 21 A right-aligned table, complete with placeholder icon.

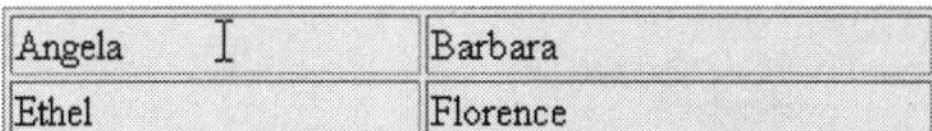

Angela	Barbara
Ethel	Florence

Figure 22 Place the insertion point above where you want the new row to appear.

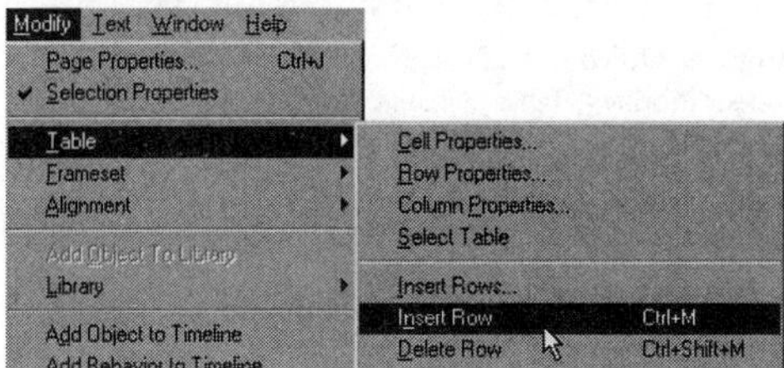

Figure 23 From the Document window menu bar, select Modify > Table > Insert Row.

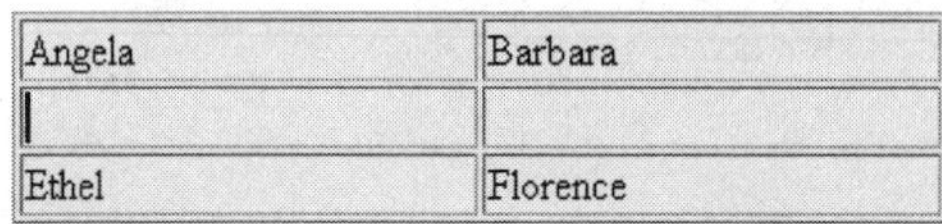

Angela	Barbara
Ethel	Florence

Figure 24 The new row appears below the cell you selected.

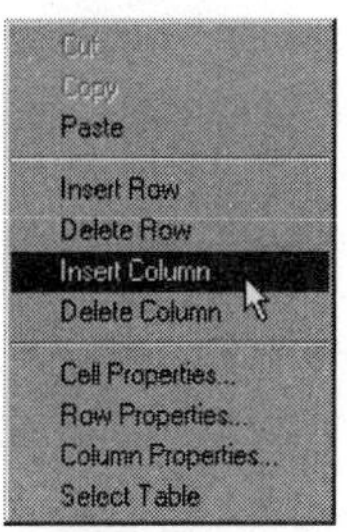

Figure 25 Choose Insert Column from the pop-up menu. You can also add a single row below the insertion point this way.

Angela		Barbara
Ethel		Florence

Figure 26 A new column appears to the right of the column you selected.

To add a single row:

1. Click in the table to place the insertion point in a table cell above where you want the new row to appear (**Figure 22**).
2. From the Document window menu bar, select Modify > Table > Insert Row, or press Ctrl+M (Command+M) (**Figure 23**). The new row will appear below the insertion point (**Figure 24**).

To add a single column:

1. Right-click on the column directly to the left of where you want the new column to appear (as in **Figure 22**).
2. From the pop-up menu that appears, choose Insert Column (**Figure 25**).

A new column will appear to the right of the column you clicked on (**Figure 26**).

To add more than one row:

1. Click in the table to place the insertion point adjacent to where you want the new rows to appear.
2. From the Document window menu bar, select Modify > Table > Insert Rows (**Figure 27**). The Insert Rows dialog box will appear (**Figure 28**).
3. In the Number of Rows text box, type the number of rows you want to add.
4. If you want the new rows to appear above the row containing the insertion point, click on the Before Current Row radio button.

   or

   If you want the new rows to appear below the row you selected, click on the After Current Row radio button.
5. Click on OK to close the dialog box and add the new rows to your table.

To add more than one column:

1. Click to place the insertion point adjacent to where you want the columns to appear.
2. From the Document window menu bar, select Modify > Table > Insert Columns. The Insert Columns dialog box will appear.
3. In the Number of Columns text box, type the number of columns you want to add.
4. If you want the new columns to appear to the left of the column you selected, click on the Before Current Column radio button.

   or

   If you want the new columns to appear to the right of the column containing the insertion point, click on the After Current Column radio button.
5. Click on OK to close the dialog box and add the new columns to your table.

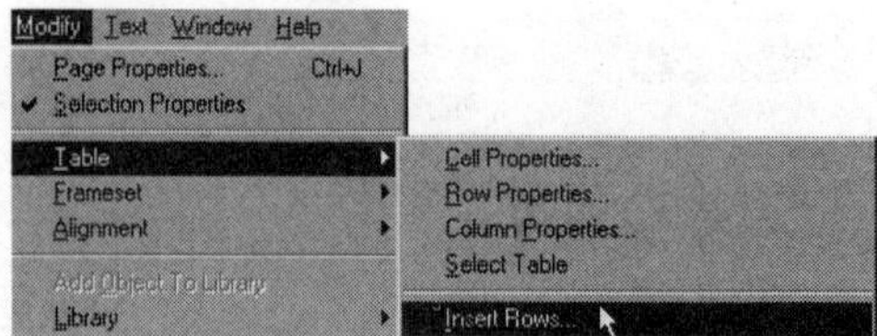

Figure 27 From the Document window menu bar, select Modify > Table > Insert Rows.

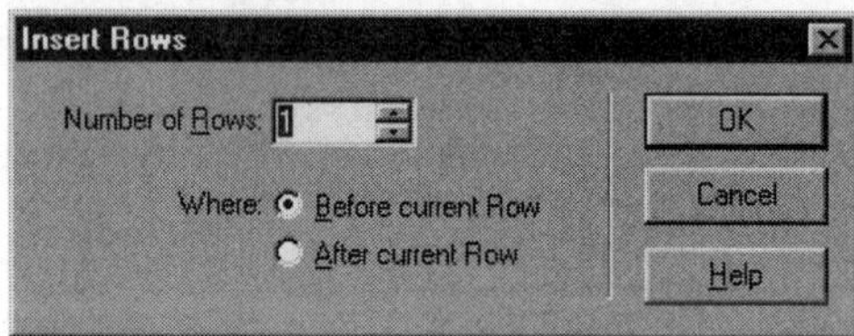

Figure 28 Use the Insert Rows dialog box to add more than one row to your table.

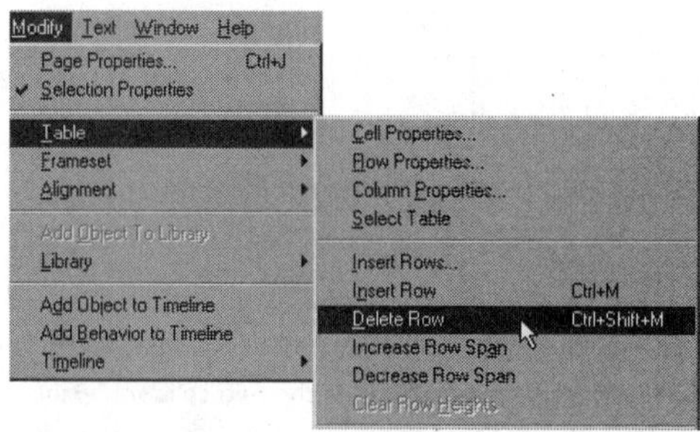

Figure 29 From the Document window menu bar, select Modify > Table > Delete Row, and the row will disappear. (You can select Delete Column, too.)

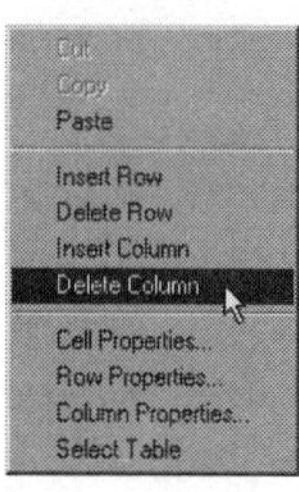

Figure 30 Choose Delete Column from the pop-up menu, and the column will disappear. (You can select Delete Row, too.)

To delete a row:

1. Click in the table to place the insertion point within the row you want to delete.
2. From the Document window menu bar, select Modify > Table > Delete Row (**Figure 29**), or press Ctrl+Shift+M (Command+Shift+M). The row and all its contents will disappear.

To delete a column:

1. Right-click on some empty space in the column you want to delete.
2. From the pop-up menu that appears, select Delete Column (**Figure 30**). The column and all its contents will disappear.

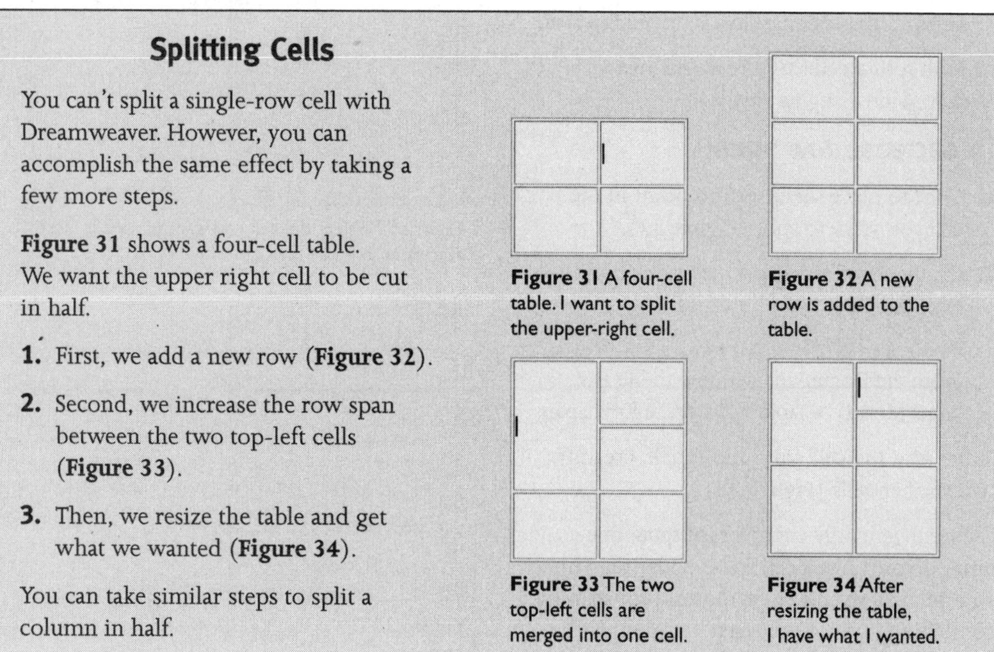

Splitting Cells

You can't split a single-row cell with Dreamweaver. However, you can accomplish the same effect by taking a few more steps.

Figure 31 shows a four-cell table. We want the upper right cell to be cut in half.

1. First, we add a new row (**Figure 32**).
2. Second, we increase the row span between the two top-left cells (**Figure 33**).
3. Then, we resize the table and get what we wanted (**Figure 34**).

You can take similar steps to split a column in half.

Figure 31 A four-cell table. I want to split the upper-right cell.

Figure 32 A new row is added to the table.

Figure 33 The two top-left cells are merged into one cell.

Figure 34 After resizing the table, I have what I wanted.

CHANGING TABLE SIZE AND LAYOUT

Each cell generally occupies, or *spans*, one row. If you'd like a cell to be taller than one row high, you can increase the row span by combining two cells to make one cell that's twice as tall.

To increase row span:

1. Click to place the insertion point in the upper of the two cells you want to combine (**Figure 35**).
2. On the Property inspector, click on the Increase Row Span button: ▣.

   or

   From the Document window menu bar, select Modify > Table > Increase Row Span.

Either way, the two cells will merge, creating one cell that spans two rows (**Figure 36**).

✔ Tip

- You can repeat these steps to make a cell that spans the entire height of a table.
- If you change your mind, just follow the steps in the section called *To Decrease Row Span*.

You can split a cell that already spans two rows by decreasing its row span.

To decrease row span:

1. Click to place the insertion point in the cell you wish to split (**Figure 37**).
2. On the Property inspector, click on the Decrease Row Span button: ▣.

   or

   From the Document window menu bar, select Modify > Table > Decrease Row Span.

Either way, the cell will split in half, creating two smaller cells (**Figure 38**).

Each cell generally occupies, or *spans*, one column. If you'd like a cell to be wider than one column, you can increase the column span by combining two cells to make one cell that's twice as wide.

Figure 35 Select the upper of the two cells you want to combine.

Figure 36 Cells in two rows merge to create one large cell that spans two rows.

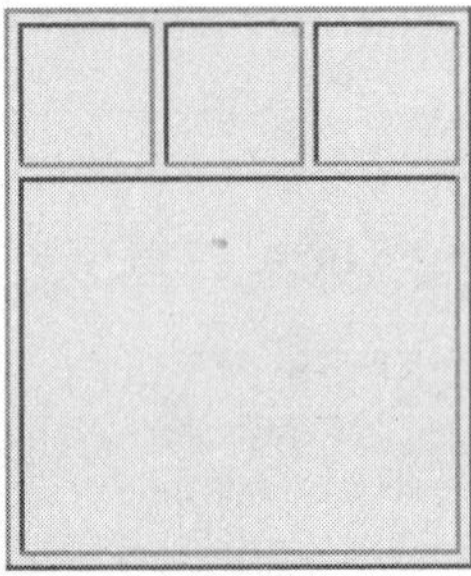

Figure 37 Select the cell you want to split. It must already span more than one row.

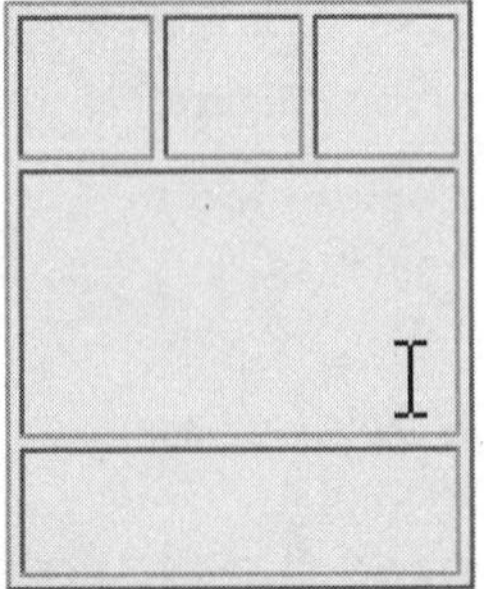

Figure 38 This cell splits and two smaller cells are created.

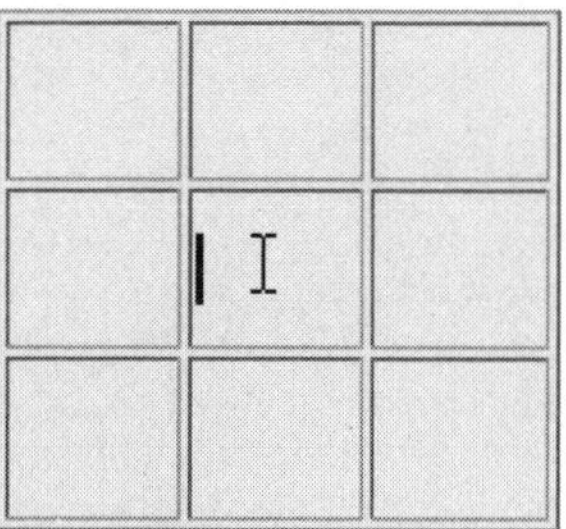

Figure 39 Select the leftmost of the two cells you want to combine.

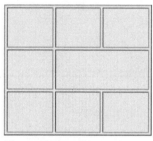

Figure 40 The cells merge to create one large cell that spans two columns.

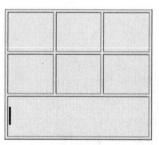

Figure 41 Select the two-column cell you want to split.

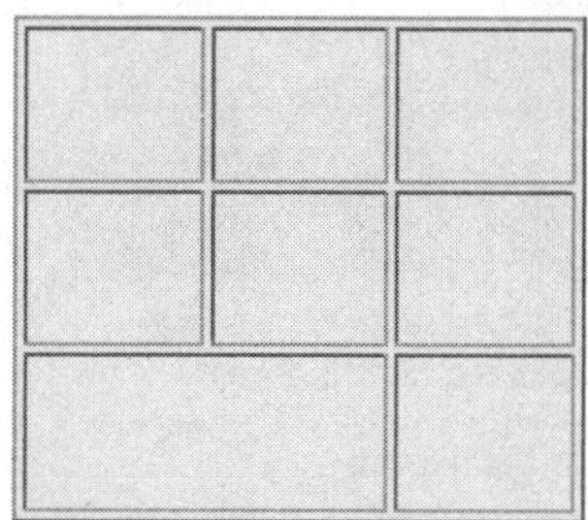

Figure 42 The cell splits in half, creating two smaller cells.

To increase column span:

1. Click to place the insertion point in the leftmost of the two cells you want to combine (**Figure 39**).
2. On the Properties inspector, click on the Increase Column Span button: .

   or

   From the Document window menu bar, select Modify > Table > Increase Column Span.

Either way, the two cells will merge, creating one cell that spans two columns (**Figure 40**). You can split a cell in two to create two smaller cells, each of which spans half a column.

To decrease column span:

1. Click to place the insertion point in the two-column cell you wish to split (**Figure 41**).
2. On the Properties inspector, click on the Decrease Column Span button: .

   or

   From the Document window menu bar, select Modify > Table > Decrease Column Span.

Either way, the cell will split in half, creating two smaller cells (**Figure 42**).

Adjusting the Table Size

Besides adding and removing elements from the table, you can adjust the table's size and appearance by increasing or decreasing the height and width of the entire table, as well as the size of the columns and rows within it.

You may have set a width for your table when you created it, but you can easily adjust the width of the table at any point after that. The width of your table will be in either pixels or percent of screen width.

To set the table width:

1. Select the entire table to display the Table Properties in the Properties inspector (as seen previously in **Figure 18**). From the drop-down menu to the right of the Width text box, choose either Pixels or Percent (%).
2. Type a number in the Width text box.
3. Click on the Apply button, and the width of your table will change.

Adding a Single Cell to a Table

While Dreamweaver doesn't directly support the addition of a single cell to a table, you can do it by adding a single line of code.

1. From the Document window menu bar, select Window > HTML. The HTML inspector appears.
2. To add a cell at the end of a table, locate the closing table tag, </TABLE>, and type the following line of code just before it:

   ```
   <tr><td> </td></tr>
   ```

   This adds a new row <tr> with only one cell in it <td>. The   gives the cell some content so it will show up.
3. Press Ctrl+S (Command+S) to save the changes to the HTML, and the new cell will appear in the table, as seen in **Figure 45**.

Figure 45 A single cell has been added to this table. Notice the funny looking blank space that appears in the rest of the row.

You can experiment with placing this code at other places in the table to see the results.

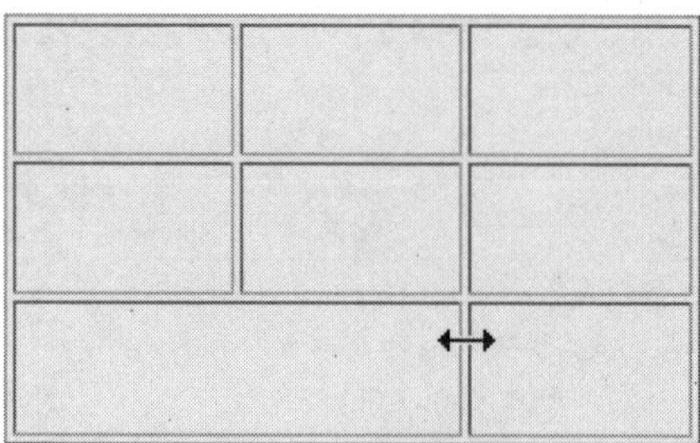

Figure 43 Mouse over the table border, and the pointer will turn into a double-headed arrow.

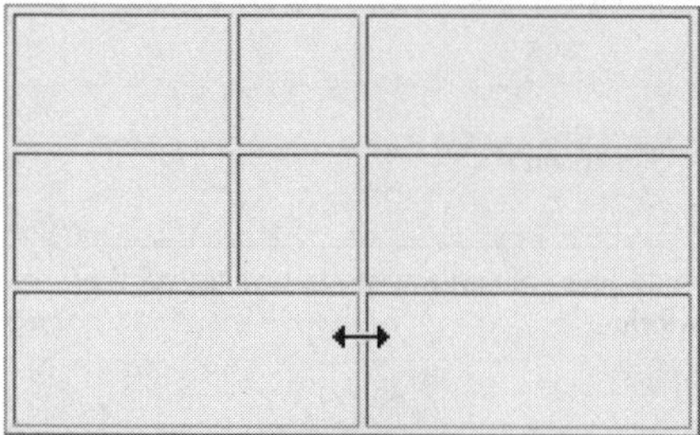

Figure 44 Use the double-headed arrow to drag the border to a new location.

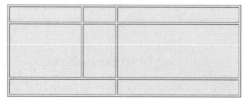

Figure 45 We put an image in this table, and then cut it. Now we're left with all this space we don't need!

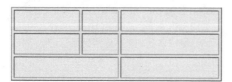

Figure 46 After you reset the row heights, the table will resize itself. We saw this table in Figure 44; notice how the column widths remain the same.

One way to adjust the width of columns or the height of rows is by simply clicking and dragging.

To drag columns and rows:

1. When you move the mouse over a border between cells, the pointer will turn into a double-headed arrow (**Figure 43**).
2. Click on the border and drag it to a new location (**Figure 44**). This will set the specifications for the dimensions of the table elements involved.

✔ Tip

- There are no specific options you can set for row height. A row's height will expand to fit the content you put in it. You can also drag the border between rows to adjust the dimensions.

If you have previously inserted some tall content, and the table's row heights have not contracted to fit the current content, you can clear row heights to shrink the table back down.

To clear row heights:

1. Select the entire table (**Figure 45**), and the Properties inspector will display Table Properties (as shown back in **Figure 18**).
2. In the Properties inspector, click on the Clear Row Heights button: [icon].

   or

   From the Document window menu bar, select Modify > Table > Clear Row Heights.

Any row heights previously set will be cleared (**Figure 46**).

To set column width:

1. Click to place the insertion point in the column whose width you'd like to specify.
2. If the Properties inspector is collapsed, expand it by clicking on the Expander arrow in the lower-right corner.
3. Click on the Table Col... button [Table Col...], and the Table Column Properties dialog box will appear (**Figure 47**).
4. In the Column width area of the dialog box, choose from one of three options by clicking on its radio button:
   - Browser default
   - Pixels
   - Percent of table width
5. If you chose one of the latter two options, type a number in the associated text box. **Figure 48** shows a column set to occupy 50 percent of the table width.

✔ Tip

- While most of the images in this chapter show little bitty tables, they can easily be translated into full-page layouts by setting the table width to 100 percent.

To clear column widths:

1. Select the entire table, and the Properties inspector will display Table Properties.
2. In the Properties inspector, click on the Clear Column Widths button: .

   or

   From the Document window menu bar, select Modify > Table > Column Widths.

Any column widths set by you (either in a dialog box or by dragging a cell's border) or by Dreamweaver (when the table was created) will be reset to no value (**Figure 49**).

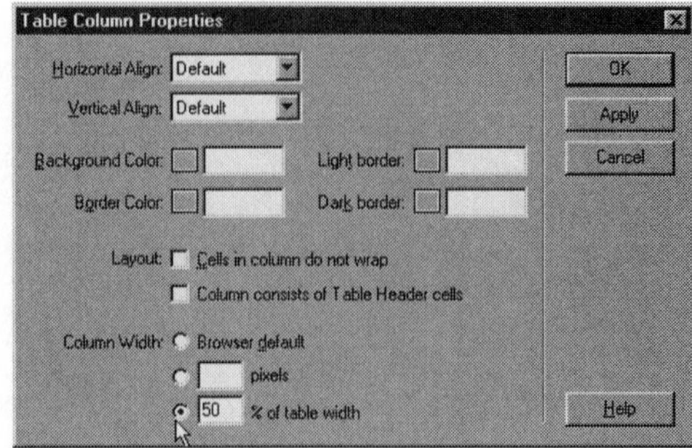

Figure 47 The Table Column Properties dialog box lets you set column width, among other things.

Figure 48 This column was set to occupy half the table width.

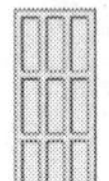

Figure 49 After column widths are cleared, the table will resize itself.

You Ought to Be in Pixels

If you set a column's width in pixels, the text you type or paste into the cells in that column will wrap to fit in the column. However, if you place an image wider than the column in one of those cells, the column will still expand to fit the image.

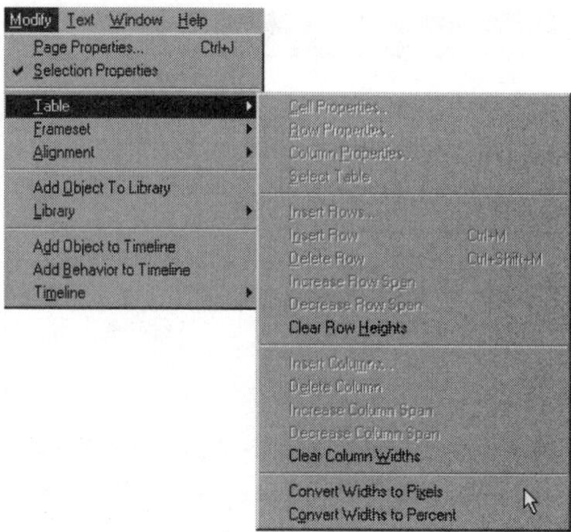

Figure 50 With the table selected, choose Modify > Table > Convert Widths to Pixels from the Document window menu bar.

You can convert any width or height measurements in your table from percentages to pixels. This is especially useful if you're working with tables created in another environment.

To convert from percentages to pixels:

1. Select the entire table, and the Property inspector will display Table Properties.
2. In the Property inspector, click on the Convert Table Widths to Pixels button: [icon].

   or

   From the Document window menu bar, select Modify > Table > Convert Widths to Pixels (**Figure 50**).

✔ Tip

- While the changes won't be visible in the Document window, you can look at the changes in the HTML window by selecting Window > HTML from the Document window's menu bar.

To convert from pixels to percentages:

1. Select the entire table, and the Properties inspector will display Table Properties.
2. In the Properties inspector, click on the Convert Table Widths to Percent button: [icon].

   or

   From the Document window menu bar, select Modify > Table > Convert Widths to Percent.

Creating a Table within a Table

When you have some complex design ideas to accomplish, you can insert a table within a larger (full page size, for example) table.

To insert a table within a table:

1. Click in the table cell where you'd like to insert a new table (**Figure 51**).
2. Click on the Table button on the Objects palette, and the Insert Table dialog box will appear.
3. Type a number of columns and a number of rows in the appropriate text boxes.
4. Click on OK to close the dialog box.

You'll see your new table inside the old table (**Figure 52**).

You can also drag and drop a table into an existing table.

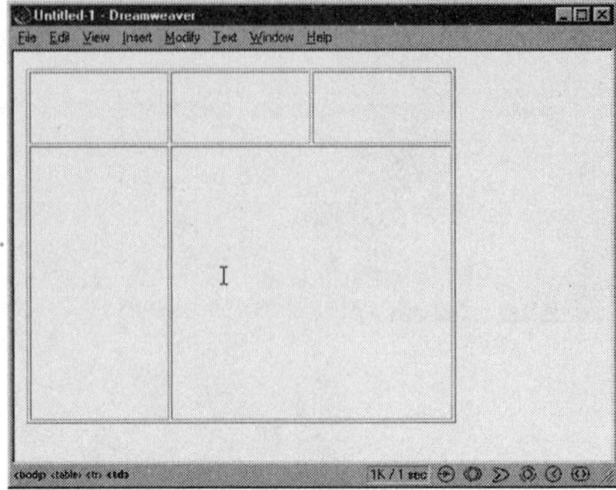

Figure 51 Select the table cell you want to hold the new table.

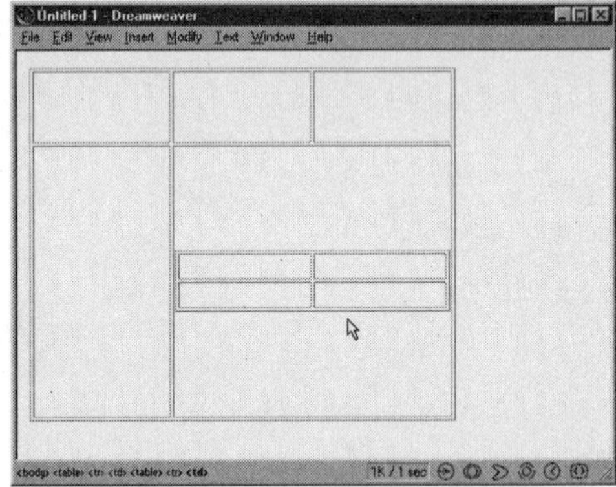

Figure 52 Your new table appears inside the old table.

Using Excel Spreadsheets and Word Tables as HTML Tables

Although you can't paste spreadsheet data into Dreamweaver like you can into FrontPage, you can still use your Excel spreadsheets as tables.

Both Excel 95 and Excel 97 have utilities to save a range of a spreadsheet as HTML. In Excel 95, choose Tools > Internet Assistant Wizard from the menu. For Excel 97, the command is File > Save as HTML. Both of these programs use Wizards that will guide you through the process.

You can also save Microsoft Word table data as HTML. In Word 95, you select File > Save As from the menu bar, and choose HTML (*.htm) as the file type. In Word 97, the command is File > Save as HTML.

Once you have one of these Office-created documents saved, you can open it in Dreamweaver, and edit the page or cut and paste the table onto an existing page.

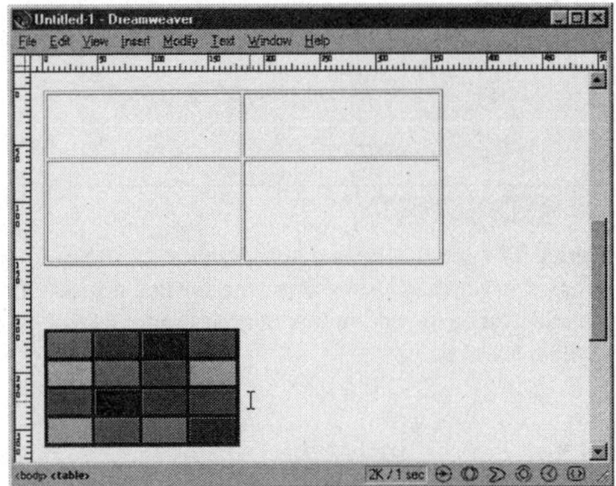

Figure 53 Select the table you want to move.

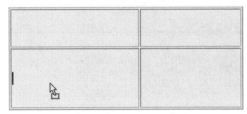

Figure 54 As you drag, the pointer displays the Object icon.

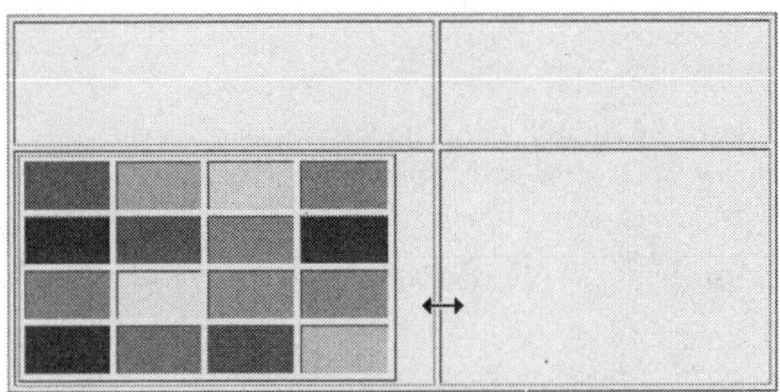

Figure 55 Let go of the mouse button, and table number two (with all its contents intact) appears inside table number one.

To drag and drop a table into another table:

1. Select the secondary table (**Figure 53**).
2. Click on it and drag it until you see the Object icon (**Figure 54**).
3. Drag it into the desired cell in the primary table, and let go of the mouse button.

The table will appear inside the other table (**Figure 55**).

Name That Table

If you're planning on working with table code directly, it may help to know which table you're working on, particularly if you've inserted a table within a table. You can name your table, in which case the table code will say something like

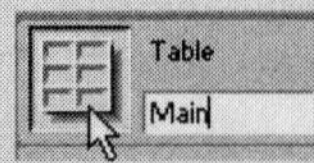

Figure 57 Type a name for your table in the little text box.

<table name="main">

To name your table, first select it. Then, in the Properties inspector, type a name in the text box to the right of the Apply button (**Figure 56**), and click on the Apply button. The name will be inserted into the code.

Working with Table Borders

By default, when you insert a table with Dreamweaver, a 1-pixel line, called a *border*, will delineate the cells and the edges of the table, but you can easily change the width of this border. (See the sections on cell padding and cell spacing for more about table spacing.)

To adjust border size:

1. Select the table to display table properties in the Property inspector.
2. In the Border text box, type a number and press Enter (Return), or click on the Apply button.

You'll see your border adjustments immediately (**Figure 57**); if you set the border width to zero, you'll see a light dashed line (**Figure 58**). No worries: it won't show up in your browser (**Figure 59**).

✔ Tips

- You can change the border width to whatever you want, or you can set the border width to zero.
- Setting the border width to zero is also known as turning off table borders, and it's what you want to do if you're using tables to lay out pages rather than display tabular information.
- It's useful to work with borders turned on (set to at least one) while you're designing pages, so you can see what's going on. Sometimes the dashed lines are difficult to see onscreen.
- To find out about coloring table borders, skip ahead to the section called *Coloring Tables*.

Figure 57 I gave my table a border width of 10. Borders larger than 1 only affect the outside edge of the table, while border widths of zero render all borders invisible.

Month	Birthstone
January	Garnet
February	Amethyst
March	Aquamarine
April	Diamond
May	Emerald
June	Pearl
July	Ruby
August	Peridot
September	Sapphire
October	Opal
November	Yellow Topaz
December	Blue Topaz

Figure 58 A table with a border width of zero is shown in Dreamweaver with dashed lines.

Month	Birthstone
January	Garnet
February	Amethyst
March	Aquamarine
April	Diamond
May	Emerald
June	Pearl
July	Ruby
August	Peridot
September	Sapphire
October	Opal
November	Yellow Topaz
December	Blue Topaz

Figure 59 This is the same table we saw in **Figure 58**, but in the browser window, the borders are invisible.

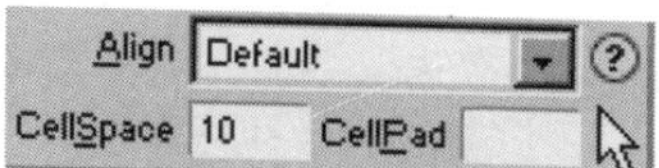

Figure 60 Type values for cell padding and cell spacing in the Table Properties inspector.

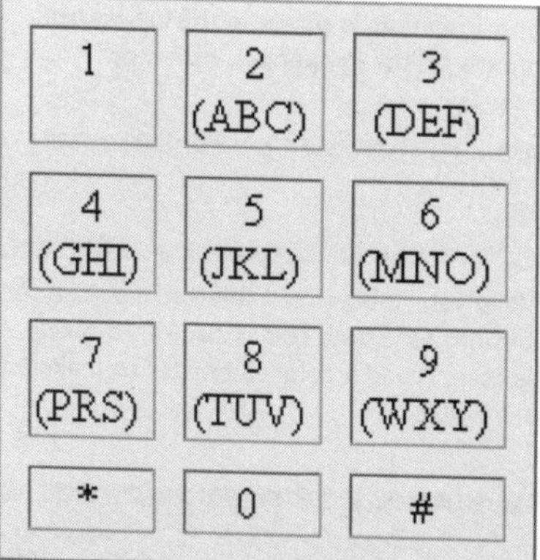

Figure 61 We made the cell spacing 10 pixels wide. If we make the border width zero, the cell spacing will be invisible.

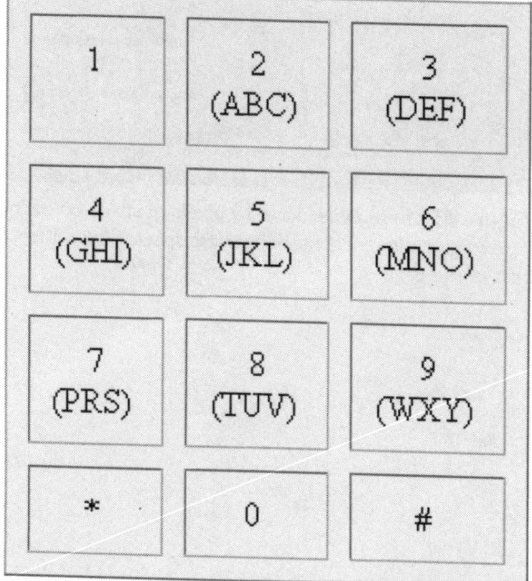

Figure 62 This is the same table we saw in **Figure 61**, but we added 10 pixels of cell padding. Notice the space between the characters and the walls of the cells.

Adjusting Table Spacing

When you're using a table as a page layout tool, it's important to be able to control the space between elements in a table. We've already talked about table borders, which in part control the space between the table and the rest of the page.

Cell spacing is the amount of space between cells—sort of like table borders, but between the cells in a table rather than around the outside of the table. *Cell padding* is the amount of space between the walls of the cells and the content within them.

To adjust cell spacing:

1. Select the table to display Table Properties in the Properties inspector.
2. In the CellSpace text box, type a number (in pixels) (**Figure 60**).
3. Click on the Apply button.

Your changes will be visible in the width of the table's borders (**Figure 61**).

✔ Tip

- Cell spacing changes may not be immediately visible on pages with table borders set to zero.

To adjust cell padding:

1. Select the table to display Table Properties in the Properties inspector.
2. In the CellPad text box, type a number (in pixels).
3. Click on the Apply button.

You'll notice a difference in the spacing between the content and the borders (**Figure 62**). If there is no content in your table at this point, you can see the changes by clicking within the cells and examining the distance between the cursor and the walls of the cell.

If you want a certain amount of space around the edges of your table, you can adjust the Vspace (vertical spacing) and Hspace (horizontal spacing). Vspace inserts blank space above and below your table, and Hspace inserts space to the left and right of it.

To adjust Vspace and Hspace:

1. Select the entire table so that the Properties inspector displays Table Properties.
2. Expand the palette to display the lower half, if necessary.
3. Type a number, in pixels, in the Vspace text box to add space above and below your table (**Figure 63**).
4. Type a number, in pixels, in the Hspace text box to add space to the left and right of your table.
5. Click on the Apply button to add the spacing to your page.

You'll see the otherwise invisible Vspace and Hspace while your table is still selected (**Figure 64**).

Using cell padding and cell spacing is particularly useful if you're going to use tables in close proximity to other elements on your page, as shown in **Figure 65**.

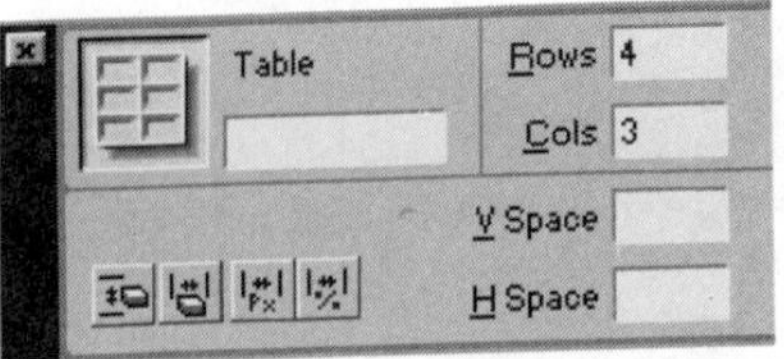

Figure 63 Type a number, in pixels, in the Vspace and Hspace text boxes on the Properties inspector.

Figure 64 While your table is still selected, you can see the space dedicated to Vspace and Hspace—10 pixels of each, in this case. I used a colored border to make the space more visible.

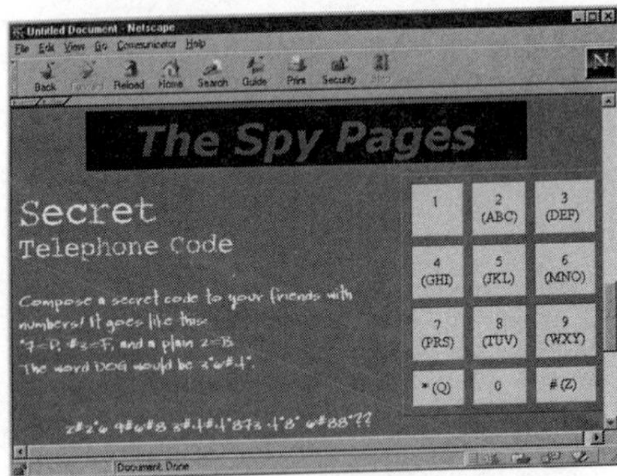

Figure 65 These tables have 10 pixels of space on each side to give them natural, borderless spacing from the rest of the page.

ADJUSTING TABLE SPACING

Figure 66 Click on the Table Cell, Table Row, or Table Col button to open the associated dialog box.

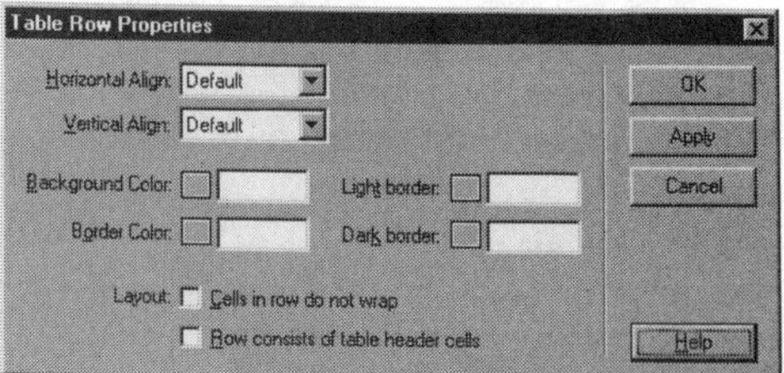

Figure 67 The Table Row Properties dialog box, like the properties dialog boxes for columns and cells, offers two alignment drop-down menus.

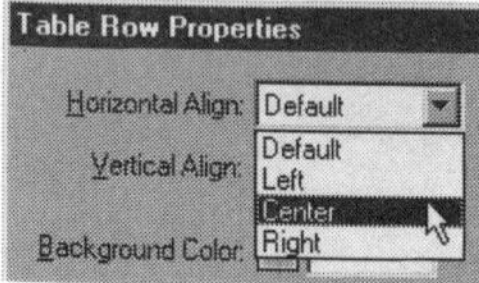

Figure 68 Horizontal Alignment options include Default, Left, Center, and Right.

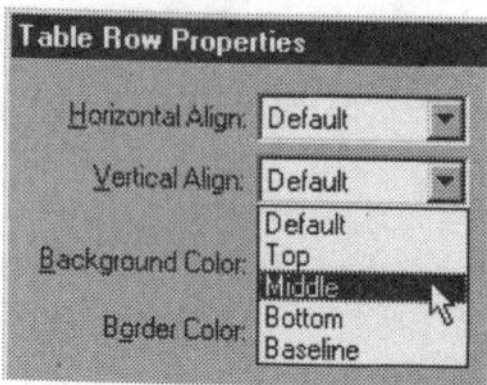

Figure 69 Vertical Alignment options include Default, Top, Middle, Bottom, and Baseline.

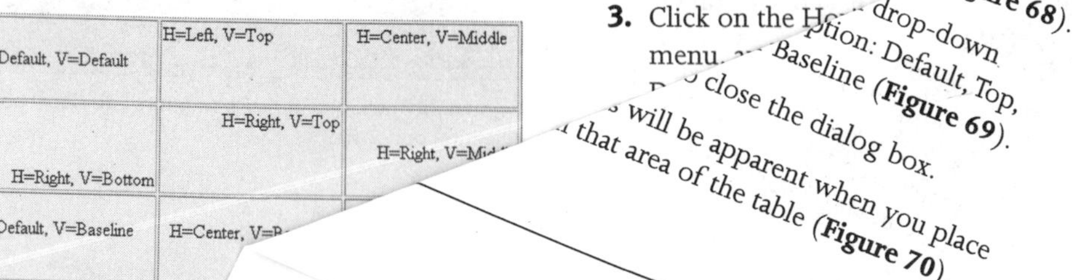

H=Default, V=Default	H=Left, V=Top	H=Center, V=Middle
H=Right, V=Bottom	H=Right, V=Top	H=Right, V=Mi[illegible]
H=Default, V=Baseline	H=Center, V=B[illegible]	

Figure 70 This table ru[illegible] ment options. The posi[illegible] alignment is based on [illegible] characters rest on, a[illegible] of the bordering ce[illegible]

Adjusting Content Spacing

In addition to table spacing, you can adjust where the content in your table's cells is placed:

- In both horizontal and vertical alignment, choosing Default sets the alignment to the browser's default—usually left (horizontal) and center (vertical).
- In most cases, then, you won't need to set alignment specifications for left or center unless you're "changing it back" from a previous adjustment.
- Cell alignment properties override row and column specs, and column specs override row specs.

Horizontal alignment within a cell is the same as regular alignment on a page: the text is aligned with the left, right, or center of the cell. Vertical alignment controls the position of the text between the top and bottom of a cell.

To change content alignment:

1. Click to place the insertion point in the column, row, or cell whose horizontal alignment you want to adjust.
2. In the expanded Properties inspector, click on the appropriate button, Table Cell, Table Row, or Table Col (**Figure 66**). The corresponding dialog box will app[ear] (**Figure 67**).
3. Click on the Ho[rizontal] [illegible] menu [illegible]

[illegible] drop-down [illegible] ption: Default, Top, [illegible] Baseline (**Figure 69**). [illegible] close the dialog box. [illegible] will be apparent when you place [illegible] that area of the table (**Figure 70**).

[illegible] own [illegible] ion: (**Figure 68**).

Coloring Tables

You can give a table a background color or background image that differs from the background of the overall page. You can also use different backgrounds in individual table cells.

To choose a table background color:

1. Select the table, and the Properties inspector will display the Table properties.
2. If the Table Properties inspector is collapsed, expand it by clicking on the Expander arrow.
3. In the Bg Color text box:
   - Type or paste a hex value for the background color.

   or

   - Click on the gray color selector button to pop up the colors palette (**Figure 71**). Hold down the mouse button and drag the pointer to select a color (**Figure 72**).

   or

   - From the color palette, click on the Colors button to open up the Color dialog box (**Figure 73**). For more on using the Color dialog box, see Chapter 2.

...you're finished making your selection, ...ur color choice, and click on OK to ...dialog box, if necessary. The ...be apparent immediately.

...the table ...ck-

✓ **Tip**

- Since y... before you... ground colo... rectly until yo... palette and desel...

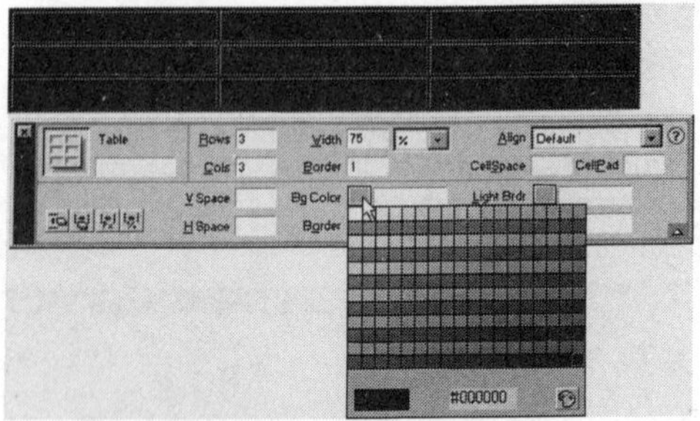

Figure 71 Click on the color selector button to pop up the Colors palette.

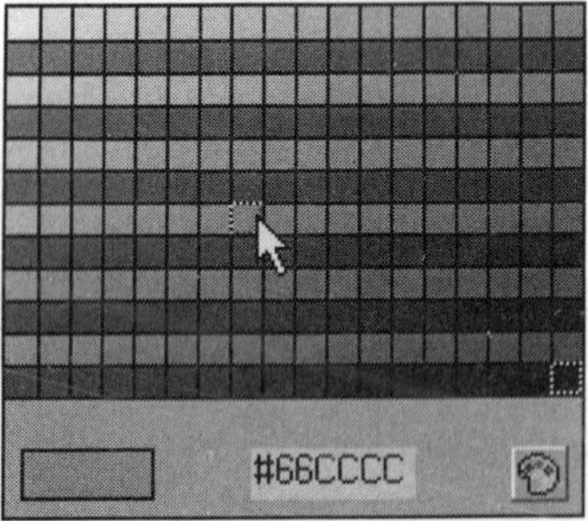

Figure 72 Choose a color from the Colors palette by clicking on it.

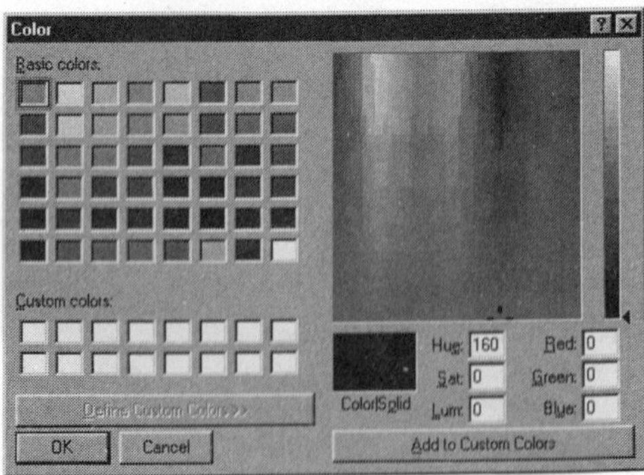

Figure 73 The Color dialog box offers additional color selection options.

Figure 66 Click on the Table Cell, Table Row, or Table Col button to open the associated dialog box.

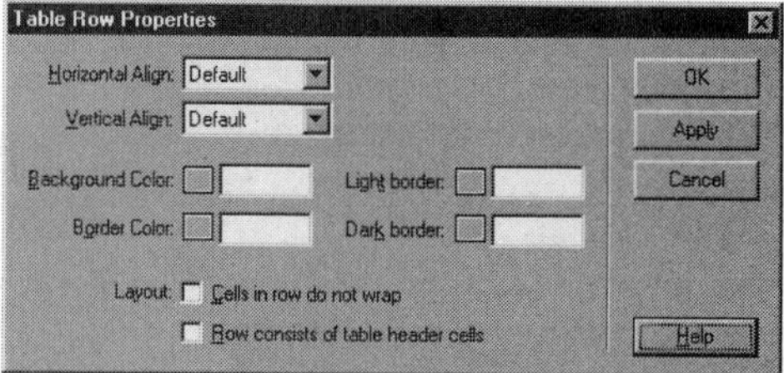

Figure 67 The Table Row Properties dialog box, like the properties dialog boxes for columns and cells, offers two alignment drop-down menus.

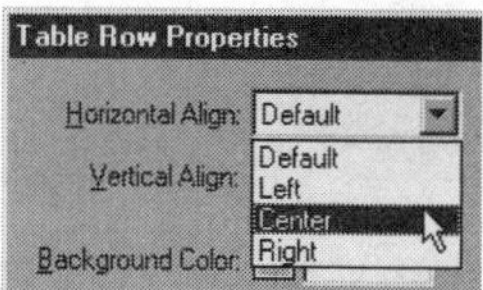

Figure 68 Horizontal Alignment options include Default, Left, Center, and Right.

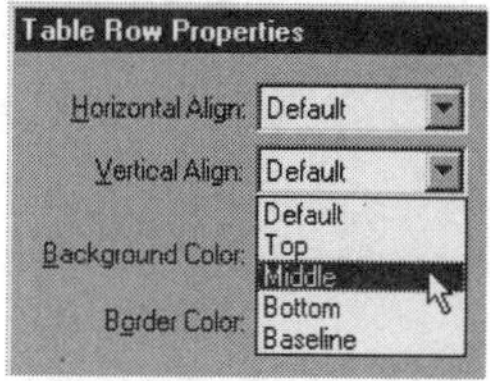

Figure 69 Vertical Alignment options include Default, Top, Middle, Bottom, and Baseline.

H=Default, V=Default	H=Left, V=Top	H=Center, V=Middle
H=Right, V=Bottom	H=Right, V=Top	H=Right, V=Middle
H=Default, V=Baseline	H=Center, V=Baseline	H=Right, V=Baseline

Figure 70 This table runs the gamut of content alignment options. The position of the Baseline vertical alignment is based on the imaginary lines that the characters rest on, and it generally follows the baseline of the bordering cells.

Adjusting Content Spacing

In addition to table spacing, you can adjust where the content in your table's cells is placed:

- In both horizontal and vertical alignment, choosing Default sets the alignment to the browser's default—usually left (horizontal) and center (vertical).
- In most cases, then, you won't need to set alignment specifications for left or center unless you're "changing it back" from a previous adjustment.
- Cell alignment properties override row and column specs, and column specs override row specs.

Horizontal alignment within a cell is the same as regular alignment on a page: the text is aligned with the left, right, or center of the cell. Vertical alignment controls the position of the text between the top and bottom of a cell.

To change content alignment:

1. Click to place the insertion point in the column, row, or cell whose horizontal alignment you want to adjust.
2. In the expanded Properties inspector, click on the appropriate button, Table Cell, Table Row, or Table Col (**Figure 66**). The corresponding dialog box will appear (**Figure 67**).
3. Click on the Horizontal Align drop-down menu, and select an alignment option: Default, Left, Center, or Right (**Figure 68**).
4. Click on the Vertical Align drop-down menu, and select an option: Default, Top, Middle, Bottom, or Baseline (**Figure 69**).
5. Click on OK to close the dialog box.

Your changes will be apparent when you place content in that area of the table (**Figure 70**).

Coloring Tables

You can give a table a background color or background image that differs from the background of the overall page. You can also use different backgrounds in individual table cells.

To choose a table background color:

1. Select the table, and the Properties inspector will display the Table properties.
2. If the Table Properties inspector is collapsed, expand it by clicking on the Expander arrow.
3. In the Bg Color text box:
   - Type or paste a hex value for the background color.

   or

   - Click on the gray color selector button to pop up the colors palette (**Figure 71**). Hold down the mouse button and drag the pointer to select a color (**Figure 72**).

   or

   - From the color palette, click on the Colors button to open up the Color dialog box (**Figure 73**). For more on using the Color dialog box, see Chapter 2.

When you're finished making your selection, click on your color choice, and click on OK to close the Color dialog box, if necessary. The color change should be apparent immediately.

✔ Tip

- Since you selected (highlighted) the table before you chose a color, the table background color you chose won't appear correctly until you finish with the Color palette and deselect the table.

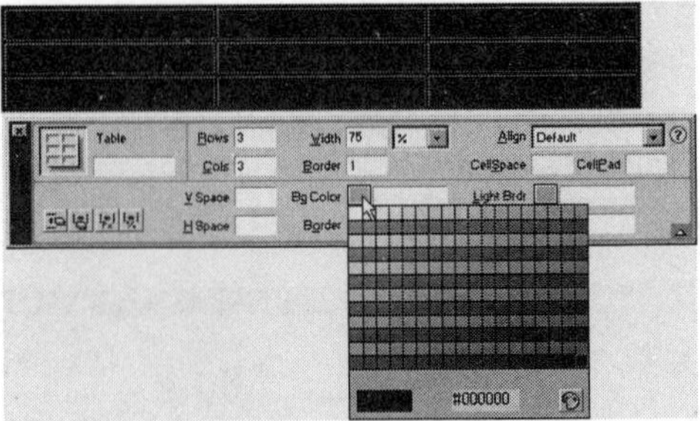

Figure 71 Click on the color selector button to pop up the Colors palette.

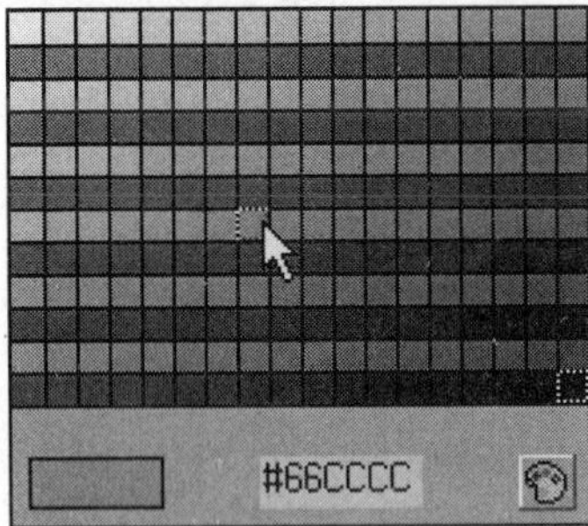

Figure 72 Choose a color from the Colors palette by clicking on it.

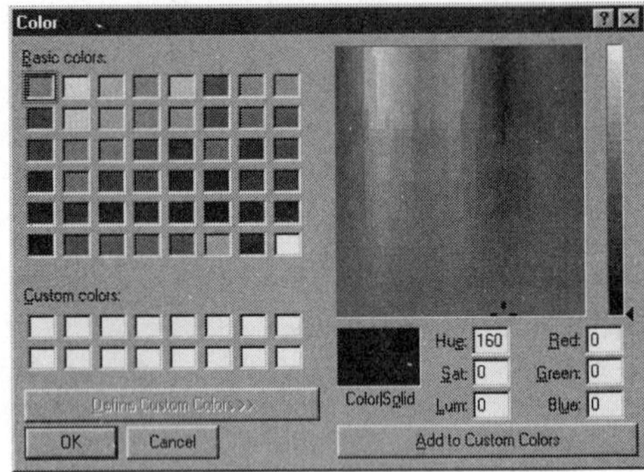

Figure 73 The Color dialog box offers additional color selection options.

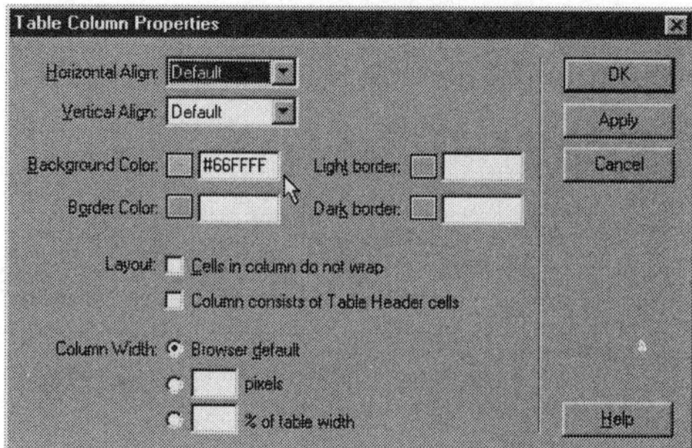

Figure 74 The Properties dialog box includes a text box and pull-down menu labeled Background Color.

Figure 75 I colored one column in this table. Notice that the table, the page, and the column use three different colors.

To color individual columns, rows, or cells:

1. Click within the row, column, or individual cell whose background you wish to modify.
2. From the Document window's menu bar, select Modify > Table > and then either Cell Properties, Row Properties, or Column Properties, depending on your selection.
3. In whichever dialog box appears (Column properties, in **Figure 74**), you'll see a text box marked Background Color.
4. Follow Step 3 in the section called *To Choose a Table Background Color*.
5. When you've made your selection, click on OK to close the Properties dialog box. You'll see your changes in the window. **Figure 75** shows a table with one column colored blue.

There are three possible border color selections you can make: Border, Light Border, and Dark Border.

To adjust border colors:

1. Select your table to change the Properties inspector to the Table Properties view.
2. For one (or all) of the color choices, Border, Light Border, and Dark Border, follow Step 3 in the section called *To Choose a Table Background Color*.

Figure 76 shows a table with colored borders, and **Figure 76** shows a table with light and dark border colors.

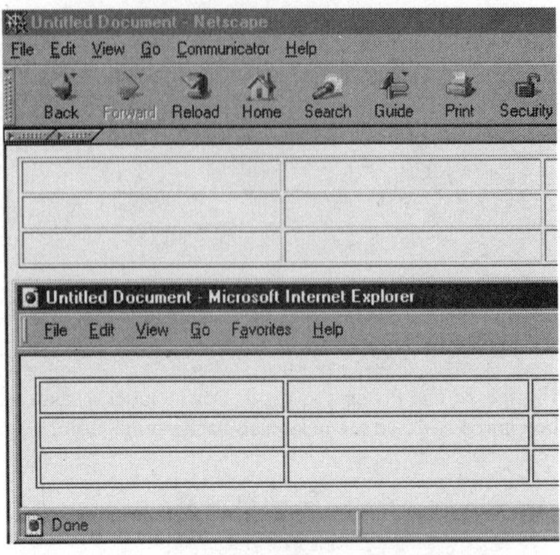

Figure 76 This table, seen in Navigator 4 on top and IE 4 below, has colored borders. In Navigator, the color appears only on the table's upper left edges.

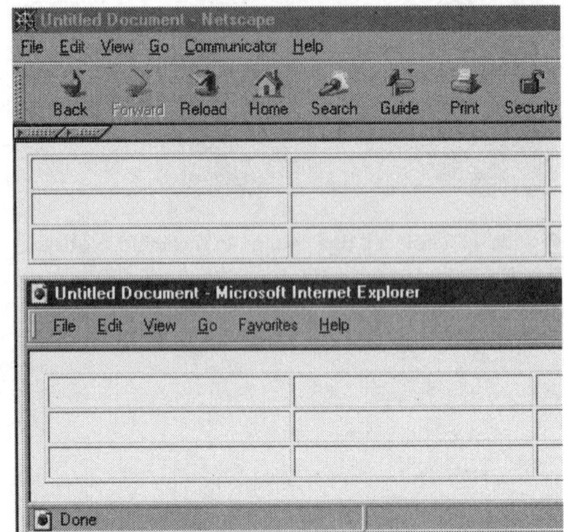

Figure 77 I used yellow for the light border color and dark gray for the dark border colors. Navigator 4 doesn't display light or dark border colors, and IE 4 displays both.

✔ Tips

- You can adjust the color of the border, the light border, or the dark border for a row, a column, or a single cell as well. To do so, use the appropriate Properties dialog box, by selecting Modify > Table > and then the name of the entity.
- Navigator version 4 or later will display the Border color, but not the Light and Dark Border colors. Those are conventions of Internet Explorer.
- You can set the Border, Light Border, and the Dark Border, but all three of them will not show up at once. However, this is the only way to get shaded borders in both Navigator and IE.

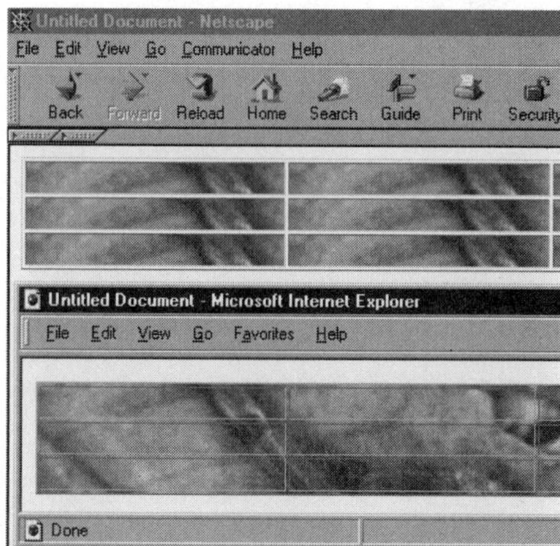

Figure 78 I used a table background image in this table. Navigator 4 (top) tiles the image in each cell, while IE 4 (bottom) uses the image as a background for the entire table.

While Dreamweaver doesn't provide direct support for using table background images, you can use one by working directly with the table code.

To use a table background image:

1. From the Document window menu bar, select Window > HTML to view the HTML for your page.
2. Find the opening code for your table. It should start with

   `<TABLE>`

   although there will probably be plenty of other attributes between the word TABLE and the closing bracket.
3. Add the following code to the TABLE tag:

   `background="bg.gif"`

   where `bg.gif` is the name and location of the background image file.
4. Press Ctrl+S to save the changes to the code. The background file will be visible immediately.

Figure 78 shows a table that uses a background image.

✔ Tips

- You can also use a table background image in an individual row `<TR>` or cell `<TD>`. Find the element you're looking for in the HTML code, include the background instructions in the element's tag:

  `<TR background="bg.gif">`

- To use a table background image for a column, you must apply the code to all the cells in that column.

8

USING FRAMES

Figure 1 Each frame is a distinct document with its own content—including different link and background colors and background images.

Web pages that use frames can be extremely versatile. A frames-based page is divided into several windows-within-windows, like the panes in an old-fashioned window (**Figure 1**).

While a frames-based page acts like a single Web page, each frame contains a single HTML document that can include completely separate contents and independent scrollbars. The glue that holds these documents together is called the *frameset definition document*, or the *frameset page*—a frameset is a set of frames, and the frameset page is what defines them as a set.

Frames and Navigation

You can use frames to create some nifty layouts. Since each page is a discrete HTML document, it can contain any HTML element except the <FRAMESET> tag—although we'll find out how to embed frames within frames later in this chapter.

Frames are best used when you want part of your page, like a toolbar or a table of contents, to be visible the entire time the page is in the window—regardless of what kind of scrolling your visitors do.

✔ Definition

- The frameset page is called that because it includes the <FRAMESET> tag, which defines the layout of the frames-based page, the location and names of the initial pages that occupy each frame, and details about the appearance and actions of the frames. You can see the code for a frameset page in **Figure 2**. **Figure 3** presents a diagram of frame structure.

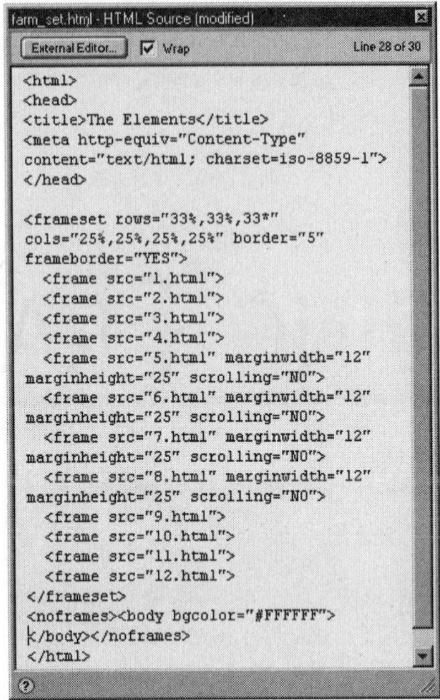


```
<html>
<head>
<title>The Elements</title>
<meta http-equiv="Content-Type"
content="text/html; charset=iso-8859-1">
</head>

<frameset rows="33%,33%,33*"
cols="25%,25%,25%,25%" border="5"
frameborder="YES">
  <frame src="1.html">
  <frame src="2.html">
  <frame src="3.html">
  <frame src="4.html">
  <frame src="5.html" marginwidth="12"
marginheight="25" scrolling="NO">
  <frame src="6.html" marginwidth="12"
marginheight="25" scrolling="NO">
  <frame src="7.html" marginwidth="12"
marginheight="25" scrolling="NO">
  <frame src="8.html" marginwidth="12"
marginheight="25" scrolling="NO">
  <frame src="9.html">
  <frame src="10.html">
  <frame src="11.html">
  <frame src="12.html">
</frameset>
<noframes><body bgcolor="#FFFFFF">
</body></noframes>
</html>
```

Figure 2 A frames-based page is held together behind the scenes by a frameset page, which keeps track of what belongs where. This is the frameset page code for the page in Figure 1.

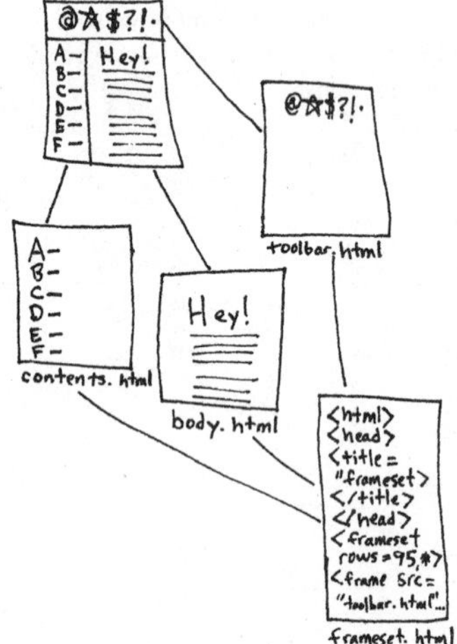

Figure 3 Each document in a frameset is an individual HTML document. In the background, the frameset page acts as mission control, holding together all the documents. Each frame has a default document anchored to it so that something will load when the frames page is loaded. An infinite number of pages can be associated with a frames page via links.

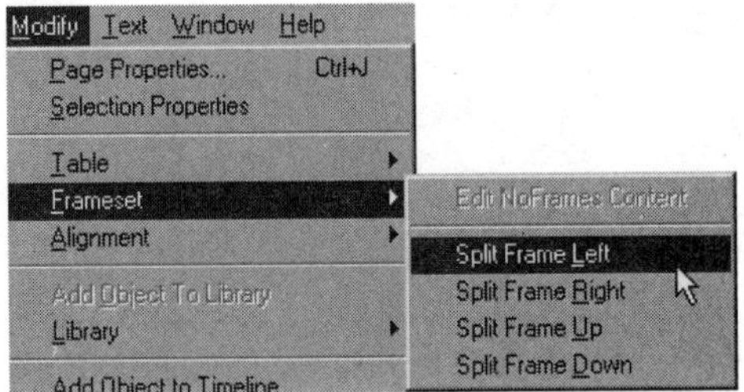

Figure 4 Choose Modify > Frameset from the Document window menu bar.

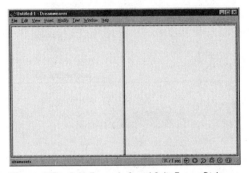

Figure 5 The Split Frame Left and Split Frame Right commands both split the current frame in half with a vertical frame border.

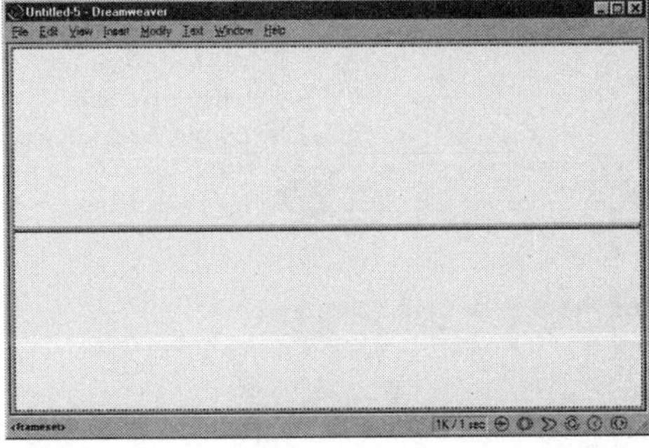

Figure 6 The Split Frame Up and Split Frame Down commands both split the current frame in half with a horizontal frame border.

Setting Up a Frames Page

Dreamweaver will automatically create a frameset when you divide a page into more than one frame.

To create frames by splitting the page:

1. Start Dreamweaver, and open a blank window, if necessary.
2. From the Document Window menu bar, select Modify > Frameset > (**Figure 4**).

   And then choose one of the following options:
   - Split Frame Left (**Figure 5**)
   - Split Frame Right (**Figure 5**)
   - Split Frame Up (**Figure 6**)
   - Split Frame Down (**Figure 6**)
3. The window will split to display two frames.

Creating Frames by Dragging

You can also drag the frame border to create multiple frames on a page.

To create a frame by dragging:

1. From the Document window menu bar, select View > Frame Borders. A heavy outline will appear around the blank space in the window (**Figure 7**).
2. Hold down the Alt (Option) key and click on one of the borders.
3. Drag it to a new location (**Figure 8**), and release the mouse button when you've positioned the border where you choose (**Figure 9**).

You now have two frames in the window.

✔ Tip

- You can drag the corner where the borders intersect to create four new frames at once (**Figure 10**).

Figure 7 After you view frame borders for your page, a heavy outline will appear around it. It should look similar to the frame borders you've seen on pages around the Web.

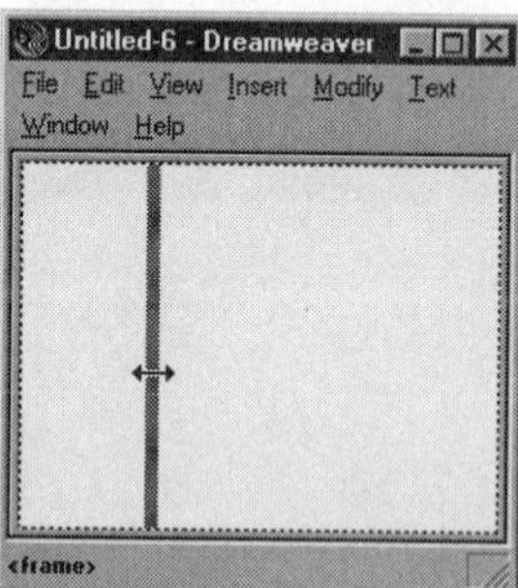

Figure 8 Hold down the Alt (Option) key and click on the border, and you can create a new frame by splitting the original page.

Figure 9 Let go of the mouse button when the frame border is where you want. Ta-da! You now have two frames.

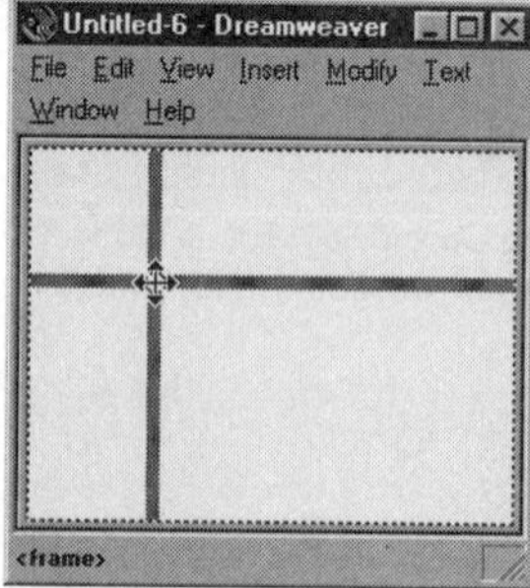

Figure 10 If you hold down the Alt (Option) key and click the corner of a frame border, you can drag it to split the page into four frames.

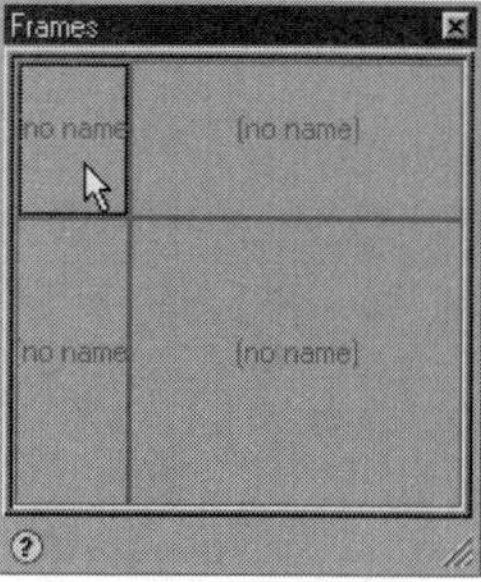

Figure 11 The Frames inspector is a handy little window that you can use to select frames just by clicking on the corresponding frame.

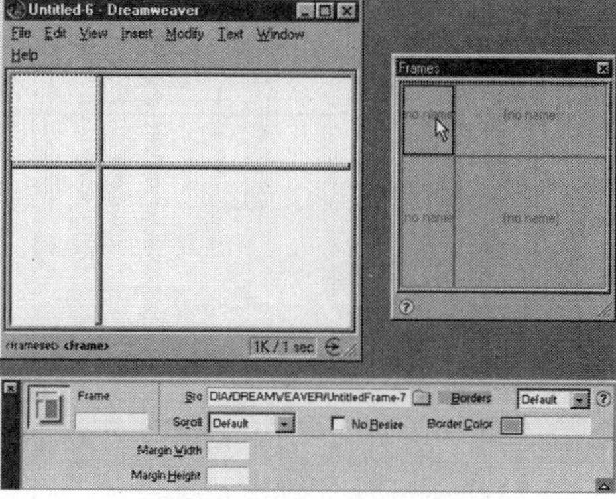

Figure 12 When you select a frame, a heavy line appears around the frame in the Frames inspector, and a dashed line appears around it in the Document window. Additionally, the Properties inspector displays Frame properties for the frame you selected.

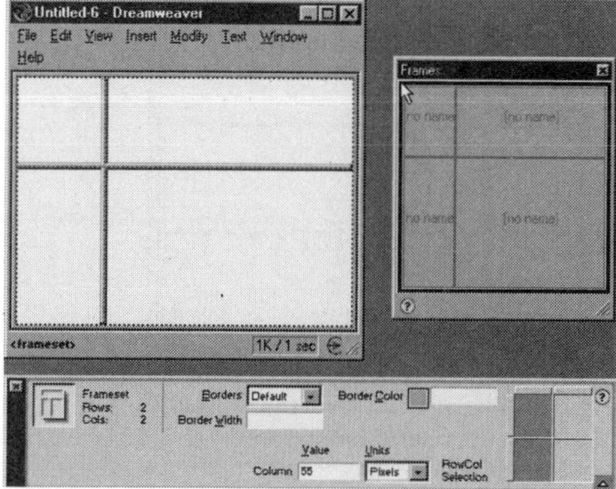

Figure 13 When you select an entire frameset by clicking on the frame border in the Document window or Properties inspector, the Properties inspector displays properties for the frameset.

The Frames Inspector

The Frames inspector is a useful tool for selecting individual frames or entire framesets. To view the Frames inspector, select Window > Frame from the Document window menu bar. The Frames inspector will appear (**Figure 11**).

To view frame properties, you need to select the frame.

To select a frame:

1. Hold down the Alt (Option) key and click on the frame in the Document window.

   or

   In the Frames inspector, click on the frame you want to select (**Figure 11**).
2. In either case, a dashed line will appear in the Document window around the frame you selected, and the Properties inspector will display properties for that frame (**Figure 12**).

Selecting a Frameset

You can select an entire frameset in one of two ways:

- Click on any of the frame borders in the Document window.

  or
- In the Frames inspector, click on the border around the frames.

Either way, the Properties inspector will display properties for the frameset, and a dashed line will appear around all the frames in the frameset (**Figure 13**).

Note that the Properties inspector displays all the columns and rows in a frameset, but that all frames are shown as having the same dimensions.

Modifying the Frame Page Layout

You have limitless options when it comes to laying out pages with frames. You can divide frames the same way you created them initially: by splitting or by dragging. You'll probably do some experimenting before you achieve the layout you want.

To split frames:

1. In the Document window, click within the frame you want to split.
2. From the Document window menu bar, select Modify > Frameset > (as shown earlier in **Figure 4**), and then choose one of the following options: Split Frame Left, Split Frame Right, Split Frame Up, or Split Frame Down.

Splitting left or right, up or down may look exactly the same unless there is already content in the frame. For example, the left window in **Figure 14** shows a frame that was split left, and the right window shows the same frame split right instead.

To drag frame borders:

1. Mouse over the border between two frames, and the pointer will turn into a double-headed arrow (**Figure 15**).
2. Click on the border, and drag it to a new location. When the border appears where you want it to, release the mouse button.

✔ Tip

- To split a frame while dragging it, hold down the Alt (Option) key while you click the mouse button (**Figure 16**).

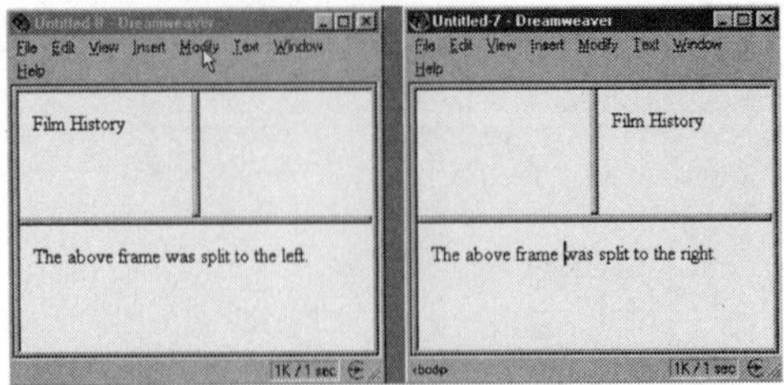

Figure 14 These two frames pages are pretty much the same. In the one on the left, the top frame was split left, while in the right-hand window, the same frame was split right. Which option you choose depends on where you want any content in the frame to land.

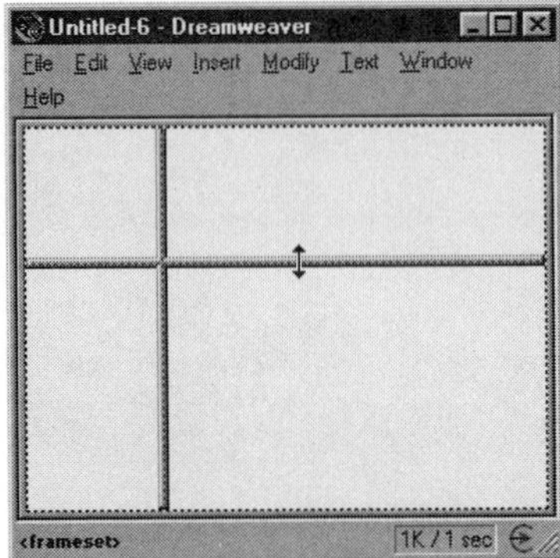

Figure 15 When you mouse over a border between frames, the pointer becomes a double-headed arrow that you can use to drag the border.

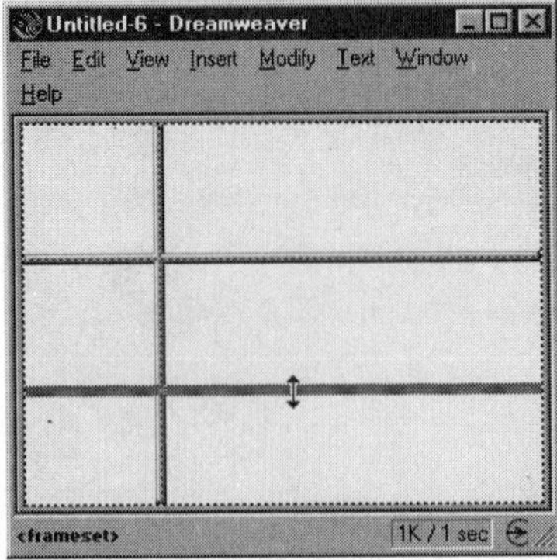

Figure 16 If you hold down the Alt (Option) key while clicking on the frame border, you can split a frame by dragging the border.

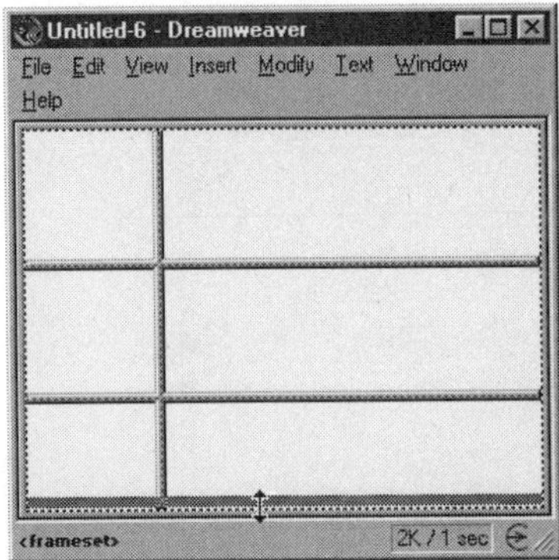

Figure 17 Click on the border of the unwanted frame, and drag it off the page—you'll get rid of both the frame and the border.

Figure 18 You can also drag a frame border into another frame border to get rid of it.

Figure 19 Either way, you'll be free of the unwanted frame.

Deleting a Frame

You can keep splitting frames until you achieve the layout you want, but if you create a few frames too many, getting rid of them is easy.

To delete a frame:

1. Click on the frame border, and drag it off the page (**Figure 17**).

   or

   Click on the frame border, and drag it until it meets another border (**Figure 18**).

2. Let go of the mouse button. The frame will disappear (**Figure 19**).

Dragging Content between Frames

Before you delete that frame, you can drag its content into another frame on the page. This works for all sorts of objects, including text, images, multimedia objects, and form fields. Click on the object to select it, or highlight the text you wish to move. Click and hold down the mouse button while you drag the object to a new frame. When the stuff is where you want it, let go of the mouse button, and it will reappear in the new location.

Nested Framesets

Once your initial frame page layout is created, you can divide the space within any individual frame by inserting another frameset that is *nested* within the original frameset. Dreamweaver creates nested framesets automatically when you split a frame. The original frameset is called the *parent*, and the frameset within the parent set is called the *child*. You can theoretically keep nesting framesets until the cows come home, and the hierarchy always has the child frameset reporting to its immediate parent.

Creating a nested frameset uses the same tasks as creating any other frameset. You can watch how Dreamweaver modifies the code by keeping the HTML inspector open while you follow these steps.

To create a nested frameset:

1. Open (or create) a frameset page in the Dreamweaver window (**Figure 20**).
2. Click in one of the frames, and then split it by selecting, from the Document window menu bar, Modify > Frameset > and then Split Frame Left, Right, Up, or Down. In **Figure 21**, we selected Split Frame Up.

Dreamweaver has created a second frameset nested within the original frameset. You can examine the structure of the document by using the Frames inspector.

Figure 20 Here's our original frameset. In framesets with no nested framesets inside them, *all* frame borders go from one edge of the window to the other.

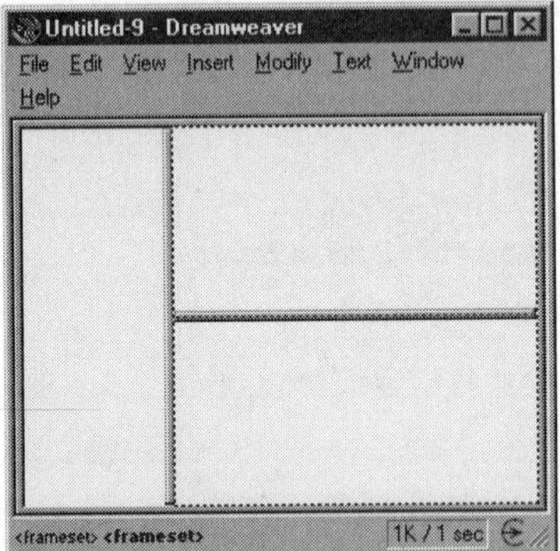

Figure 21 We split the frame on the right into two halves.

NESTED FRAMESETS

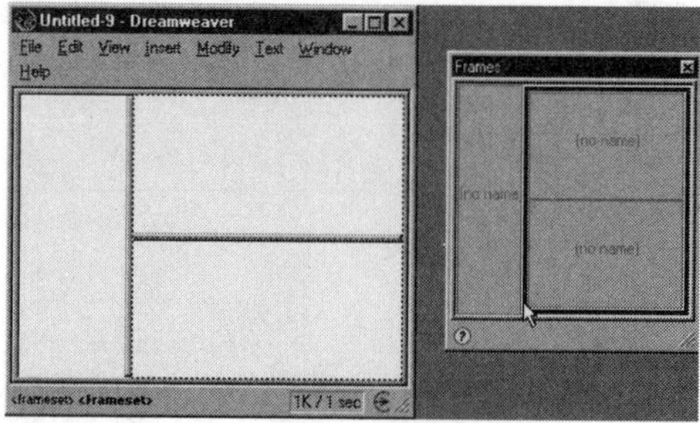

Figure 22 Dreamweaver automatically nests a new frameset inside the original, and you can select the child frameset with the Frames inspector.

To view the structure of a document:

1. Display the Frames inspector, if necessary, by selecting Window > Frames from the Document window menu bar.
2. As you click on each frame in the Frames inspector, it becomes highlighted. Additionally, a dashed line appears around the frame in the Document window.
3. To select an embedded frameset, click on the heavy border around the frameset in the Frames inspector (**Figure 22**). A dashed line will appear around each frame in the embedded frameset.

Setting Column and Row Sizes

Frames, just like tables, are divided into columns and rows. You could think of the individual frames in a set as cells, each of which occupies a certain number of columns and rows (See Chapter 7 for more on cells, columns, and rows).

When you split a frame or drag a frame border, Dreamweaver translates the information about the position of the frame border into a height or width amount for each frame, in pixels or percent of the window. To adjust the height or width of a frame, you can adjust the row height or column width.

The page in **Figure 23** is comprised of two framesets (look at the Frames inspector to see this more clearly). The first frameset is made up of two rows. The top frame, or row, is 68 pixels high. The bottom row is relative to that height; it will take up the rest of the browser window, however small or large (**Figure 24**).

The embedded frameset is made up of two columns. The left column occupies 25 percent of the available space—in this case, it's both 25 percent of the parent frame and 25 percent of the window. The right column, then, can be set to either 75 percent or to relative to the parent frameset's width.

✔ Tips

- Since the dimensions of a column or row affect the dimensions of the entire table, row height and column width are frameset properties, rather than frame properties.
- It makes sense to set the height and width for one column or row in particular, and to set all other heights and widths as relative to that area of the page.

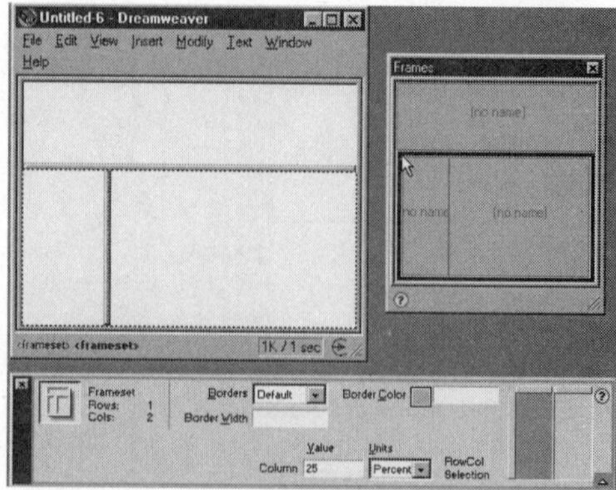

Figure 23 This frameset is made up of two rows (across the window), and a nested frameset that has two columns (vertical divisions of the lower frame). In this figure, the Properties inspector is displaying Frameset properties for the child (nested) frameset.

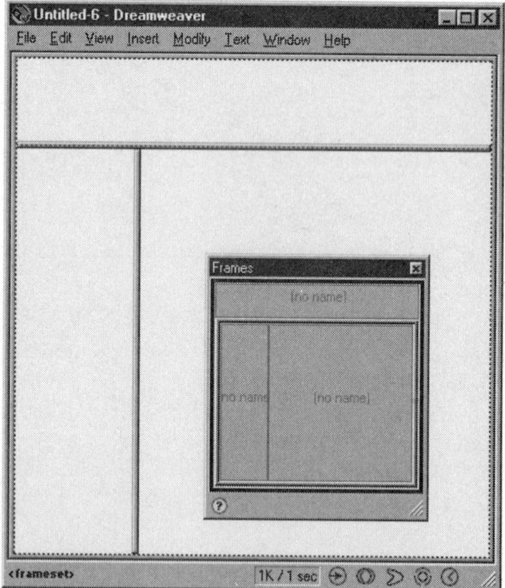

Figure 24 Here you see the same frameset resized. Notice how the top frame retains the same pixel size, while the bottom frames retain their proportional settings.

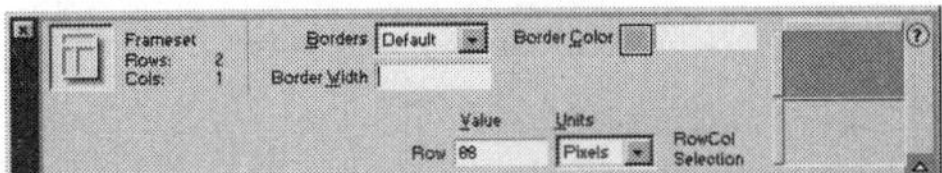

Figure 25 The Properties inspector displays frameset options when you click on a frame border in the Document window.

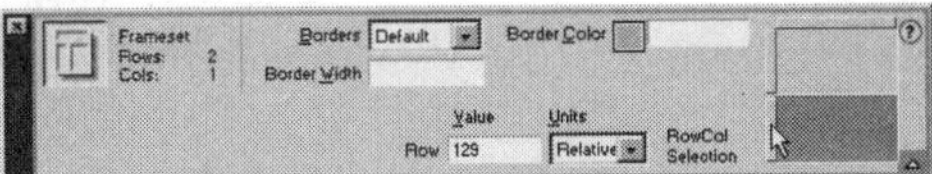

Figure 26 Click on a tab in the frameset preview of the Properties inspector to adjust settings for that column or row.

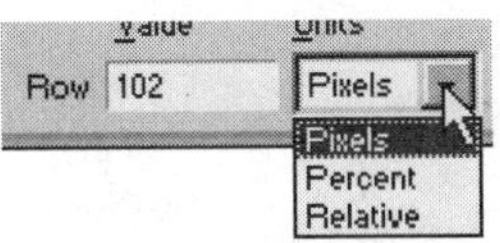

Figure 27 Select either pixels, percent, or relative as the units for the height or width measurement.

To adjust row height and column width:

1. Select the frameset by clicking on a frame border. The frameset properties will appear in the Properties inspector (**Figure 25**).
2. If necessary, display the entire inspector by clicking on the Expander arrow in the bottom-right corner of the inspector. The Properties inspector will display column or row values, depending on your selection.
3. Select the column or row whose area you wish to define by clicking on the associated tab, above the column or to the left of the row, in the Properties inspector (**Figure 26**).
4. Type a value for the column or row in the associated text box and select one of the following units from the drop-down menu (**Figure 27**):
   - *Pixels* set an exact height or width. When the frameset is loaded in the browser, pixel measurements are followed exactly.
   - *Percent* refers to a percentage of window (or frameset) size.
   - *Relative* means that the height or width is relative to the elements in the frameset that have been given pixel or percent measurements.
5. Click on the Apply button to apply the height or width changes to the frameset.
6. Repeat these steps for the remainder of the elements in the frameset.

✔ Tip

- When a browser is loading a frameset page, it draws the layout in the following order:
  - *Pixel* measurements are given their space allotment first.
  - Columns or rows with *percentage* measurements are drawn next.
  - Frames with *relative* settings are drawn to fill the rest of the available space.

Setting Content Pages

There are two ways you can go about putting content into those pretty, blank frames. One way is to open an existing page in the framework of the frameset; the other way is to create your new page right now in the Dreamweaver window.

In either case, to determine what your frames page will display when it's loaded into a Web browser, you'll attach a URL to each of the frames in the set.

To attach a page to a frame:

1. Select the frame you want to put some content in. The Properties inspector will display the properties of that frame (**Figure 28**).
2. The SRC text box currently displays the pathname of the blank, untitled, unsaved page that's in it currently. You can:
   - Type (or paste) a location of an existing page—on the Web or on your computer—into the text box.
   - Click on the Properties inspector's Browse icon to open up the Select HTML File dialog box (**Figure 29**).
   - From the Document window menu bar, select File > Open in Frame to display the Select HTML File dialog box.

If you use one of the latter two options, locate the file on your computer, and then click on Open to attach the file to the frame you selected. (See Chapter 2 if you need more information on using the Select HTML File dialog box.)

If the file you selected is on your local machine, it will appear in the frame within the Document window.

If the file is on the Web, you'll see a message that says "Remote File" (**Figure 30**).

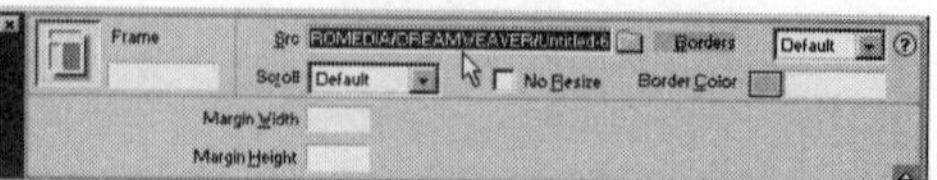

Figure 28 When the Properties inspector displays frame properties, you can set the location for the default frame document in the SRC text box.

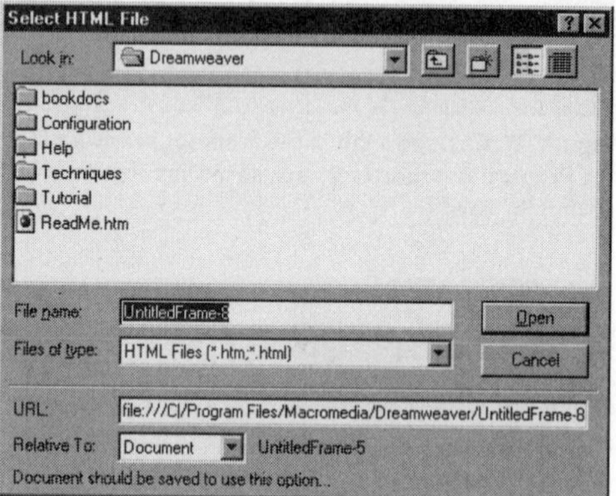

Figure 29 Use the Select HTML File dialog box to choose a file to load in the frame.

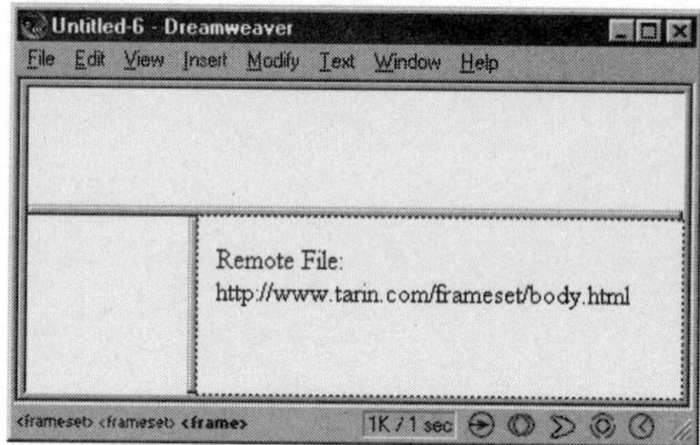

Figure 30 If you type an Internet URL in the Frame Properties SRC text box, the Document window will display the "Remote File" message. If you're online when you preview this page in your browser, the browser should load the remote file in the frame.

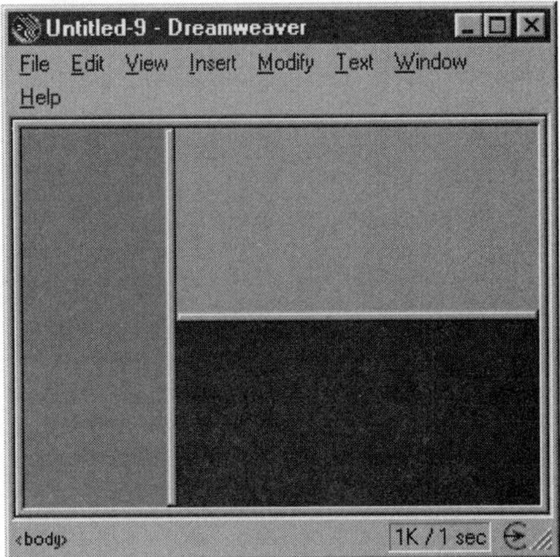

Figure 31 This page has three frames, each of which uses a different background color. Back in **Figure 1**, 8 of the 12 frames used different background images.

Creating Content within a Frame

Creating and editing content within one of the frames in a frameset is the same as doing so in a blank Dreamweaver window, only with less screen real estate.

On these pages you can put text, images, multimedia objects, and tables—anything that you can use on a non-frames page.

✔ Tip

- Of course, you can create a page in Dreamweaver, save it, and then attach it to a frameset (as described in the preceding section), but if you're creating simple content, you can easily work in the frameset.

Setting the background color for a frame is just like setting the background color for a standalone page. Each frame, remember, is a single HTML document, or page, and each page in the frameset has its own page properties. **Figure 31** shows a frames page in which every frame has a different background.

To set a frame background:

1. Display the page properties for the frame in one of two ways:
   - Right-click on the frame and select Page Properties from the pop-up menu.
   - From the Document window menu bar, select Modify > Page Properties.

   Either way, the Page Properties dialog box will appear.

2. From here, you can adjust page properties for that frame, including background color, background image, text colors, and link colors.

For more on working with Page Properties, see Chapter 2.

Saving Your Work

Since frames pages are made up of multiple documents, saving them is a multistep process. If you just press Ctrl+S (Command+S), you might not be quite sure of which page you're saving, because Dreamweaver's Save dialog box doesn't offer any distinguishing marks.

You can skip these steps for any previously completed pages you attached to the frameset, as described in the section *Setting Content Pages*.

To save each frame:

1. Select the frame that you want to save by clicking on it in the Frames inspector.
2. From the Document window menu bar, select File > Save, or press Ctrl+S (Command+S). The Save As dialog box will appear (**Figure 32**).
3. Type a meaningful filename in the File Name text box. You'll want to be able to distinguish one frame file from another when dealing with these documents later, so choose a name such as left.html or main_body.html rather than frame1.html.
4. Make sure that the Save In list box displays the folder you want to save the files in; otherwise, browse through the folders on your computer until you find the one you want.
5. Click on Save to close the Save As dialog box and return to the Document window.
6. Repeat these steps for each frame in the window.

✔ Tip

- If you create work within a frame in the Document window, you can save your work, and Dreamweaver will automatically set the URL for that page as the default page for that frame.

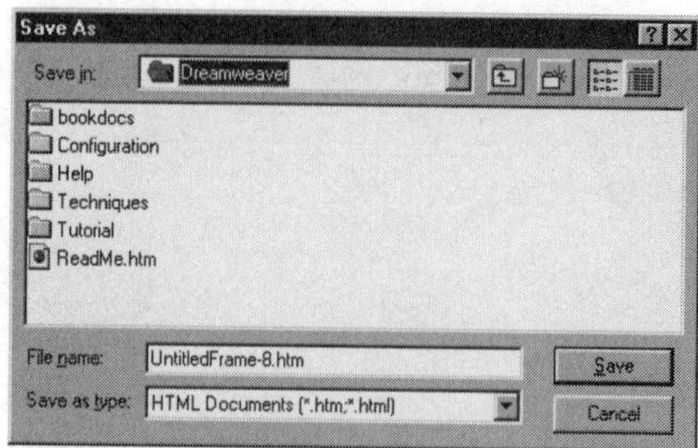

Figure 32 You need to save each frame separately, since they are distinct documents. This Save As dialog box is no different from any other Dreamweaver Save As dialog box. (Some other Web page programs, such as Microsoft FrontPage, have distinct Save As dialog boxes for the different parts of a frameset.)

Saving All Your Work at Once

After you've saved all the pages in your frameset once, you can periodically save all of them at the same time.

From the Document window menu bar, select File > Save All. Changes to documents currently open in any Dreamweaver window will be saved. A Save As dialog box will appear for any previously unsaved documents open in Dreamweaver.

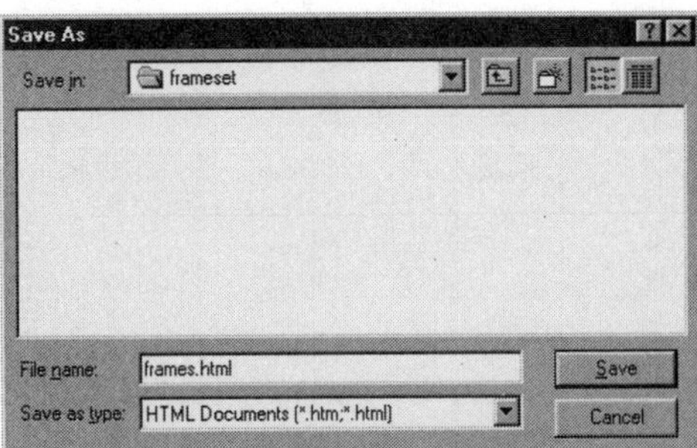

Figure 33 The filename for the frameset page will ultimately appear as the URL of your frames-based site. For instance, in this case the URL of the page will end up being something like http://www.yoursite.com/frameset/frames.html.

Titling the Frameset Page

Since the frameset page is the one whose URL you'll point to, and since it's the page-in-charge, you need to give it a title:

1. Select the frameset by clicking on the outside frame border in the Document window or in the Frames inspector.
2. From the Document window menu bar, select Modify > Page Properties. The Page Properties dialog box will appear.
3. Type the title for your page in the Title text box.
4. Click on OK to close the Page Properties dialog box.

You'll see the title in the title bar when you preview the page in the browser window.

Saving the Frameset Page

The frameset page, which contains all the behind-the-scenes data that makes the page function as a frames page, needs to be saved separately as well.

To save the frameset page:

1. With your frames page visible in the Document window, choose File > Save Frameset from the Document window menu bar. The Save As dialog box will appear.
2. Type a meaningful filename in the File Name text box. This filename will be part of the URL, or pathname, for the entire frames page (**Figure 33**).
3. Make sure that the Save In list box displays the folder you want to save the files in; otherwise, browse through the folders on your computer until you find the one you want.
4. Click on Save to close the Save As dialog box and return to the Document window.

✔ Tips

- It's helpful not only to save all the files in a frameset in the same folder, but to keep those files separate from the rest of the HTML files on your computer.
- That way, not only will you be able to locate the files easily and distinguish them from your other projects, you'll have them tidily in their own folder when you get ready to upload them all to the Web.
- Of course, if you also place frameset files in their own directory on your Web site, you can use relative filenames to keep everything tidy.
- When you open your site in the browser window, it's the frameset document that you're using as the URL.

Frameset Options

There are several options you can set for the frames in your page, including options for scrollbars and borders, whether the frames can be resized, and margin settings for each frame.

You can set scrollbar options for each frame on a page. **Figure 34** demonstrates these options.

To set scrollbar options:

1. Select the frame whose scrollbar settings you want to change.
2. In the Properties inspector, choose a scrollbar option from the Scroll drop-down menu (**Figure 35**):
   - *Yes* (the frame will always have scrollbars, whether they're needed or not)
   - *No* (the frame will never have scrollbars, whether they're needed or not)
   - *Auto* (the frame will display scrollbars when they are needed)
   - *Default* (uses browser default settings, which are usually Auto)

Note that these scrollbar settings affect both horizontal and vertical scrollbars. The Yes and No settings should be used with discretion.

Generally, when a frames page is loaded into a browser window, the user can resize the frames to personal taste or viewing convenience. If you want some or all of the frames in your page not to be resized, you can set the No Resize option.

Using the no resize option:

1. Select the frame whose scrollbar settings you want to change. The Properties inspector will display settings for that frame.
2. Place a checkmark in the No Resize checkbox.

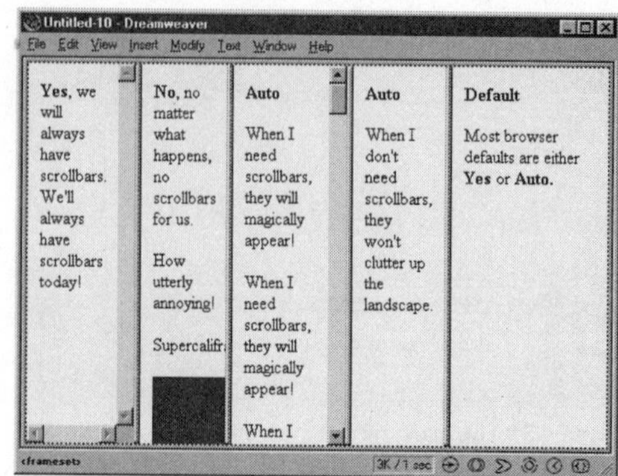

Figure 34 Scrollbar options demonstrated here are, from left to right, Yes, No, Auto (with scrollbars), Auto (without scrollbars), and Default. Obviously, Auto makes the most sense most of the time.

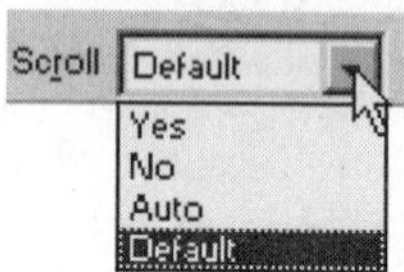

Figure 35 Choose one of the scrollbar options from the drop-down menu on the Properties inspector.

Figure 36 Here's the same page we saw in **Figure 1**, with a normal, default frame border. (To "change back" to this setting after a departure, use a frame border of 5.)

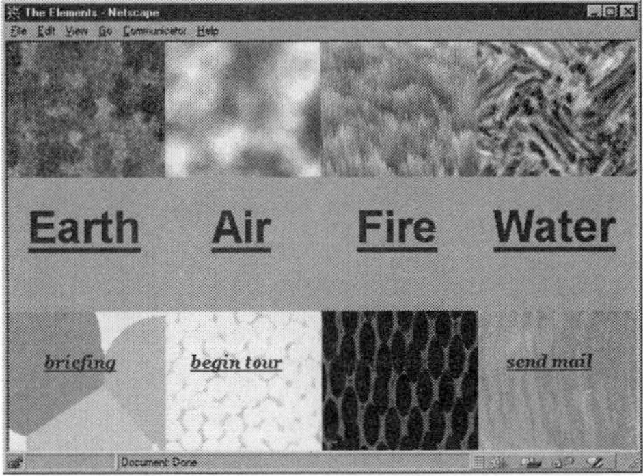

Figure 37 Here's the same page with a border width of zero.

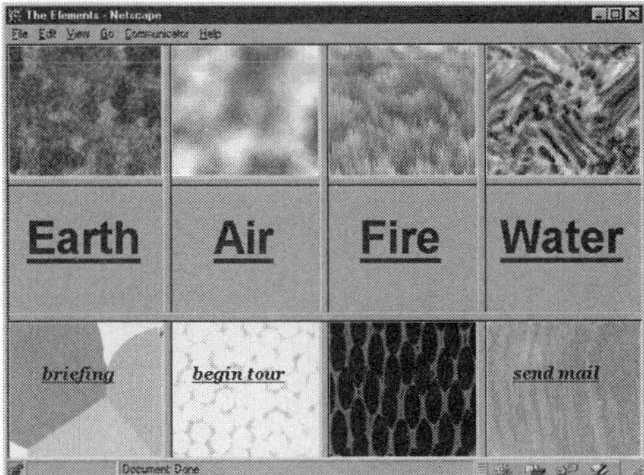

Figure 38 Same thing, with a rather thick border of 10. Play around with it; the most interesting effects are between 0 and 10.

Obviously, all frames that border frames with the No Resize option selected will not be able to be resized on that border. In **Figure 34**, it sure would be nice to be able to resize some of those frames.

You can turn off borders for the frames on a page, and you can set the width of all the borders on a page. These are frameset options rather than a single-frame option.

Figures 36–38 show the same page, with frame borders turned off in **Figure 37**, and a border width of 10 in **Figure 38**.

To set border options:

1. Select the frameset. The Properties inspector will display frameset options (as shown earlier in **Figure 13**).
2. From the Properties inspector's Borders drop-down menu, choose one of the following options:
   - *Yes* (displays all frame borders)
   - *No* (hides all frame borders)
   - *Default* (uses browser default settings, usually displaying borders)
3. Type a number, in pixels, in the Border Width text box.
4. Press Enter (Return), or click on the Apply button to apply your changes to the page.

✔ Tips

- In case you change your mind and want to go back to "normal" frame borders, the default border width is 5.
- You can display or hide borders while you're working in Dreamweaver, regardless of what your final browser settings are. Just select View > Frame Borders to toggle the borders on and off.
- Border width affects the spacing between the frames on a page whether or not the borders themselves are displayed.

To choose a border color:

1. Select the frameset, and the frameset properties will appear in the Properties inspector.
2. Choose a border color by:
   - Typing or pasting a hex code in the Border Color text box Border Color ;
   - Clicking on the Border Color button to display the Colors palette, and then clicking on a color in the Colors palette ; or
   - Displaying the Colors palette, clicking on the Colors button, and using the Colors dialog box to select a specific color (see Chapter 2).

The color you selected will be displayed on the frame borders (**Figure 39**); the appearance will differ depending on border width.

✔ Tips

- You can set border colors for individual frames, which will override any border color settings you made for the entire frameset, although your mileage may vary (**Figure 40**).
- Border colors will not display if the borders are turned off.

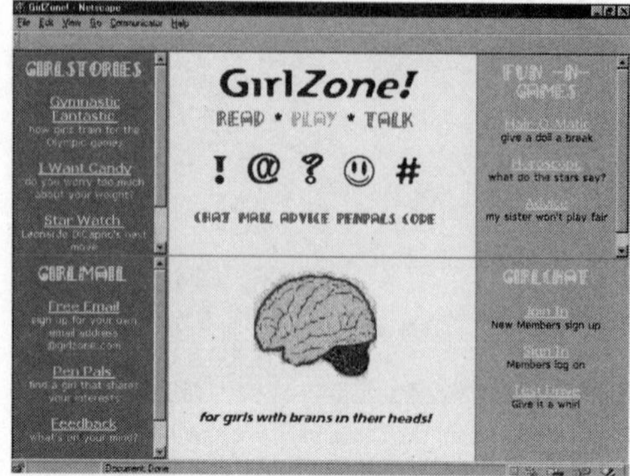

Figure 39 This frameset has colored borders and a border width of 3.

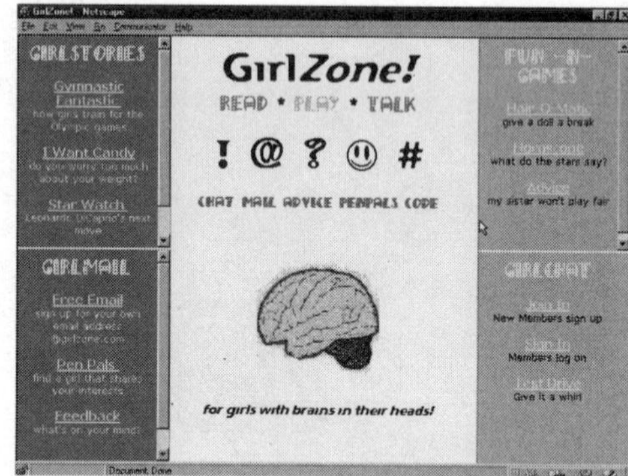

Figure 40 We changed the border color setting *only* for the top-left frame, and all the borders were affected except the border between the middle and right frames.

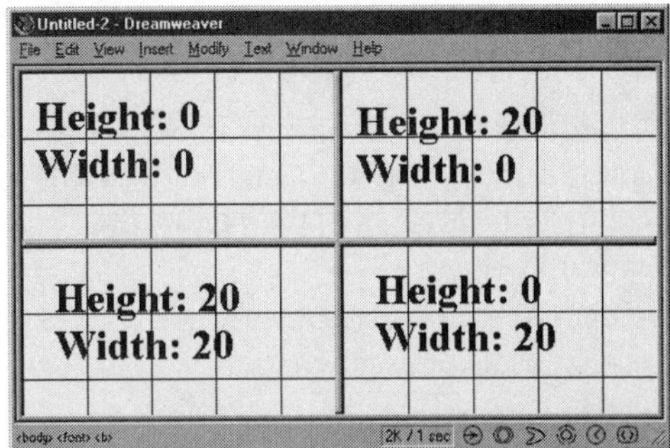

Figure 41 I turned on the grid in this view (View > Grid > Show) so you can see the difference that margin settings make. Each of these four frames has different margin settings; experiment with different settings for pages that use images or different sizes of text.

Setting Margins

Before Dynamic HTML, the only way to set page margins was by using frames. You can set two border values for each frame in a set: Margin Width (left and right margins) and Margin Height (top and bottom margins).

To set margins:

1. Select the frame whose margins you'd like to set.
2. In the Properties inspector, type a number (in pixels) in the Margin Width and/or Margin Height text boxes.
3. Press Enter (Return), or click on the Apply button to see your changes take effect.

Figure 41 demonstrates the effect that margins can have. See Chapter 10 for much more on style sheets.

Targeting Links

Now you have a frames page that looks exactly like you want it to, and you have a default document attached to all the frames in your page. Before you can call your page finished, you need to set targets for the links in your pages.

What's a Target?

When you click on a link in a regular Web page, it generally opens in the same window as the last document you were viewing. In a frames page, however, in which several documents occupy the same window, you don't always want the result of the user's next click—the *target* page—to appear in the same frame as the link they clicked on. A target tells the link in which window it should open.

Target Options

- If you don't declare any targets for a particular frame, the target page will open in the same frame as the link.
- You can set targets so that clicking on a link in one frame opens the page in another frame. Or you can use one of the special targets (see the sidebar on this page) to control where a document opens.
- You can set a default, or base target, for all your frames; you only need to set individual targets for links that differ from the frame's default target.

Specialized Targets

In addition to targeting links to open in a specific frame, you can set targets that will control which window the pages will appear in.

- target=_blank makes the link open in a new, blank browser window.
- target=_top makes the link replace the content of the current window
- target=_parent makes the link open in the parent frame, in cases where you're using nested framesets
- target=_self makes the link open in the same frame as the link.

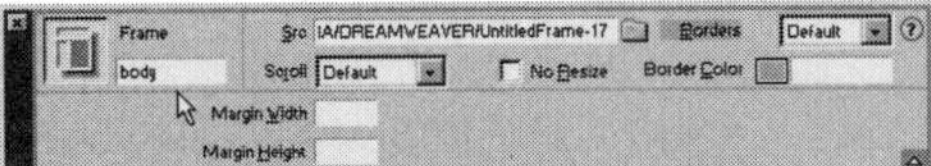

Figure 42 Name each frame by selecting it and then typing a meaningful word in the Frame text box.

Figure 43 After you've named your frames, the Frames inspector will display the name of each frame.

Naming Frames

Before you can set targets, you need to name each frame. A frame name is different from a filename or a page title. The frameset page needs to know both the filename and the frame name of each page in order to be able to load the pages in the proper position and order. (The page title, in cases of frames pages, is mostly cosmetic for all but the frameset page.)

To name a frame:

1. Select the frame you want to name by clicking on it in the Frames inspector. The Frame properties will appear in the Properties inspector.
2. Type a meaningful name in the Frame text box (**Figure 42**). You should be able to distinguish one frame from another by their names; for example, upper_left, main, or toolbar.
3. Press Enter (Return), or click on the Apply button. The name will remain in the Frame text box.
4. Repeat these steps for all the frames in the window.

When you open the Frames inspector, the names of the frames will be displayed there (**Figure 43**).

✔ Tips

- As is the case with most HTML entities, no spaces are allowed in frame names. Underscores are okay, but hyphens are not. Try to restrict yourself to lowercase letters and numbers.
- Another great Dreamweaver advantage: you don't have to remember, memorize, write down, or tattoo the names of your frames on your forehead; just refer to the Frames inspector.

Setting a Base Target

By default, the target for each frame is the frame itself. To set a different default target, you need to specify the name of the target in the code.

To set a target:

1. Click in the frame whose base target you want to set.
2. Open the HTML window for that frame by pressing F10, or by selecting Window > HTML from the Document window menu bar.
3. Locate the <HEAD> tag, near the top of the HTML window. It should look something like this:

```
<head>
<title>Untitled Document</title>
<meta http-equiv="Content-Type" ¬
content="text/html; charset=iso-8859-1">
</head>
```

4. Within the <HEAD> tag, but after the <title> tag, type the following line of code:

   `<base target="name">`

   Where **name** is replaced by the name of the frame you want to make the default target, or one of the special targeting instructions, such as "_top" (quotation marks included).
5. Your code should now look something like this:

```
<head>
<title>Untitled Document</title>
<base target="main_frame">
<meta http-equiv="Content-Type"
content="text/html; charset=iso-8859-1">
</head>
```

6. Press Ctrl+S (Command+S) to save the changes to your code. You can close the HTML window, if you like.

While behind-the-scenes changes like this one won't show up visibly in the Dreamweaver window, you can preview your frames page in the browser window and test them to make sure they work.

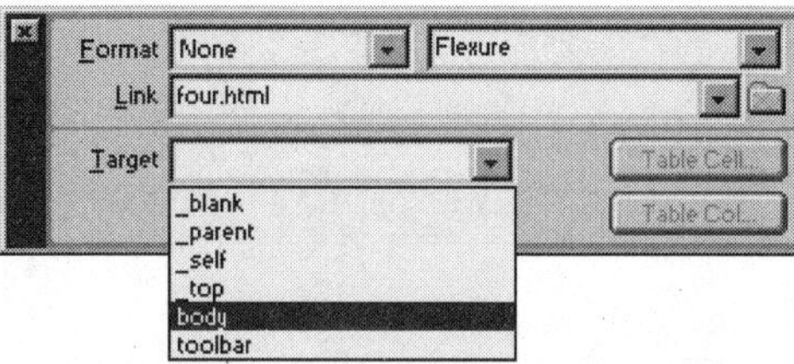

Figure 44 Select the desired target from the Target drop-down menu.

Testing Your Targets

It's vitally important, more so than with almost any other kind of Web page, that you test every link on your frames-based pages. You need to make sure that the links open where you think you told them to open. Targets can be tricky—they don't need to be difficult, but they absolutely must be done correctly if you don't want to drive your visitors away for good. **Figure 45** shows the evil recursive frame problem: a link to the entire frameset was accidentally targeted to open in one of the frames.

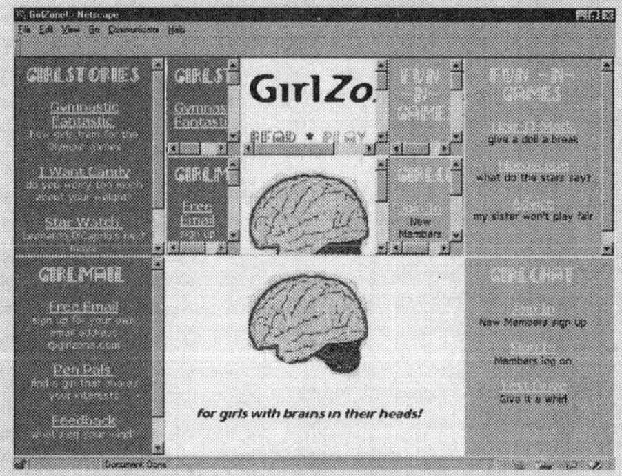

Figure 45 A misplaced target can be ugly, at best. Here we see a recursive frameset—a link to the entire frameset was accidentally targeted to open in the top, center frame.

When you want to set a target for a link that differs from the default, or base target, you use the Properties inspector to select a target for the link.

To target individual links:

1. Select the text or image that you want to target. The Properties inspector will display properties for that object.
2. If there's not a link specified for that object as yet, type or paste the URL for the link in the Link text box.
3. From the Target drop-down menu (**Figure 44**), select a target. This can be either the name of one of the other frames on the page, or one of the special targets discussed in the section called *Target Options*.

You're all set.

Figures 46 and **47** demonstrate a simple, common use of targeting: click on a link in the top frame, and it opens in the bottom frame.

Figure 46 Here's what you'll see when you first visit numbers.html: two frames introducing you to the site.

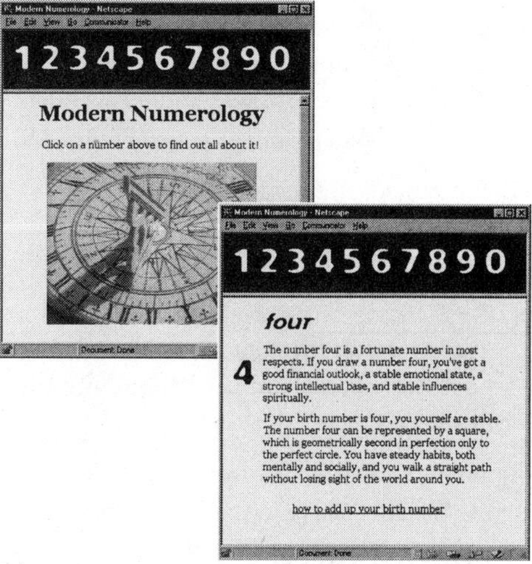

Figure 47 Click on one of the numbers in the top frame, and a new page opens in the bottom frame. The top frame has a base target of body, which is the name of the bottom frame.

Creating No-Frames Content

Not everyone who visits your site will have a frames-capable browser. While most people are using some version or other of Netscape Navigator or Internet Explorer, not everyone is. See Appendix C on the Web site for the details. The point is that if you don't offer your non-frames visitors something, they won't see anything at all.

At the very least, you need to leave a message that says something like "This site requires a frames-capable browser, such as Netscape Navigator 2 or later, or Internet Explorer 3 or later." Providing links to a site where they can download this software is also a good idea.

But even that is shortchanging your guests, in a way. Without much work at all, you can give them a fully functional page that will connect them with much of the same information.

To create a no-frames page from scratch:

1. To view the no-frames page, From the Document window menu bar, select Modify > Frameset > Edit No Frames Content. The Document window will display the blank no frames page (**Figure 48**).
2. You can edit this page, including page properties such as background color, the same way you'd create a page from scratch.

   or

   You can select the contents of an existing page, copy them, and paste them into the no-frames page.

Figure 49 shows the no-frames page we created as the alternative to the frames-based page shown in **Figures 46** and **47**.

To return to the frames view, just select Modify > Frameset > Edit No Frames Content again.

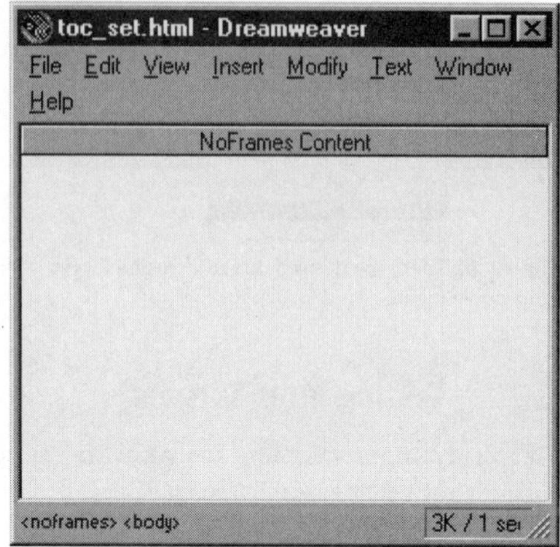

Figure 48 From the Document window menu bar, select Modify > Frameset > Edit No Frames Content, and the Document window will display the blank no-frames page.

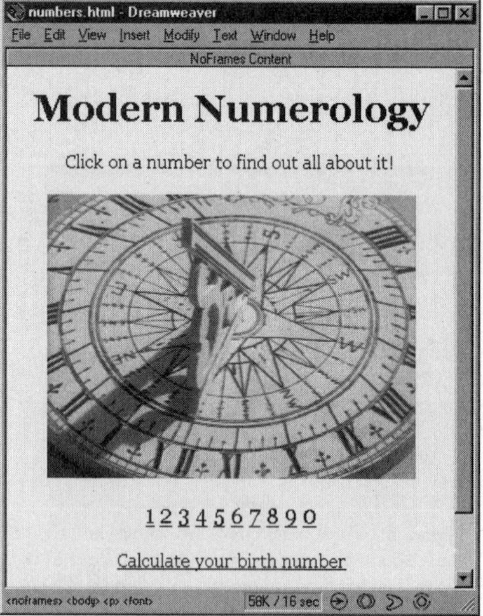

Figure 49 With very little effort, I created a no-frames page that includes all the same links as the frameset page. To appease very old browsers, I also avoided frills like tables, background images, and imagemaps—see Appendix C on the book's Web site for more details.

No-Frames Tips

- Check to make sure that:
  - You don't include any <html> or </html> tags within the <noframes> tags
  - You include one, and only one set of <body> and </body> tags between the <noframes> tags.
- When you preview no-frames content in your regular browser, it won't show up. Why? Because your regular browser is probably frames-capable, and it will load the frames-based page instead—they are the same document, after all.
- See Chapter 16 for information about getting and using a non-frames browser for previewing your documents.

To use existing code in a no-frames page:

1. In the HTML inspector or your favorite code editor, open the code for the page you want to use.
2. Select all the code between (and including) the <body> and </body> tags, and copy it to the clipboard.
3. In the Dreamweaver Document window, View the no frames page by selecting Modify > Frameset > Edit No Frames Content from the menu bar. The Document window will display the no-frames page.
4. View the HTML for this page—which is really just part of the frameset document. The empty no-frames code should look like this:

   ```
   <noframes><body bgcolor="#FFFFFF">
   </body></noframes>
   ```

5. Select everything between the <noframes> and </noframes> tags, and delete it.
6. Paste in the HTML from the code you copied in step 2. You should get something like this:

   ```
   <noframes>
   <body bgcolor="#000000">
   This is all the neat content that's on my
   frames page, including
   <A HREF="links.html">links</A>
   and everything!
   </body>
   </noframes>
   ```

7. Save the changes to your HTML, and close the HTML window. The page you pasted in should show up in the No Frames Content window.

Inline Frames

Internet Explorer has introduced a proprietary tag called <IFRAME> to make frames appear within a page (**Figure 50**). This technique, called *inline frames* or *floating frames*, only works with Internet Explorer version 3 or later.

To use inline frames:

1. With the appropriate page open in the Document window, view the HTML code by selecting Window > HTML from the Document window menu bar.
2. Insert the following code:

   ```
   <IFRAME SRC="float.html">
   </IFRAME>
   ```

   where "float.html" is replaced by the URL for the content to appear in the floating frame.
3. Type or paste some no-iframes content between the two tags, such as "To view this page, you need MSIE 3 or later."
4. Press Ctrl+S (Command+S) to save the changes to the code.

You'll need to view this page in IE to see the iframe.

This is the code for the iframe in **Figure 50**:

```
<IFRAME name="toc" src="toctoc.html"
frameborder=1 height="80%" width=200
scrolling=yes align=center, bottom>
You must use Internet Explorer to view the inline
frames on this page, but you can get the same
content <a href="toctoc.html">here</a>.
</IFRAME>
```

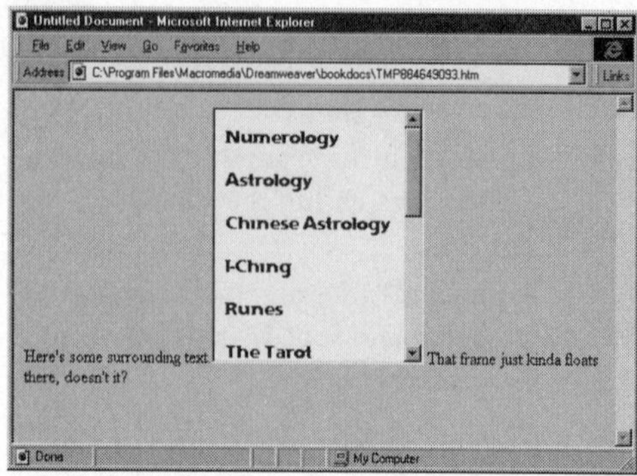

Figure 50 The inline frame is a particular feature of Internet Explorer—you'll need to experiment with the IFRAME attributes quite a bit to figure out how they work.

Other IFRAME Attributes

You can adjust the appearance and behavior of an IFRAME by using these other attributes within an IFRAME tag. You should recognize most of these attributes from this and other chapters. As always, the pipe | means "or."

name="name"

align=top|middle|bottom|left|right|center
(pick two, as in align="top, center") This has more to do with the relationship between the frame and the other content than with the position of the frame.

frameborder=1|0 (1=yes, 0=no)

height=x|"x%"

width=x|"x%"

marginheight=x

marginwidth=x

scrolling=yes|no|auto

FILLING OUT FORMS

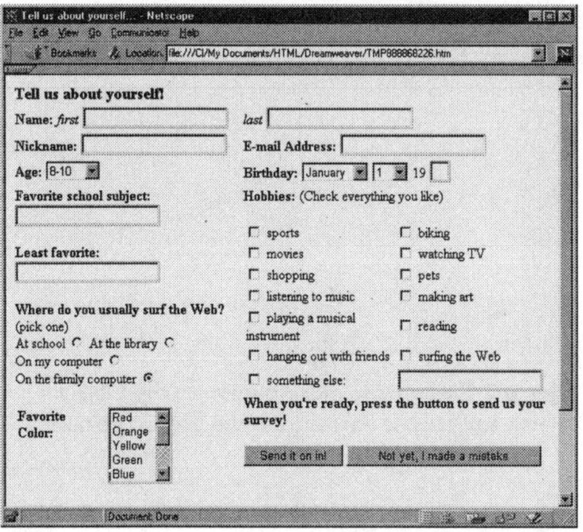

Figure 1 This feedback form includes most of the different kinds of form fields you can have in a form. I laid out the form using tables.

Forms are what you fill out when you apply for a driver's license. They're also what you want your visitors to fill out to give you feedback about your site or about who your users are (**Figure 1**). Online shopping, user surveys, interactive scripts, search engines, and guestbooks all use forms to collect data (called *input*) from your users.

This data is then sent to a form handler—usually a CGI script, although other custom scripts can be used—which does something with this data. In some cases, like surveys, it simply saves the input for you to look at later. In other cases, such as search engines, it takes the input and immediately uses it to provide some response or results for the user's edification.

Forms are made up of various widgets and thingies that your users will click on or type in, and these are known as *form fields*, or—in Dreamweaver parlance—*form objects*.

Creating a Form

The first thing you need to do to create a form is to put the form itself, represented by the <FORM></FORM> tags, on your page. The form will be delineated, in the Document window, by a dashed red line that will be invisible when the page is loaded in the browser window (**Figure 2**).

Forms are easy to create with Dreamweaver, and the Object palette is especially handy for automating the process.

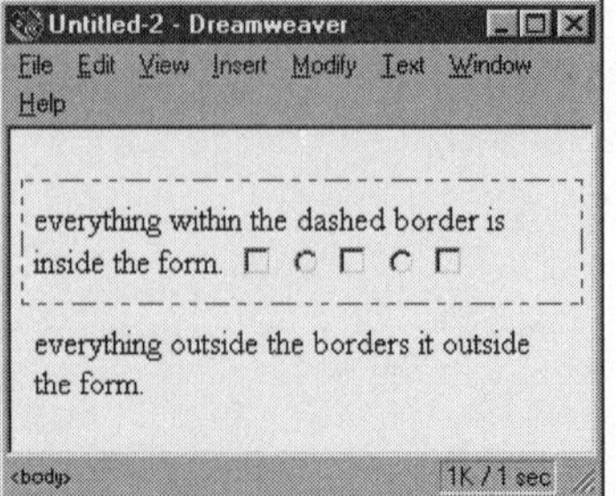

Figure 2 In the Document window, forms are outlined by a red, dashed border.

To display form objects on the Object palette:

1. Display the Object palette by selecting Window > Objects from the Document window menu bar.
2. On the Object palette, click on the menu button at the top.
3. From the pop-up menu that appears, choose Forms (**Figure 3**).

The Object palette will display form objects (**Figure 4**).

Figure 3 Click on the menu button on the Object palette, and choose Forms from the pop-up menu.

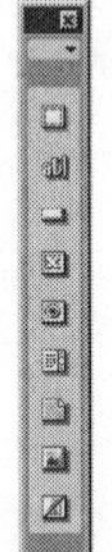

Figure 4 The Object palette, with form objects displayed. Note that I resized the palette—you can do that by clicking and dragging the lower-right corner.

To create a form:

1. From the Document window menu bar, select Insert > Form.

   or

   On the Object palette, click on the Insert Form button: .

The form will appear (**Figure 5**). By default, your form will occupy 100 percent of the page width. The height is determined by the content you place within the form borders. You cannot resize forms with Dreamweaver, although you can format their content using tables.

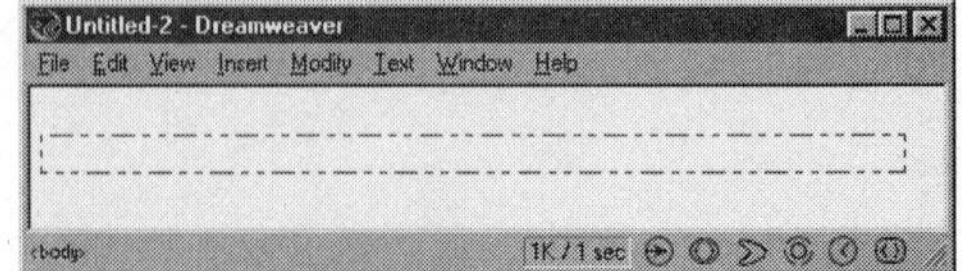

Figure 5 A new, blank form.

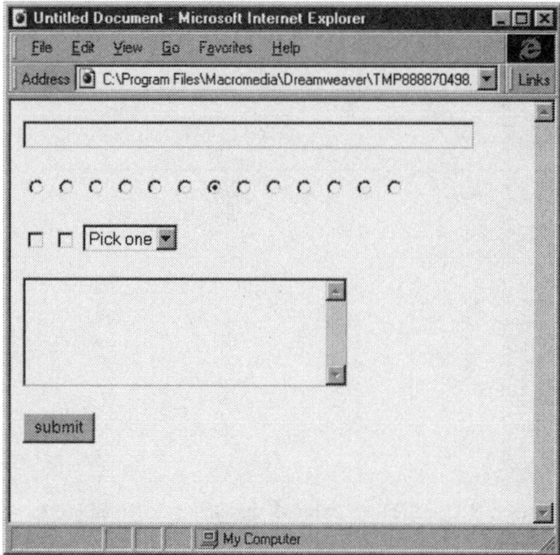

Figure 6 What is this form for? Without labels, it's impossible to tell.

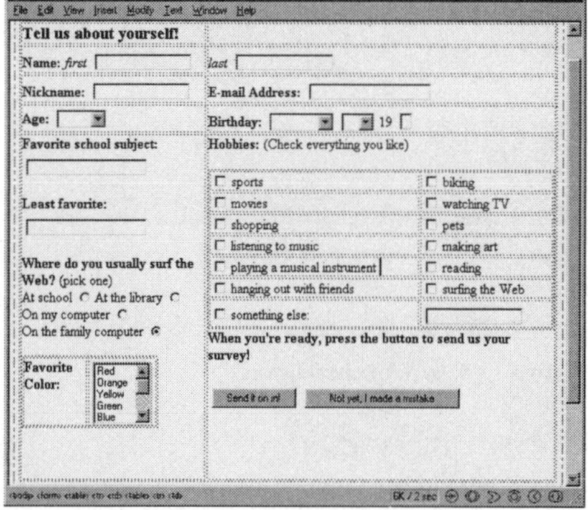

Figure 7 This is the same form we saw in Figure 1, with the table and form borders revealed in the Document window.

Formatting Forms

It's essential to label each field in a form; otherwise the users won't know what the heck they're supposed to do (**Figure 6**). I don't specify this in the steps for adding each field, because it's pretty unlikely that you're going to forget.

You can use line breaks, paragraph breaks, preformatted text, or tables to format the stuff in your forms (**Figure 7**). A form can include nearly any HTML entity—text, images, tables—except another form. You can put a form in a table, or a table in a form, but you can't put a form within a form. You can, however, include more than one form on a page—just don't overlap them.

✔ Tip

- You can find out about working with tables in Chapter 7. I discussed text formatting in Chapters 3 and 4.

Adding Form Objects

Form objects, commonly referred to as form fields, are the nuts and bolts of a form. They're the boxes and buttons that people click on or type in to make their mark (technically called their *input*) on a form.

There are five different flavors of form objects, each of which has its own button on the Object palette (**Figure 8**), as well as its own entry in the Insert > Form Object menu.

Text Fields (also called text boxes) come in two flavors: single-line and multi-line. If a form was a test, single-line would be a short answer question (**Figure 9**), and multi-line would be an essay question (**Figure 10**).

Checkboxes are always used in groups of two or more (**Figure 11**). Checkboxes allow the user to select more than one of a set of options.

Radio buttons, named after the buttons on old-fashioned console radios, also come in groups of two or more (**Figure 12**). They allow you to choose only one of a set of options—when you push in one button on a radio, the other buttons pop out.

Lists and *menus* allow the user to choose from a long list of options that don't take up too much space on the page. A list, also called a drop-down list, drops down when you click on it to reveal the full set of options, while a menu offers several choices at once, and the user can choose more than one item from a menu, in some cases (**Figure 13**).

Buttons are what makes the form do something. A *submit* button sends the form off over the wires to its final destination. A *reset* button clears all the values entered in a form and resets the form to its default, or starting, values (**Figure 14**).

I'll also tell you about *hidden fields, file fields*, and *image fields*.

Figure 8 The Object palette, displaying form objects

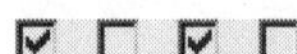

Figure 9 A one-line text box

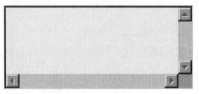

Figure 10 A multi-line text box

Figure 11 A flock of checkboxes

Figure 12 A gaggle of radio buttons

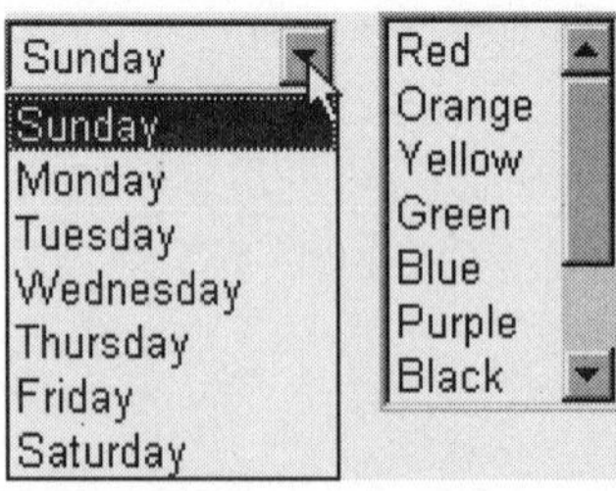

Figure 13 A drop-down menu and a list box

Figure 14 Submit and reset buttons

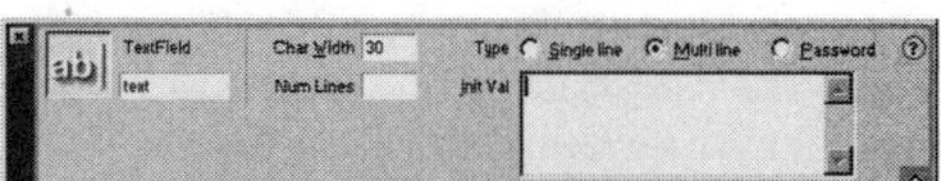

Figure 15 The Properties inspector, displaying properties for a multi-line text field

Names and Values

Each gadget, or form field, in a form is also known as an input item (the HTML tag is **<input>**). That means that it's used to collect input from the people who use it.

Each input item is represented in the form results by a name and a value. The name is a unique signifier that tells you (or the script handling the form) which field is which. The value is the content of the field.

Names and values are required for form fields, and if you forget to add them, Dreamweaver will provide sequential names and values, such as **radiobutton**, **radiobutton2**, **radiobutton3**, and so on.

In a text box, the value of the input is equal to what the users type; in other words, the form submission contains their words. In a checkbox, on the other hand, you really need to specify what value the checkbox has by providing unique text that says what the checkbox means. This is particularly important if you're using several checkboxes; a value of "checkbox5" won't tell you anything.

As in most cases in Dreamweaver, the Properties inspector will come in handy for formatting just about everything—both the text and the form fields. The Properties inspector will display unique properties for each form field—this is what you'll use to specify names and values.

To display the Properties inspector:

1. From the Document window menu bar, select Modify > Selection Properties.

   or

   From the Document window menu bar, select Window > Properties.

Either way, the Properties inspector will appear (**Figure 15**). (One of my only real complaints about Dreamweaver is the lack of a Properties inspector key command.)

Text fields are used to collect data that you can't predict. You can't offer a multiple choice menu for every possible name or e-mail address, for instance. For short answers, such as address information or favorite TV show, you'll use a single-line text field.

To create a single-line text field:

1. In the Document window, click within the form boundaries.
2. From the Document window menu bar, select Insert > Form Object > Text Field.

   or

   On the Object Palette, click on the Text Field button, or drag the button to the page.
   A single-line text field will appear:

   You can resize it, if you like.
3. Display the Properties inspector, if necessary (**Figure 16**).
4. To resize the text field, type a number, in characters, in the Char Width text box.
5. Click on the Apply button, and your text field will resize.

You can use a single-line text box to collect password information, in which case the stuff they type in the box will become *** or •••.

To create a password box:

1. Click on the text field to select it, and display the Properties inspector, if necessary (**Figure 16**).
2. In the Type area of the Properties inspector, click on the Password radio button.

There won't be any visible change, but when your page is on the Web, the stuff the user types in it will be replaced by asterisks or bullets (**Figure 17**).

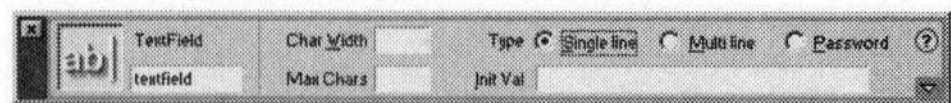

Figure 16 The Properties inspector, displaying properties for a single-line text field

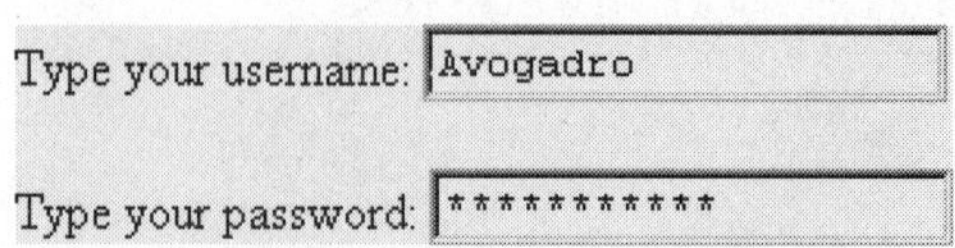

Figure 17 The first text box is a normal single-line text box, while the second text box is a password box—the browser will display asterisks or bullets instead of the typed characters, so that a snoop can't see the password over the user's shoulder.

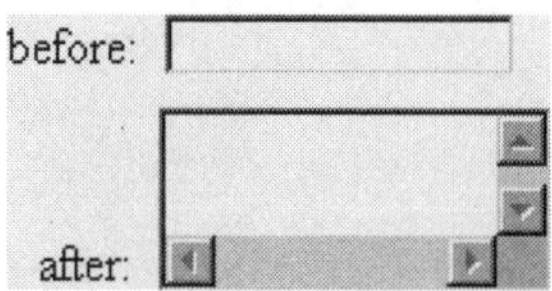

Figure 18 Change a single-line text field into a multi-line text field by clicking on the Multi-line radio button in the Properties inspector.

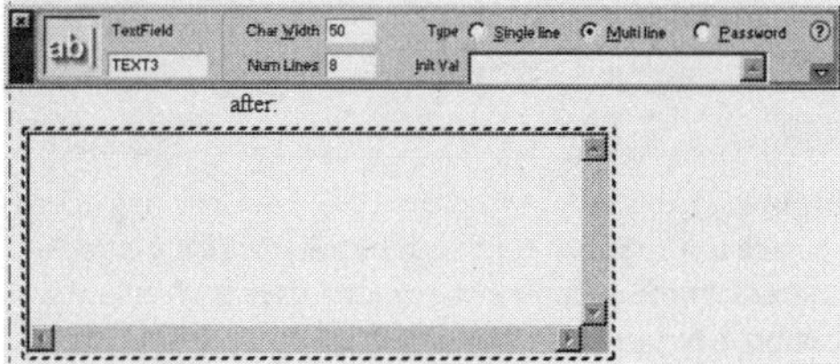

Figure 19 To change the dimensions of the multi-line text box, type a character width and a line height in the Properties inspector.

A multi-line text field will create a "feedback box" that you can use to elicit longer responses from your users. Multi-line text boxes are commonly used for guestbooks, e-mail forms, and any other case in which you want more than a few words from your visitors.

To create a multi-line text field:

1. Create a single-line text field, as described on the previous page.
2. Select the text field, and display the Properties inspector, if necessary.
3. In the Type area of the Properties inspector, click on the Multi-line radio button. The text field will change appearance (**Figure 18**).

To resize a multi-line text field:

1. Select the multi-line text field.
2. In the Properties inspector, type a number (in characters) in the Char Width text box.
3. Type a number of lines in the Num Lines text box.
4. Click on the Apply button. The text box will resize to your specifications (**Figure 19**).

✔ Attention!

■ If you try to resize a multi-line text field by clicking and dragging, you may crash the program.

To restrict the number of characters allowed:

1. Click on the text field to select it, and display the Properties inspector, if necessary.
2. In the Max Chars text box, type the maximum number of characters you'll allow in this field.
3. Click the Apply button.

In a Web browser, the user will not be able to type more than the number of characters you specified. (Generally, they'll hear beeping when they try to type past the limit.)

If you want to give your visitors an example of what kind of input you're expecting, you can set an initial value for either kind of text box.

To set an initial value:

1. Select the text box, and view the Properties inspector.
2. In the Init Val text box, type the text you want to have displayed in the text box.
3. Click on the Apply button.

The text will show up in the text box in the Document window (**Figure 20**) (and in the Web browser).

✔ Tip

- Beware of using the initial value. While it might seem like a great idea at the time, a lot of wise guys (or dumb guys) won't bother to change something that's already filled in. It might be better, in some cases, to use example text *outside* the box, as shown in **Figure 21**.

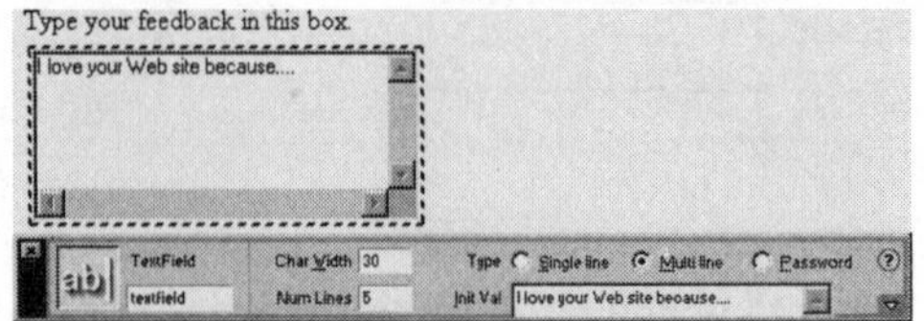

Figure 20 The text you type in the Properties inspector's initial value text box will be included in the form field.

Figure 21 In the first text box, the user may neglect to replace the supplied text with his or her real e-mail address. In the second instance, the user is given a visual example, but the text box is left blank.

File Fields

One kind of form field you may have reason to use, albeit rarely, is the *file field*. The file field consists of a text box and a button marked **Browse**. This file is used when you want your visitors to be able to upload files from their local computer to your remote server. The Browse button will open the Open File dialog box in their Web browser, which they will use to select the file; then they will use the form's Submit button to send you the file.

To insert a file field, click on the Insert File Field button on the Forms panel of the Object palette, or select Insert > Form Object > File Field.

The file field will appear:

You can set a maximum character width and a maximum number of characters for this field in the Properties inspector.

As with all form fields, it's a good idea to name your text fields so you can tell them apart.

To name a text field:

1. Select the text box, and view the Properties inspector.
2. In the TextField text box, highlight the textfield text and type over it, replacing it with a meaningful word that will indicate the purpose of the field.
3. Click on the Apply button.

Your text field will be named in the code, as well as in the form results that your users will submit.

Checkboxes, which often appear in groups, allow users to make one or more selections from a set of options. You can use a single checkbox for a yes/no question, or you can use a group of checkboxes and allow users to pick and choose between options in a group.

To create a checkbox:

1. Click to place the insertion point within the form in the Document window.
2. From the Document window menu bar, select Insert > Form Object > Checkbox.

   or

   On the Object Palette, click on the Insert Checkbox button, or drag the button to the form in the Document window.

   The checkbox will appear: .
3. Repeat step 1 for each checkbox in the set.

Remember to give each checkbox a unique name and value; checkbox1 and checkbox2 won't tell you much when you're looking at results.

To specify name and value:

1. Select the checkbox by clicking on it.
2. Display the Properties inspector, if necessary (**Figure 22**).
3. In the Checked Value text box, type the text you want to see if the user checks the box. Good examples include `send_info` or `owns_dog`.
4. Name the checkbox by typing a name for it in the CheckBox text box. For example, the name could be `mail` or `dog`.
5. Click on the Apply button.

Figure 22 The Properties inspector, displaying checkbox properties

✔ Tips

- If the user does not check off the checkbox, there will be no indication of the checkbox at all in the form results.
- If the user does check off the checkbox, the results will say something like `NAME=VALUE`. In our example above, the results would be `mail=send_info` or `dog=owns_dog`.
- If you want the checkbox to appear checked when the page is loaded, click on the Checked radio button in the Initial State area of the Properties inspector.

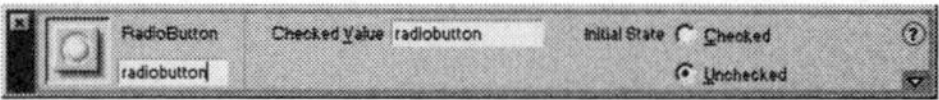

Figure 23 The Properties inspector, displaying radio button properties

While checkboxes can appear either singly or in groups, radio buttons *always* appear in groups. You can use radio buttons for yes/no, true/false, or multiple-choice questions.

To insert a radio button:

1. Click to place the insertion point within the form in the Document window.
2. From the Document window menu bar, select Insert > Form Object > Radio button: .

   or

   On the Object Palette, click on the Insert radio button button, or drag the radio button button to the form in the Document window.

   A radio button will appear:
3. Repeat step 2 for each radio button in the set.

You must name each radio button in a group with the same name, and you must give each radio button in a group a different value.

To specify names and values:

1. Select a radio button, and display the Properties inspector, if necessary (**Figure 23**).
2. Type a name for the group of radio buttons in the RadioButton text box.
3. Type a value for that particular radio button in the Checked Value text box.
4. Repeat steps 1–3 for each radio button in the set. Be sure to spell the name exactly the same, and to give each button a different value.
5. Select one of the buttons to be initially selected when the page is loaded. Click on that button and, in the Properties inspector, click on the Checked radio button.
6. Click on the Apply button to apply your changes to the form.

✔ Tips

- You can check to make sure you've grouped your radio buttons properly by previewing the page in a browser and making sure that, when you click on each button in turn, the other buttons in the set become deselected.
- If you use more than one group of radio buttons in a single form, be sure to give each group a unique name.

You can offer a range of choices by using drop-down menus, also called pull-down menus or pop-up menus.

To create a menu:

1. Click to place the insertion point within the form in the Document window.
2. From the Document window menu bar, select Insert > Form Object > List/Menu.

   or

   On the Object Palette, click on the Insert List/Menu button, or drag the button to the form in the Document window.

An itty-bitty drop-down menu will appear:

To fill the menu with menu items:

1. Click on the list to select it, and display the Properties inspector, if necessary (**Figure 24**).
2. Click on the List Values button. The Initial List Values dialog box will appear (**Figure 25**).
3. Click on the Item Label menu button, and a text field will appear beneath it.
4. Type a menu item (what you want to appear in the menu) in the Item Label text field.

   If you want the values (the information that will appear in the form results) to be the same as the item labels, you can skip steps 5 and 6.
5. Press the Tab key or click on the Value menu button, and a text field will become visible (**Figure 26**).
6. Type the value of the menu item in the Value text field.
7. Repeat steps 2–6 for each menu item you want to include. (Press the Tab key or click on the + button to create a field for each new menu item.)

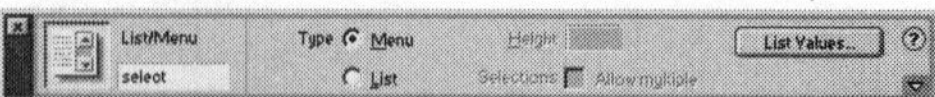

Figure 24 The Properties inspector, displaying menu properties

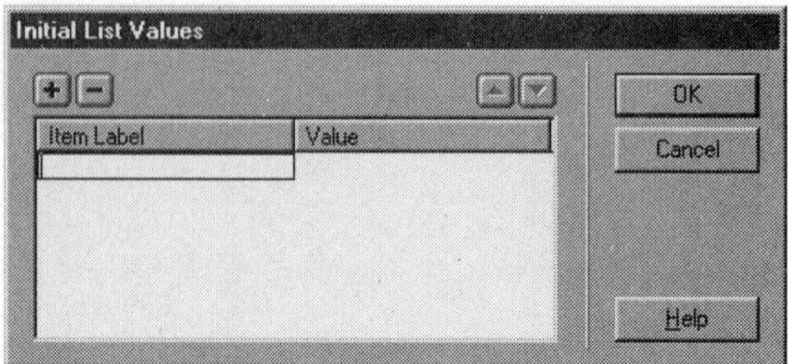

Figure 25 The Initial List Values dialog box is where you add menu items to your menus and lists.

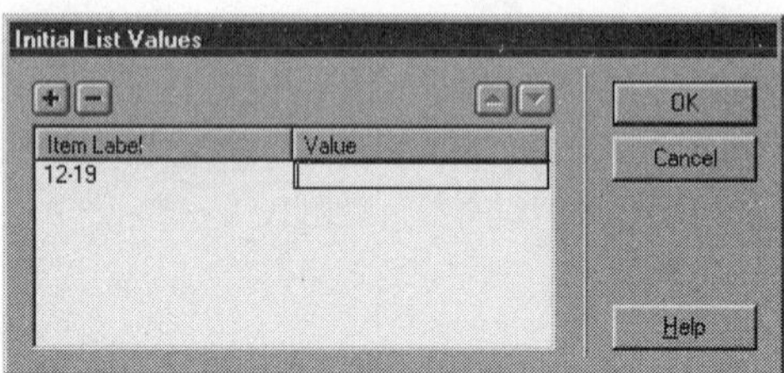

Figure 26 Press the Tab key to move to the next column and type the value for the menu item.

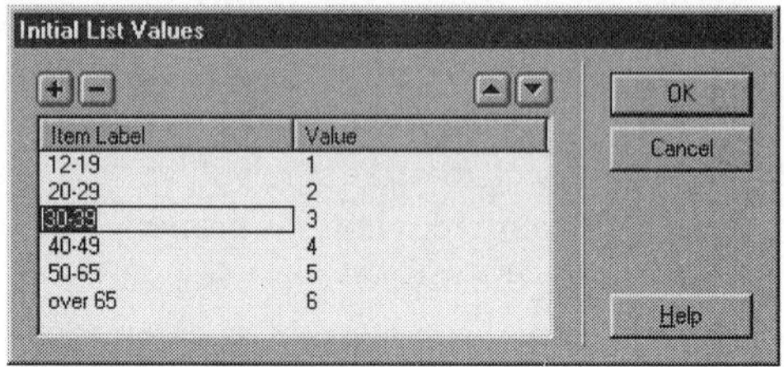

Figure 27 Use the + and – buttons to add and delete items—and the up and down arrow buttons to rearrange the order of the list.

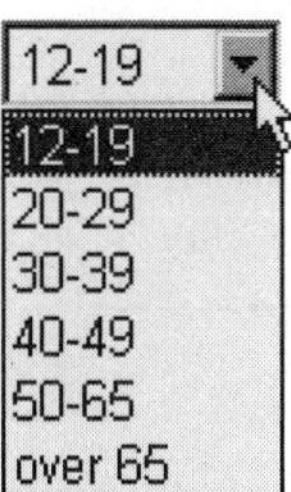

Figure 28: When you load the page in the browser window, you can click on the menu to make sure it looks the way you want it to look.

You can edit this list before you close the dialog box (**Figure 27**).

To edit the menu items:

1. You can rearrange the menu items by moving them up and down through the list.
   - To move an item up through the list, click on the Up arrow button.
   - To move an item down through the list, click on the Down arrow button.
2. You can add or delete items as necessary.
   - To delete an item, click on it, and then click on the – (minus) button.
   - To add an item, click on the + button, and then move the item to a new location in the list, if desired.
3. And of course, you can edit the text of the menu items themselves. Just click on the item, and type your changes in the text field.

When you're all done with the Initial List Values dialog box, click on OK to close it. You'll return to the Document window. The menu will appear larger than it was before, which indicates that it contains multitudes, but Dreamweaver doesn't display the menu as active—you won't see the menu items themselves.

✔ Tips

- To proofread your menu, you need to preview it in the browser window (**Figure 28**). Once there, you can click on it to drop down the menu and scroll through the list of items.
- Don't forget to name your menu by typing a name in the List/Menu text box on the Properties inspector.

The drop-down menu is one kind of list-type form field you can create; the other kind is the list box. List boxes can be several items high, and can offer the possibility of multiple selections.

To create a list box:

1. Create a menu, as described in the section *To create a menu*. (You can input the menu items at any point.)
2. Display the Properties inspector, if necessary, by selecting Modify > Selection Properties from the Document window menu bar.
3. In the Properties inspector, click on the List radio button (**Figure 29**). The menu will change appearance in the Document window (**Figure 30**).
4. To adjust the height of the list, type a number of lines in the Height text box (**Figure 31**).
5. To allow multiple selections, make sure the Selections checkbox is checked. To disallow multiple selections, deselect the Selections checkbox.
6. Name your list by typing a name in the List/Menu text box and clicking on the Apply button.

✔ Tip

- To add menu items to a list box, follow the steps in the section *To fill the menu with menu items*. The dialog boxes are identical.

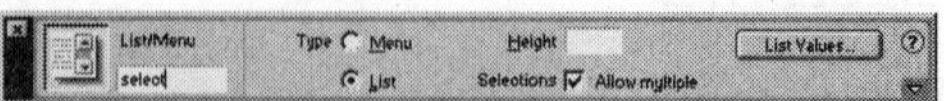

Figure 29 The Properties inspector, displaying list properties

Figure 30 The menu turns into a list.

Figure 31 I gave the list a line height of 5. Since I have more than 5 items, scrollbars appear in the list box.

Tweaking Your Menus and Boxes

Dreamweaver doesn't support two rather handy attributes for your menu items, but you can easily add these attributes in the code.

One is the checked attribute, which allows you to specify which item will be preselected when the form loads in the Web browser—by default, the first menu item in the list will be the selection.

The other is the disabled attribute, which allows you to keep a user from selecting a particular menu item. If the first item in your drop-down menu is something like "Click here to pick your favorite color," you want to make sure they can't submit that item.

To add these items to your list or menu, follow these steps:

1. Click on the list or menu in the Document window.
2. View the code for your page by selecting Window > HTML from the Document window menu bar. The code for the list or menu should be highlighted in the HTML inspector.

The code for the menu or list should look something like this:

```
<select name="menu">
<option value="">red</option>
    <option value="">white</option>
    <option value="">blue</option>
</select>
```

Each option is a list item.

- To make one of the selections the preselected item, add the checked attribute to the option tag:

  ```
  <option checked value="">red</option>
  ```

- To prevent users from submitting a particular selection, add the disabled attribute to the option tag:

  ```
  <option disabled value="">red</option>
  ```

Save your changes to the HTML, and be sure to test the form to make sure these changes work the way you want them to.

Besides the regular widgets you can use on a form, you can place hidden form fields in the code so that some fixed information is passed along with the rest of the data. This information might include the URL of the form, the version of the form, or any other information you want to receive with the form results.

To create a hidden form field:

1. Click to place the insertion point at the place on the form where you want the invisible field to be inserted.
2. From the Document window menu bar, select Insert > Form Object > Hidden Field

   or

   Click on the Insert Hidden Field button on the Forms panel of the Object palette, or drag the button to the page.

   If you have Invisible Element viewing turned on, a Hidden Field icon will appear:
3. Display the Properties inspector, if necessary.
4. Type the value of the hidden field in the Value text box.

You won't see the hidden fields on the Web page (duh!), but the value will be sent with the rest of the data when the user submits the form.

✔ Tip

- If you use more than one hidden field, be sure to give each one a different name.

Covering Your Assets

Although most browsers these days support forms, some browsers can't deal with them—they display them improperly or not at all. Even some versions of Internet Explorer have bugs which prevent proper handling of forms, as well as of **mailto:** addresses. If getting input (or orders!) from your visitors is important to you, be sure to include an e-mail address on your site—not just a hidden **mailto:** link.

✔ Tips

- It's a convention on most Web pages that the Submit button appears to the left of the Reset button at the bottom of the form.
- Dreamweaver displays push buttons with a smaller font face than either Navigator or MSIE uses.

There are three kinds of buttons you can put at the bottom of a form for your visitors to make use of.

Submit buttons are what you push to send the form off to the form handler, which compiles all the input and then does something with it.

Reset buttons clear the form of any new input and reset the form to its initial state.

The last kind of button has no action; that is, it will neither reset nor submit the form, but it can be used with JavaScript or other active content to do *something*.

To create a button:

1. Click to place the insertion point within the form in the Document window.
2. From the Document window menu bar, select Insert > Form Object > Button

   or

   On the Object palette, click on the insert button button, or drag the insert button button to the form in the Document window.
3. A submit button will appear: submit
4. Display the Properties inspector, if necessary, by choosing Modify > Selection Properties from the Document window menu bar.
5. Choose the type of button you want:
   - If you want a Submit button, click on the Submit radio button.
   - If you want a Reset button, click on the Reset radio button.
   - If you want a Nothing button, click on the Nothing radio button.
6. Click on the Apply button to apply your changes to the button.

BUTTONS

You can call your buttons whatever you want. By default, the Submit buttons will say Submit, and the reset buttons will say Reset, but that's an option, not an imperative. Instead of Submit, you can have the button say "Deliver me from evil." Instead of reset, the button could read, "Absolve me of my sins." I've seen reset buttons named Gorilla and submit buttons named Fish.

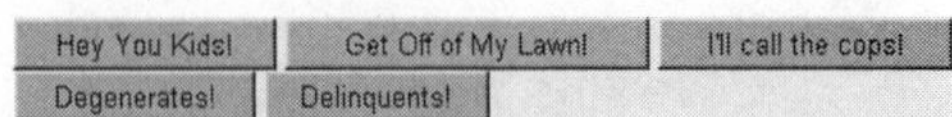

Figure 32 Your buttons can say anything you want.

To rename your button:

1. Click on the button to select it, and display the Properties inspector, if necessary.
2. In the Label text box, type the text you want to appear on the button, and click on the Apply button.

Your button will be renamed (**Figure 32**).

✔ Attention!

- Dreamweaver has the default text in the buttons say submit with a small s and Reset with a capital R. To make them consistent, pick a case and make the appropriate changes using the steps laid out on this page.

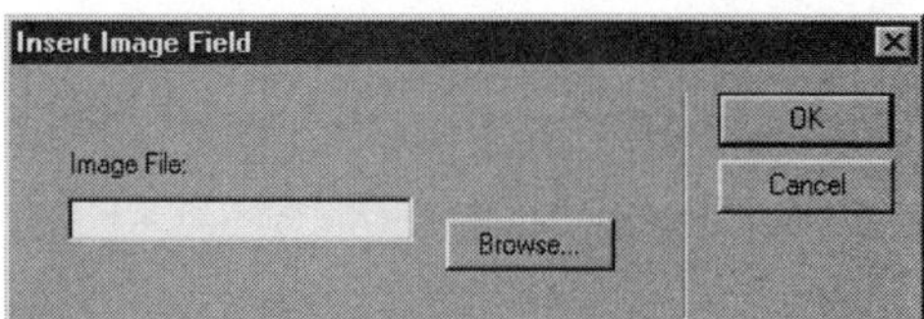

Figure 33 The Insert Image Field dialog box is exactly like the generic Insert Image dialog box.

Figure 34 The Properties inspector, displaying Image Field properties. The dashed border around the image at left indicated that it's an image field rather than a plain old image.

The Button Tag

Another way to use images as buttons is by using the button tag instead of the input tag. The button tag allows images to be used as Reset and Nothing buttons, too.

1. Follow steps 1-4, at right.
2. Select the image field in the Document window.
3. View the HTML inspector by pressing F10. The code for the button will be highlighted in the inspector.
4. Replace the button code with this code:

   ```
   <button type=submit name="name"
   value="value">
   <img src=button.gif">
   </button>
   ```

   The button type can be submit, reset, or button (for forms that call a script—the "nothing button"). The name is the name of your button image; the value can reflect the value you want to be transmitted; and the src is the source of your image.
5. Save the changes to the code, and preview the page in a browser to make sure it works.

Instead of the standard, boring gray push buttons that usually appear in forms, you can use images as buttons. This method only works for Submit buttons, not Reset or Nothing buttons.

To create an image field:

1. Click to place the insertion point at the place on the form where you want the image button to appear.
2. From the Document window menu bar, select Insert > Form Object > Image Field

   or

   Click on the Insert Image Field button on the Forms panel of the Object palette, or drag the button to the page.

   The Insert Image Field dialog box will appear (**Figure 33**).
3. This dialog box is just like the Insert Image dialog box. Type the pathname of the image in the Image File text box, or click on Browse to choose the image from your hard drive.
4. Click on OK to close the Insert Image Field dialog box. The image will appear in the Document window with a dashed line around it.
5. Display the Properties inspector, if necessary (**Figure 34**). The Src text box will display the source of the image.
6. Type a name in the Name text box and a value in the Value text box (both optional).
7. Type the alternate text for the image in the Alt text box.

Along with the results of your form, you'll get coordinates that say where on the image the user clicked, appended to the *name* text (name.x and name.y).

Making It Go

Figure 35 When the Properties inspector displays Form properties, you can choose the method and action of the form handler.

In order to make a form actually do something, you have to set it up to work with a CGI script or other custom script, called a *form handler*. Dreamweaver can't write the script for you—you have to take care of this part on the server end. Many Internet service providers make available standard scripts for common forms like mail forms and guestbooks, and they may offer other scripts as well. If you're working on a larger project, you may need to consult with a programmer, your systems administrator, or both.

Forms are sent by one of two methods: GET, which sends the results of the form in the URL submitted to the script; and POST, which encodes the material sent to the script. Check with your sysadmin to see which method you should use.

To set up the form handler:

1. In the Document window, select your form by clicking on the dashed border around it.
2. If necessary, display the Properties inspector (**Figure 35**).
3. Choose the method and action of the form handler.
4. Click on the Method drop-down menu, and choose either GET or POST.
5. In the Action text box, type the URL of the CGI script that will be processing the form.
6. Click on the Apply button to apply these changes to the form.

You won't see any changes, but you can examine the HTML to make sure they're there.

Stylin' with Style Sheets

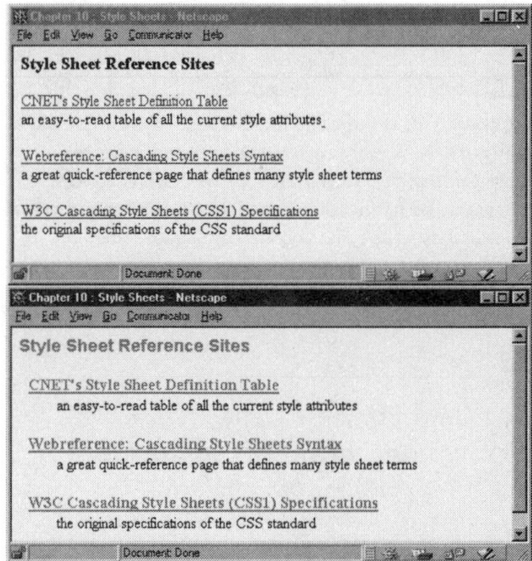

Figure 1 All I had to do was create four simple styles to completely redo the look of this page (top is pre-styles, bottom is with styles). Rather than applying color, font, and text style changes by hand, I created a style sheet. (You can't specify exacting indents without using styles.)

Backwards Compatibility

Dreamweaver 1.2 has a new command (File > Convert > 3.0 Browser Compatible) that allows you to save a version of style sheet pages so you retain as much of your formatting as possible when the pages are viewed using a pre-4.0 browser. For details about this feature, see the companion Web site for this book.

After years of grumbling about the design limitations of HTML, and despite the debate from the old-school digerati about how HTML is a mark-up language, not a layout language, Cascading Style Sheets (CSS) have become a standard.

A *style* is a group of attributes that are called by a single name, and a *style sheet* is a group of styles. Style sheets simplify the formatting of text, as well as extending the kinds of formatting you can apply (**Figure 1**). When you update a style, all instances of that style are automatically updated as well.

Style sheets are used primarily to format text, although some style attributes, such as positioning, can be used to format images and other objects as well.

✔ Notes

- One of the properties that style sheets add to HTML is the ability to better control positioning of elements on the page. Because style sheets cover so much territory, I cover positioning in Chapter 11.
- Style sheets only work in 4.*x* browsers such as Navigator 4 and MSIE 4. Some properties of style sheets are recognized by generation 3.*x* browsers, but most earlier browsers simply ignore them.

In This Chapter

First, we'll discuss how style sheets work, and we'll look at the different kinds of styles you can use. Then we'll go over the basics of creating and editing style sheets. After that, we'll learn how to apply style sheets to your Web pages. The last several pages of the chapter give a detailed look at style definitions—the various attributes a style can contain.

Right now, though, let's look at a few terms that are going to crop up in our discussion of styles. This chapter is a bit more code-heavy than previous chapters. You still don't have to *write* code—Dreamweaver takes care of that—but I will be discussing behavior of styles at the tag level (**Figure 2**), rather than just the way they look or act.

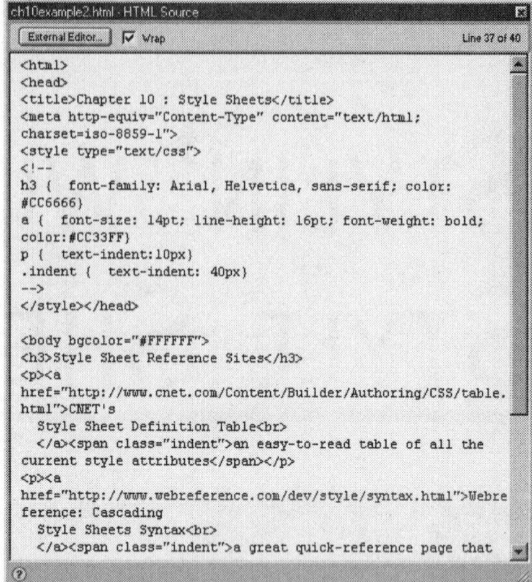

Figure 2 This is the code for the second example page in **Figure 1**. As you can see, styles operate, for the most part, on tags rather than on selections, (p for paragraph, h3 for heading 3, and so on), so I spend more time discussing specific tags in this chapter than in other chapters.

Definitions

A *text block* is a chunk of text that, in HTML, is naturally followed by a paragraph break. Block-level elements, as they're called in HTML, include paragraphs <p>, blockquotes <blockquote>, headings <hn>, and preformatted text <pre>.

Block-like elements include lists, tables, and forms, which are somewhat self-contained structures that envelop a group of other line-level (rather than block-level) elements.

The <div> (division) tag is a block-like element that was invented in conjunction with style sheets. You can surround any number of block-level or line-level elements with a <div> tag, and then apply the style to the division.

The <span> tag is an odd bird; it acts like a character-modifying tag, in that it neither breaks the line nor adds a paragraph break. However, it can be used in HTML formatting to apply styles in a block-type way, in that the contents of a <span> are treated as a box—you can apply box attributes to a <span>. (See the section called *Style Definitions* at the end of this chapter.)

Parent tags, simply put, are the tags that surround an element. On a Web page, all content tags are surrounded by the <html> and <body> tags. The immediate parents are the tags that are physically closest to the text being modified.

Inheritance is the process by which text blocks inherit properties from the various tags and styles that envelop them.

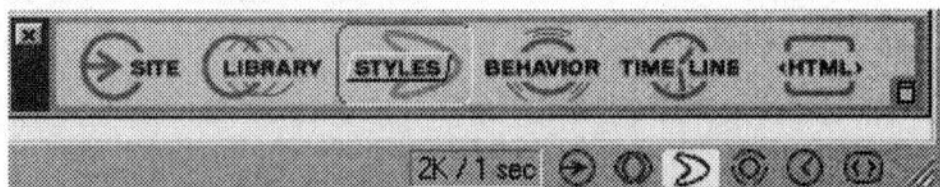

Figure 3 Click on the Styles button on the Launcher (or on the Launcher bar in the Document window status bar) to launch the Styles palette.

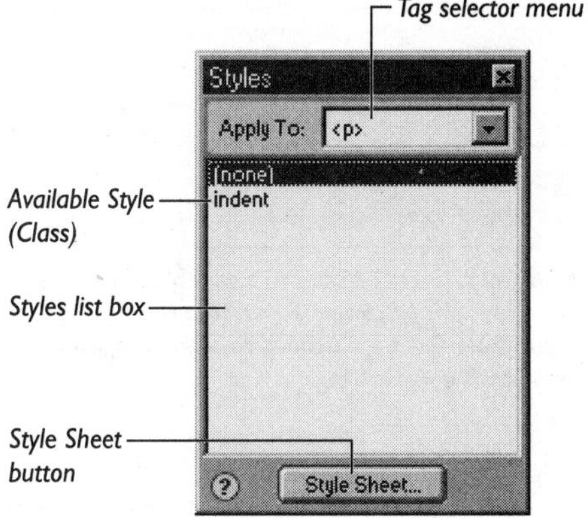

Figure 4 The Styles palette will be blank when you first open it; I've included a style here for labeling purposes.

How Style Sheets Work

With regular HTML, if you wanted all your links to appear italic, you had to apply italic formatting to each tag separately:

```
<i><a href="link.html">link</a></i>
```

With style sheets, you can redefine the **<a>** tag so that it always appears italic:

```
a { font-style: italic}
```

Even better than that: if you later decide that you'd rather have all the links bold instead of italic, you simply change the style rather than changing all the instances:

```
a { font-weight: bold}
```

Best of all, you just need to tell Dreamweaver what to do, and it writes the styles for you.

The Styles Palette

Like other specialized tasks in Dreamweaver, writing style sheets is made easier by using a palette—in this case the Styles palette.

To display the Styles palette:

1. From the Document window menu bar, select Window > Styles.

   or

   Press the F7 Key.

   or

   Click on the Styles button on the Launcher (**Figure 3**).

   The Styles palette will appear (**Figure 4**).

You'll use the Styles palette for three things:

- Clicking on the Style Sheet button is the fastest way to open the Edit Style Sheet dialog box, which you'll use quite a bit in this chapter.
- Choosing a tag from the drop-down menu is the same as clicking on the tag selector in the Document window status bar.
- Once you write some styles, you can choose style classes from the palette's list box.

Kinds of Style Sheets

There are four kinds of styles you can use, and Dreamweaver supports all of them.

The first kind, which we looked at on the previous page, involves *redefining an HTML tag* so that it includes new properties, as well as retaining its own. For example, you can redefine the <h2> tag so that it always appears red and it always uses the Arial font face (**Figure 5**).

```
h2 { color: red font-family: Arial}
```

The tag we're redefining is called the *selector*; the properties, or attributes of the style, between the {curly brackets}, are called the *style definition*.

The second kind of style is called a *class*. In this case, you name and define a style, which you then apply to blocks or spans of text (**Figure 6**). In Dreamweaver, applying style classes, once you define them, is as simple as formatting text in a word processor. Instead of applying bold, you apply the **.heavy** class, which may include properties for color, font face, paragraph formatting, or any number of style attributes.

In Dreamweaver these first two styles, redefining an HTML tag and defining a class, are delineated in the <head> tag of the document (which comes before the <body>).

✔ Tip

- In most cases, tag redefinitions and classes are located in the <head> tag of the document. You can define a style within a single tag, but that sort of preempts the entire reason for style sheets in the first place. In Chapter 11, you'll see instances of this in which each layer's style is defined within the <div> or <layer> tag.

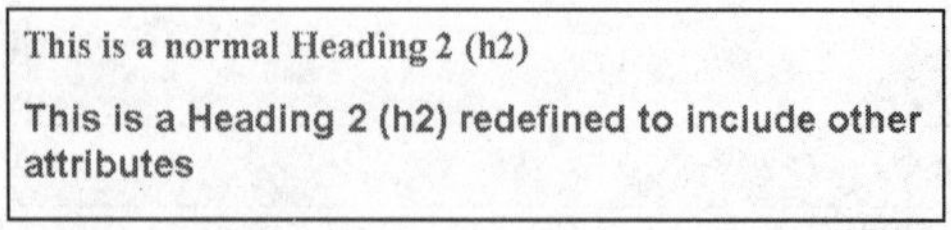

This is a normal Heading 2 (h2)

This is a Heading 2 (h2) redefined to include other attributes

Figure 5 When you redefine the H2 tag, it retains its original properties, such as its boldness, its size, and the paragraph breaks that surround it.

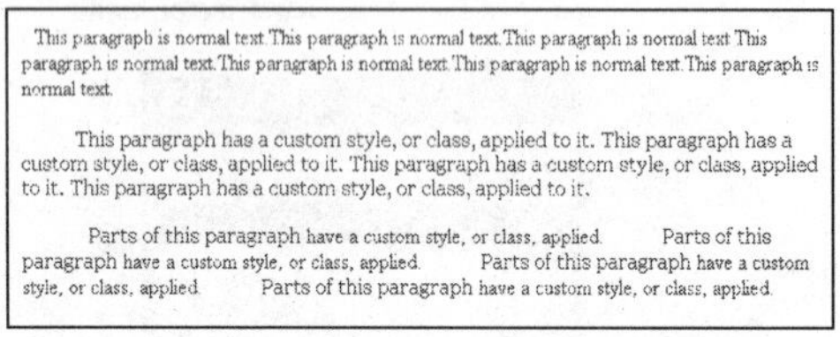

This paragraph is normal text This paragraph is normal text This paragraph is normal text This paragraph is normal text This paragraph is normal text This paragraph is normal text This paragraph is normal text.

This paragraph has a custom style, or class, applied to it. This paragraph has a custom style, or class, applied to it. This paragraph has a custom style, or class, applied to it. This paragraph has a custom style, or class, applied to it.

Parts of this paragraph have a custom style, or class, applied. Parts of this paragraph have a custom style, or class, applied. Parts of this paragraph have a custom style, or class, applied. Parts of this paragraph have a custom style, or class, applied.

Figure 6 You can apply a class to a text block (the second paragraph) or to a selection (the third paragraph). Selections are defined as spans and are enveloped by the <span> tag.

The third and fourth kinds of styles involve creating a more literal style sheet, which is a separate document that defines your styles. In your Web pages themselves, you *link to* or *import* the style sheet. (Linked and imported styles can include both the first two kinds.)

The implication, of course, is that once you create a style sheet document, you can link to it from any number of Web pages. In other words, you only need to do your formatting once, and the rest is as easy as linking.

In this chapter, we'll cover all four of these methods.

Creating a Style

Every move you make in creating and editing style sheets starts with the Edit Style Sheet dialog box.

To open the Edit Style Sheet dialog box:

1. From the Document window menu bar, select Text > Custom Style > Edit Style Sheet, or press Ctrl+Shift+E (Command+Shift+E).

   or

   On the Style palette, click on the Edit Style button.

   Either way, the Edit Style Sheet dialog box will appear (**Figure 7**).

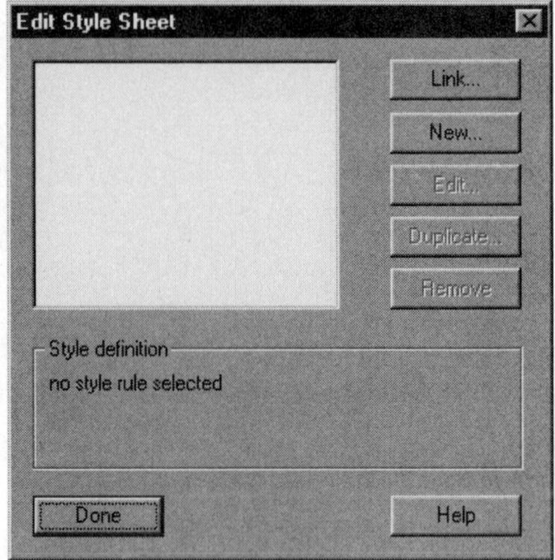

Figure 7 The Edit Style Sheet dialog box is where you make your first move.

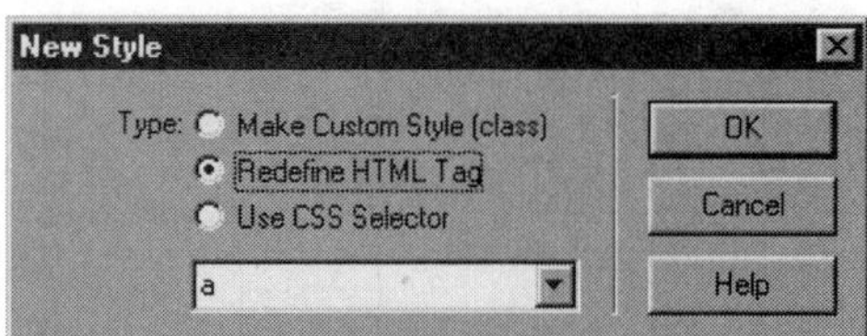

Figure 8 The New Style dialog box lets you choose which kind of style sheet you're going to create.

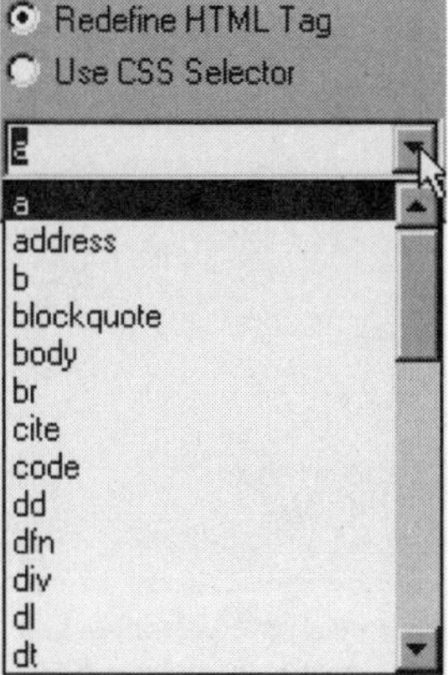

Figure 9 Choose an HTML tag, from a to var, from the drop-down menu. The menu doubles as a text box where you can type any HTML tag.

To redefine an HTML tag:

1. Open the Edit Style Sheet dialog box.
2. Click on New. The New Style dialog box will appear.
3. Click on Redefine HTML tag (**Figure 8**).
4. Select a tag from the drop-down menu (**Figure 9**), or type a tag in the text box (without the <brackets>).
5. Click on OK. The New Style dialog box will close, and the Style definition dialog box will open (see **Figure 11**, next page).
6. Select the attributes you want to add to the tag, using the guidelines in the *Style Definitions* section of this chapter. To move from one panel of the dialog box to another, click on the name of the category in the list box at the left of the Style definition dialog box.
7. When you're finished making your selections, click on OK. The Style definition dialog box will close, and you'll return to the Edit Style Sheet dialog box.
8. Click on Done to close the Edit Style Sheet dialog box and return to the Dreamweaver window.

✔ Tip

- The HTML tag will retain its intrinsic properties, as well as taking on the new attributes you define.

To create a Style Class:

1. Open the Edit Style Sheet dialog box.
2. Click on New. The New Style dialog box will appear.
3. Click on the Make a Custom Style (Class) radio button (**Figure 10**).
4. Type a name (one word, all lowercase) for the class in the text box. The name must start with a period (.), but if you leave it out, Dreamweaver will add it for you.
5. Click on OK. The New Style dialog box will close, and the Style definition dialog box will appear (**Figure 11**).
6. Select the attributes you want to add to the tag, using the guidelines in the Style Definitions section of this chapter. To move from one panel of the dialog box to another, click on the name of the category in the list box at the left of the Style definition dialog box.
7. When you're finished making your selections, click on OK. The Style definition dialog box will close, and you'll return to the Edit Style Sheet dialog box.
8. Click on Done to close the Edit Style Sheet dialog box and return to the Dreamweaver window.

The names of the classes you create will be added to the styles list box in the Styles palette (**Figure 12**).

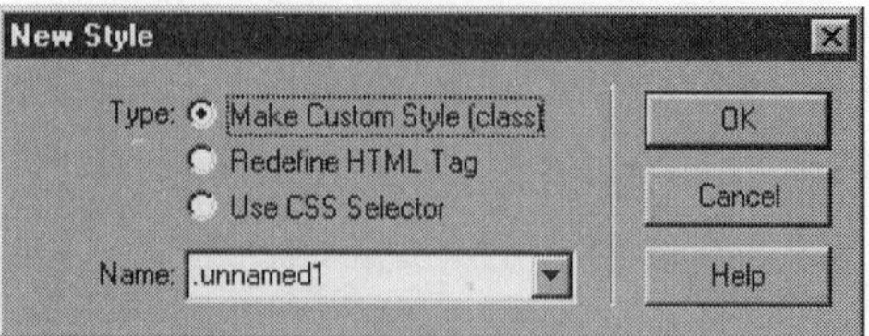

Figure 10 Click on the Custom Style (class) radio button to create a class, or custom style, to be applied to certain tags or selections on your page.

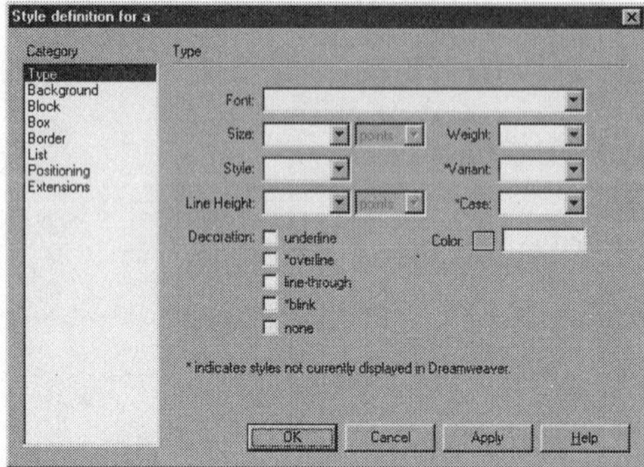

Figure 11 The Style definition dialog box is where you choose the attributes of your style. Since there are so many attributes, I define them all in the Style Definitions section at the end of this chapter.

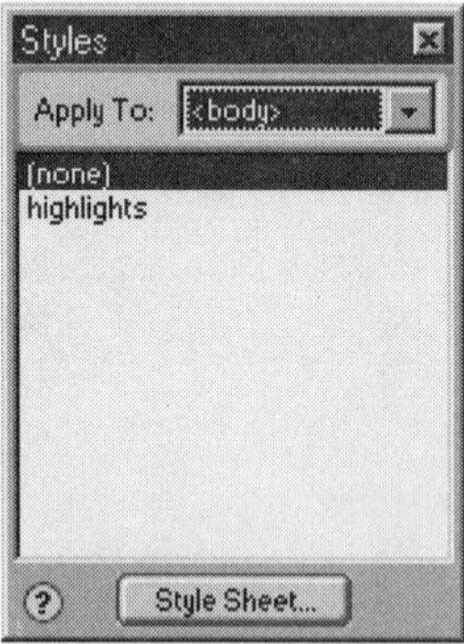

Figure 12 As you add classes to the style sheet, they will appear in the Styles palette.

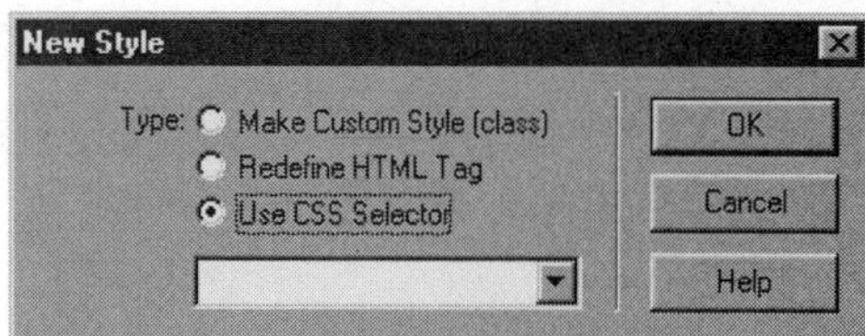

Figure 13 What does that third button do?

Defining New Selectors

You may have been wondering about that third option on the Create New Style dialog box: CSS Selector (**Figure 13**). As I've said previously, one way to create a style is to redefine an HTML tag, called a *selector* in that context.

You can also create a style for more than one selector at a time. There are two instances in which you would to this: One is when you want to define a style that would apply to several different tags. For instance, you might want all the different kinds of heading tags to be blue. Instead of setting a style for each <hn> tag individually:

```
h1 { color: blue }
h2 { color: blue }
```

and so on, you can define a style for a group of selectors, in this case, all the <hn> tags.

```
h1, h2, h3, h4, h5, h6 { color: blue }
```

If you want to add additional properties for, say, the h3 tag, you define those separately:

```
h1, h2, h3, h4, h5, h6 { color: blue }
h3 { font-family: Courier, Courier New }
```

Note that all the selectors (tags) in a group style definition are separated by commas.

To define a style for more than one selector:

1. Open the Edit Style Sheet dialog box.
2. Click on New. The New Style dialog box will appear.
3. Click on the CSS Selector radio button.
4. Type all the tags, separated by commas, that you want to create a style for. For example: h1, h2, h3 (**Figure 14**).
5. Click on OK, and create the style as usual.

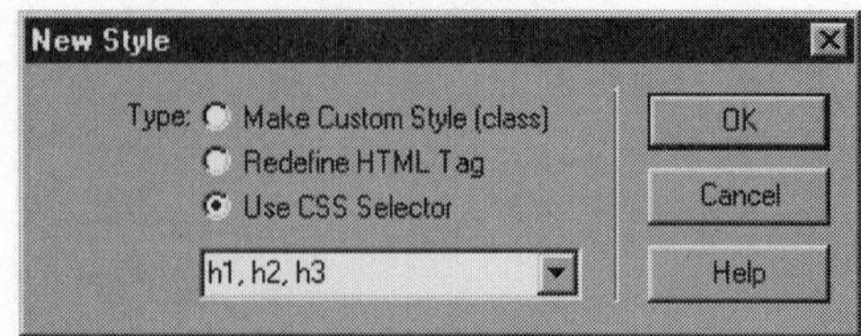

Figure 14 Type the tags, separated by commas, for which you want to define group properties.

Anchor Color Pseudoclasses

The style sheet standard defines a class that is applied to entities other than HTML Specification Standard tags as a *pseudoclass*. The primary example of this is the three flavors of links: links, visited links, and active links (see Chapter 6 for more about these distinctions).

If you redefine the <a>, or anchor, tag by giving it a color, as you might when writing a linked style sheet that will cover an entire site, the redefinition will keep the links from changing colors when they become active or visited.

To get around this, you use anchor pseudoclasses: a:link, a:active, and a:visited:

1. Open the Edit Style Sheet dialog box.
2. Click on New. The New Style dialog box will appear.
3. Click on the Use CSS Selector radio button (as shown in **Figure 13**).
4. The text box is also a drop-down menu; click on it and select one of the anchor pseudoclasses.
5. Click on OK. The Style definition dialog box will appear. To define a color for this pseudoclass, use the color option in the Text panel of the dialog box (see the section called *Text Attributes*, later in this chapter, for more information).
6. Click on OK to close the Style definition dialog box.
7. Repeat steps 2–6 for the other two pseudoclasses, if you like.

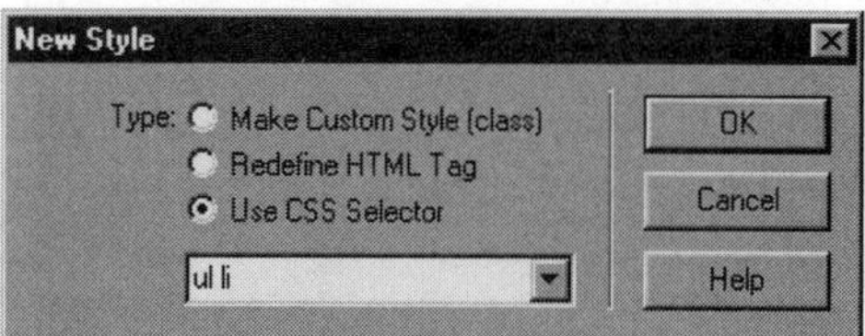

Figure 15 Type the contextual selectors, in the order they will be nested and separated only by a space, in the text box.

Examples of Contextual Styles

ul li or ol li for items in an unordered or ordered list (your mileage may vary)

td a for links that appear within table cells

td p for paragraphs within table cells (would not effect paragraphs not in a table)

b a for bold links

blockquote blockquote for nested indents

center img for centered images

Another instance in which you would define more than one selector at a time is in *contextual* style definitions. These apply to nested HTML tags. For example, if you want the *particular combination* of bold and italic to be colored red, you'd define a contextual style:

```
b i {color: red}
```

In this case, text nested in both the bold and italic tags would turn red, but other bold or italicized text would not:

```
<b><i>this text is red</i></b>
<i>this text is not red</i>
<b>and neither is this</b>
```

Note that contextual selectors are separated by only a single space.

To define a style for a contextual selector:

1. Open the Edit Style Sheet dialog box.
2. Click on New. The New Style dialog box will appear.
3. Click on the CSS Selector radio button.
4. Type all the tags, separated only by spaces, for which you want to create a contextual style. For example: b i (**Figure 15**).
5. Click on OK, and create the style as usual.

Linked and Imported Style Sheets

Style sheets for individual pages are nifty, but if you want to create a style sheet that can be used on more than one page (actually, on as many pages as you want), then you should create a linked or imported style sheet.

To create a new linked or imported style sheet:

1. Save the page you are working on. Dreamweaver prefers that you add linked style sheets only to saved pages.
2. Open the Edit Style Sheet dialog box (**Figure 16**).
3. Click on Link. The Add Remote Style Sheet dialog box will appear (**Figure 17**).
4. Type a filename for your new file, ending in .css, in the File/URL text box. If your style sheet will not be located in the same directory as your page, include the directory information in the pathname (as in /styles/master.css).
5. Choose a linking method:
   - To use the new file as a linked style sheet, click on the Link radio button.
   - To use the new file as an imported style sheet, click on the Import radio button.
6. Click on OK to close the Add Remote Style Sheet dialog box. You'll return to the Edit Style Sheet dialog box, where you'll see the name of the style sheet you just created (**Figure 18**).

✔ Tip

- The kinks aren't yet worked out of style sheet importing in either Navigator or Explorer, so linking to the style sheet is recommended rather than importing it.

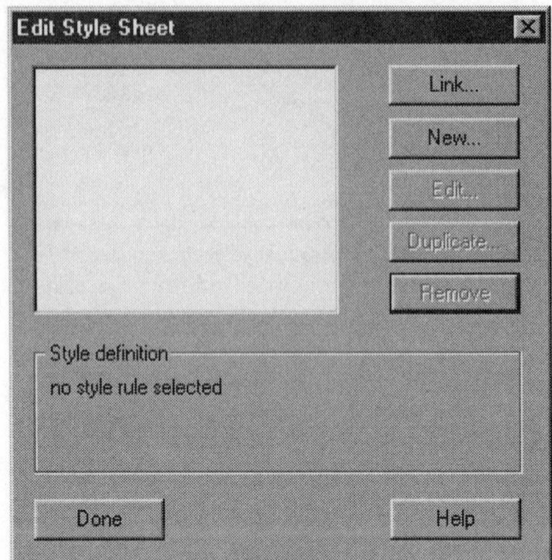

Figure 16 In the Edit Style Sheet dialog box, click on Link.

Figure 17 Type the pathname for your new style sheet in the Add Remote Style Sheet dialog box. Dreamweaver will create the file in the location you specify.

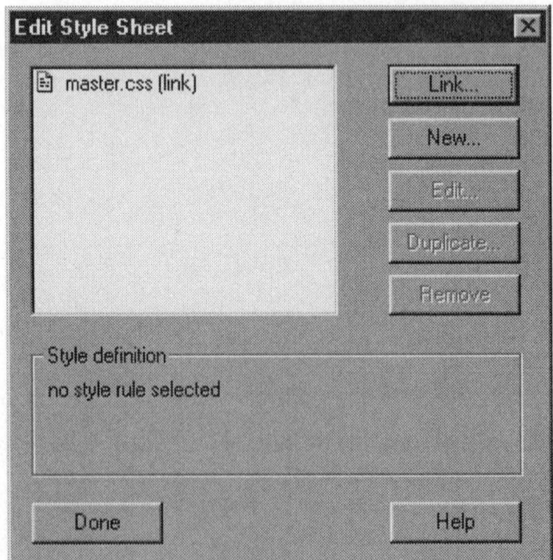

Figure 18 The name of the linked style sheet you created will appear in the Edit Style Sheet dialog box.

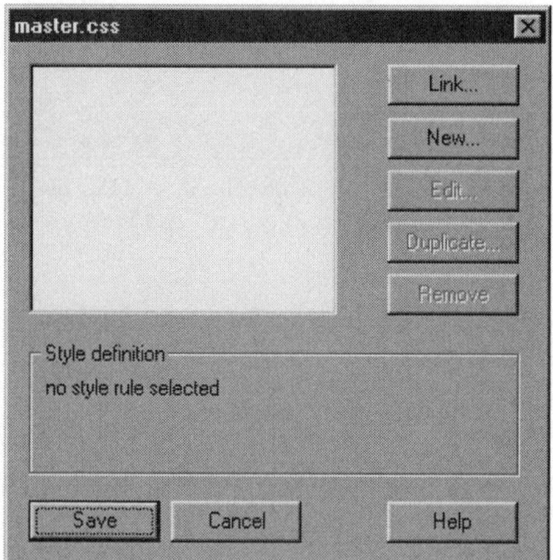

Figure 19 Use the Style Sheet dialog box to add styles to your linked style sheet.

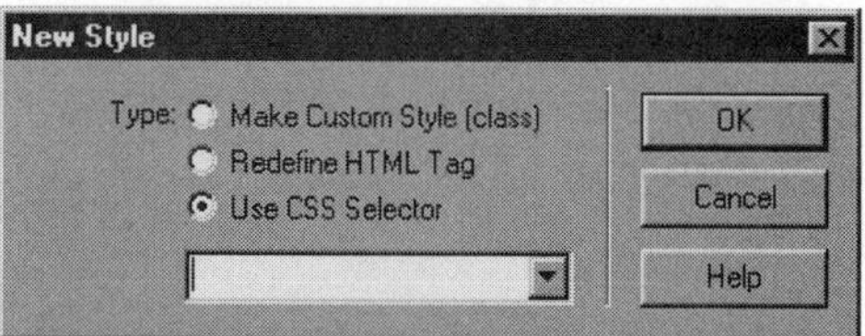

Figure 20 The New Style dialog box. From here on out, adding stuff to a linked Style Sheet is the same as creating new styles for a single page.

Before you can save your style sheet, you need to add at least one style to it.

To add styles to a linked style sheet:

1. In the Edit Style Sheet dialog box, click on the name of your style sheet in the styles list box.
2. Click on Edit. The Style Sheet (name) dialog box will appear (**Figure 19**).
3. Click on New. The New Style dialog box will appear (**Figure 20**).
4. Now you can add styles to your style sheet in the same way you'd add them to an individual page:
   - To redefine HTML tags, follow steps 3–7 in the section called *To redefine an HTML tag*.
   - To create a class, follow steps 3-7 in the section called *To create a style class*.
   - To create a new selector, refer to the section called *Defining a New Selector*.
5. Follow steps 3 and 4 for every style you want to add to your style sheet.
6. When you have added some styles to your style sheet that you want to save, click on Save in the Style Sheet (name) dialog box (**Figure 19**). The styles will be added to the style sheet.

Now you have an external style sheet linked to the current page. Be sure to check the link URL when you upload the page to your Web site. It's in the code and looks something like this:

```
<link rel="stylesheet" href="/styles/master.css">
```

For imported styles, the code will look something like this:

```
@import "import.css"
```

After you initially create and link to an external style sheet, Dreamweaver will save it on your hard drive, and you can link to it over and over again.

To link to an existing style sheet:

1. Open the Edit Style Sheet dialog box.
2. Click on Link. The Add Remote Style Sheet dialog box will appear (**Figure 21**).
3. Click on Browse. The Select Stylesheet File dialog box will appear (**Figure 22**).
4. Browse through the files and folders on your computer until you locate the .CSS file you want to link to.
5. When you locate the file, click on it, and then click on Open. The dialog box will close, and you'll return to the Add Remote Style Sheet dialog box.
6. Choose a linking method:
   - To link to the style sheet, click on the Link radio button.
   - To import the style sheet, click on the Import radio button.
7. Click on OK. The Add Remote Style Sheet dialog box will close, and you'll return to the Edit Style Sheet dialog box, where you'll see the name of the style sheet you selected (**Figure 23**).

What Little Style Sheets Are Made Of

An external style sheet, or .CSS document, is just made up of a few lines of style definition code. If you use only one style in an external style sheet, it will only contain one line of code. Try opening a .CSS document in your text editor to see how simple it is—that's why linked style sheets don't add much load time to Web pages.

Figure 21 In the Add Remote Style Sheet dialog box, click on Browse to select an existing Style Sheet from your hard drive.

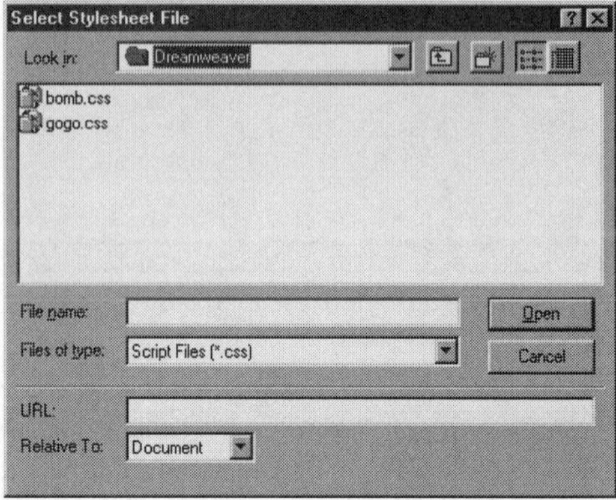

Figure 22 The Select Stylesheet dialog box is just like the Open dialog boxes you're familiar with.

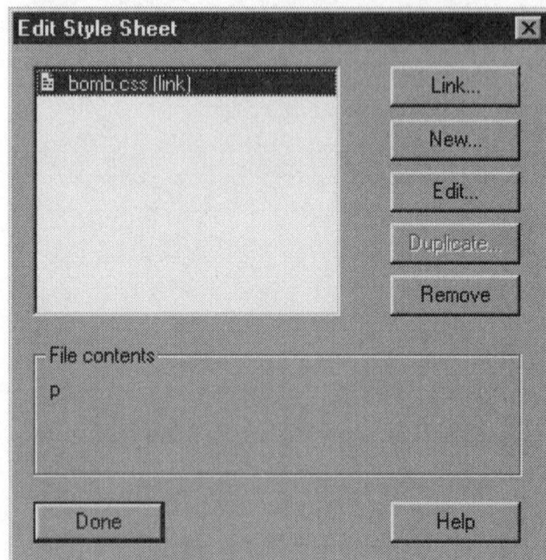

Figure 23 After you link to an existing Style Sheet, you'll see its filename displayed in the Edit Style Sheet dialog box.

LINKED AND IMPORTED STYLE SHEETS

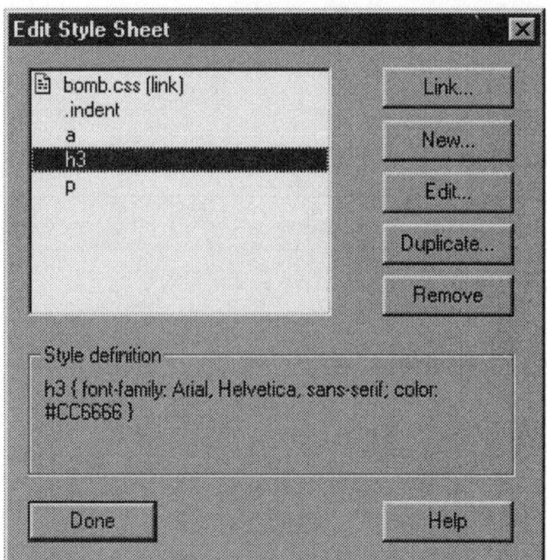

Figure 24 Click on the name of the style that you want to edit. A summary of its attributes will appear in the Style definition area of the dialog box to remind you of what it already contains.

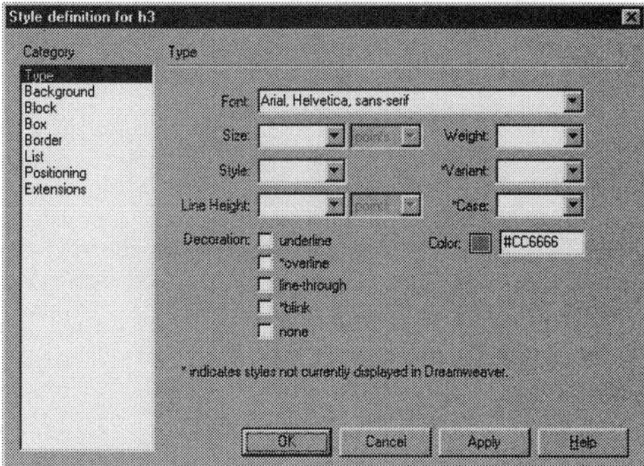

Figure 25 In the Style definition dialog box, you make your changes to the style.

✔ Tips

- When you select a style in the Edit Style Sheet dialog box, a summary of the attributes it contains will appear in the Style definition area of the dialog box.
- To edit the styles in an external style sheet, follow steps 1 and 2. When you click on Edit, the Style Sheet (name) dialog box will appear, which lists the names of all the styles in the external style sheet. From there, follow steps 2–6 for the styles in the external style sheet that you wish to edit.

Editing Style Sheets

When you edit a style sheet, all instances of that style will automatically be updated on the pages to which it applies. Whether you change from brown to green, right-aligned to justified, Arial to Courier, or scrap a style entirely, your changes will be reflected instantly.

To edit a style sheet:

1. Open the Edit Style Sheet dialog box by selecting Text > Custom Styles > Edit Style Sheet from the Document window menu bar; by pressing Ctrl+Shift+E (Command+Shift+E); or by clicking on the Style Sheet button on the Styles palette.
2. Click on the name of the style sheet you wish to edit in the styles list box (**Figure 24**), whether that style is an HTML tag you have redefined; a class; or a group of selectors.
3. Click on the Edit button. The Style definition dialog box will appear (**Figure 25**).
4. Make your changes to the style in the Style definition dialog box. (See the *Style Definitions* section at the end of this chapter for details.)
5. When you're done, click on OK to close the Style definition dialog box and return to the Edit Style Sheet dialog box.
6. Click on Done to close the Edit Style Sheet dialog box and return to the Document window. Your changes will take effect immediately.

   or

   You can click on another style sheet and click on Edit to edit that style sheet; or you can click on New to create a new style sheet.

You may want to create two styles that are very similar. You can make a copy of a style and then edit it. You can duplicate tag and selector styles as classes, or vice versa.

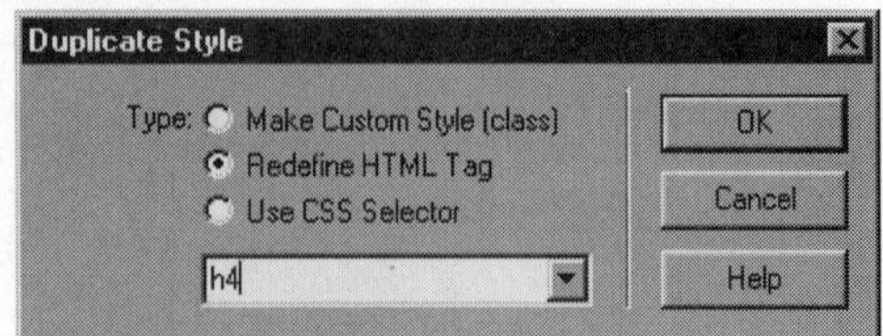

Figure 26 The Duplicate Style Sheet dialog box is pretty much the same as the New Style dialog box.

To make a copy of a style:

1. Open the Edit Style Sheet dialog box.
2. Click on the name of the style in the list box. (You can't duplicate external style sheets this way).
3. Click on Duplicate. The Duplicate Style dialog box will appear (**Figure 26**); this is pretty much the same as the New Style dialog box.
4. You must rename the style before you can duplicate it.
   - To save the duplicate style as a class, click on the Class radio button, and type a name for the style in the text box.
   - To apply the duplicate style to a different HTML tag, click on the Redefine HTML tag radio button, and select a tag from the drop-down menu (or type a tag without the <brackets> in the text box).
   - To apply the duplicate style to a set of tags, type the tags, either a group (such as `h1, h2`) or a contextual set (such as `b i`) in the text box.
5. Click on OK. The Duplicate Style Sheet dialog box will close, and you'll return to the Edit Style Sheet dialog box, where you'll see the name of your new style selected in the list box.

Now you can edit your new style, if you wish, by clicking on the Edit button.

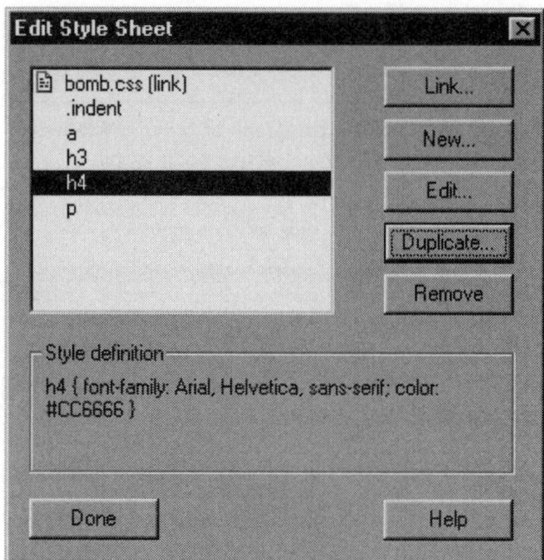

Figure 27 In the Edit Style Sheet dialog box, click on the name of the style you want to delete.

To delete a style sheet:

1. Open the Edit Style Sheet dialog box.
2. Click on the name of the style you want to delete (**Figure 27**).
3. Click on Remove.
4. Click on Done to close the Edit Style Sheet dialog box.

✔ Tip

- Deleting an external style sheet doesn't remove it from your hard drive, it simply removes the links to it from the current page.

Applying Style Sheets

So now that you've made all these styles, how do you use them?

To apply a redefined HTML tag:

1. Simply use the tag.

✔ Tip

■ You may need to view the page in Navigator 4 or MSIE 4 to see all the attributes of the style sheet.

To apply an external style sheet:

1. You apply external style sheets by linking to them, as described in the section called *Linked and Imported Style Sheets*.

To apply a class:

1. Select the text to which you want to apply the class.
   - To select an entire paragraph (or other block-level element), simply click to place the insertion point within the paragraph (**Figure 28**).
   - To select the text within a particular tag, click on the text, and then click on the tag selector in the status bar of the Document window. Or you can use the tag selection menu in the Styles palette (**Figure 29**).
   - To select a span of text within a paragraph or other tag, select the text with the mouse or arrow keys (**Figure 30**).
2. From the Document window menu bar, select Text > Style > Custom Style, and then choose the class from the submenu.

   or

   In the Styles palette, click on the name of the class in the list of styles.

The style will be applied to your selection.

This paragraph is normal text. This paragraph is normal text. This paragraph is normal text. This paragraph is normal text. This paragraph is normal text. This paragraph is normal text. This paragraph is normal text.

Figure 28 To select a paragraph or other block-level element, simply click the insertion point within it.

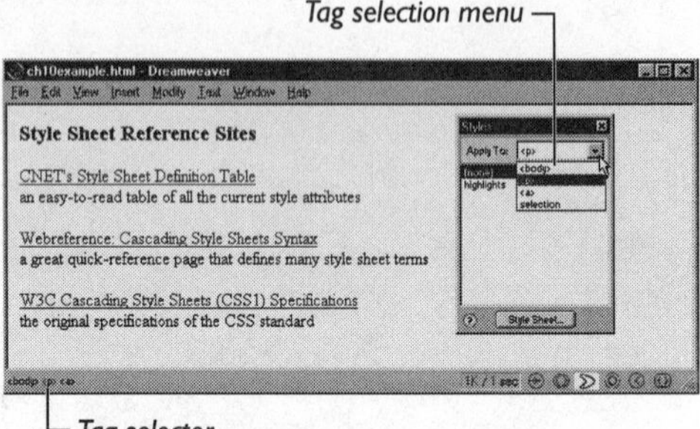

Figure 29 To select a particular tag, click on the text within the tag, and then choose a tag from one of the tag selectors: either in the Document window's status bar or in the Styles palette.

This paragraph is normal text. This paragraph is normal text. This paragraph is normal text. This paragraph is normal text. This paragraph is normal text. This paragraph is normal text. This paragraph is normal text.

Styles
Apply To: selection
(none)
indent

Figure 30 To select a span of text, simply select the text you want to modify—notice how the tag selection menu in the Styles palette reads "selection." Dreamweaver will add a <span> tag automatically.

Spanning

Styles can be applied to any tag, but they must be applied to an existing tag—not just to freewheeling text. If the selection to which you apply a class is not confined by a parent tag, Dreamweaver will automatically insert a <span> tag to which the class will be applied—this is one of Dreamweaver's most profoundly convenient style editing features. The <span> entity is a non-breaking, non-intrusive way to define a text block without creating a new paragraph.

To remove class formatting:

1. Select the text or tag from which you want style formatting removed.
2. From the Document window menu bar, select Text > Custom Style > None.

   or

   In the Styles palette, click on (none) in the class list box.

About Conflicting Styles

What happens when you apply two conflicting styles to the same text?

Suppose you have defined the paragraph style with the following properties:

```
p { font-family: "Courier New, Courier, mono;
font-size: 14pt}
```

And then, suppose your link style is as follows:

```
a { font-family: "Arial, Helvetica, sans-serif;}
```

Who would win? That's where the *cascading* in cascading style sheets comes in. Styles, like tags, are nested around elements. The style that's closest, physically, to the text that it modifies has precedence over the other styles that might effect it. So in our example, the <a> tag would have precedence in this instance:

```
<p>All of this text is in the same paragraph, but
this <a href="piece.html">piece</a> is also
linked.</p>
```

In the following example, no matter what style modifications have been made to the <body> and <h3> selectors, the <span> tag will dominate them in the hierarchy for the word "favorite."

```
<head>
<style type="text/css">

<!--
body { color: white; background-color: red}
h3 {color: yellow}
.fav {color: black text-decoration: underline}
-->
</style>
</head>
<body>
<h3>This is my <span class=.fav>favorite</span>
headline</h3>
</body>
```

Your Parents' Inheritance

Tags that surround a piece of text are called *parents*. Parent tags also have parent tags, the whole way up through the <body> and <html> tags that surround all the content in a document. While the cascading rule applies to these nested tags, what about nested styles? In other words, what happens when you have a style sheet that has a linked style sheet as well as style sheets located on that page?

Again, the closer the style is, the more influence it has. Modifications made to particular pieces of text win out over modifications made to an entire document (called *global styles*); and global styles win out over imported styles; and imported styles win out over linked styles.

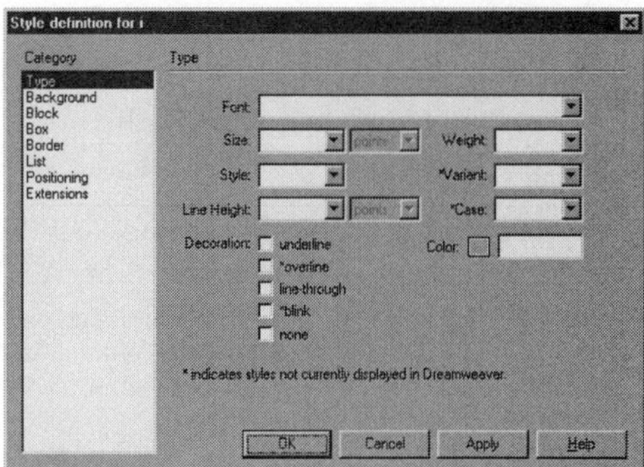

Figure 31 All the attributes you could ever want, eight categories high.

Style Definitions

Now, at last, we come to the closing section of the chapter, where I finally describe the style attributes you can use in your custom styles. There are eight different categories of custom styles in Dreamweaver (**Figure 31**), each of which contains several different single attributes you can apply to a block of text. The categories are:

- **Type** attributes refer to font formatting properties, such as font face, font size, font color, and text weight and style.
- **Background** attributes, such as background color and image, can be applied either to the <body> tag, to a text block, or to control an entire page.
- **Block** attributes control the spacing and shape of text within a block. Alignment and indent are block attributes.
- **Box** attributes are applied to the box that surrounds a block element, and can also be applied to <span> selections. Box attributes such as padding and margin controls shape the space around a block-type element.
- **Border** attributes are a subset of box attributes. Border attributes can make the usually invisible box around a style box visible with borders and colors.
- **List** attributes affect the formatting of ordered and unordered lists, including the appearance of the numbers or bullets in those lists.
- **Positioning** controls allow you to determine the location of elements on the page. (Because there are so many, and because this chapter is quite long enough already, I discuss positioning in the next chapter, Chapter 11.) Dreamweaver's **Extensions** to style sheets are generally unsupported, although the visual effects are supported by MSIE 4.

To use the Style definition dialog box:

1. To move from one panel of the dialog box to another, click on the category's name in the list box on the left side of the dialog box.
2. Select items from pull-down menus, check checkboxes, and type number values, as needed.
3. Some pull-down menus double as text boxes.
4. To select units for an attribute, first select *value* from the drop-down menu, then type a number (you can change it later) over the word *value* in the text box, and then choose a unit from the units pull-down menu.
5. Leave any items blank that aren't needed.

Units

The following units are used to define various spatial relationships in style sheets:

pixels (px) are the little dots that make up the picture on your computer monitor. At a monitor resolution of 600x800, a line 100 pixels long would be roughly 1½ inches long.

inches (in), **centimeters (cm)**, and **millimeters (mm)** are the same as their real-world equivalents.

picas and **points** are typographical measurements from the days of hand-set type. There are six picas in an inch, 12 points in a pica, and 72 points in an inch. (That's why most font sizes are based on the number 12.)

ems and **exs** are also handset-type measurements. An em, as in the letter m, is a square piece of type. The width of an em is one pica in a monospace font; in digital terms, this width may vary slightly from font to font and should be treated as a relative measurement. An ex, on the other hand, is the height of the letter x, which is shorthand for "average height of the lowercase alphabet in this font without any ascenders or descenders."

percent (%), in the case of style sheets, refers to percentage of the parent tag. If the only parent tag is the <body> tag, then % will apply to the width of the screen. If the parent tag is a table cell, then the style block will occupy x% of that cell. If the parent unit is a text block such as a paragraph or <span>, things might get funky. Experiment with percentages to see what happens.

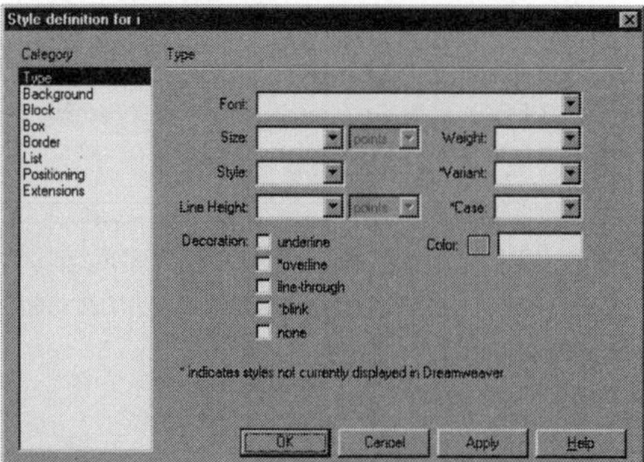

Figure 32 The Font panel of the Style definition dialog box

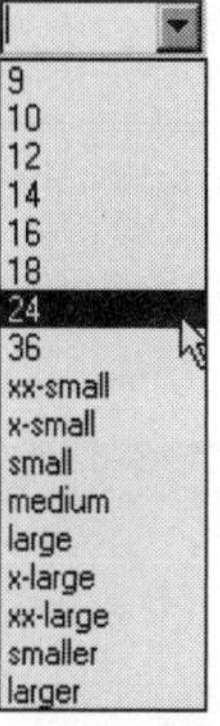

Figure 33 The whole family of font sizes

Type Attributes

Type attributes are probably the styles you're going to use most often, and they include those previously defined by the **<font>** tag (now deprecated). The Type panel of the Style definition dialog box is shown in **Figure 32**.

Type attributes include:

Font chooses a font face or a font family.

✔ Tip

- To find out about adding fonts or font families to this dialog box, see the section of Chapter 3 called *To Define a Font Combination.*

Size (**Figure 33**) sets a font size for the text. You can choose from number of different units to set the size for the text.

The size attribute offers point sizes ranging from 36 (largest) to 9 (smallest), which roughly correspond to the 1–7 font size scale in basic HTML.

If point sizes don't do it for you, you can set a size in a number of other units, including pixels (px), inches (in), centimeters (cm), millimeters (mm), picas, ems, and exs.

Additionally, you can set relative sizes ranging from "largest" to "xx-small."

* Attributes with an asterisk * are not displayed properly in the Document window.

☞ Attributes with a ☞ pointer are not supported by current browsers.

Style, as in regular text style, lets you set text as Normal, Italic, or Oblique (**Figure 34**).

☞ Normal, or "upright," italic, and oblique are three font styles; oblique means "slanted." Navigator follows the rule for font selection literally here: it looks for a font with "oblique" properties in the selected font family, and if it doesn't find one, it uses a normal font, whereas Explorer will display oblique text as italic.

☞ **Line Height**, a typographical setting not available in regular HTML, determines the height of each line in the text block (**Figure 35**). If the font size is 12 points, and the line height is 16 points, you'll have a good bit of extra space between each line. (Normal line height provides an offset of approximately two points.) Browsers may interpret "normal" line height however they choose. This setting may cause problems with IE3.

Decoration (**Figure 36**) can apply underlining, overlining*, strikethrough (line-through), or blinking* to the text.

✔ Tip

- Since the default for regular text is no decoration, and the default for linked text is underlining, you can remove the default underlining from links by selecting None from the Decoration category and applying it to the <a> tag. (Text decoration is not inherited, so if you apply it simply as a paragraph style, links will still appear underlined.)

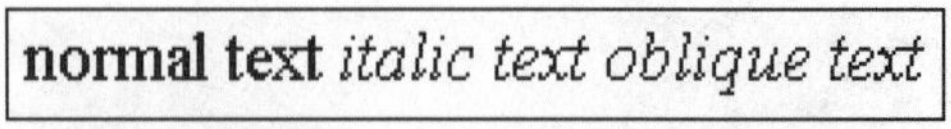

normal text *italic text oblique text*

Figure 34 Font styles in Internet Explorer: Normal, Italic, and Oblique

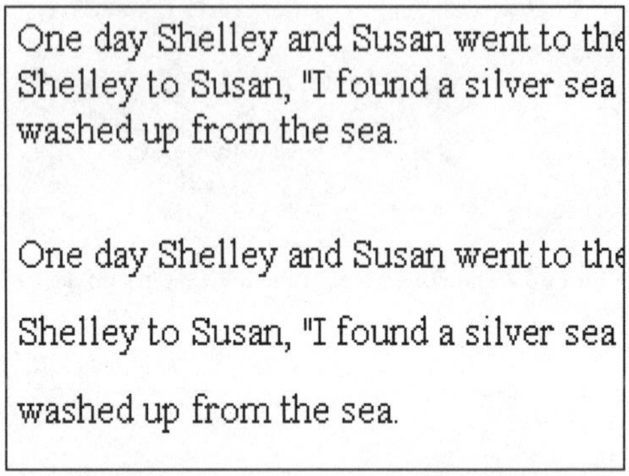

One day Shelley and Susan went to th
Shelley to Susan, "I found a silver sea
washed up from the sea.

One day Shelley and Susan went to th

Shelley to Susan, "I found a silver sea

washed up from the sea.

Figure 35 Line height as interpreted by Navigator. The top paragraph has no line height set. The second paragraph has a line height of 24 points (to a font size of 14 points).

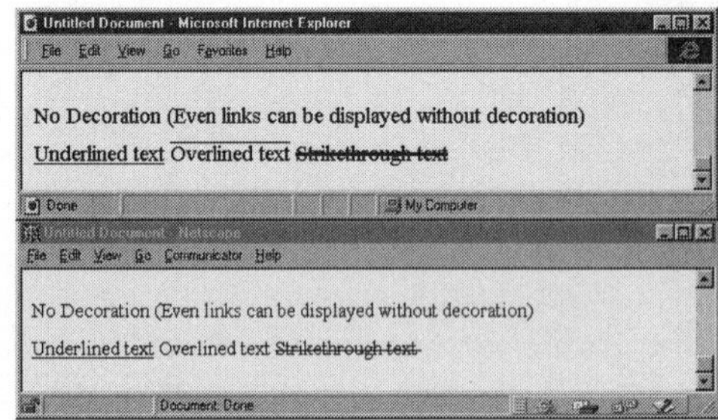

Figure 36 Text decoration, as displayed by Internet Explorer (above) and Netscape Navigator (below). Note that Navigator does not display overline.

* Attributes with an asterisk * are not displayed properly in the Document window.

☞ Attributes with a ☞ pointer are not supported by current browsers.

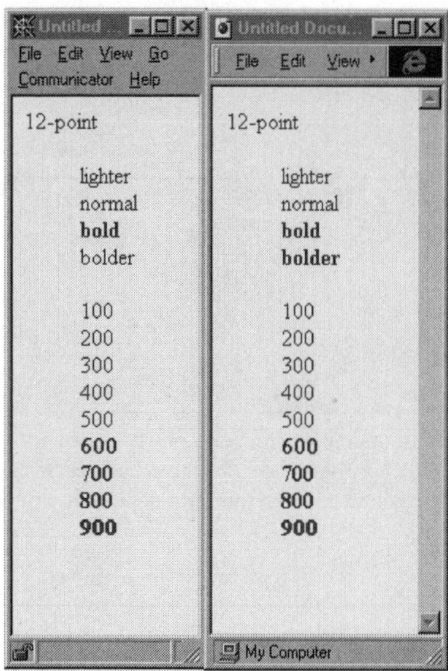

Figure 37 Weight variations, at 12 points. Neither browser does much with lighter weights, and Navigator also handles "bolder" unpredictably (I've seen it read that attribute just fine, but sometimes it doesn't).

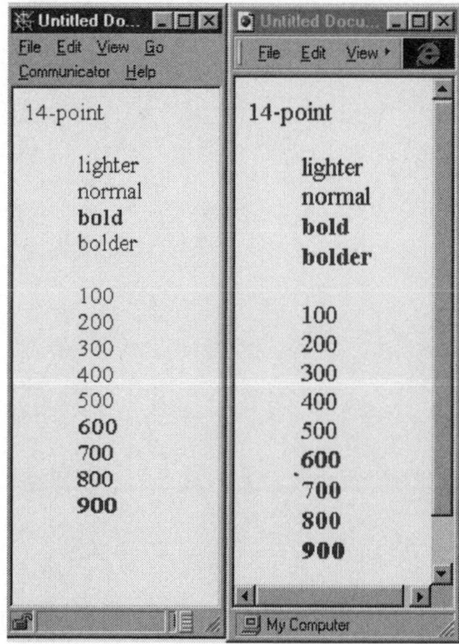

Figure 38 The differences between how Navigator and Explorer handle text are apparent in this figure. While the treatment of the fonts was practically the same at 12 points, at 14 points, Explorer (on the right) gets decidedly heavier with its text weights.

Weight (**Figure 37**) is the same as **boldness** <b>, or <strong>. You can apply a relative weight (lighter, normal, bold, bolder), or a numerical weight from 100–900 (**Figure 38**). The weight of normal text is generally 400, while boldface text has a weight of about 700.

The only font **Variant*** currently supported by Dreamweaver is SMALL CAPS.

Case* allows you to apply all-lowercase, all-uppercase, or title case (The First Letter In Each Word) to a text block. This would come in especially handy for setting headers or captions.

Color, of course, acts the same as <font color=n>.

✔ Tip

- To find out about selecting colors, see the sections of Chapter 2 called *Colors and Web Pages* and *Modifying the Page Background*.

TYPE ATTRIBUTES

* Attributes with an asterisk * are not displayed properly in the Document window.

☞ Attributes with a ☞ pointer are not supported by current browsers.

Background Attributes

Background attributes allow you to place a background color or image behind a text block. They will be superimposed over any other background color or image on the page. The Background panel of the Style definition dialog box is shown in **Figure 39**.

✔ Tips

- To set the background color or image for a page, see the section called *Modifying the Page Background* in Chapter 2.
- To set the background color or image for a table, see the section called *Coloring Tables* in Chapter 7.
- To use style sheets to apply a background color or image to an entire page, apply the style to the **<body>** tag.

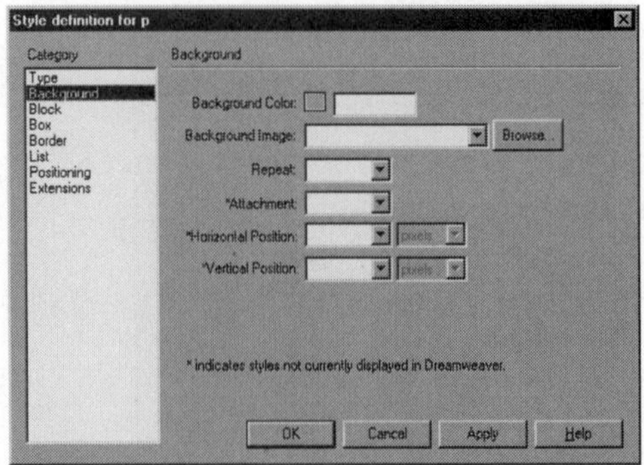

Figure 39 You can define properties of a background color or image for either a text block or the page body using the Background panel of the Style definition dialog box.

* Attributes with an asterisk * are not displayed properly in the Document window.

☞ Attributes with a ☞ pointer are not supported by current browsers.

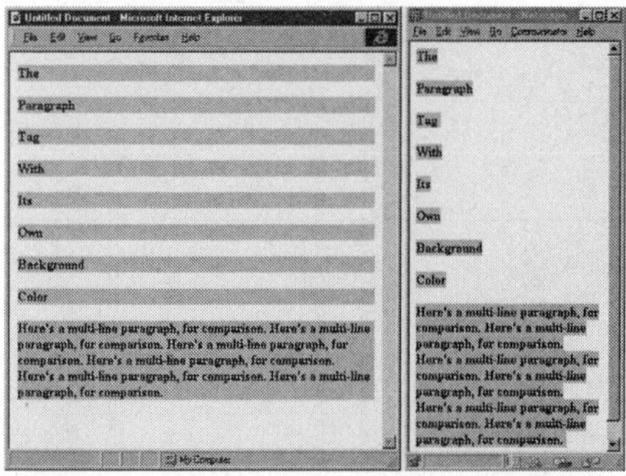

Figure 40 I redefined the paragraph tag to have its own background color. Explorer (on the left) makes paragraphs occupy 100 percent of the parent tag (the page body, in this case) by default, and colors in the entire width. Navigator (on the right) colors in only the part of the paragraph that contains content.

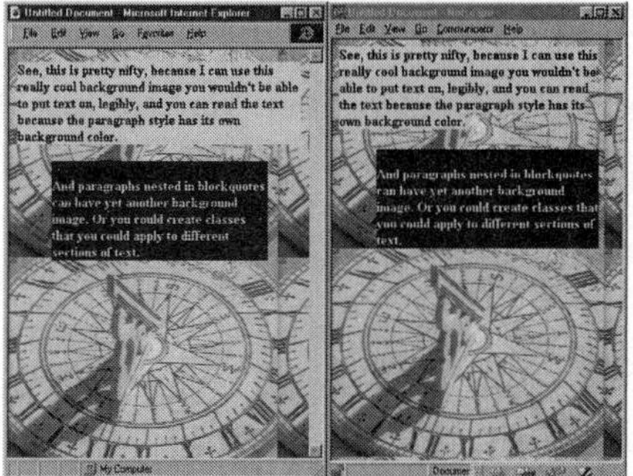

Figure 41 If you use a background color (first paragraph) or background image (second paragraph) for a text block, it will be superimposed over the page background. Note how the blockquote style (second paragraph) is rectangular in both Explorer and Navigator (right).

* Attributes with an asterisk * are not displayed properly in the Document window.

☞ Attributes with a ☞ pointer are not supported by current browsers.

Background attributes include:

Background color and **background image** can be applied to an entire page or to a text block (**Figure 40**). If both are used, the text block background will be superimposed over the page background (**Figure 41**).

The rest of the attributes all apply to a background image.

Repeat (**Figure 42**) determines whether the background image is tiled, and if so, how. If the image is displayed in an element that is smaller than the image dimensions, the image will be cropped to fit the element's dimensions.

*No-repeat** prevents the image from tiling.

Repeat tiles the image as it would be tiled in a page background image: from left to right in columns proceeding down the page.

*Repeat-x** displays a horizontal "band" of images; the image is tiled in one row across the page.

*Repeat-y** displays vertical "band" of images; the image is tiled in one column down the page.

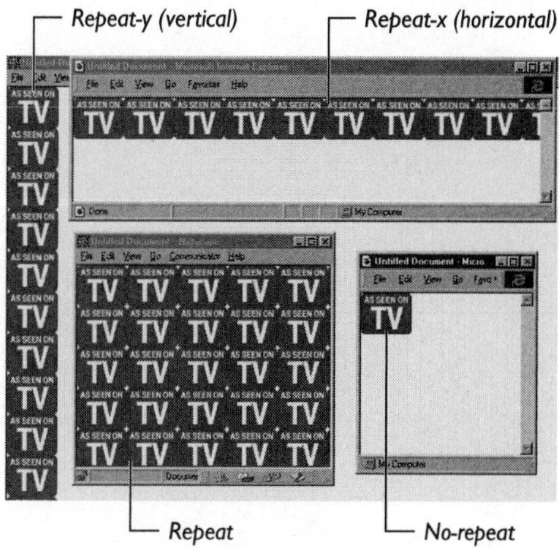

Figure 42 The four flavors of background repeat

Attachment* means the relative attachment of the background image to the page, in particular for full-page background images. Normally, when you scroll through a page, the background image moves, and so does the content—this is both default and scroll. The *fixed* attachment attribute fixes the background image in place, so that when you scroll through a page, the content "moves," and the background image "stands still" (**Figure 43**). ☞ Currently, IE4 supports the fixed option, but Navigator 4 treats fixed as scroll.

Horizontal position and **vertical position** mark the position of the background image, relative to the element. I discuss positioning in Chapter 11.

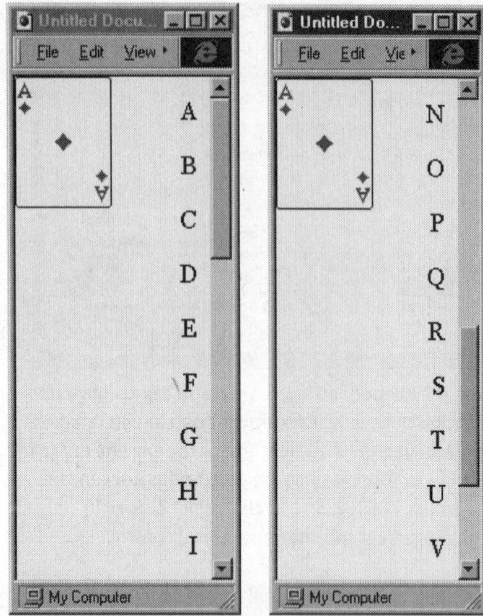

Figure 43 A demonstration of the fixed attachment background attribute in Internet Explorer. The image of the Ace is set not to repeat. Normally, a tiny background image like this one would scroll off the screen. With fixed attachment set, the ace stays in place while you scroll through the text at right.

BACKGROUND ATTRIBUTES

* Attributes with an asterisk * are not displayed properly in the Document window.

☞ Attributes with a ☞ pointer are not supported by current browsers.

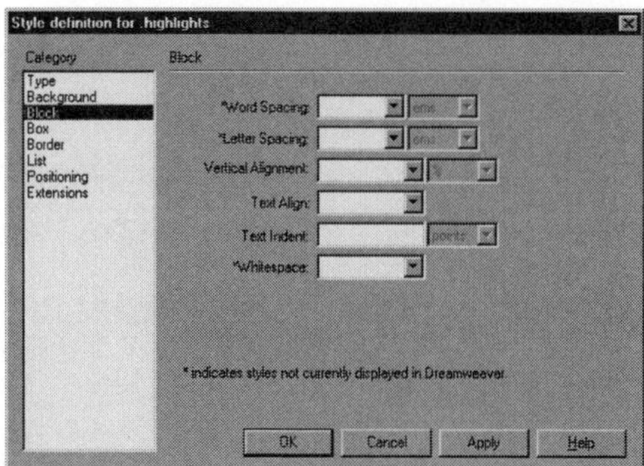

Figure 44 The Block attributes panel of the Style dialog box

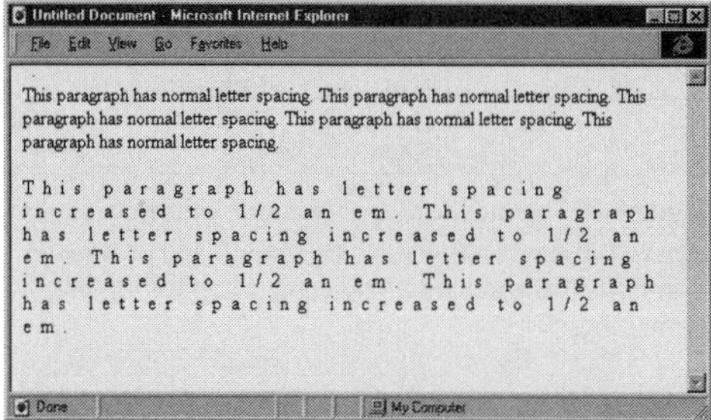

Figure 45 Explorer 4 processes letter spacing, but neither browser supports word spacing as of yet.

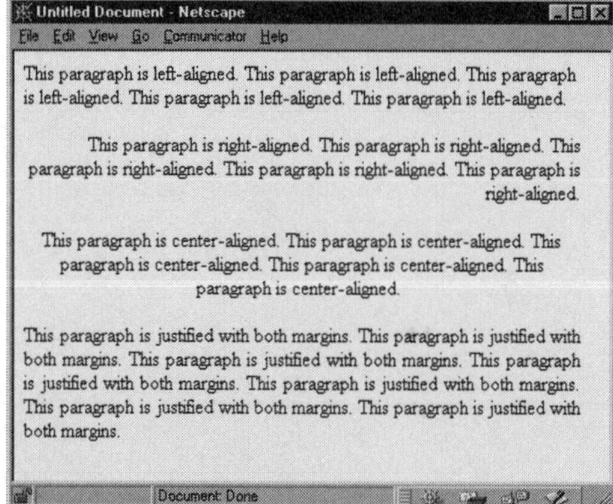

Figure 46 Text block alignment options, from top to bottom, are left, right, center, and justify. Note that the margin gutter is greater on the right than on the left; Navigator is leaving room for a scrollbar. (Explorer displays vertical scrollbars whether they're needed or not.)

Block Attributes

Block attributes apply typographical constraints to the alignment and spacing of words and characters within the selected element. The Block panel of the Style definition dialog box is shown in **Figure 44**.

Block attributes include:

Word spacing* is used to adjust the space between words, and **Letter spacing*** is used to adjust the space between characters.

Units available for using word and letter spacing include "normal" (no units), pixels, inches (in), centimeters (cm), millimeters (mm), picas, ems, and exs.

☞ I could not produce appreciable changes in word spacing in either Navigator or MSIE, which places this attribute in the "real soon now" category. Explorer deals with letter spacing (**Figure 45**), and Navigator does not.

☞ You can specify either positive or negative values, although not all browsers will support the latter.

☞ If property alignment is set to justify, this will most likely overrule word spacing, while letter spacing will override justification.

☞ The "normal" settings for word and letter spacing are left up to the individual browser.

Vertical alignment* controls the vertical position of the selection. Vertical alignment is related to positioning, which I discuss in Chapter 11.

Text align sets alignment for the text within the margins of the page or the block unit. As in regular HTML, alignment options are left, right, and center, with the additional justify option (**Figure 46**).

* Attributes with an asterisk * are not displayed properly in the Document window.

☞ Pointer items discuss how different browsers may treat an attribute.

Text indent* applies a tab-like indent to the first line of a block-type element (**Figure 47**).

*Dreamweaver displays indents unpredictably.

Units available for using indents include "normal" (no units), pixels, inches (in), centimeters (cm), millimeters (mm), picas, ems, and exs.

☞ You can use negative values to create a hanging indent, but not all browsers will support this.

✔ Tip

- Indents are not inherited, which means that line breaks used within paragraphs can cause unpredictable indent behavior. You might experiment with applying a class with indent properties to spans within paragraphs, which is what I did to get the indents in **Figure 48**.

Whitespace* controls the use of spacing within the selection. *Normal* ignores extra spaces and text-based breaks; *Pre* treats the text as if it were enclosed in <pre> tags, conserving the use of spaces and text-based breaks; *Nowrap*, similar to the nowrap setting for table cells, allows the line to break only when a <br> tag is used. This last setting is useful particularly for layers and block elements with dimensions smaller than 100 percent of the page.

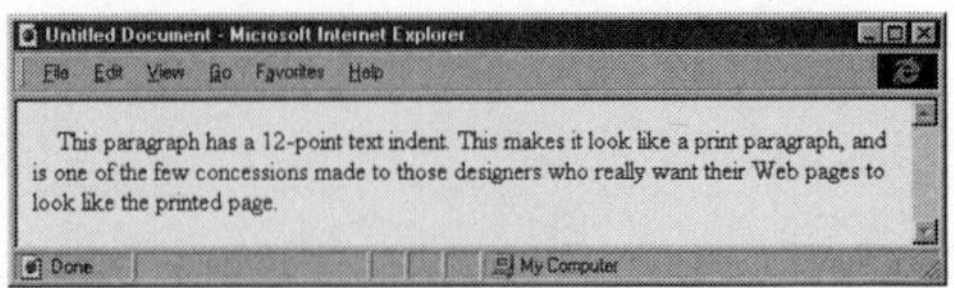

Figure 47 A paragraph with a 12-point indent

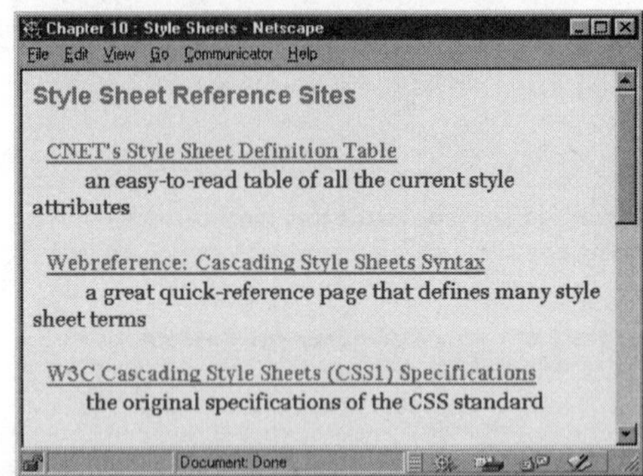

Figure 48 The indent property is not inherited, so tags within the block element—the <p> in this case—won't be indented unless you apply separate <span> formatting.

* Attributes with an asterisk * are not displayed properly in the Document window.

☞ Pointer items discuss how different browsers may treat an attribute.

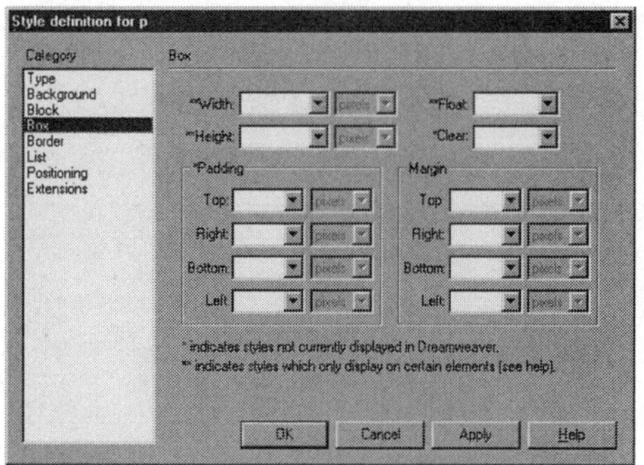

Figure 49 The Box attributes panel of the Style definition dialog box allows you to define the dimensions of the imaginary box that surrounds text blocks.

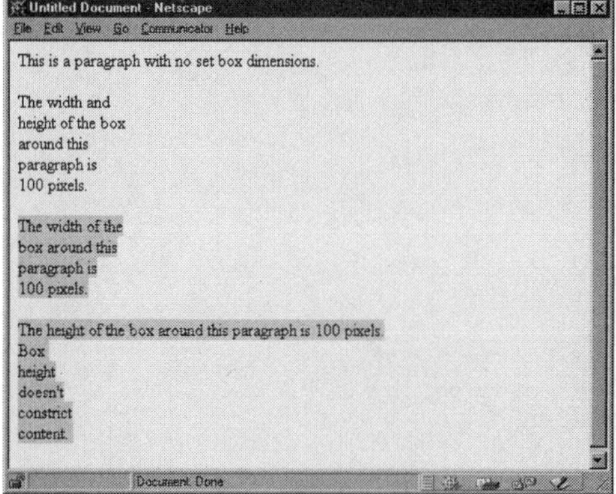

Figure 50 The box attributes of these paragraphs, from top to bottom: None, 100x100 pixels, 100 pixels across, and 100 pixels high. Horizontal measurements will break a line, but vertical measurements will not crop content. I used a background color on the bottom two paragraphs so you could see the dimensions more clearly.

Box Attributes

You can imagine all style modifications to HTML elements as being rectangular, or box-shaped. Box attributes, then, are styles applied to the (generally invisible) box that surrounds a block (or span) of text. The Box panel of the Style definition dialog box is shown in **Figure 49**.

Box attributes include:

Height* and **Width*** of the box can be expressed in a number of units, including pixels, inches (in), centimeters (cm), millimeters (mm), picas, ems, and exs, and percentage of the parent unit (%). To use the default dimensions of the box, leave these spaces blank, or choose *Auto*. Dreamweaver handles box dimensions correctly only for images and layers.

Box width will break a line, but box height will not crop the content of the box to fit within the box (**Figure 50**).

☞ Navigator respects box dimensions, but Explorer does not. Navigator only displays boxes as true rectangles if borders are applied (see next section).

Float* places the entity at the left or right margin, effectively separating it from the regular flow of the page. Other elements will wrap around floating elements. *Dreamweaver displays floating images correctly, but not other elements.*

* Attributes with an asterisk * are not displayed properly in the Document window.

☞ Pointer items discuss how different browsers may treat an attribute.

The **Clear*** setting determines the relationship of floating elements to the selected entity. A clear setting of *both* keeps objects from occupying the margins on either side of a selected entity. A clear setting of *none* allows floating entities to occupy either margin. Settings of *left* or *right* protect the respective margin. *Dreamweaver only displays this attribute correctly when it is applied to images.*

✔ Tip

- To apply the *both* setting, you need to type the word "both" (without the quotes) in the Clear text box, because it is not available from the drop-down menu.

Padding* is similar to cell padding used in tables. Padding is blank space between an object and its margin or visible border. Padding is set as a unit value in pixels, inches (in), centimeters (cm), millimeters (mm), picas, ems, and exs, and percentage of the parent unit (%).

✔ Tips

- To set percentage values, you need to type the % directly into the code.
- Padding is only visible when you use a visible border (see the next section, *Border Attributes*).
- You can specify padding for the **top**, **bottom**, **left**, and **right** independently.

* Attributes with an asterisk * are not displayed properly in the Document window.

☞ Pointer items discuss how different browsers may treat an attribute.

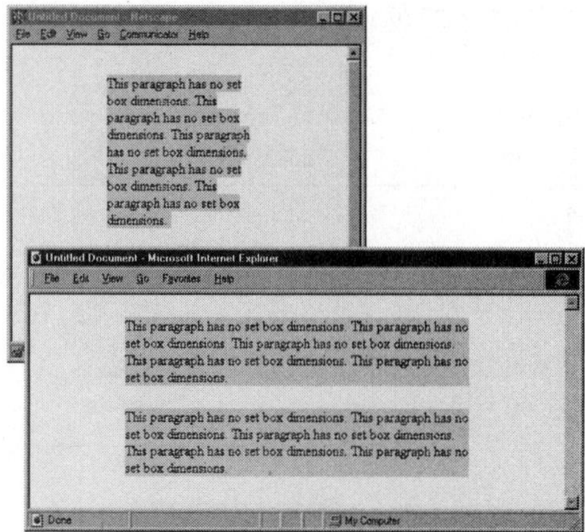

Figure 51 In this example, I added the following margins to the **<p>** tag: 100 pixels on the left and right, and 25 pixels at the top. I showed two different window sizes here (Navigator is at the top) to show how window size affects left and right margins.

Margins* (**Figure 51**) are the location of the border around the box (whether or not that border is visible). Margins are set as either *auto*, or as a number of units, including pixels, inches (in), centimeters (cm), millimeters (mm), picas, ems, and exs, and percentage of the parent element (%). *Dreamweaver displays margins properly only when they are applied to block elements.*

✔ Tips

- Setting top and bottom margins is a nice alternative to line spacing; you can subtly increase the spacing between paragraphs.
- You can set margins for the **top**, **bottom**, **left**, and **right** independently.

* Attributes with an asterisk * are not displayed properly in the Document window.

☞ Pointer items discuss how different browsers may treat an attribute.

Border Attributes

Border attributes are a subset of box attributes, but in the interests of space and neatness, Dreamweaver displays them in their own panel in the Style definition dialog box (**Figure 52**).

Border elements are not displayed by Dreamweaver in the Document window.

Borders are composed of four entities: the **top**, **right**, **bottom**, and **left**.

You can set a **width** and a **color** for each entity (**Figure 53**).

☞ Navigator will display different border widths, but not different border colors.

☞ Navigator will only display box borders if a box width is specified (You can specify 100 percent). Explorer ignores box widths.

☞ Navigator and Explorer deal with color combinations differently.

You can also choose from a number of border **styles** (**Figure 54**).

✔ Tip

- Padding, a box property, starts doing its thing when you use visible borders.

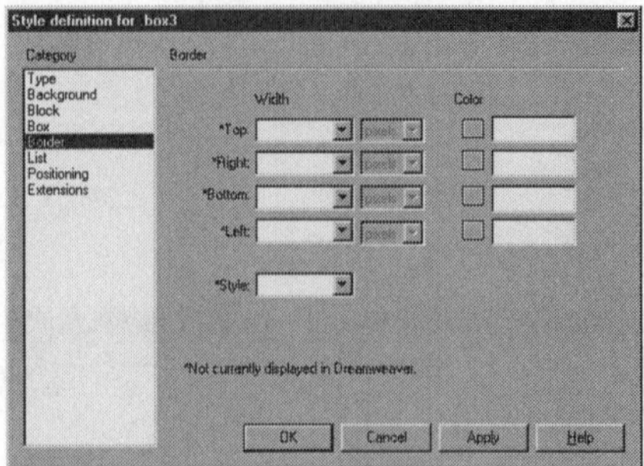

Figure 52 Box attributes allow you to make the border around the box visible.

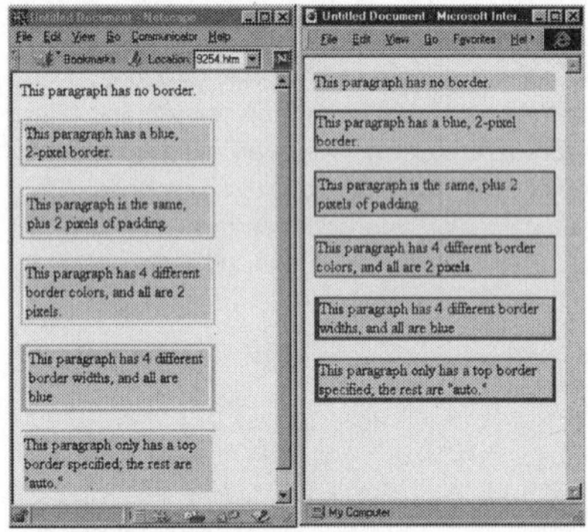

Figure 53 How Navigator (left) and Explorer (right) treat the same border settings. I set a box width of 200 pixels, which Navigator requires and Explorer ignores. You can't see this in black and white, but the border colors are treated differently by the two browsers.

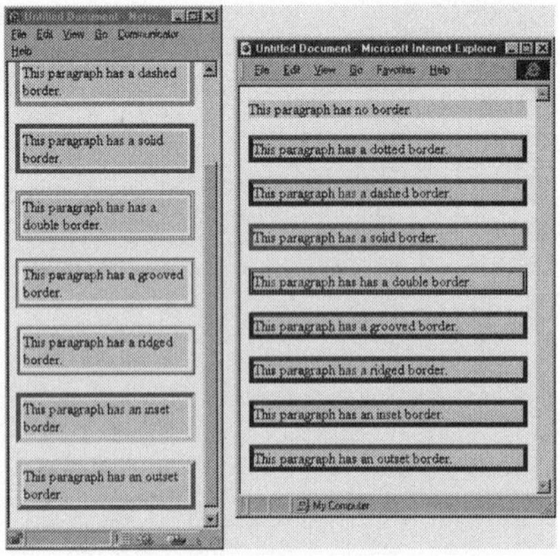

Figure 54 Border styles, as displayed by Navigator (left) and Explorer (right). Neither browser displays all border styles as described; for instance, "dotted" and "dashed" don't look like their names.

* Attributes with an asterisk * are not displayed properly in the Document window.

☞ Pointer items discuss how different browsers may treat an attribute.

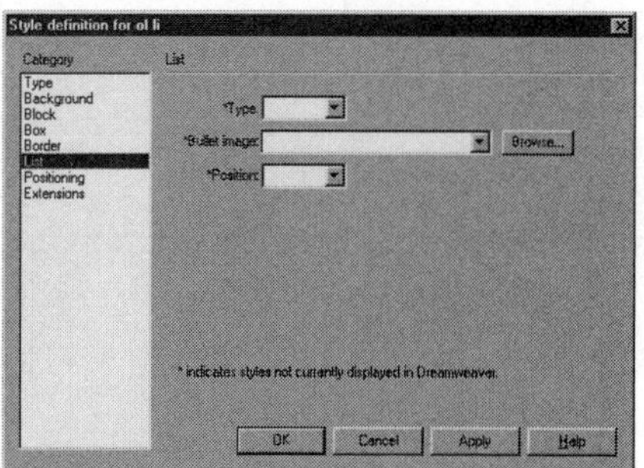

Figure 55 The List panel of the Style definition dialog box lets you define the format of ordered (numbered) or unordered (bulleted) lists.

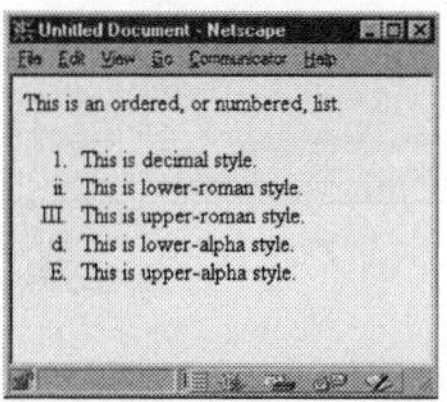

Figure 56 An ordered list, formatted with the five different types of ordered list styles

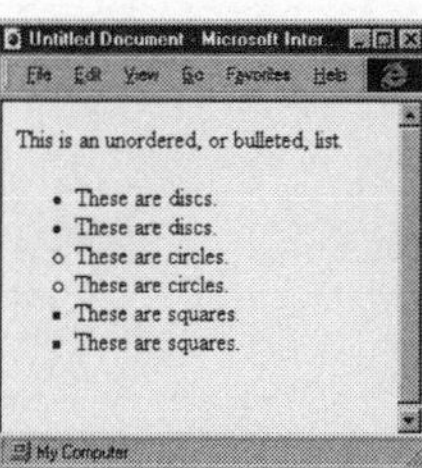

Figure 57 An unordered list, formatted with the three different types of unordered list styles.

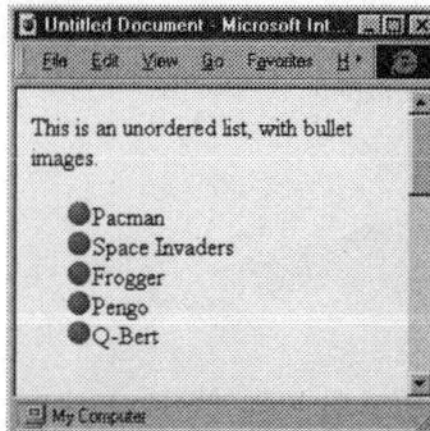

Figure 58: An unordered list, using bullet images.

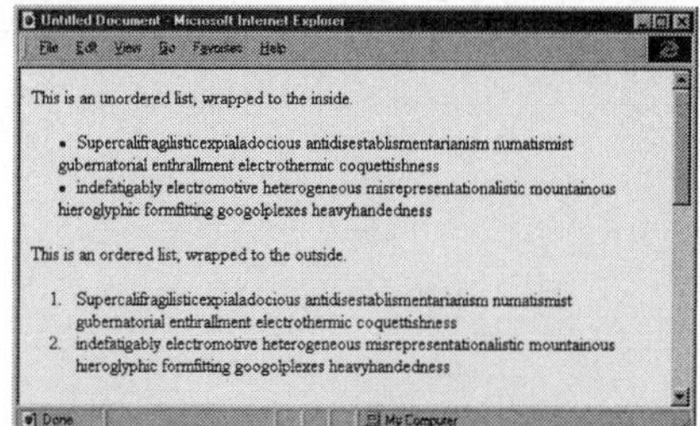

Figure 59 The first list is wrapped to the inside, and the second list is wrapped to the outside.

List Attributes

List attributes are applied to ordered (numbered) and unordered (bulleted) lists, The List panel of the Style definition dialog box is shown in **Figure 55**.

*List attributes are not displayed by Dreamweaver in the Document window.

The **Types*** of list attributes that apply to **Ordered Lists** (**Figure 56**) are *decimals* (1., 2., etc.) *lower-roman* (i., ii., etc.), *upper-roman* (I, II, etc.), *lower-alpha* (a., b., etc.), and *upper-alpha* (A., B., etc.).

For **unordered lists**, the **Types*** of bullets available include *discs*, *circles*, and *squares* (**Figure 57**).

You can also apply a **Bullet Image*** (**Figure 58**) to unordered lists, for which you supply an image URL. ☞ Navigator does not display bullet images.

The **Position*** of the list items applies to what the text will do when it wraps. *Inside* will indent all the text to the bullet point, while *outside* will wrap the text to the margin (**Figure 59**). ☞ Navigator does not display inside wrapping.

* Attributes with an asterisk * are not displayed properly in the Document window.

☞ Pointer items discuss how different browsers may treat an attribute.

Extensions

The attributes in the Extensions panel of the Style definition dialog box (**Figure 60**) are not supported by most browsers.

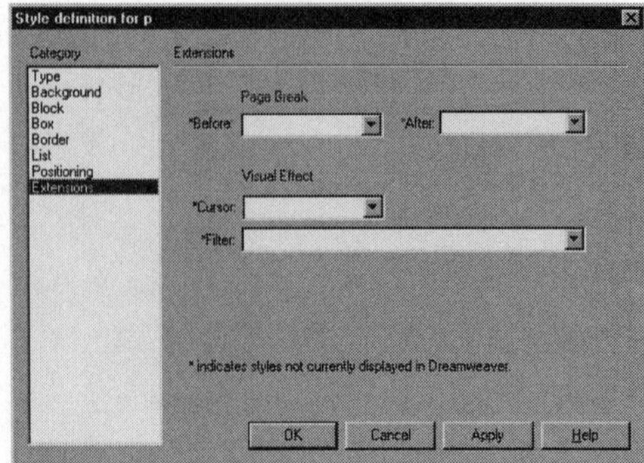

Figure 60 The Extensions panel offers extensions to the W3C style sheet specifications.

The **Page Break** extension is a proposed style attribute that is not currently supported by *any* browser. This extension will allow you to recommend a page break before or after a given style that would break the page when printing the document.

The **Cursor** extension is supported by MSIE4. When the user mouses over a style callout, the cursor (pointer) changes into an icon other than the pointer.

The **Visual Effects Filters** are *supposedly* supported by MSIE4. I had extremely mixed results using these filters, and I suggest you experiment with them rather than count on them. To apply a visual effects filter, choose it from the drop-down menu (**Figure 61**). You need to replace any question marks with values. I'm guessing that you use hex codes for colors; the units for the other values are anyone's guess, as these are not covered in the Dreamweaver manual or help files.

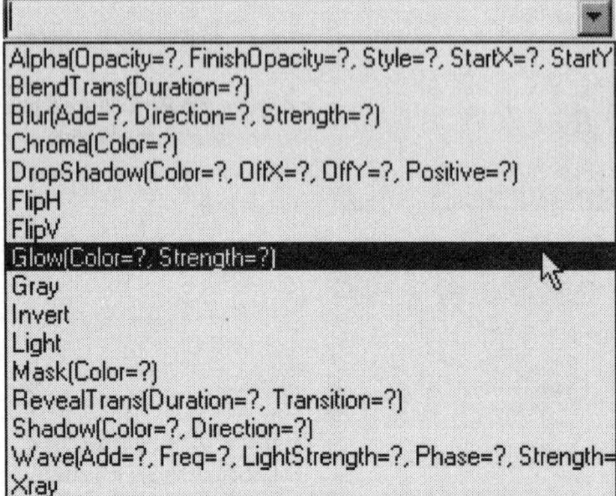

Figure 61 The visual effects filters are proprietary, unsupported gimmicks that only work in Internet Explorer.

As with all things, in style sheets and in general Web design, experimentation is the key.

LAYERS AND POSITIONING

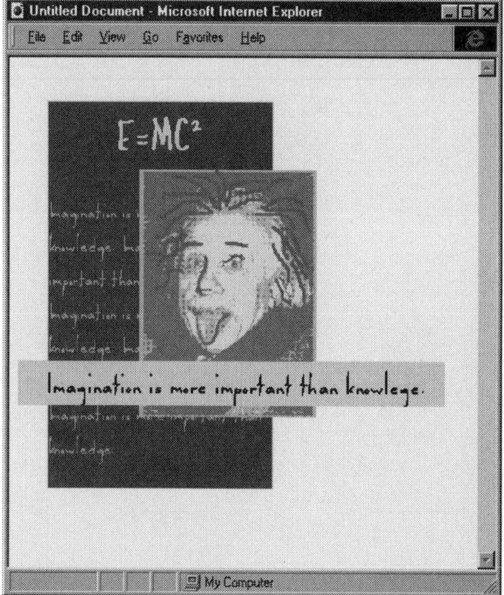

Figure 1 This little collage is made with three layers, positioned so that they overlap in the browser window. Can't do *that* with tables!

Backwards Compatibility

Dreamweaver 1.2 has a new command (File > Convert > 3.0 Browser Compatible) that allows you to save a version of pages that use layers so you retain as much of your formatting as possible when the pages are viewed using a pre-4.0 browser. For details about this feature, see the companion Web site for this book.

Layers are part of the nifty world of Cascading Style Sheets and Dynamic HTML. A layer is a container for HTML content, usually delineated by the <div> or <span> tag, that you can position anywhere on a page.

Layers are called layers because they can be positioned in three dimensions. You can set an absolute or relative location for a layer along the page's *x* and *y* axes. The third dimension is called the Z-index and allows layers to overlap one another (**Figure 1**).

Designers really love layers for their versatility: you can hide layers (through visibility), or even parts of layers (with the Z-index or with clipping areas) when a page initially loads. Then you can write a script that will cause the hidden areas to appear after a certain amount of time or when a certain user event happens (see Chapters 12 and 13 for information on Behaviors and Timelines).

✔ Tip

- Browsers that don't support layers will display the content of a layer, but will ignore most layer properties, including positioning. See Appendix C on the Web site. to find out how to accommodate older browsers.

CSS Positioning

Cascading Style Sheets Positioning, or CSS-P, allows the most specific positioning in HTML to date. Earlier methods, using tables, frames, and frame margins, don't approach the specificity you can reach with CSS-P.

You can apply CSS Positioning to a block of text, a block-type element, an image, or a layer. There are two ways to apply positioning: one is to create a style class and apply it to the selections or text blocks you want to position on the page (at which point, the object becomes a layer, for all practical purposes). The other is to create a layer in the Document window that you can modify independently of creating a style.

X and Y coordinates

A layer or other positioned element is positioned using X and Y coordinates. X and Y correspond to Left and Top. This can be the left and top of the page itself or of another parent container, such as another layer or a text block.

Layers and Animation

Dynamic HTML means that you can make layers change or move after the page is finished loading. Timelines, discussed in Chapter 13, are used to animate layers over time. The Show Layer Behavior, described in Chapter 12; and the Drag Layer Behavior, detailed on the companion Web site for this book, allow layers to change when the user performs an action.

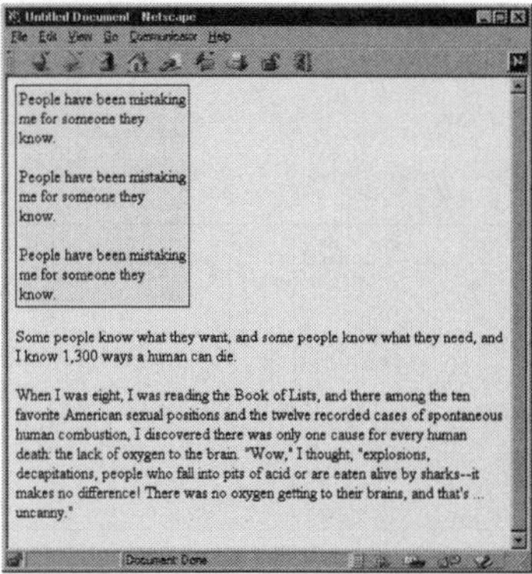

Figure 2 In static positioning, a layer can have all the layer properties you want, *except* the biggie—positioning coordinates. The layer is simply treated as a text block and thrown into the normal flow of text.

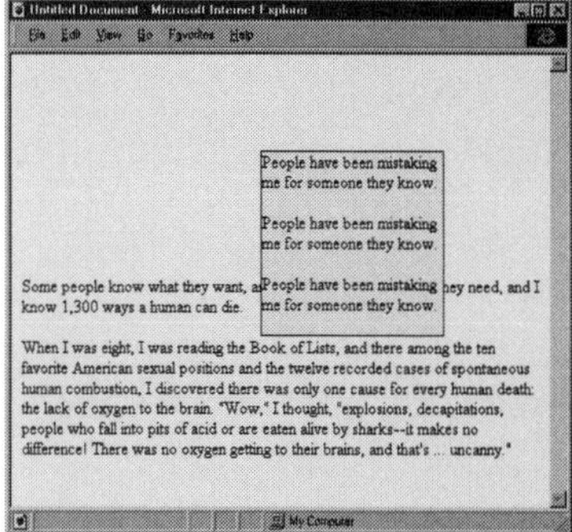

Figure 3 Relative positioning places the layer according to the specified *x* and *y* coordinates, but it still affects the flow of text on the page. I used a **<div>** tag in this instance, which causes a paragraph break after the layer. Compare this to **Figure 4**.

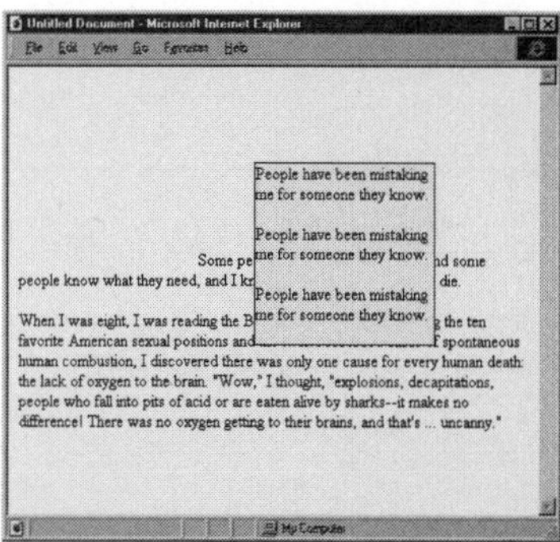

Figure 4 The code in this page is exactly the same as the code in Figure 3, except that the layer uses a **<span>** tag instead of a **<div>** tag.

Absolute vs. Relative Positioning

The position of an element in an HTML document can be either absolute, relative, or static.

Normal positioning is called *static*, and causes the element to be positioned within the normal flow of text. Specifying coordinates for static positioning does you no good, as they will be ignored (**Figure 2**).

Relative positioning means that a layer or other element is given a position relative to the top-left corner of the parent container. However, the relative element is included in the flow of the page, and is also inline—it does not automatically cause any line breaks (**Figure 3**). To guarantee the inline properties, a <span> tag should be used instead of a <div> tag (**Figure 4**).

An element, such as a layer, which is positioned *absolutely* is completely outside of the flow of the document. The regular flow of the material on the page neither contains the layer, nor is it interrupted by the layer (**Figure 5**).

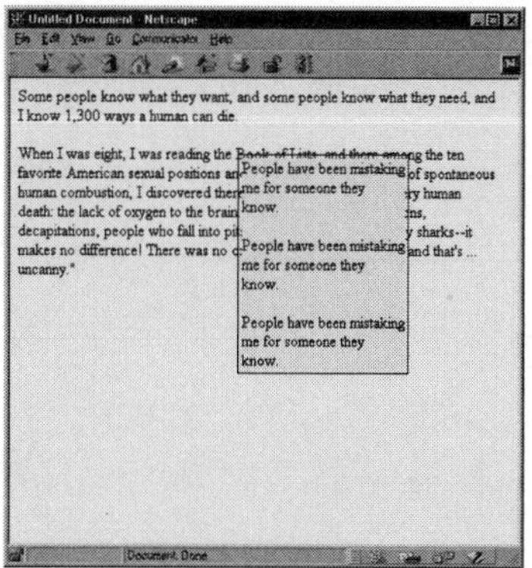

Figure 5 The layer is back to being a **<div>** now, and it's positioned absolutely. That means that the regular text flow once again starts at the top of the page, and the layer simply overlaps it.

Positioning Properties

Positioning properties can be applied to any object, but when you set these properties, the behavior of the object becomes similar to layer behavior, and Dreamweaver treats it as a layer, although the browsers may respond differently to positioned elements that are not enclosed in <div> or <span> tags.

To apply positioning to objects other than layers, create and apply a style, as described in Chapter 10, using the Positioning Properties in the Style definition dialog box (**Figure 6**).

The following properties are discussed more fully throughout this chapter in terms of layers.

Type lets you designate the positioning as *absolute*, *relative*, or *static*.

Visibility determines whether the element will be visible on load. You can declare an element as *visible* or *hidden*, or you can allow it to *inherit* its properties from the parent element.

Z-Index determines the stacking order of overlapping elements; the Z index is the third coordinate, combined with X and Y, that determines the location of the layer on the page in three dimensions. The higher the number, the higher priority the element is given (a layer with a Z-index of 3 will be stacked on top of elements with a Z-index of 1 and 2).

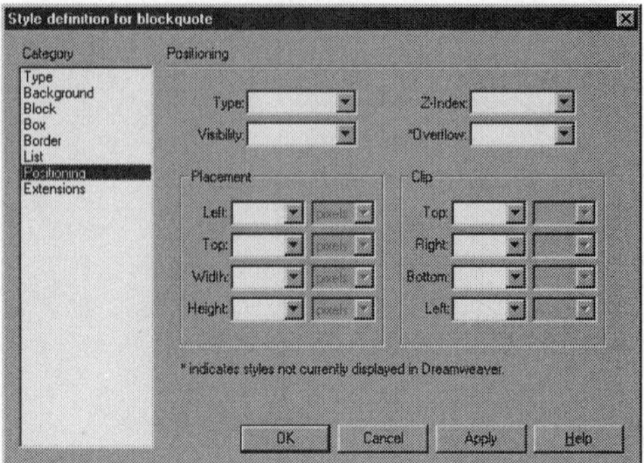

Figure 6 The Positioning Properties panel of the Style definition dialog box. I describe everything else to do with styles in Chapter 10; positioning is discussed in this chapter in terms of layers.

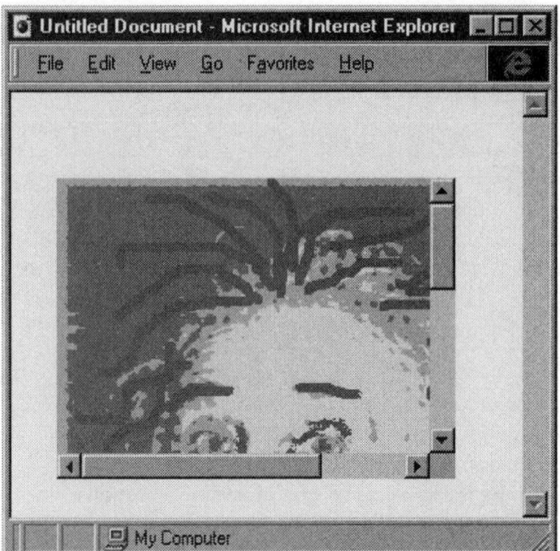

Figure 7 Internet Explorer will provide scrollbars for content that exceeds the dimensions of the layer. You can also designate this content as visible or hidden.

Figure 8 The clipping area or clipping region allows you to define which areas of the layer are visible or hidden when the page loads. In this instance, only the top half of the image is being displayed on load.

Overflow determines the behavior of the layer when the content exceeds the borders of the layer. You can designate the out-of-bounds content as *visible* or *hidden*; or the layer can be given *scrollbars* to make the rest of the content accessible (generally, *auto* also provides scrollbars) (**Figure 7**). *Overflow treatment is not displayed properly in Dreamweaver or supported by Navigator. In Navigator, overflow content is visible, even if another option is set.*

Placement of a layer is determined by its distance from the *Left* and *Top* of the parent unit. The *Width* and *Height* measurements are related to placement in that they determine the position of the lower-right corner of the layer.

Clip refers to the clipping area of the layer; the area of the layer in which content shows through (**Figure 8**). You could give a layer an area of 200 pixels by 200 pixels, and then allow only a 100x100 pixel area to show through. You set a clipping area as a rectangular area comprised of four measurements (Top, Right, Bottom, Left).

✔ Tip

- The clipping area is unrelated to overflow. Overflow is simply related to the layer's dimensions, regardless of whether a clipping region is defined.

Other CSS Attributes Related to Positioning

In Chapter 10, I described most style sheet attributes, except positioning attributes. I also relegated vertical alignment attributes to this chapter, since you'll most often use them to align text and images within a layer.

Vertical alignment attributes can be found in the Block attributes panel of the Style definition text box (**Figure 9**).

These include:

Superscript text is smaller text raised above the baseline text, as in E=mc^2. **Subscript** text dips below the baseline, as in H_2S_{04}.

The other vertical alignment options are used with text and images in combination (**Figure 10**), or with two images aligned within a parent layer.

The **baseline** is the imaginary line that text sits on. (*Descenders*, as in the letters j and g, dip below the baseline, while *ascenders*, as in the letters l and d, rise above lowercase text.) Baseline alignment makes text vertically align to the baseline of nearby text, or the bottom of an image align to the text baseline.

Top, **middle**, and **bottom** are pretty self-explanatory.

Text-top and **text-bottom** align an image or another object with the tallest ascender in the text or the lowest descender in the text, respectively.

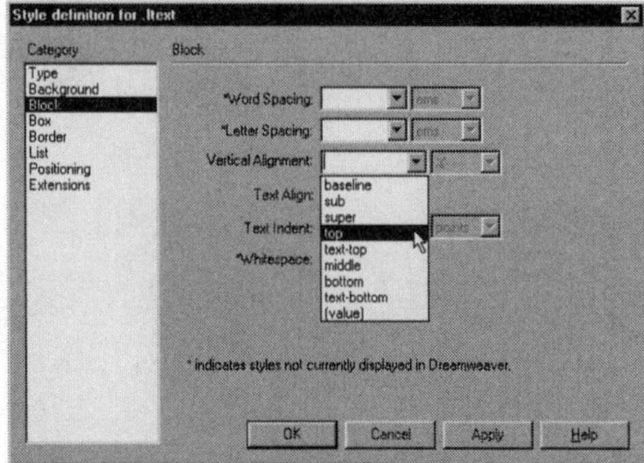

Figure 9 The Block Properties panel of the Style definition dialog box is where you apply vertical alignment attributes to text blocks or selections.

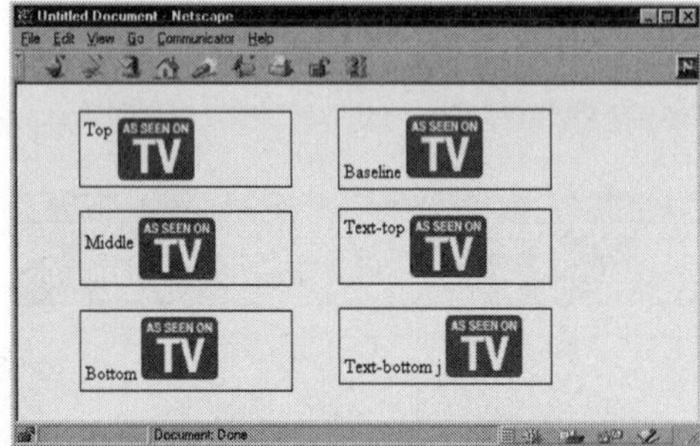

Figure 10 Vertical alignment options using styles.

✔ Tips

- Other style-sheet attributes are somewhat related to positioning, although they may position text rather than anything else. Still, here's a list for reference: All Block attributes, particularly Text Align; Line Height, which is a Text attribute; the Position List attribute, which relates to indents; and most Box attributes, particularly Float, Clear, Margins, and Padding.
- All of these style attributes are described in Chapter 10.

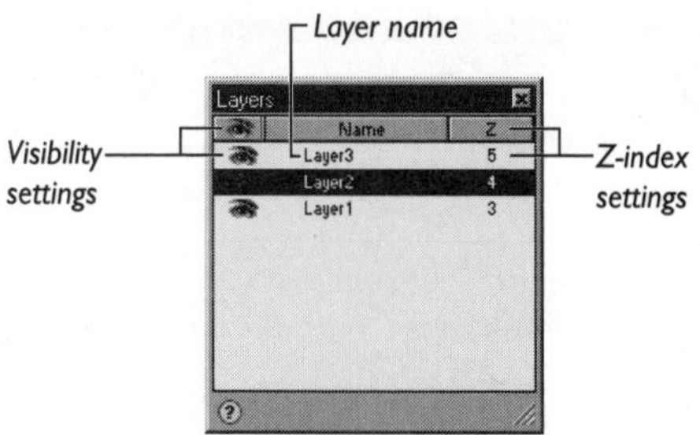

Figure 11 The Layers inspector lists all the layers on the current page.

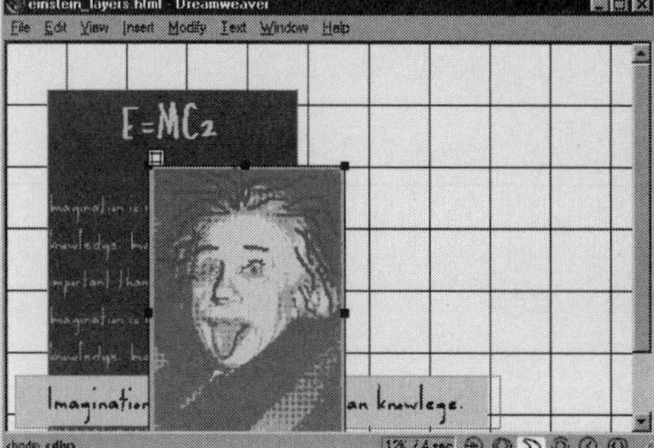

Figure 12 Viewing the grid can give you a better idea of the position of things.

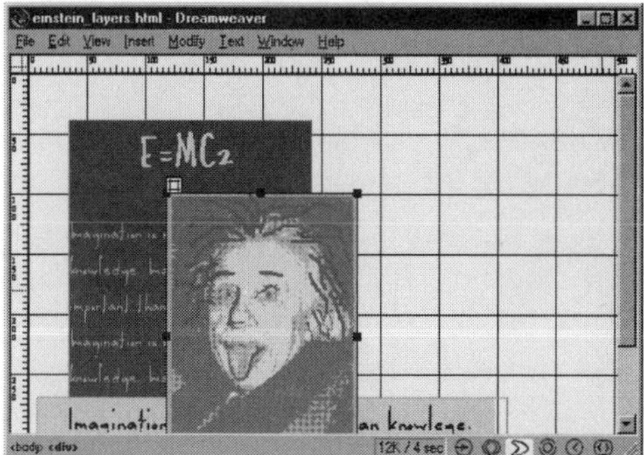

Figure 13 View the rulers, with or without the grid, when you want to measure exactly where things are.

About the Layers Inspector

The Layers inspector (**Figure 11**) lists all the layers on the current page. When you create a new layer, its name will appear in the Layers inspector.

To view the Layers inspector:

1. From the Document window menu bar, select Window > Layers.

   or

   Press F11.

Either way, the Layers inspector will appear.

About the Grid

The grid displays an incremental series of boxes that look like graph paper. You can use grid lines to guide you in positioning or resizing layers.

To view the grid:

1. From the Document window menu bar, select View > Grid > Show.

The grid will appear (**Figure 12**).

About the Rulers

The rulers can be displayed along the top and left of the Document window to guide you in positioning and resizing layers.

To view the rulers:

1. From the Document window menu bar, select View > Rulers > Show.

The rulers will appear (**Figure 13**).

✔ Tip

- I discuss changing the preferences, snap-to settings, and units of the grid and rulers in the section of Chapter 1 called *Customizing the Document Window.*

Creating Layers

Before you can dig your fingers into all the nifty layer features, you need to put a layer on the page. You can insert a layer using the Object palette, in which case you draw the layer on the page; or you can use the Insert menu, which places a default layer. In either case, you can modify the layer's size and location after placing it.

✔ Tip

- You can modify the default layer properties. See the section called *Dreamweaver's Layer Preferences*, near the end of this chapter.

To place a layer using the Insert menu:

1. From the Document window menu bar, select Insert > Layer.

A layer will appear at the top-left corner of the Document window (**Figure 14**).

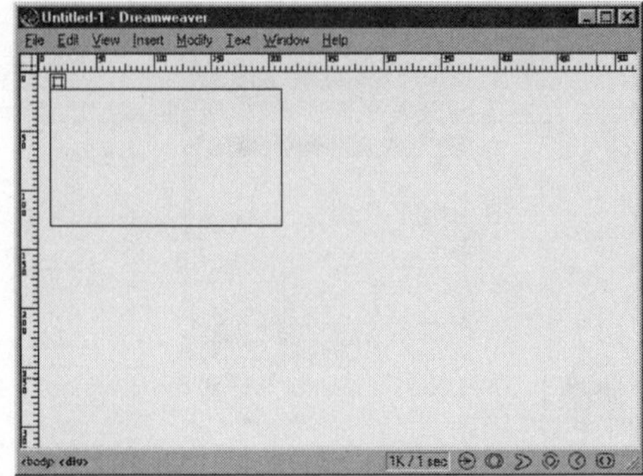

Figure 14 When you place a layer using the Insert menu, a default layer appears. You can change the properties of this layer after placing it.

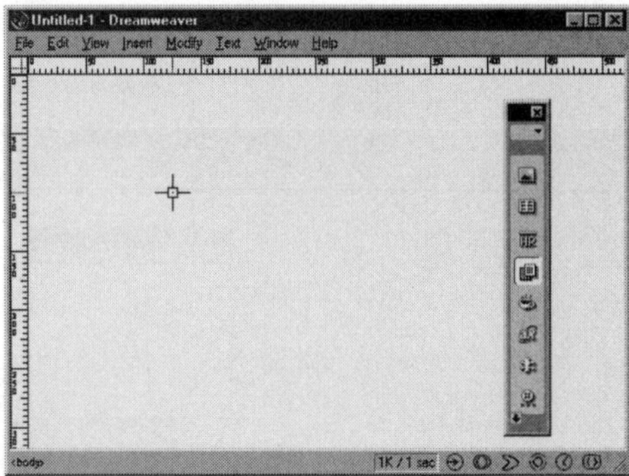

Figure 15 After you click on the Insert Marquee Layer button, the pointer will turn into crosshairs you can use to draw the layer.

Figure 16 After you draw a layer, it appears exactly where you positioned it. A layer marker also appears in the window, indicating the layer's location in the code.

To place a layer using the Object palette:

1. View the Object palette, if necessary, by selecting View > Objects from the Document window menu bar.
2. Click on the Insert Marquee Layer button: . The cursor will appear as crosshairs in the Document window (**Figure 15**).
3. Click the cursor at the point where you want the top-left corner of the layer to begin, and drag the cursor to where you want the bottom-right corner to be.
4. Let go of the mouse button, and a layer will appear in the Document window (**Figure 16**).

Along with the layer, a layer marker will appear that shows where the layer's code appears within the code of the page.

✔ Tip

- If the layer markers aren't visible, view them by selecting View > Invisible Elements. You can toggle the markers on and off this way as often as you choose.

Selecting Layers

In order to delete, move, or resize a layer, you need to select it. Clicking within a layer does not select it automatically. There are several ways you can select a layer.

To select a layer:

1. Click on the layer.
2. Click on the layer's selection handle at the top, left of the layer (**Figure 17**).

   or

   Click on the name of the layer in the Layers inspector.

   or

   Alt-click (Option-click) within the layer.

   or

   Click on the layer's marker in the Document window.

   or

   Click on the layer's tag (<span>, <div>, <layer>, or <ilayer>) in the tag selector at the left of the Document window's status bar (**Figure 17**).

Eight points, called handles, will appear on the edges of the layer (**Figure 18**), and the name of the layer will become selected in the Layers inspector. And, of course, our good old friend the Properties inspector will display Layer properties (**Figure 19**).

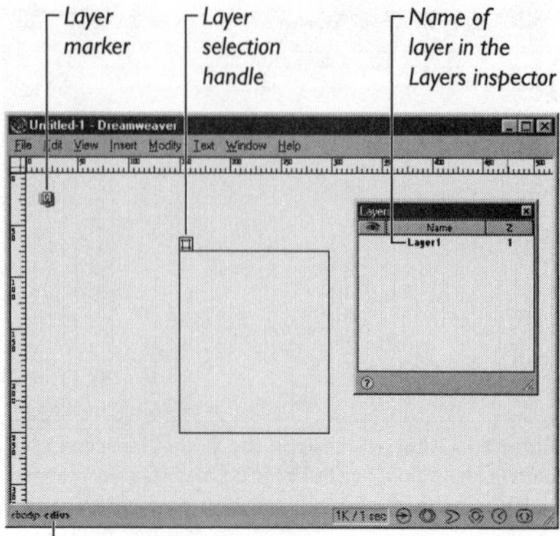

Figure 17: To select a layer, you can click on the layer's selection handle; the layer marker in the Document window, the **<div>** or **<span>** tag in the tag selector; or the layer's name in the Layers inspector.

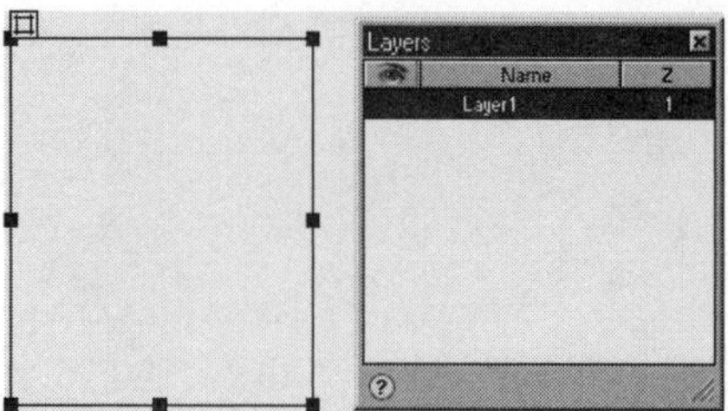

Figure 18 When a layer is selected, eight handles will appear around the borders of the layer, and its name will appear highlighted in the Layers inspector.

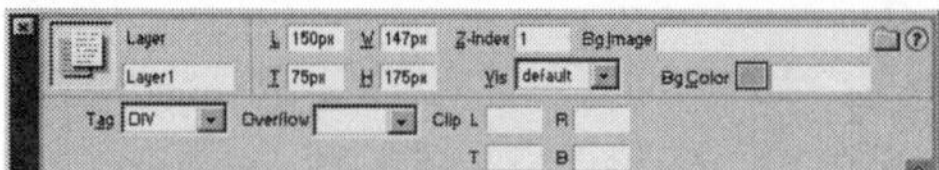

Figure 19 The Properties inspector, displaying Layer properties.

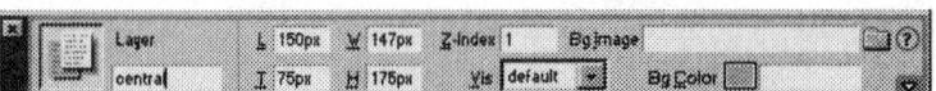

Figure 20 Type a new name for your layer in the Properties inspector's Layer text box.

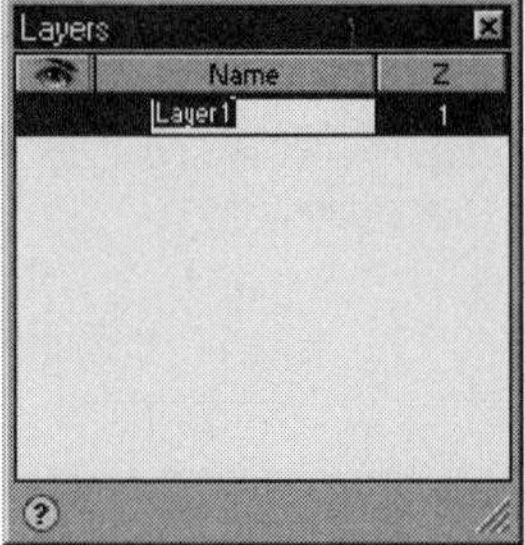

Figure 21 Type a new name for your layer in the Layers inspector.

Deleting a Layer

When a layer is selected, you can delete it if you choose.

To delete a layer:

1. Select the layer.
2. Press the Delete or Backspace key.

The layer will go away.

Renaming a Layer

Layer names are used by the browser and by any scripts which treat the layer as a script object. By default, Dreamweaver names each successive layer "Layer1," Layer2," and so on.

You may want to give your layers more meaningful names.

To rename a layer:

1. Select the layer.
2. In the Properties inspector, select the old layer name and delete it (**Figure 20**).

   or

   In the Layers inspector, click on the name of the layer and hold down the mouse button. The row holding the name of the layer will become highlighted, and the name of the layer will appear in a text box.
3. Type the name of the layer in the text box (**Figure 21**).

The layer will be renamed.

Choosing Tags

There are four tags used in creating layers. The <div> and <span> tags create what is called a marquee layer. The <div> tag is more closely associated with absolute positioning; a paragraph break surrounds the <div> tag. If you prefer to create a layer that's inline, without paragraph breaks, then you want to use the <span> tag, which works well with relative positioning.

To change tags:

1. Select the layer.
2. In the Properties inspector, choose either <div> or <span> from the Tag drop-down menu (**Figure 22**).

The tag will change to reflect your choice.

✔ Tip

- The other available tags, <layer> and <ilayer>, are Netscape tags. I discuss those in the section called *Netscape's Layer Tags*, near the end of this chapter.

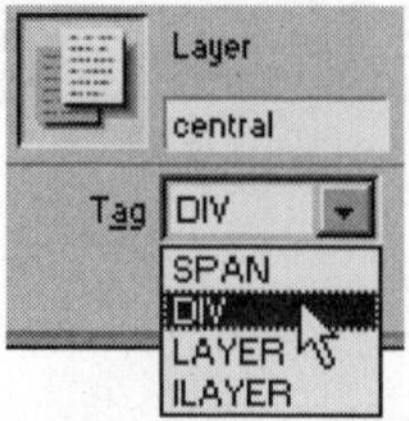

Figure 22 You can change tags by clicking on the Tag drop-down menu in the Properties inspector.

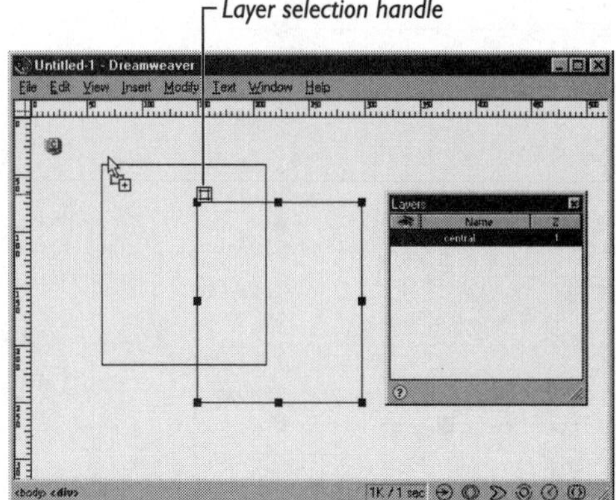

Figure 23 Click on the layer's selection handle and drag it to a new location.

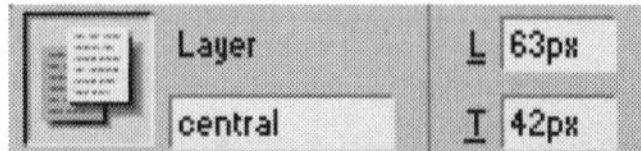

Figure 24 Type the X and Y (Left and Top) coordinates in the Properties inspector's L and T text boxes.

Moving Layers

The location of a layer on the page is measured by its distance from the top-left corner of the page or the parent layer, to the top-left corner of the layer itself. You can change the location of a layer at any point—before or after you put content in it.

To change the layer's location by dragging:

1. Select the layer.
2. Click on the layer's selection handle and drag it to its new location.

   or

   Use the arrow keys to move the layer in one-pixel increments.

✔ Tip

- To move the layer using the grid's snapping increment, select the layer and hold down the Shift key while using the arrow keys to move the layer.

To change a layer's location using the Properties inspector:

1. View the Properties inspector, if necessary.
2. Select the layer.
3. In the properties inspector, type the distance of the layer from the left margin in the L text box, and the distance of the layer from the top margin in the T text box (**Figure 24**).
4. Press Enter (Return), or click on the Apply button.

The layer will change position on the page.

Resizing Layers

You can change the height and width of a layer at any time, before or after you add content to the layer. You can resize a layer by clicking and dragging, by using the keyboard, or by using the Properties inspector.

To resize a layer by dragging:

1. Select the layer. The handles will appear.
2. To change both the height and width of the layer, click on one of the corner handles and drag it (**Figure 25**).

   To change only one of the dimensions, click on one of the side handles and drag it (**Figure 26**).

When you let go of the mouse button, the layer will be resized.

To resize a layer using the keyboard:

1. Select the layer.
2. To resize by eyeballing it, press Ctrl+arrow (Option+arrow).

   To resize using the grid's snapping increment, press Shift+Ctrl+arrow (Shift+Option+arrow).

✔ Tip

- To find out how to change the grid settings, refer to the section in Chapter 1 called *Customizing the Document Window*.

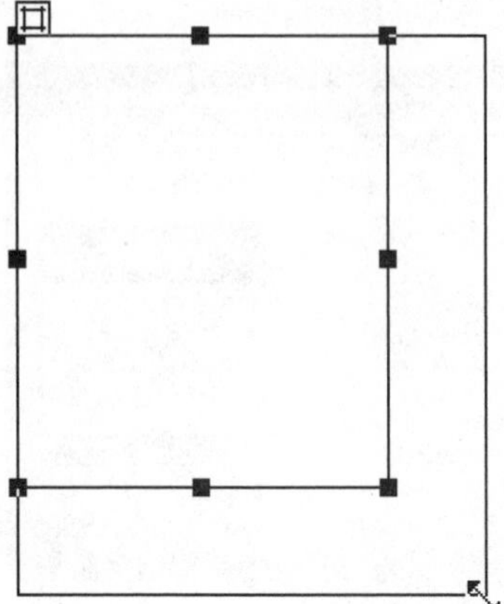

Figure 25 Click on a corner handle and drag it to resize two sides of a layer at once.

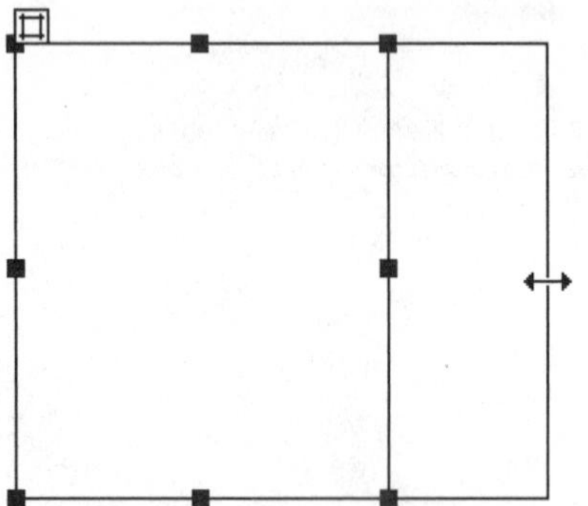

Figure 26 Click on a side handle and drag it to move one side of a layer.

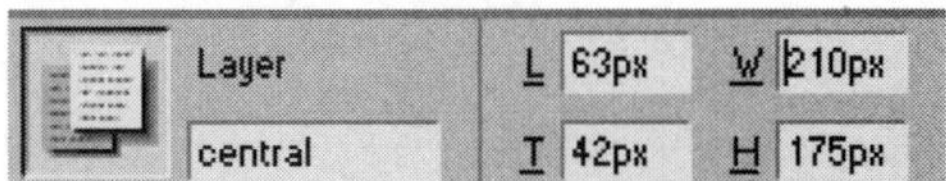

Figure 27 You can type new dimensions for your layer in the W(idth) and H(eight) text boxes in the Properties inspector.

To resize a layer using the Properties inspector:

1. View the Properties inspector, if necessary.
2. Select the layer.
3. In the Properties inspector, type the width of the layer in the W text box, and the height of the layer in the H text box (**Figure 27**).
4. Press Enter (Return), or click on the Apply button.

✔ Tip

- You cannot resize a layer so that it's smaller than the content it contains without changing the layer's clipping area (see the section called *The Clipping Area*, later in this chapter).

Nesting and Overlapping Layers

The neato thing about layers is that you can put a layer within a layer, or you can create two layers that overlap.

To overlap two or more layers:

All you need to do is move two layers so that they overlap, or create a layer which shares page area with another layer (**Figure 28**).

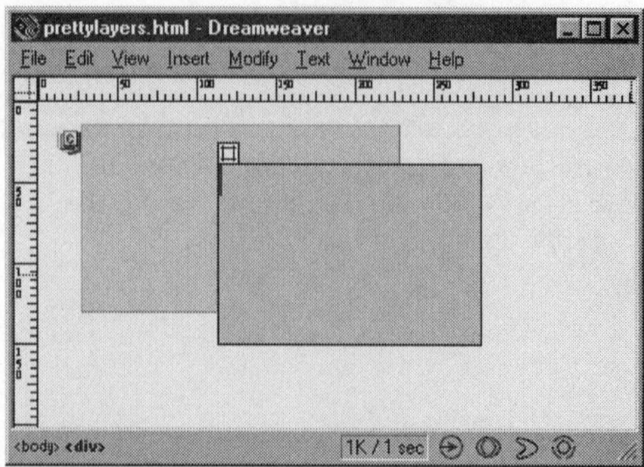

Figure 28 Two overlapping layers.

To nest a layer within a layer:

1. Create the first layer.
2. Click to place the insertion point within the existing layer.
3. Create a second layer inside the first (**Figure 29**).

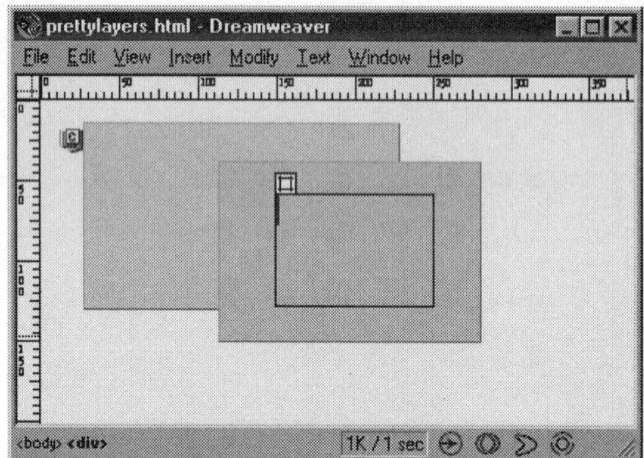

Figure 29 I drew one layer nested inside the other.

The Layers inspector will display nested layers indented beneath the name of the layer that contains them (**Figure 30**).

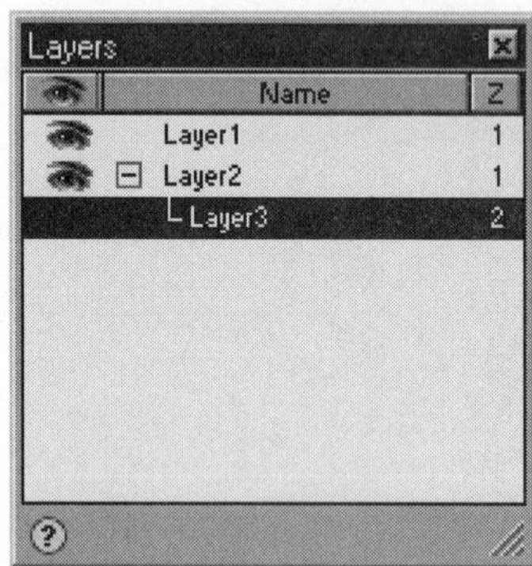

Figure 30 The Layers inspector displays nested layers indented beneath their parent layer.

✔ Tip

- If you draw the layer, you may have to hold down the Ctrl (Command) key while you're drawing in order for the layers to be nested. See the section on *Dreamweaver's Layer Preferences* for more details.

To nest two existing layers:

1. In the Layers inspector, click on the name of the layer you wish to nest inside another layer. A layer icon will appear.
2. Drag the name of the layer on top of the name of the parent layer. A box will appear around the name of the new parent.
3. Let go of the mouse button. The name of the layer you dragged will appear indented beneath the name of the new parent.

You may decide that you don't want one layer to be nested inside the other.

To un-nest a layer:

1. Click on the layer's name in the Layers inspector.
2. Drag the layer's name so that it's no longer indented beneath the parent layer's name.

✔ Tips

- A layer that contains one or more additional layers is called a *parent layer*.
- In the Layers inspector, you can collapse or expand the list of layers that are nested within the layer. Just click on the + sign next to the parent layer's name to expand the list, or the – sign to collapse the list.
- When you're working with nested layers, the easiest way to select a layer is to click on its name.
- You can also determine the stacking order of layers by dragging their names around. To find out about stacking order, refer to the section called *Stacking Order*, later in this chapter.

Changing Layer Visibility

When you're working on a page with lots of layers, you may want to show or hide various layers depending on what area of the page you're working with. This is especially convenient when you're working with overlapping or nested layers.

Layer visibility also determines whether a layer will be visible when a page loads.

The layer's visibility is determined by its "eyeball status" in the Layers inspector. The eyeball is a three-way toggle switch:

- A closed eyeball means the layer is hidden.
- An open eyeball means the layer is visible.
- No eyeball means that the layer's visibility is determined by the status of the parent layer, if any.

To show or hide a layer:

1. In the Layers inspector, click on the name of the layer you wish to view or hide.
2. Click within the leftmost column to change the eyeball status: closed, open, or none.

The layers will appear or disappear, as indicated by the eyeball (**Figure 31**).

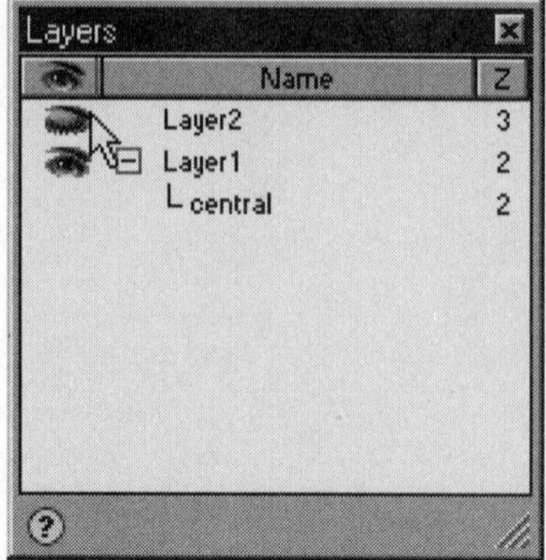

Figure 31 You can set the visibility of each layer individually by changing the status of the eyeball in the visibility column.

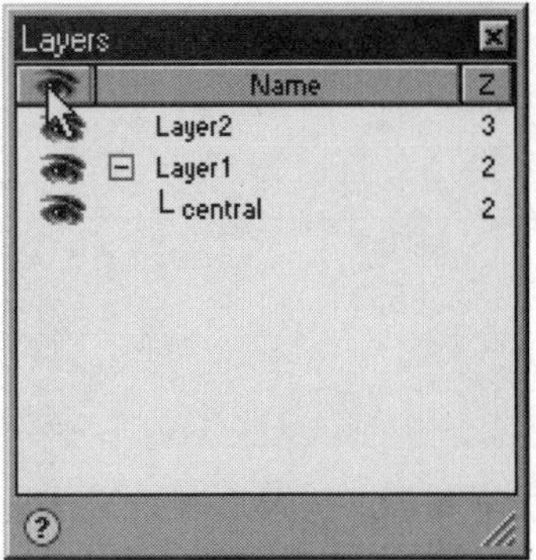

Figure 32 Click on the eyeball button at the top of the visibility column to show or hide all layers at once.

To show or hide all layers:

1. Click on the eyeball button at the top of the leftmost column in the Layers inspector (**Figure 32**).

All the layers will appear with an open eyeball, or disappear with a closed eyeball.

✔ Tips

- Layer visibility is not used simply in working with Dreamweaver; hidden layers will not appear on the page when viewed in the browser window.
- You can use hidden layers with Timelines or Behaviors (see Chapter 12), so that layers become visible over time, or when certain actions are performed.

Stacking Order

The stacking order, or Z-index, of layers, determines the order in which the browser will draw them, as well as their stacking priority (**Figures 33–35**).

✔ Tip

- While Dreamweaver uses the term "stacking order" to describe the Z-index, that doesn't mean that it's an exclusive scale. If you have three layers on different parts of the page, you can make the Z-index 1 for all of them.
- If two layers with the same Z-index (or with no Z-index specified) overlap, the first layer listed in the code will be placed on the top of the heap.

Figure 33 The little person has the highest Z-index in this cheesy little montage.

Figure 34 In Figure 33, the person had a Z-index of 3, and the text banner had a Z-index of 2. In this figure, the text banner has the highest Z-index.

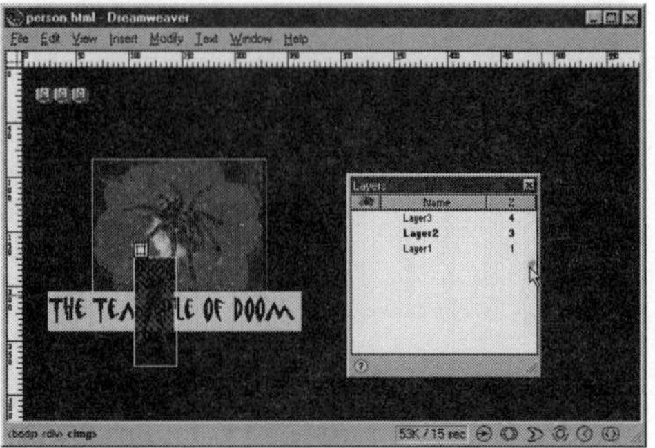

Figure 35 This is what the carnage looks like in Dreamweaver.

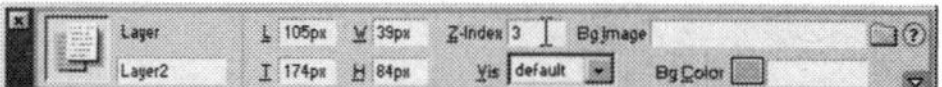

Figure 36 You can set the Z-index by typing a number in the Properties inspector's Z-index text box.

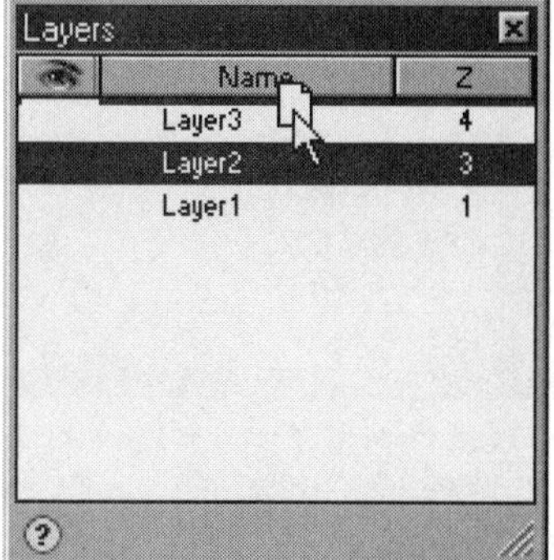

Figure 37 You can move the order of the layers in the Z-index by dragging their names in the Layers palette.

You can change a layer's Z-index individually or you can determine the stacking order of all the layers in the Layers inspector.

To change the Z-index of a single layer:

1. Display the Properties inspector, if necessary, by selecting Window > Properties from the Document window menu bar.
2. Select the layer.
3. In the Properties inspector, type a Z-index for the layer: the bigger the number, the higher the priority (a Z-index of 2 goes on top of a Z-index of 1).

To rearrange the stacking order in the Layers inspector:

1. Click on the names of a layer in the Layers inspector, and drag it up or down to change its position (**Figure 37**).

The first layer listed in the Layers palette (and therefore, listed first in the code) has the highest priority in the stacking order, and so on down the line.

✔ Tips

- Take care not to drag the layer's name onto the name of another layer; this will indent one layer beneath the other and thereby nest the layers (see the section on *Nesting and Overlapping Layers*, earlier in this chapter).
- The Layers inspector may renumber the Z-index strangely when you drag layers; you might start out with index numbers of 3, 2, and 1 and end up with 6, 4, and 1. You can reset these in the Properties inspector, if you want.

Content and Layers

A layer can hold nearly any other kind of HTML content: text, images, tables, forms, multimedia content, and, as discussed, other layers.

To add content to a layer, click on the layer so that the insertion point appears within it, and then add your content as you would to any other part of a Web page (**Figure 38**).

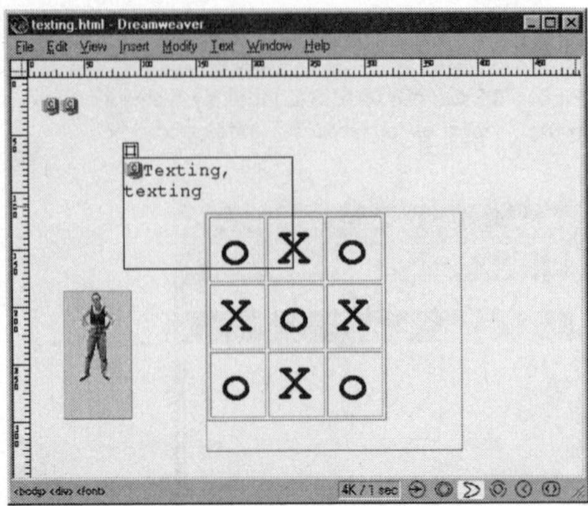

Figure 38 You can add any kind of content you want to a layer. Here we've added a table, some text, and an image to the various layers on this page. Just about the only thing you can't put in a layer is a frame.

✔ Tip

- You can drag content from outside a layer to within the layer's borders. Just select the object you wish to move, hold down the mouse button, and drag it within the borders of the layer.
- You can put nearly anything in a layer, except a frame. You can put a form in a layer, but you cannot spread out form content over more than one layer.
- If a layer contains less content than the layer's borders would indicate, Navigator displays only the content (not the entire layer), but the layer's dimensions will still be considered in the layout. Explorer displays the entire layer dimensions, regardless of the content (**Figure 39**).

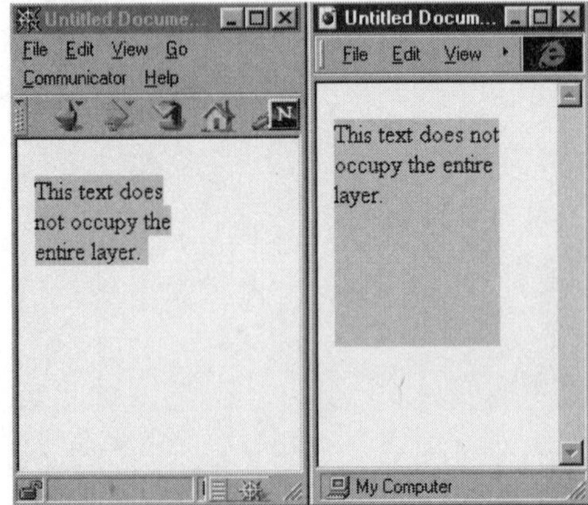

Figure 39 Navigator (on the left) only displays the part of the layer that contains content, not the entire layer.

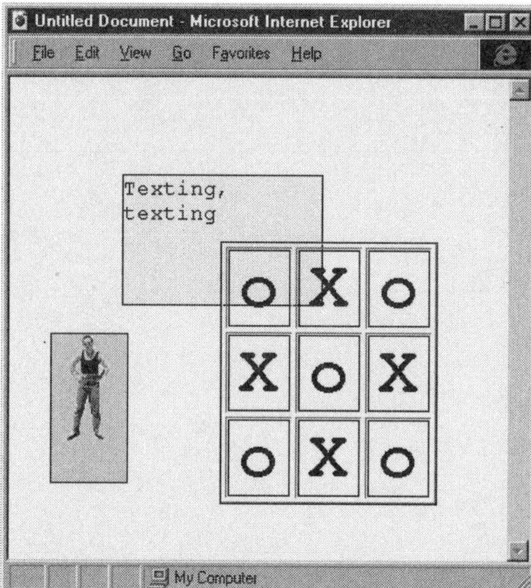

Figure 40 On this page, I redefined the <div> tag using style sheets so that all layers made with the <div> tag would have a one-pixel-wide black border.

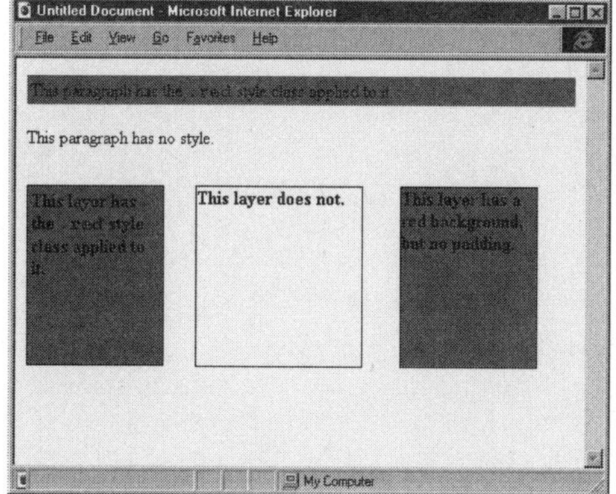

Figure 41 On this page, I assigned the .red class to the first paragraph and to the first of the three boxes. The third box has a red background color, but it is not modified by the .red class.

Layers and Styles

All the nifty style sheet attributes that I discussed in Chapter 10 can be applied to layers—not just positioning.

When you create a layer in Dreamweaver, the style attributes that guide the layer's behavior generally appear directly within the <div> tag (rather than as a class or tag redefinition, in which case the attributes would appear in the <style> area of the <head> tag).

You can, as I discussed in Chapter 10, redefine the <div> or <span> tag so that it attains new properties that will be applied to every layer you create using those tags (**Figure 40**).

You can also create a style class that you can apply to a layer by selecting the <div> or <span> tag and then applying the class to the tag (**Figure 41**).

Or, let's say you were playing along at home by following up your experiments with styles in Chapter 10 by viewing the source code and learning how to write style sheets on your own. You can type additional styles into the code for your layers.

Layer code—pre-content—might look something like this:

```
<div id="Layer2" style="position:absolute;
left:23px; top:155px; width:358px; height:33px;
z-index:2; background-color: #FFCC33">

</div>
```

All that stuff in the <div> tag is style sheet code. You can apply as many additional style attributes to a layer as you want.

The Clipping Area

Layers are somewhat like table cells in that they expand to fit the content you put in them. While you can specify an exact size for a layer, it will expand beyond those dimensions if you place larger content in it.

A layer is unlike a table cell, however, in that you can specify a clipping area for it. As I mentioned earlier, the clipping area is the part of the layer that is visible; it's somewhat like cropping an image, only the rest of the content remains hidden rather than being deleted out of the file. (The file size of clipped content remains the same as if you hadn't clipped it.)

✔ Tip

- To find out more about what you can do with content that exceeds a layer's dimensions, see the section called Content Overflow, later in this chapter.

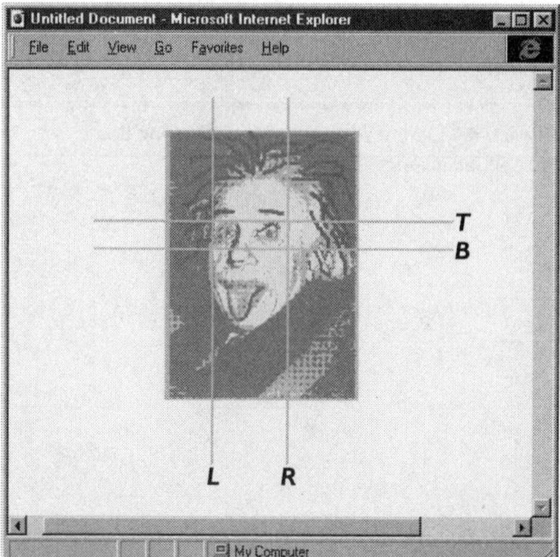

Figure 42 Clipping explained: The layer is the same size as the image. Lines T and B are measured from the top of the layer. T is 70 pixels from the top, and B is 96 pixels from the top. Lines L and R are measured from the left of the layer. Line L is 30 pixels from the left, and Line R is 101 pixels from the left. The rectangular area framed by these lines is what will be left visible. (I drew these lines; you're not going to see them when you clip a layer.)

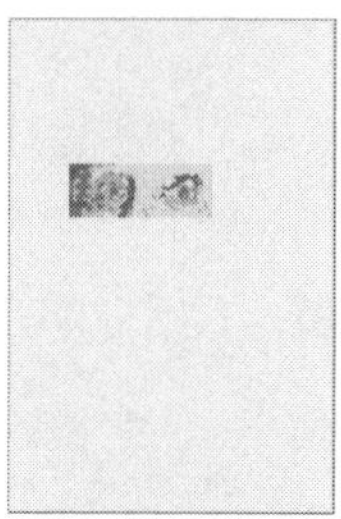

Figure 43: The layer as it looks post-clip (in Dreamweaver, so you can see the outlines of the layer).

You can make your clipping area the same size as the layer's area, or smaller than those dimensions. (You could make it larger, but that kind of defeats the purpose of having a layer of that size.)

✔ Tips:

- In the Clip area of the Properties inspector, you specify four measurements: L (Left), T (Top), R (Right), and B (Bottom).
- The L and R measures are from the left edge of the layer, and the T and B measures are from the top edge of the layer (**Figure 42**).
- The clipping occurs as follows: The area from the left margin of the layer to the L measurement is clipped out, and the area from the R measurement to the right margin is also clipped out. The area between L and R, therefore, is visible. The same goes for T and B, respectively (**Figure 43**).
- Unspecified units are in pixels; you define other units in the following format: `1.5cm` (no space between the number and the unit).

To define the clipping area:

1. Display the Properties inspector and expand it so that all the properties are displayed, if necessary.
2. Select the layer.
3. Define the clipping area by typing the numbers that define the region in the T, L, R, and B text boxes (**Figure 44**).
4. Press Enter (Return), or click on the Apply button to apply the changes to the layer.

The area defined by the clipping area will be visible, and the rest will be hidden.

✔ Navigator vs. Explorer Tips:

- For Navigator, you can define all four of these areas, or you can define only the bottom and right (the top and left will be set to zero, which is the top-left margin of the layer.)
- For Explorer, however, you *must* indicate a measurement of zero for the top and left, if that's what you want.

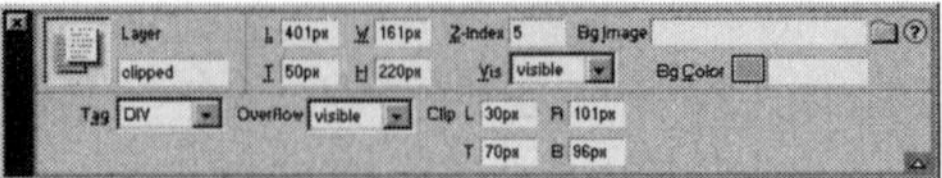

Figure 44 Define your clipping area using the Properties inspector.

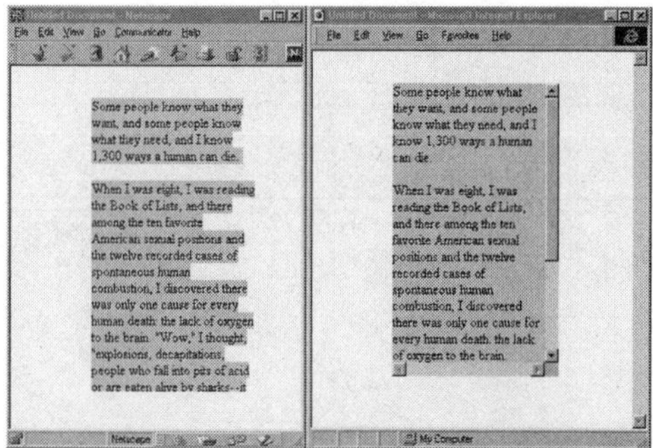

Figure 45 Navigator (left) displaying the hidden setting, and Explorer displaying the scroll setting for the same layer.

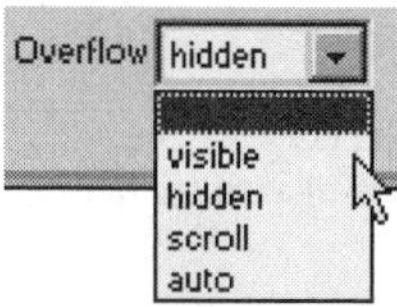

Figure 46 Select a content overflow setting from the Overflow drop-down menu on the Properties inspector.

Content Overflow

When the content of a layer is larger than the layer's dimensions (independent of the layer's clipping area), you have what is called *content overflow*.

You can let the browser defaults take care of content overflow in their own ways, or you can set one of three properties for content overflow: *hidden*, *visible*, or *scroll*. The last option adds scrollbars to the layer so that users can scroll to see the rest of the layer's content (**Figure 45**).

To control content overflow:

1. Select the layer.
2. In the Properties inspector, choose *hidden*, *visible*, or *scroll* from the Overflow drop-down menu (**Figure 46**).
3. Click on the Apply button.

Dreamweaver doesn't display content overflow—it always displays all the contents of the layer, regardless of whether they exceed the layer's dimensions.

✔ Tips

- If you don't choose a setting (if you leave the drop-down menu blank), the browser will display all the contents of the layer, regardless of the layer's dimensions.
- The *auto* setting translates as *hidden* in Navigator and *scroll* in Explorer.
- Navigator 4 does not support the *scroll* setting.

Setting a Background

Layers, like tables, table cells, and CSS text blocks, can have their own background colors or background images. Layer backgrounds will be layered over other background colors or images on the page (**Figure 47**).

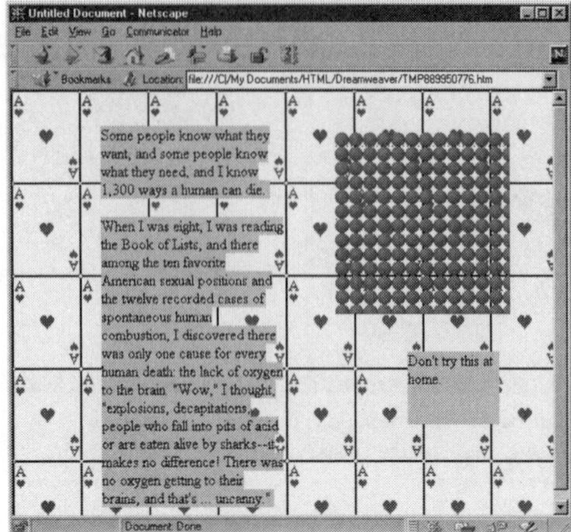

Figure 47 This self-consciously ugly page has a background image, over which the three layers are superimposed. In the layer at the upper right, the background image is a transparent GIF through which the background of the page shows.

To set a layer background color:

1. Select the layer.
2. In the Properties inspector, type a hex code or color name in the Color text box.

   or

   Click on the Color button to pop open the Colors palette, and choose a color by clicking on it (**Figure 48**).

   or

   In the Color selection menu, click on the Colors palette button to open the Colors dialog box.

✔ Tip

- For information about using the Colors text box, see Chapter 2.

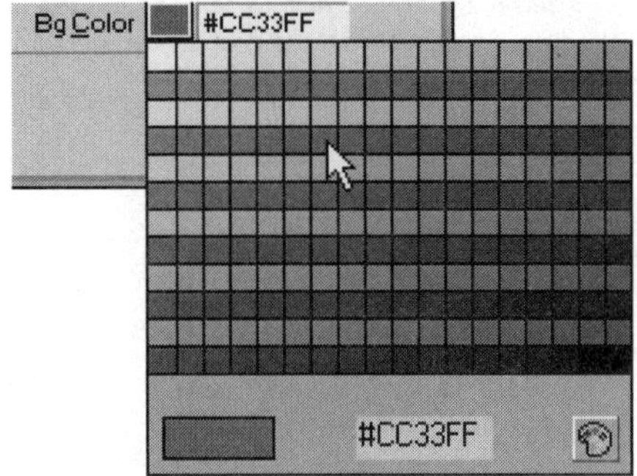

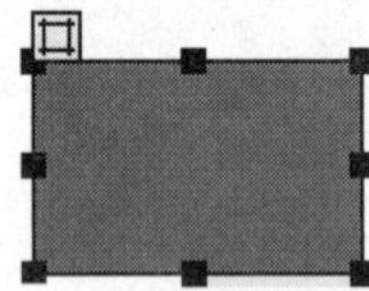

Figure 48 You can set a layer background color by clicking on the Color button and choosing a browser-safe color from the Colors palette.

To set a layer background image:

1. Select the layer.
2. In the Properties inspector, type the URL of the background image in the Bg image text box.

   or

   Click on the folder icon to open the Select Image File dialog box. Browse through the files and folders on your computer until you find the image file you want to use; then click on Open to select the file.

✔ Tip

- You can apply additional attributes to a background image using Style Sheets. See the section of Chapter 10 called *Background Attributes.*

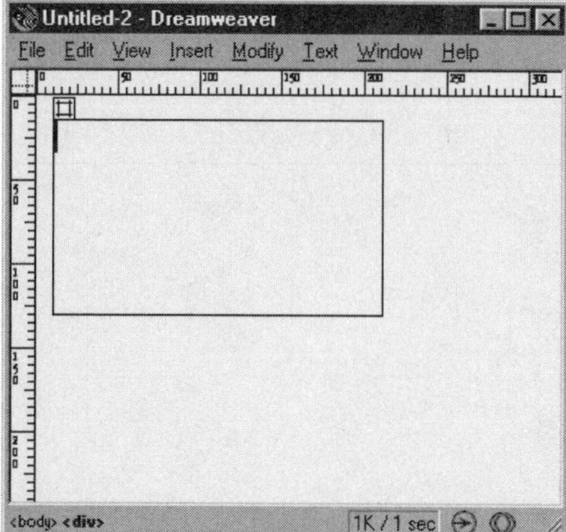

Figure 49 A default layer placed using the menu command Insert > Layer.

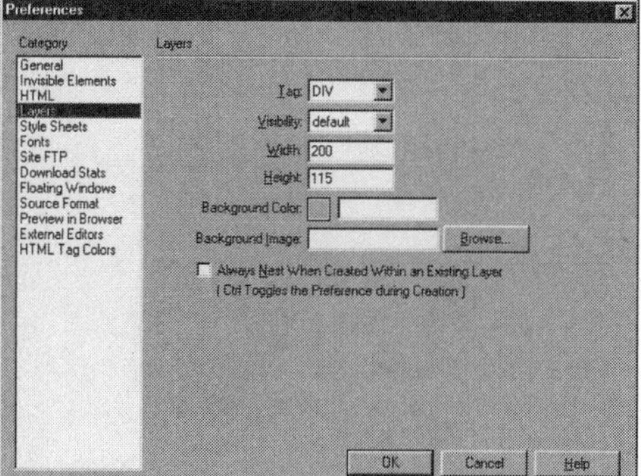

Figure 50 The Layers panel of the Preferences dialog box.

Dreamweaver's Layer Preferences

When you insert a layer using the Insert menu, Dreamweaver plunks down a default layer whose properties you can then adjust (**Figure 49**). Of course, Dreamweaver being so clever, you can adjust those default properties, too. All the default properties except size properties will also be applied to layers you draw using the Insert Marquee Layer button on the Object palette.

To set default layer properties:

1. From the Document window menu bar, select Edit > Preferences. The Preferences dialog box will appear.
2. In the Category list box at the left of the dialog box, click on Layers. The Layers panel of the dialog box will appear (**Figure 50**).
3. You can decide whether to use a <div>, <span>, <layer>, or <ilayer> tag for your layers by default. To change the default, choose one of these options from the Tag drop-down menu.
4. By default, visibility of the layers is controlled by the activity on the page. To make all layers visible or hidden by default, choose one of those options from the Visibility drop-down menu. You can also choose Inherit to have nested layers inherit their visibility from their parents.
5. The dimensions of a default layer are 200x115 pixels. To change these, type new dimensions in the Width and Height text boxes.

6. You can set a default background color or image for all new layers. Set these attributes as described in the section called *Setting a Background*.

7. The last option, when checked, makes all overlapping layers nested by default.

8. When you're all hunky-dory with your choices, click on OK to close the Preferences dialog box. Your choices will be applied to your next new layer.

✔ Tip

- You can toggle the automatic nesting of layers on and off by holding down the Ctrl (Command) key.

Figure 51 An Ilayer (inline layer) nested within a Layer.

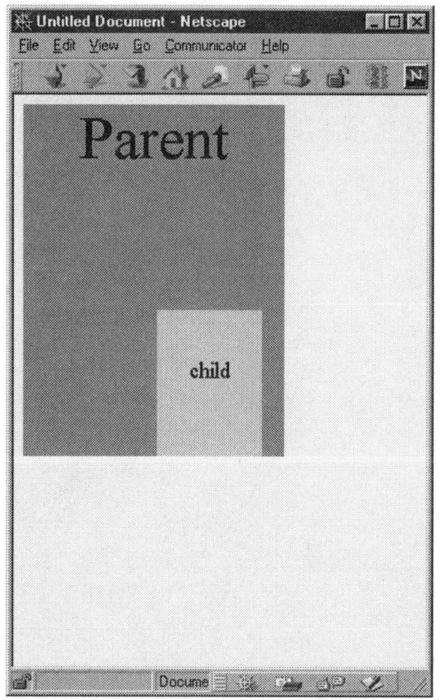

Figure 52 A Layer nested within a Layer.

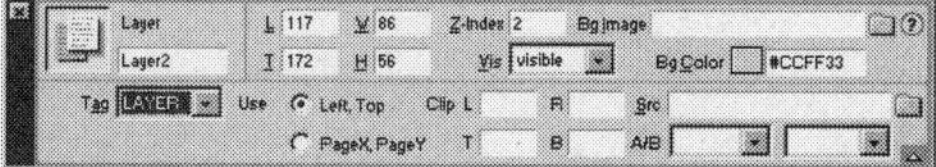

Figure 53: The Properties inspector displays extra options for Layer and Ilayer tags.

Netscape's Layer Tags

While layers are normally created by applying positioning attributes to <div> and <span> tags, the concept of layers is named after two proprietary tags introduced by Netscape with its first beta release of Navigator 4.

The <layer> and <ilayer> tags act similarly to CSS-P layers, although they also possess a few additional properties. The **<ilayer>** tag is for inline layers, which are embedded in the parent layer (**Figure 51**). You can also nest two layer tags; nesting behavior is somewhat different with Netscape Layers (**Figure 52**).

Neither the <layer> nor <ilayer> tag is supported by Explorer. Their behavior in Dreamweaver is vaguely related to the way they appear in Navigator.

To create a Layer or Ilayer:

1. Create a layer as you normally would.
2. With the layer selected, choose Layer or Ilayer from the Tag drop-down menu in the Properties inspector.

The marquee layer will become a Layer or Ilayer, and the Properties inspector will display additional properties for the layer (**Figure 53**).

Additional Netscape Layer Properties

The additional properties of Netscape's <layer> and <ilayer> tags are as follows:

When you're nesting two Netscape Layers, you can choose between two x-y relationships for the two layers. **Top, Left** refers to the regular relationship a nested layer's position has to the top-left corner of its parent layer. Choosing **PageX, PageY** instead changes a nested layer's location so that it relates to the top-left corner of the page rather than to the parent layer. (Your mileage may vary.)

Netscape Layers can also have a relative Z-index relationship. You can position a layer as appearing **Above** or **Below** a "sibling" layer—that is, a layer that shares a parent container, whether that's a parent layer or the page itself. Both layers must already exist when you create above and below settings.

✔ Tips

- When working with nested layers, parents automatically appear below children in the Z-index.
- Netscape Layers and <div> tag layers don't nest together very nicely.

You can display an entirely other HTML document as the content of the layer by specifying the URL of the document in the **Layer Source** text box.

The <nolayer> Tag

Layers are proprietary, and importing layer source code is really, really proprietary.

Browsers that don't support the <layer> and <ilayer> tags, including Explorer 4, will display the content of a Netscape Layer, completely devoid of positioning and of any scripting effects applied to it.

You can use a <nolayer> tag to either insult or "enlighten" users with browsers that don't support the <layer> and <ilayer> tags. Just add some code similar to the examples below.

For instance:

```
<LAYER SRC=monkey.html></LAYER>
<NOLAYER>
You could see my dancing monkey if you had
Netscape 4, but you don't. Neener neener.
</NOLAYER>
```

Or you could be a bit nicer:

```
<LAYER SRC=monkey.html></LAYER>
<NOLAYER>
<img src=/images/monkey.gif>
This monkey would really put on a show if
you downloaded
<a href="home.netscape.com/">Netscape
4</a>.
</NOLAYER>
```

To set Netscape Layer properties:

1. Create the <layer> or <ilayer> and select it.
2. To set the Top, Left or PageX, PageY relationship, click on the associated radio button in the Properties inspector.
3. To set the Above/Below relationship, choose Above or Below from the A/B drop-down menu, and then choose the name of the associated sibling layer from the drop-down menu to the right of the A/B menu.
4. To choose a source page for layer content, type the URL of the page in the Src text box.

   or

   Click on the folder icon to pop open the Choose HTML File dialog box, and browse through the files and folders on your computer to locate the file. When you find the file, click on Open to select it.

Behavior Modification

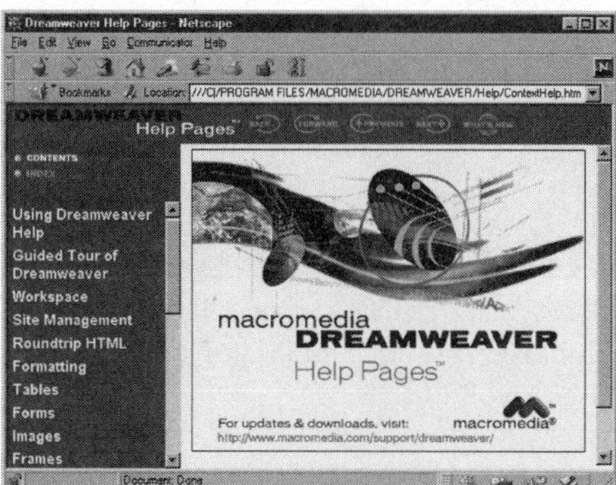

Figure 1 I'm going to use Dreamweaver's help pages for many examples in this chapter, because they use lots of JavaScript, they're not going to change anytime soon, and you can load them at any time to see what I'm talking about by pressing F1 in the Dreamweaver window.

New Behaviors

Three new Behaviors have been added to Dreamweaver with the release of version 1.2. These are Preload Images, Check Browser, and Drag Layer. Rather than adding several pages to this chapter, I put the descriptions of the latter two new actions on the Web site for this book. I cover the Preload Images action in this chapter.

Dreamweaver's Behavior tools let you apply common JavaScript actions without having to write any JavaScript. You can make something happen on a page when your users load a page, click on an object, or move the mouse around (**Figure 1**).

Obviously, I'm being simplistic here. There are a lot of really fancy things you can do with JavaScript, but this isn't a JavaScript book (see the sidebar called *Learning JavaScript*). In this chapter I discuss the stock behaviors that Dreamweaver lets you apply. In Chapter 13, you can get even fancier with Timelines.

✔ Tips

- JavaScript was introduced with Netscape 2. All the actions that Dreamweaver has packaged up for us to use are designed to work with 4.0 browsers and many also work with earlier browsers (as I note when explaining each action).
- Not all events are available to all browsers, and not all actions work in all browsers, so choosing which behaviors to use is dependent on which browsers you want to target.

JavaScript Concepts

A JavaScript Behavior is sort of like an equation:

Event + Object = Action

or

If this event happens to this object, this behavior will happen.

You can see a simple example of this relationship in **Figure 2**.

An *object* is an HTML element on a Web page, such as an image, a link, a layer, or the body of the page itself.

An *event* is shorthand for both user event and event handler. A *user event* is what happens when the user, or the user's browser, performs a common task, such as loading a page, clicking on a link, or pointing the mouse at an image. An *event handler* is the JavaScript shorthand that designates a particular user event, such as onMouseOver or onLoad.

Learning JavaScript

You've probably gotten the idea by now that if you're not used to coding HTML by hand, Dreamweaver is a great way to learn how to do so. You just highlight the objects you're curious about in the Document window, open the HTML inspector, and, *voilà*, you can see what the code behind the page is.

You can do the same thing with JavaScript by creating Dreamweaver Behaviors and viewing the code for them in the HTML inspector. If you feel lost looking at JavaScript, you might refer to one of the Web sites I link to in the supporting site for this book.

If you want a handy-dandy JavaScript reference, try *JavaScript for the World Wide Web: Visual QuickStart Guide*, Second Edition, by Tom Negrino and Dori Smith, also from Peachpit Press.

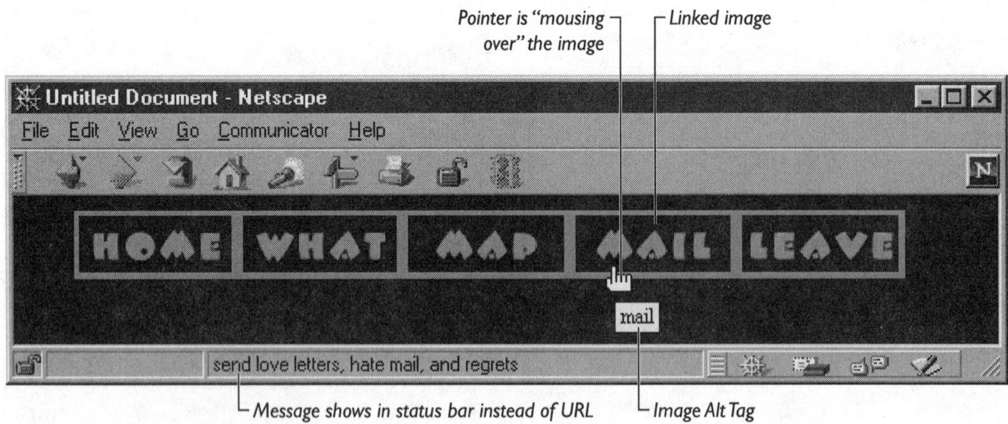

Figure 2 This button bar, shown in Navigator, is made up of five linked images (with image borders set to 0). The object is the link around the image. The event is onMouseOver, and the action is Show Status Message.

JAVASCRIPT CONCEPTS

Making Scripts Go

Dreamweaver doesn't actually run any JavaScript Behaviors. You need to preview your page in a browser to test your Behaviors. You can preview in your default browser by pressing F12, or you can choose a browser from the preview list by selecting File > Preview in Browser > Browser Name from the Document window menu bar.

Appendix C on this book's Web site includes instructions on adding browsers to the Preview list.

An *action* is where the JavaScript comes in. Normally, when you click on a link, you go to the page that's that link's target. That's a normal browser action that has nothing to do with a script. A JavaScript action might start with the click and then play a sound, or pop open a dialog box.

In Dreamweaver, to add Behaviors to a page, you choose an object and an event, based on which browsers you want to make the script available to. Then you choose an action that the object + event combination will trigger.

In this chapter, I'm first going to describe how to add a Behavior to a page, which is a pretty darn simple process. The rest of the chapter will be dedicated to listing and describing the objects, events, and actions you can combine in Dreamweaver Behaviors.

Adding Behaviors

Adding a Behavior to a page is incredibly simple—the devil is in the details. All Dreamweaver Behaviors are added and edited with the Behaviors inspector.

To view the Behaviors inspector:

1. From the Document window menu bar, select Window > Behaviors.

   or

   Click on the Behavior button (**Figure 3**) on the Launcher or the Document window Launcher bar.

   or

   Press F8.

The Behaviors inspector will appear (**Figure 4**).

To add a Behavior:

1. In the Behaviors inspector, choose the browser or set of browsers you want the Behavior to work in by selecting them from the Browser drop-down menu.
2. In the Document window, click on the object you want the Behavior to act on, or choose an entire tag (such as <body>) by clicking on the tag selector at the bottom-left of the Document window (**Figure 5**).

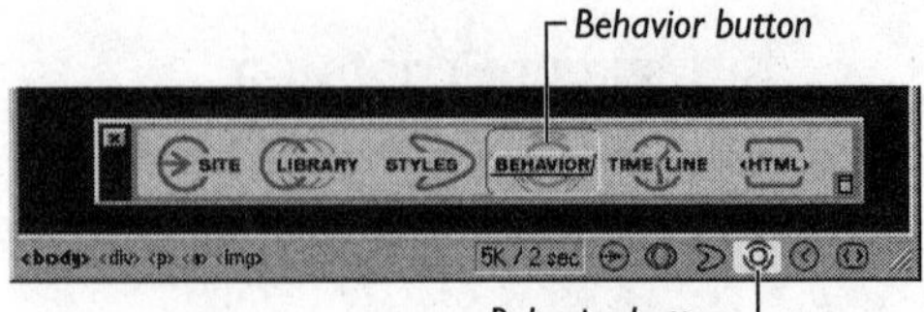

Figure 3 View the Behaviors inspector by clicking on the Behavior button on the Launcher or the Launcher bar.

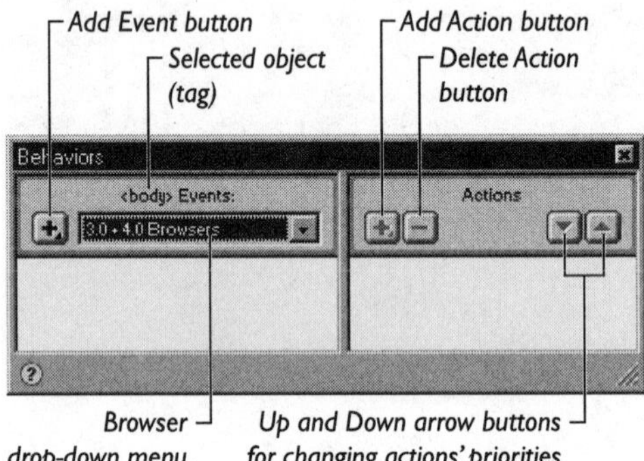

Figure 4 The Behaviors inspector is what you use to add JavaScript Behaviors.

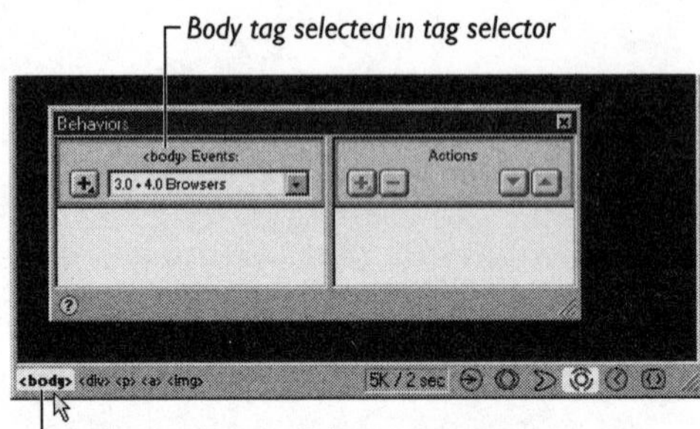

Figure 5 The tag that's selected in the tag selector is the one that will be affected by the Behaviors you apply in the Behaviors inspector.

Figure 6 Click on the Add Event (+) button to pop up a menu and add an event to the selected object. The events available depend on the selected browser + object combination.

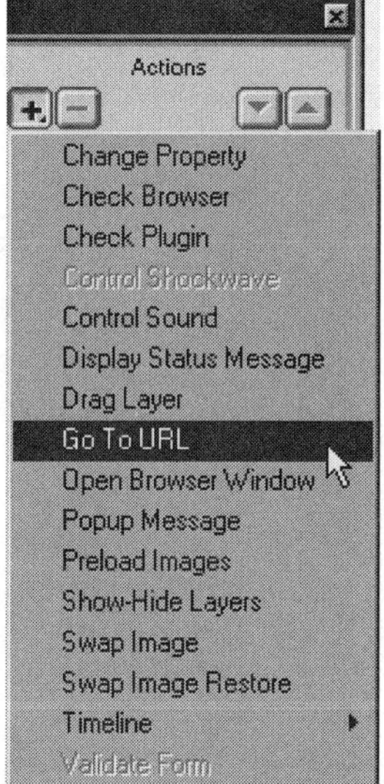

Figure 7 Click on the Add Action (+) button to pop up a menu and add an action to the selected event. The events available depend on the selected browser + object + event combination.

3. In the Events area of the Behaviors inspector, click on the Add Event button [+] to pop up a menu of events that are available for that particular browser-object combination (**Figure 6**).
4. Choose your event from the menu (they're described later in this chapter). Its name will appear in the Events list box.
5. In the Actions area of the Behaviors inspector, click on the Add Action button [+] to pop up a menu of actions that are available for that browser + object + event combination (**Figure 7**).
6. Choose your action from the menu (they're described later in this chapter). In most cases, a dialog box will appear.
7. Fill out the dialog box (guess what? I explain them later in this chapter as well), and click on OK.
8. The name of the action will appear in the Actions list box.

✔ Tips

- You can add more than one event to a single object. You might have different events for onMouseOver and onClick. Just repeat steps 3–8 for each additional event.
- You can also attach more than one action to a single event. Just repeat steps 5–7 to add additional actions to an event. For instance, you might have onMouseOver trigger both a sound and a status message.

To delete a Behavior:

1. In the Document window, click on the object to which you applied the Behavior. The name of the event associated with that object will appear in the Behaviors inspector.
2. In the Behaviors inspector's Events list box, click on the name of the event associated with the Behavior you want to delete. The actions associated with that event will appear in the Actions list box (**Figure 8**).
3. In the Behaviors inspector's Actions list box, click on the action you want to delete.
4. Click on the Delete Action button. The name of the action will disappear (**Figure 9**).

If there are no other actions associated with that event, Dreamweaver will delete the event. To make sure that it does, click on another object and then click on the object you selected in step 1. The event will have been deleted from the Behaviors inspector.

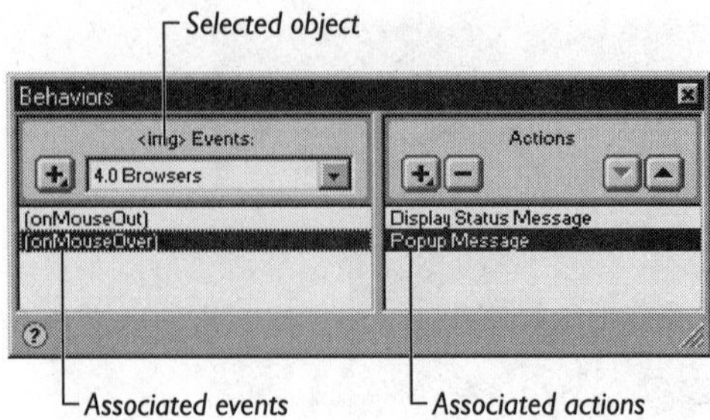

Figure 8 When an object is selected, its associated events appear in the Behaviors inspector. When one of those events is selected, its associated actions appear in the Behaviors inspector.

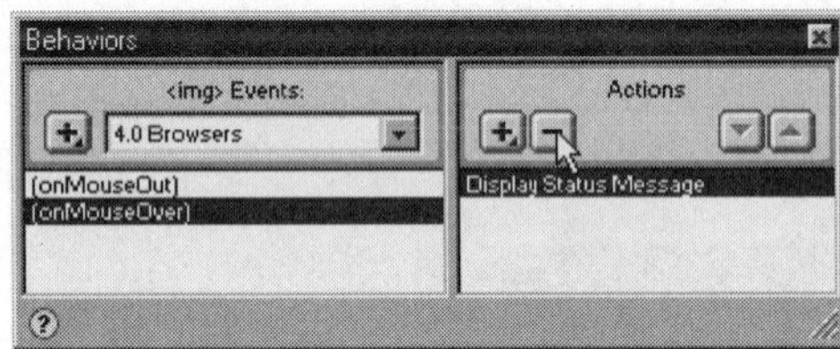

Figure 9 When I clicked on the Delete Action (minus) button, the unwanted action disappeared.

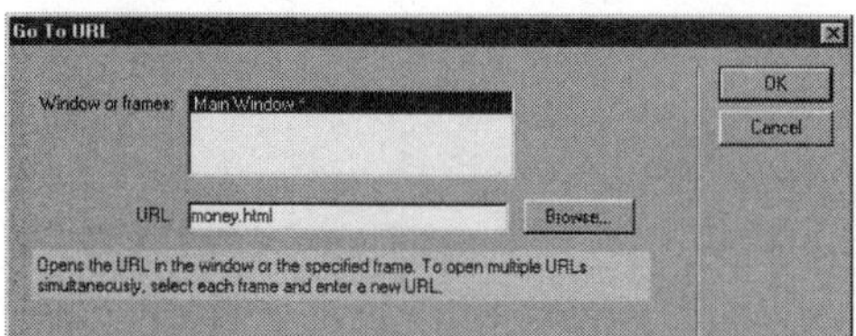

Figure 10 When you add a new action or double-click on the name of an existing action, a dialog box will appear, in which you add or edit the variables for the action. This is the dialog box for the Go to URL action.

To edit a Behavior:

1. In the Document window, click on the object to which you applied the Behavior. The name of the events associated with that object will appear in the Behaviors inspector (as we saw in **Figure 8**).
2. In the Behaviors inspector's Events list box, click on the name of the event associated with the Behavior you want to edit.
3. In the Behaviors inspector's Actions list box, click on the action you want to change.
4. Make your changes as follows:
   - To delete the action, click on the Delete Action button. The name of the Action will disappear.
   - To add an action, click on the Add Action button, and choose an action from the list.
   - To edit the action, double-click on its name.

   For the latter two choices, the associated dialog box will appear (**Figure 10**). (Dialog boxes for each the actions are explained later in this chapter.) Make your changes and then click on OK to close the dialog box.

You can edit actions as often as you want. If you have an event that triggers more than one action, you may want to set the order in which the actions occur.

To change the order in which actions occur:

1. Follow steps 1–3, above, to select the appropriate object, event, and action (**Figure 11**).
2. Change the order of the action by clicking on the arrow buttons:
   - Click on the up arrow to move the action up in the list.
   - Click on the down arrow to move the action down in the list.

The order of the actions will change immediately (**Figure 12**), and the browser will perform the actions in order from top to bottom.

That's about it for adding and editing Behaviors. The rest of the chapter is dedicated to the details.

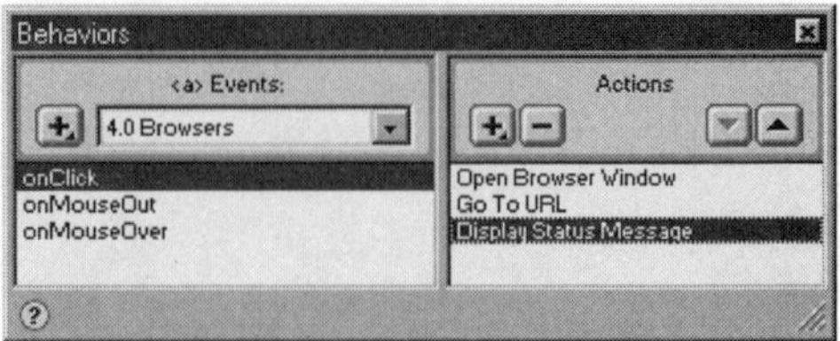

Figure 11 Select the proper object and event, and then select the action whose position you wish to change.

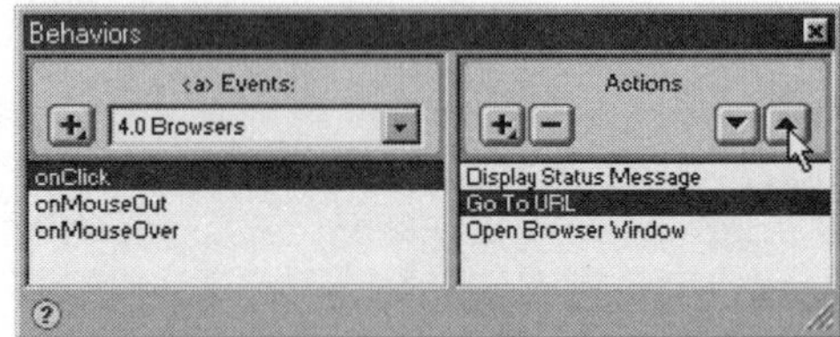

Figure 12 I moved the actions around by clicking on the up and down arrow buttons.

CHANGING THE ORDER OF ACTIONS

Common Objects

You can attach a behavior to nearly any HTML element, although some are more versatile than others. I'm going to list some of the more common objects here.

Anchors <a>

Many events are only available to the <a> tag that is usually used for links. Other objects can be attached to these events by surrounding the object with the <a> tag, which can be a null link that doesn't go anywhere.

For images that are not already linked, Dreamweaver will automatically tell you that it's going to supply an <a> tag for the object.

The anchor code for a null link will look like this:

```
<a href="#">foo</a>
```

The # (pound sign) basically means that the link doesn't do anything. You can replace the # later with an actual link, if you want.

✔ Tips

- In the Behaviors inspector's Events pop-up menu, events that can be activated by applying the <a> tag appear (in parentheses).
- You can use style sheets to apply anchors to text without underlining or color changes.

Body <body>

If you want to apply Behaviors to an entire page, the <body> tag is what you select.

Images <img>

Images have some nifty properties, one of which is that they load. A popular trick the kids are playing with these days is the *rollover*, in which mousing over an image causes another image to load in its place.

Forms <form>

You can use special form Behaviors with a form. The Behaviors available to a form include OnSubmit and OnReset.

Form Fields

You can attach Behaviors to individual fields in a form, too, such as <option> (for items in a menu or list), <textfield>, and <checkbox>. One example is the Go to URL action, which can be applied to the <option> items in a drop-down menu, so that when you select an item from the menu, a new page loads.

Event Handlers

There are many different event handlers you can use in Dreamweaver Behaviors. These events are detailed in **Table 12.1**.

✔ Tips

- Events will appear in the Add Event menu in the Behaviors inspector depending on the browser and object you've selected.
- Events surrounded (by parentheses) in the Add Event menu will become activated by adding an anchor to the selected object. Dreamweaver does this automatically.
- Internet Explorer 4 has the most available events, but it's important to remember that only a small fraction of your audience uses IE4 exclusively.

Table 12.1 User Events available in Dreamweaver. Events are arranged in logical sets rather than alphabetically. This table does not include *all* event handlers available to JavaScript; only those that Dreamweaver utilizes for behaviors.

Event Handlers

Event Handler Name	Description of the User Event (The event handler may call any number of actions, including dialog boxes.)	Browsers (According to Dreamweaver.)	Associated Tags (Other tags may be used; these are the most common associated objects.)
Page Loading Events			
onAbort	When the user presses the Stop button or Esc key before successful page or image loading	NN3, NN4, IE4	body, img
onLoad	When a page, frameset, or image has finished loading	NN3, NN4, IE3, IE4	body, img
onUnload	When the user leaves the page (clicks on a link, presses the back button)	NN3, NN4, IE3, IE4	body
onResize	When the user resizes the browser window	NN3, NN4, IE4	body
onError	When a JavaScript error occurs	NN3, NN4, IE4	a, body, img
Form and Form Field Events			
onBlur	When a form field "loses the focus" of its intended use	NN3, NN4, IE3, IE4	form fields: text, textarea, select
onFocus	When a form field receives the user's focus by being selected form fields: text, by the Tab key	NN3, NN4, IE3, IE4	textarea, select
onChange	When the user changes the default selection in a form field most form fields	NN3, NN4, IE3, IE4	
onSelect	When the user selects text within a form field	NN3, NN4, IE3, IE4	form fields: text, textarea
onSubmit	When a user clicks on the form's Submit button	NN3, NN4, IE3, IE4	form
onReset	When a user clicks on the form's Reset button	NN3, NN4, IE3, IE4	form
Mouse Events			
onClick	When the user clicks on the object	NN 3, NN 4, IE3, IE4 (IE3 only uses this handler for form fields)	a; form fields: button, checkbox, radio, reset, submit
onDblClick	When the user double-clicks on the object	NN 4, IE 4	a, img
onMouseMove	When the user moves the mouse	IE 3, IE 4	a, img,
onMouseDown	When the mouse button is depressed	NN 4, IE 4	a, img
onMouseUp	When the mouse button is released	NN 4, IE 4	a, img
onMouseOver	When the user points the mouse pointer at an object	NN 3, IE 3, NN 4, IE 4	a, img
onMouseOut	When the user moves the mouse off an object they moused over	NN 3, NN 4, IE 4	a, img
Keyboard Events			
onKeyDown	When a key on the keyboard is depressed	NN3, NN4, IE3, IE4	form fields: text, textarea
onKeyPress	When the user presses any key	NN3, NN4, IE3, IE4	form fields: text, textarea
onKeyUp	When a key on the keyboard is released	NN3, NN4, IE3, IE4	form fields: text, textarea
Internet Explorer 4 Events			
onHelp	When the user presses F1 or selects a link labeled "help"	IE4	a, img
onReadyStateChange	Page is loading	IE4	img
onAfterUpdate	After the content of a form field changes	IE4	a, body, img
onBeforeUpdate	After form field item changes, before content loses focus	IE4	a, body, img
onScroll	When the user uses the page scrollbars	IE4	body

Common Actions

In this section of the chapter I describe how to set up some common JavaScript actions in Dreamweaver. This is not meant to be an all-encompassing JavaScript reference; the language is capable of much more than I'm able to sum up in a single chapter.

Setting up Behaviors in JavaScript is very much like ordering Chinese food: you take one from Column A (objects), one from Column B (events), and one from Column C (actions). (Choosing a browser is like deciding whether Uncle Harvey's stomach can take the Mongolian beef.)

Since it would be redundant for me to repeat every detail of how to set up a behavior for each of these actions, I'm going to skip some of the basic steps, like showing the Behaviors inspector. You can review the details in the section called *Adding Behaviors.*

✔ Tips

- The objects and events that I name in the instructions for these events are suggestions; many other combinations are possible.
- Don't forget that JavaScript can crash older browsers. Heck, my computer crashed a half-dozen times just *writing about* it. Refer to Appendix C on the Web site for tips on writing pages for the masses.

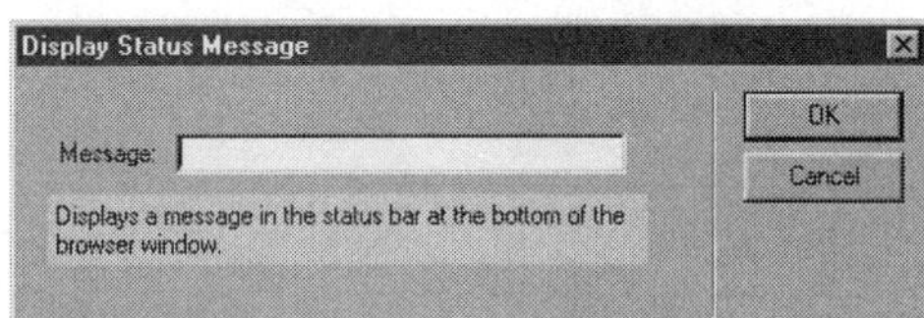

Figure 13 Type your status bar message in the Message text box.

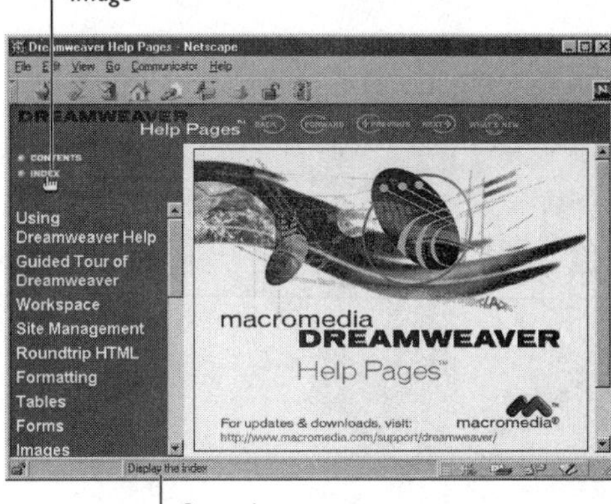

Figure 14 When the user mouses over the image, a message appears in the status bar.

The Status Bar Message

A status bar message is a little message that appears in the status bar of the browser.

Usage Example: Combine <a> and OnMouseOver with Display Status Message. When the user mouses over a link, they'll see a message in the status bar such as "Explore the Invisible Cities." This is also a great trick for hiding the target URL.

To add a status bar message:

1. In the Behaviors inspector, select a browser (3.0+4.0).
2. In the Document window, select an object (a, body, img).
3. In the Behaviors inspector, add an event (OnMouseOver, OnMouseOut, OnLoad).
4. In the Behaviors inspector, add the Action Display Status Message. The Display Status Message dialog box will appear (**Figure 13**).
5. Type your message in the Message text box.
6. Click on OK. The Display Status Message dialog box will close.

When you load the page in a browser, the message will appear in the status bar when you perform the user event you specified (**Figure 14**).

✔ Tip

- If you specify a status message for OnMouseOver, you may also want to specify a status message for OnMouseOut. This can be a blank message.

Go to URL

Obviously, links already perform this action. You can have URLs opened for other actions besides click, however.

Usage Example: Have a link open two windows at once or open a document in each of two frames. You may also want to specify URLs in this way using JavaScript; older browsers get the regular old link, while the JavaScript user goes to the JavaScript page.

To add a URL:

1. In the Behaviors inspector, select a browser (3.0 + 4.0).
2. In the Document window, select an object (a, img, body).
3. In the Behaviors inspector, add an event (OnClick, OnMouseOver, OnMouseOut).
4. In the Behaviors inspector, add the action Go to URL. The Go to URL dialog box will appear (**Figure 15**).
5. Add your URLs as follows:
   - For one window and one URL, simply type the URL in the text box.
   - For pages with more than one frame and URL, select the name of the single frame from the Window or Frames list box and type the URL in the text box.

   For pages with more than one frame and more than one URL to load, repeat the preceding instruction for each of the frames you want to load a document into.
6. Click OK. The dialog box closes.

The URL(s) will open when the user performs the event, such as a click (**Figure 16**).

✔ Tip

- Be sure to test, test, and retest these links once they're on the server, particularly if you're targeting multiple frames.

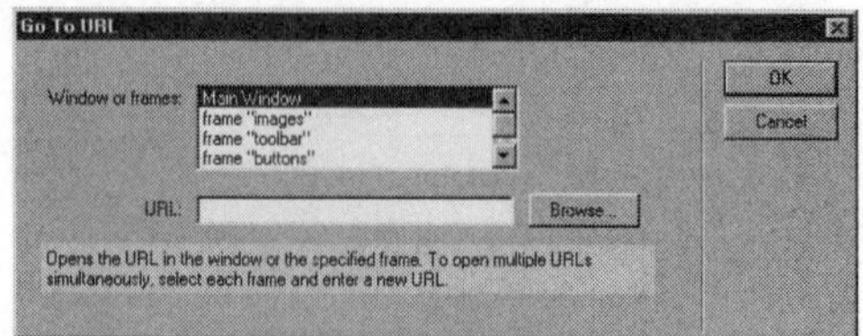

Figure 15 Select the windows (or frames) and type in the corresponding URLs that will load when the event happens.

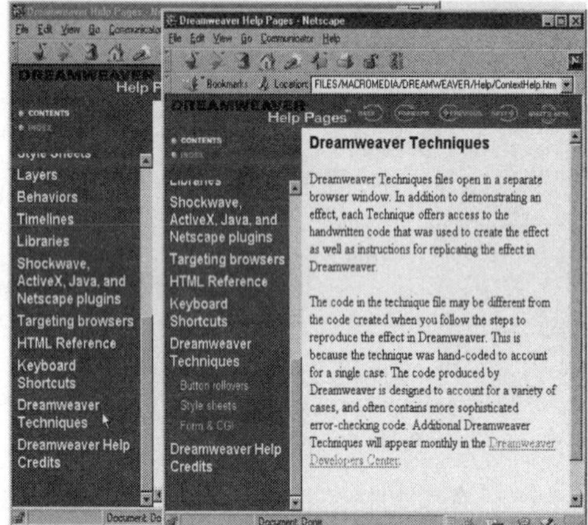

Figure 16 When you click on Dreamweaver Techniques on the Dreamweaver help page, frames on both the left and right load new content.

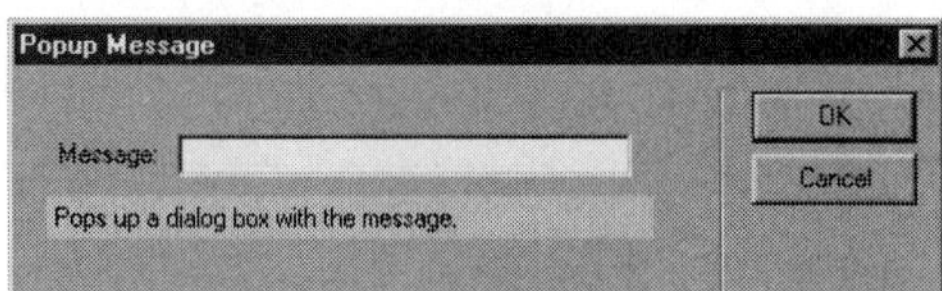

Figure 17 Type the message you want to appear in the dialog box in the Message text box.

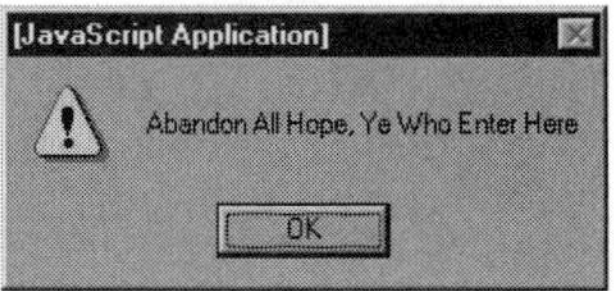

Figure 18 A pop-up message created with Dreamweaver. This message appears when the user clicks on a link. I used this in combination with the Go to URL action; when the user clicks on OK, the browser will open a new page.

Pop Up Message

In the Pop Up Message action, when the user performs an action, a pop-up message or dialog box will appear. In Dreamweaver, the only choice in this dialog box is OK.

Usage Example: Combine this action with the result of another action, such as form validation ("You forgot to type your e-mail address") or plug-in detection ("You need Shockwave to properly appreciate this page.")

To add a pop-up message:

1. In the Behaviors inspector, select a browser (3.0 + 4.0).
2. In the Document window, select an object (a, body).
3. In the Behaviors inspector, add an event (OnClick, OnMouseOver).
4. In the Behaviors inspector, add the action pop-up message. The Popup Message dialog box will appear (**Figure 17**).
5. Type your message in the Message text box.
6. Click on OK. The Popup Message dialog box will close.

When you load the page in a browser, the pop-up message or dialog box will open when the user performs the event, such as a click (**Figure 18**).

✔ Tip

- Don't overuse this one. I've seen pages where the slightest mouse movement would open a dialog box, and it was truly annoying.

Control Sound

You can use the Control Sound action to do one of two things: play a sound when a user performs an action, or stop playing an embedded sound when a user performs an action.

Usage Example: Provide a button such as "Stop the Music" for an embedded sound. Or combine a small (20KB) sound with image rollovers so that a "beep" of some kind occurs.

✔ Tip

- To use the "Stop Sound" option, the sound must be embedded in the page before you apply the Behavior.

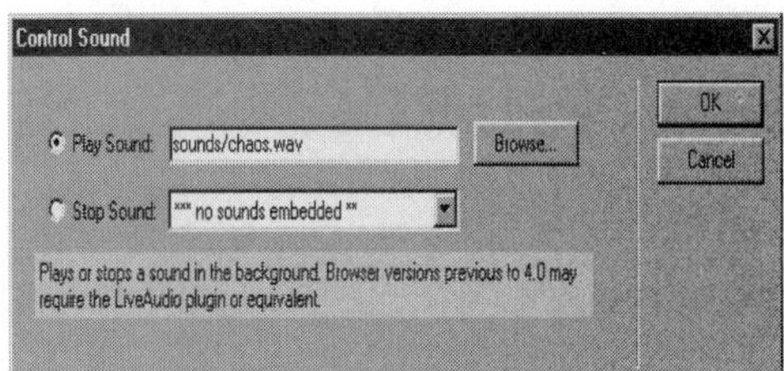

Figure 19 Using the Control Sound dialog box, you can add a sound to an event, or you can provide a control to stop an embedded sound.

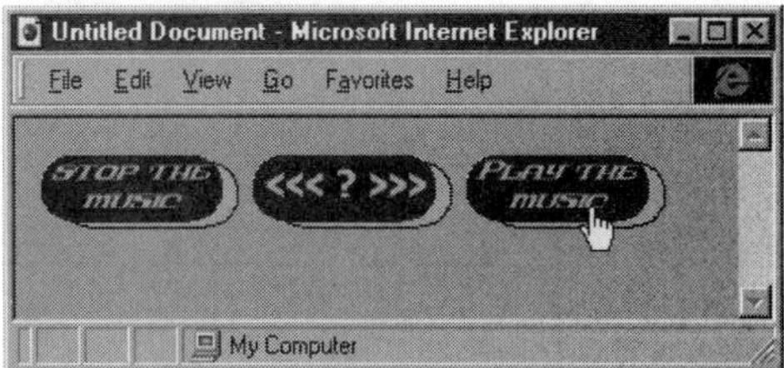

Figure 20 Using these images as the objects for the Control Sound Behavior, you can let the user play or stop a sound embedded using JavaScript.

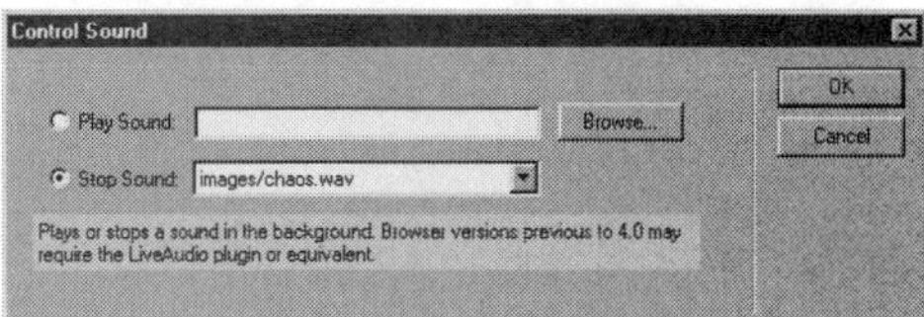

Figure 21 Here's the Sound Control dialog box again. This time, I'm using it to supply a control to turn off the sound I embedded in **Figure 19**.

To add Sound Control:

1. In the Behaviors inspector, select a browser (Netscape 3, 4.0 browsers).
2. In the Document window, select an object (a, body).
3. In the Behaviors inspector, add an event (OnClick, OnMouseOver).
4. In the Behaviors inspector, add the Action Control Sound. The Control Sound dialog box will appear (**Figure 19**).
5. To play a sound onEvent, type the URL of the sound clip in the Play Sound text box.

   or

   To stop playing a sound onEvent, click on the Stop Sound radio button, and select the URL of an embedded sound from the drop-down menu.
6. Click on OK. The Control Sound dialog box will close.

When you load this page in the browser you can play or stop a sound clip (**Figure 20**).

✔ Tips

- I had trouble getting Dreamweaver to detect sounds embedded using the `<embed>` tag in the HTML code for the page. The best way to use the Control Sound Behavior with Dreamweaver is to use one action to embed the sound and another to turn it off (**Figure 21**).
- I cover plug-ins and sound files in Chapter 15. You can refer to that chapter for information on changing HTML or JavaScript code for hidden/visible sound controls, sound loops, and the like.

Control Shockwave

You can use the Control Shockwave action to play, stop, rewind, or jump to a particular frame in a Shockwave movie.

Usage Examples: Provide buttons or links marked "Stop" and "Play." For a Shockwave game, provide a "Play Again" link that jumps back to the particular frame in which the game starts.

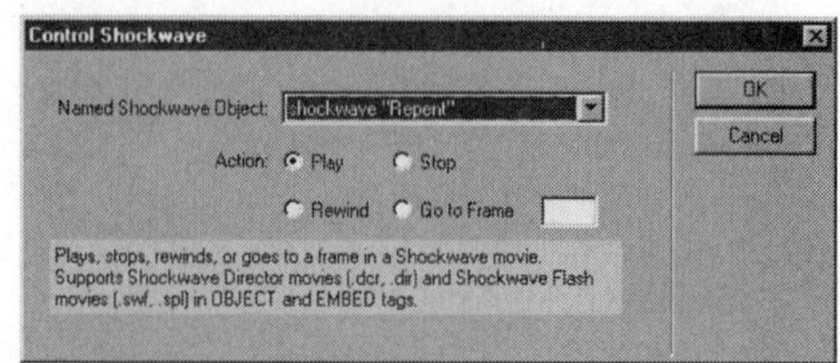

Figure 22 Using the Control Shockwave dialog box, you can provide controls to play, stop, rewind, or jump to a frame in a Shockwave movie.

✔ Tip

- To use the Control Shockwave action, you must first embed Shockwave in the page using the <embed> or <object> tags. I discuss Shockwave and other plug-ins in Chapter 15.

To add Shockwave Control:

1. In the Behaviors inspector, select a browser (3.0 + 4.0 browsers).
2. In the Document window, select an object (a, img, input).
3. In the Behaviors inspector, add an event (OnClick, OnMouseOver).
4. In the Behaviors inspector, add the Action Control Shockwave. The Control Shockwave dialog box will appear (**Figure 22**).

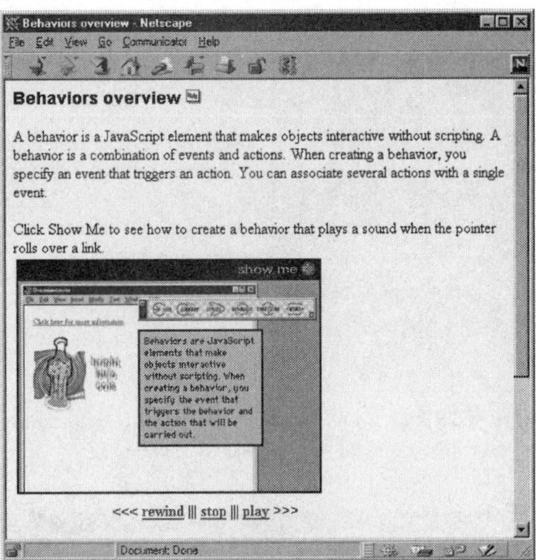

Figure 23 I modified the About Behaviors page from the Dreamweaver help files to add Shockwave controls that rewind, play, or stop the movie.

Error, Will Robinson!

You may get a JavaScript error in Dreamweaver when implementing this Behavior. If a dialog box pops up mumbling something about Netscape and objects, follow these steps:

1. In the Document window, select the Shockwave object.
2. Display the Properties inspector by selecting Modify > Selection Properties from the Document window menu bar.
3. From the TAG drop-down menu, select OBJECT and EMBED.

Now both Navigator and Explorer will load both the Shockwave movie and the Control Shockwave script properly. I explain this more thoroughly in Chapter 15.

5. If there is more than one Shockwave movie on your page, select the correct object from the Named Shockwave Object drop-down menu.
6. Click on the radio button for the control you want to add: Play, Stop, Rewind, or Go to Frame. For this last option, type the number of the Frame in the Frame text box.
7. Click on OK. The Control Sound dialog box will close.

When you load this page in the browser you can control the Shockwave movie (**Figure 23**).

✔ Tips

- Dreamweaver automatically adds a Detect Plug-in script when you add the Control Shockwave action. If the user does not have Shockwave installed, this script will send the user to a page that supplies a link for downloading the Shockwave plug-in.

Open Browser Window

You know those little bitty JavaScript windows? You can pop one open using the Open Browser Window action—or you can pop open a regular-sized window.

Usage Example: Pop open a floating toolbar, "control panel," or a window set to the exact size of a Shockwave applet or image map (**Figure 24**).

Figure 24 This sound control panel is set to pop open when a link in the parent window is clicked.

To add the Open Browser Window action:

1. In the Behaviors inspector, select a browser (3.0 + 4.0).
2. In the Document window, select an object (a, img, body).
3. In the Behaviors inspector, add an event (OnClick, OnLoad, OnMouseOver).
4. In the Behaviors inspector, add the Action Open Browser Window. The Open Browser Window dialog box will appear (**Figure 25**).
5. Type the URL of the content for the new window in the URL text box.
6. If you want to specify a window width and window height, type these dimensions (in pixels) in the appropriate text boxes. If you don't specify these dimensions, a default-sized browser window will open.

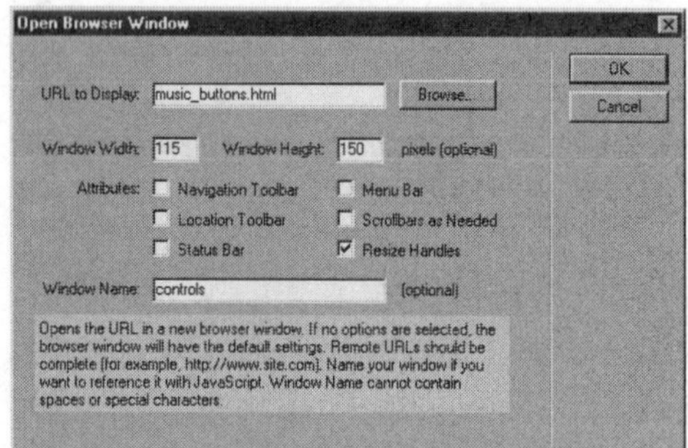

Figure 25 The Open Browser window dialog box. These are the attributes I set for the control panel in Figure 24.

Figure 26 Another floating toolbar. Note the extra space below the buttons—the window must be 100 pixels high. If I were getting this control panel ready for prime time, I'd center the buttons within the window using a table.

7. The checkboxes allow you to display regular browser features such as the status bar, toolbar, and address bar. Leave all the boxes unchecked if you want a "featureless" window.

8. To specify a window title, type the title in the Window Name text box. (You can use these window titles in other Behaviors, such as Go to URL.)

9. Click on OK. The Open Browser Window dialog box will close.

In the browser window, when the action (page loading, link clicking) occurs, the new window will open (**Figure 26**).

✔ Tip

- By trial and error, I've found that JavaScript windows must be at least 100 pixels high. The window in **Figure 24** is 115 pixels wide and 150 pixels high, and the window in **Figure 26** is 100 pixels high, although I'd like it to be about 50 pixels high.

Swap Image

Swapping images is the same as performing the famous "rollovers" I talked about earlier.

Usage Example: When the user mouses over the image, it's replaced with a "lit up" image (**Figure 27**) or another image entirely.

Images must be named for image swapping to work properly.

To name your images:

1. Select the image.
2. In the Properties inspector, name the image by typing a name for it in the Img text box and pressing Enter (Return).

To add the Swap Image action:

1. In the Behaviors inspector, select a browser (Netscape 3.0 + 4.0 Browsers).
2. In the Document window, select an image (img; Dreamweaver will add the anchor tag for Navigator).
3. In the Behaviors inspector, add an event (onClick, onLoad, onMouseOver).
4. In the Behaviors inspector, add the Action Swap Image. The Swap Image dialog box will appear (**Figure 28**).

Figure 27 The Dreamweaver help page uses image rollovers to make the buttons "light up" when you mouse over them.

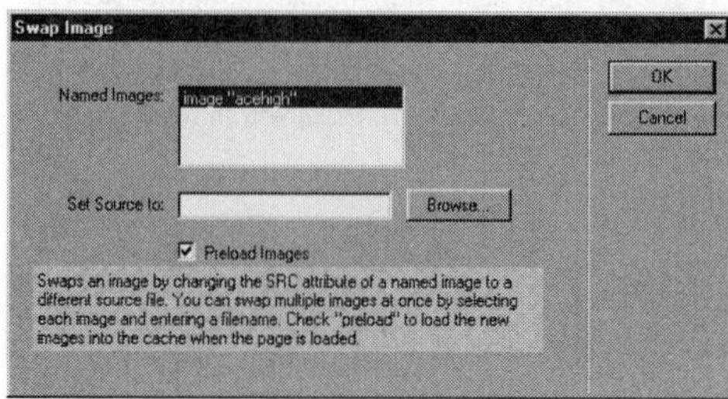

Figure 28 This is the Swap Image dialog box I used to set the rollovers in Figures 29 and 30.

Figure 29 A popular way to implement image swapping is to use an image that's the reverse of the original. When the user mouses over the image on the bottom, it's swapped with an image that's the same size and shape, with reversed colors.

Figure 30 You can set the Swap Image action to swap several images at once. In this example, when the user mouses over the image on the bottom, all three images are swapped simultaneously.

5. The Images list box displays all the named images on your page. Click on the name of the image you want to swap.
   - To swap the image you selected as an object in Step 2, be sure to select the name of that image.
   - To swap a different image when the user event occurs, select a different image.
6. Type the source for the new image (the one that will replace the named image when the action occurs) in the Set Source To text box.
7. Repeat steps 5 and 6 for each image to which you want to apply this action.
8. To have the images be swapped in preload with the page, select the Preload Images checkbox.

When you view this page in a 4.0 browser, the images you selected will be swapped (**Figure 29**).

✔ Tips

- If you set all the image rollovers in a single dialog box, all the images will roll over when you mouse over the single image you selected in Step 2 (**Figure 30**).
- To set rollovers for individual images, you need to follow steps 2–7 for each consecutive image.
- Image swapping onMouseOver is often combined with Image restoring onMouseOut.

Swap Image Restore

The Swap Image Restore action is used with Swap Image to redisplay the original image after the Swap Image action occurs.

Usage Example: Set Swap Image to occur onMouseOver, and Swap Image Restore to occur onMouseOut.

To add the Swap Image Restore action:

1. Set up the Swap Image action, as described in the preceding section.
2. In the Behaviors inspector, select a browser (Netscape 3.0 + 4.0 Browsers).
3. In the Document window, select the image you selected in step 1.
4. In the Behaviors inspector, add an event (onClick, onMouseOut).
5. In the Behaviors inspector, add the Action Swap Image Restore. The Swap Image Restore dialog box will appear (**Figure 31**).
6. Click on OK. That's all there is to it.

The combination of events in Swap Image and Swap Image Restore can make for interesting visual effects (**Figure 32**).

✔ Tip

- Repeat these steps for each additional image to which you applied the Swap Image action.

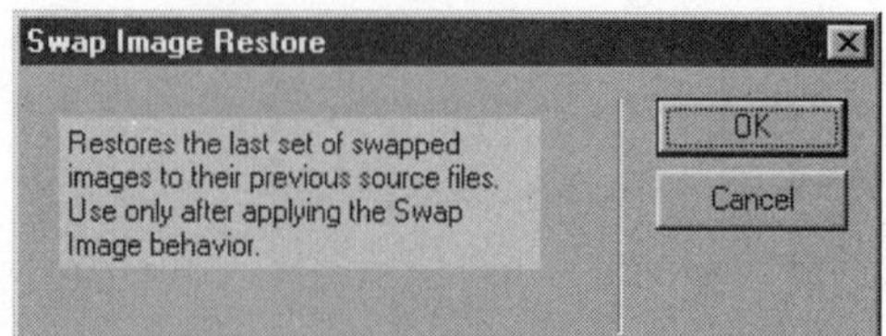

Figure 31 All you need to do with the Swap Image Restore dialog box is click on OK.

Figure 32 There's no good way to demonstrate roll-overs in print, so let's pretend that the window on the left and the window on the right are the same window. On the left, we're mousing over the image. On the right, we've just moused out, and the image is restored.

SWAP IMAGE RESTORE

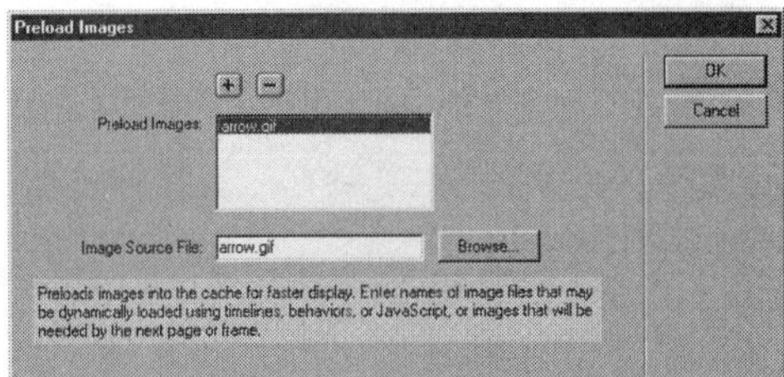

Figure 33 Set the source for all the images you want cached and ready in the Preload Images dialog box.

Preload Images

You can set up the Swap Image behavior to automatically preload images, but there are other instances in which you may want to preload images as well.

Usage Example: Preload a large image that appears in a DHTML/JavaScript window before the user ever gets there by adding this behavior to the home page.

To add the Preload Image action:

1. In the Behaviors inspector, select 4.0 browsers.
1. In the Document window, select the body of the page by clicking on the <body> tag in the tag selector.
1. In the Behaviors inspector, add the onLoad event.
1. In the Behaviors inspector, add the Action Preload Images. The Preload Images dialog box will appear (**Figure 33**).
1. Type the pathname of the image you want to preload in the Image Source File text box, or click on Browse to choose the image from your computer.
1. For every image you want to preload, click on the Plus button, and then repeat step 5.
1. To delete an image, select it and click on the Minus button.
1. Click on OK to close the Preload Images dialog box.

Dreamweaver will write what's called an array in the head of the document. All image filenames that appear in this array will be preloaded when the browser loads the page.

Check Plugin

The Check Plugin action checks the user's browser to see if they have a particular plug-in installed. After the check, the action can load one of two URLs: one for Yes, and an alternate for No.

Usage Examples: If the user has Shockwave installed, they will proceed to the Shockwave-enhanced version of the page. If not, they will be sent to a page that's designed to present the same information without Shockwave.

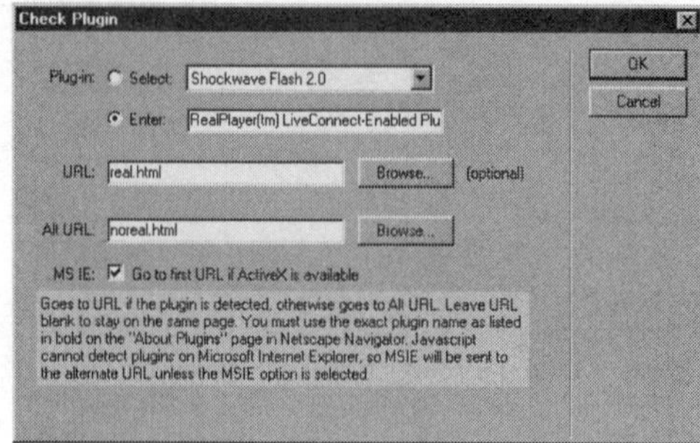

Figure 34 Choose your plug-in from the drop-down menu.

To add the Check Plugin action:

1. In the Behaviors inspector, select a browser (3.0+4.0 Browsers).
2. In the Document window, select the <body> tag by clicking on it in the Tag Selector at the bottom left of the status bar, or select an <a> tag.
3. In the Behaviors inspector, add the event (onLoad, onClick).
4. In the Behaviors inspector, add the action Check Plugin. The Check Plugin dialog box will appear (**Figure 34**).
5. Choose a plug-in from the drop-down menu.

   or

   If the desired plug-in is not available in the drop-down menu, type the name of the plug-in, *exactly as it appears on Netscape's About Plug-ins page*. For example, to look for the latest version of the RealPlayer, you'd type RealPlayer(tm) LiveConnect-Enabled Plug-In (32-bit) Version 5.0 (yes, the whole thing).

CHECK PLUGIN

6. Type the URL for the Yes page in the URL text box (for example: `shock_index.html`).
7. Type the alternate URL, for the No page, in the Alt URL text box (for example: `noshock_index.html`).
8. Click on OK to close the Check Plugin dialog box.

When the page loads or the link is clicked, the user will automatically be forwarded to the proper page.

✔ Tips

- To view Netscape's About:Plug-ins page, select Help > About Plug-ins from Navigator's menu bar, or type `about:plugins` in the address bar and press Enter (Return).
- For Internet Explorer, check the checkbox marked Go to URL if ActiveX is Available; deselecting the checkbox will send MSIE to the alternate URL. Many Netscape Plug-ins have Active-X counterparts for Internet Explorer; check the documentation for the plug-in to find out more.
- I discuss plug-ins and Active X in Chapter 15. Appendix C on the Website discusses making sites available to browsers other than the latest versions of Navigator and Explorer.

Show-Hide Layers

The Show-Hide Layers action can make certain layers appear or disappear. You must already have the layers on your page to set up this Behavior. The effectiveness of this Behavior depends on the initial visibility setting you give your layers.

Usage Examples: When a user mouses over an image or clicks on a link, one layer disappears and another appears. Since layers are loaded with a page, you can make several sets of content available on a single page and hidden in different layers.

To add the Show-Hide Layers action:

1. In the Behaviors inspector, select a browser (4.0 Browsers).
2. In the Document window that contains the layers, select an object (a, body, img).
3. In the Behaviors inspector, add an event (onLoad, onClick, onMouseOver).
4. In the Behaviors inspector, add the action Show-Hide Layers. The Show-Hide Layers dialog box will appear (**Figure 35**).

   Dreamweaver may take a moment or two to detect all the layers on the page, at which point their names (id="" or name="") will appear in the Layers list box.
5. Click on the name of the layers whose visibility you want the event to change, and then click on one of the three buttons: Show, Hide, or Default. Default will restore the layer's original visibility setting.
6. Repeat step 5 for all the layers you want this Behavior to affect.
7. Click on OK to close the Show-Hide Layer dialog box.

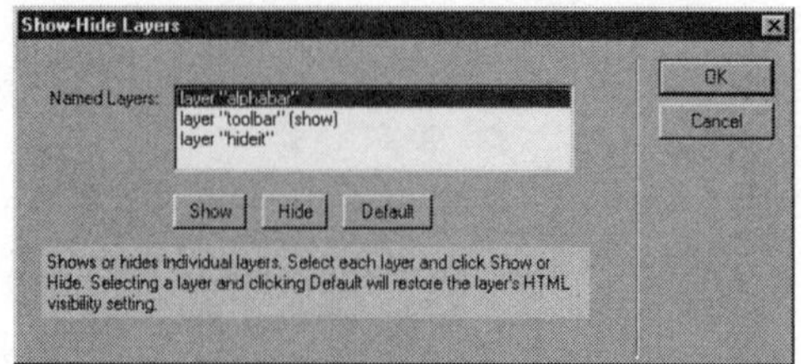

Figure 35 Set the (onEvent) visibility of your layers in the Show-Hide Layers dialog box.

SHOW-HIDE LAYERS

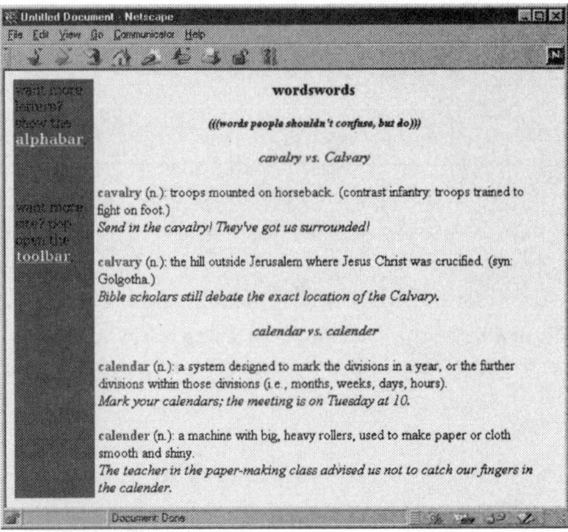

Figure 36 This page has two hidden layers. The links to them are in the table cell at the left.

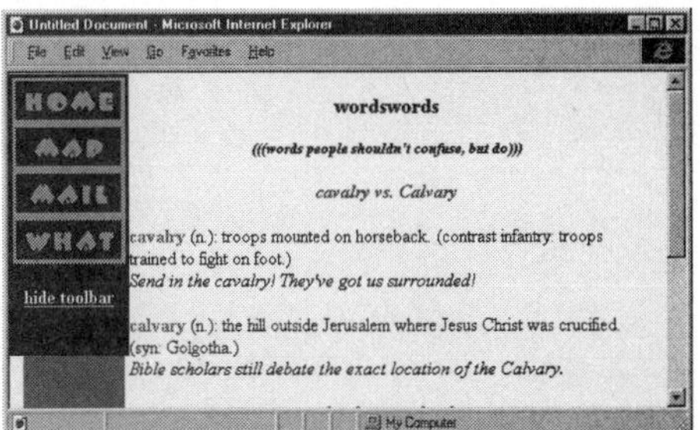

Figure 37 Click on the link that says Show Toolbar, and it calls a Behavior that shows the Toolbar layer. Notice that that layer has a link called Hide Toolbar.

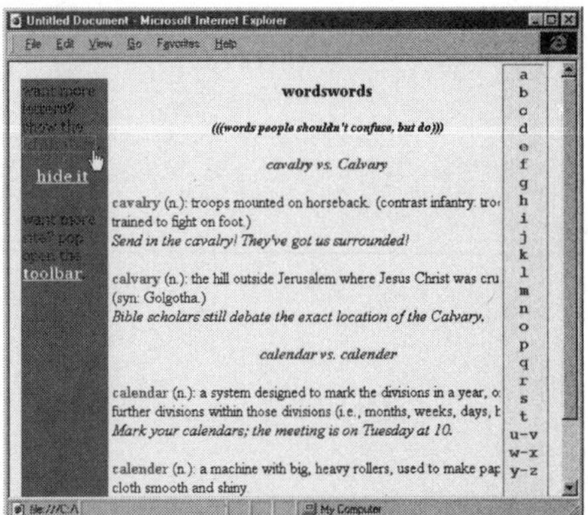

Figure 38 Here, we've hidden the toolbar again and are showing the layer called Alphabar. Notice the additional text in the left margin: that's yet another layer that has a link that will hide the Alphabar layer.

The page must be loaded in a 4.0 browser for this action to work, since earlier browsers don't show layers at all. **Figure 36** shows a page with all layers hidden. **Figures 37** and **38** show the same page with the layers showing.

✔ Tip

- Another layer animation behavior, Drag Layers, is described on the companion Web sitefor this book.

Why Default?

The *Default* setting is most useful for a second Show-Hide Layer behavior.

For instance: let's imagine a page with two layers. When the page loads, Layer Apple is showing, and Layer Banana is hidden—those are their default settings.

First behavior: When an onClick happens to a link called "Turn the Page" in Layer Apple, Apple hides and Banana appears.

Second behavior: When an onClick happens to a link called "Back to the Beginning" in Layer Banana, the Default settings of both layers are restored, and thus Apple appears and Banana hides.

Experiment with this; I got mixed results.

Form Validation

Form validation is useful—you can have JavaScript validate a form before it's even sent to the form handling script.

✔ Attention!

- You must already have the completed form on your page, with all fields named, before you can apply this Behavior.

Usage Example: You can require that certain fields be filled out, or require that data be in a certain format; for instance a full e-mail address or only numbers instead of letters.

To add the Form Validation action:

1. In the Behaviors inspector, select a browser (3.0 + 4.0 browsers).
2. In the Document window that contains the form, select the form (click on <form> in the tag selector).
3. In the Behaviors inspector, add the OnSubmit event.
4. In the Behaviors inspector, add the action Validate Form. The Validate Form dialog box will appear (**Figure 39**).
5. Dreamweaver may take a moment or two to detect all the named text form fields on the page, at which point their names will appear in the Named Fields list box.

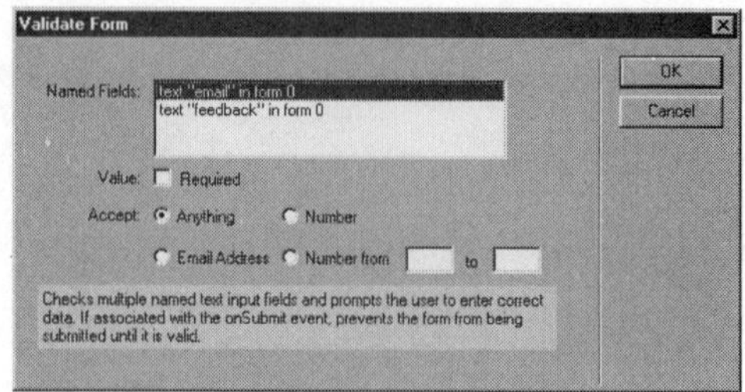

Figure 39 In the Validate Form dialog box, you can restrict the input into text or text-area form fields.

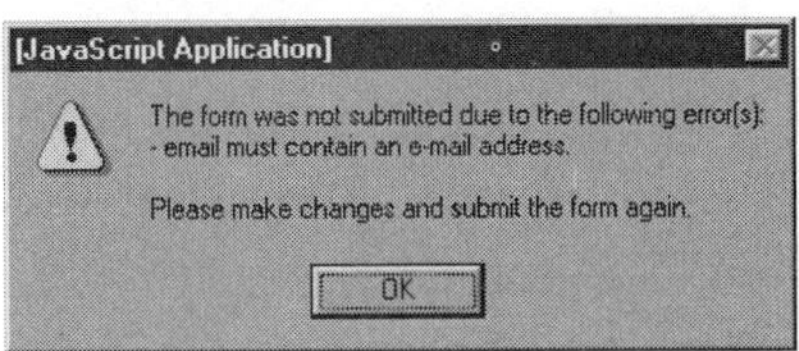

Figure 40 On my form, I required that the text in the e-mail field be in standard e-mail address format. If a user submits a form that doesn't conform to this validation requirement, they'll get a message telling them so.

The onBlur Event

The onBlur event is kind of confusing at best, but it makes a cute party trick. To "blur" a form field means that it "loses the focus" of its intent. To this end, you can mini-validate a single form field. Follow the instructions above, substituting the following variables:

1. In step 2, select a <text> or <textarea> tag as the object, instead of the <form> tag.
2. In step 3, use the onBlur event instead of the onSubmit event.

The easiest way to test out the onBlur event is to use numbers; in step 8, require a number between 1 and 10.

Now load the page in a browser, and try typing a number less than 1 or greater than 10 in the form field, and press Enter (Return). Your input will disappear. This doesn't work if you Tab out of the field, so it's only marginally useful.

6. Click on the name of the form field you want to validate.
7. To make the form field required, in which case the form will not be accepted unless this field is filled out, place a checkmark in the Required checkbox.
8. To restrict the content you'll accept, choose one of the following options:
   - Number (content must be numbers)
   - Number from n to n (range of numbers; type the range in the text boxes)
   - E-mail address (text must be in the name@address.domain format)
9. Click on OK to close the Validate Form dialog box.

When users submit the form, they'll see a dialog box informing them if they failed to meet your validation standards (**Figure 40**).

✔ Tip

- Before you unleash the form validation script on your users, test it to make sure it does what you want it to.

Change Property

I'm discussing this action last because it has the most variables. You can have an event that's associated with one object change the properties of that object or a different object. See **Table 12.2** to find out the objects available to this Dreamweaver Behavior, and their associated properties.

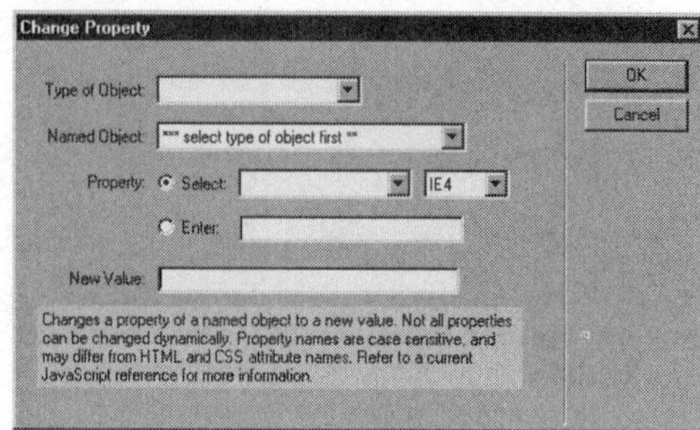

Figure 41 You can change several properties at once using the Change Property dialog box.

Usage Examples: Provide a drop-down menu from which the user can pick a background color. Change the dimensions or Z-index of a layer when the user clicks on a button image. Change the destination of a form if the user checks a particular checkbox.

1. In the Behaviors inspector, select a browser (all browsers; layer properties won't work in 3.0 or earlier browsers).
2. In the Document window that contains the layers, select an object (`a`, `body`, `img`, a form field, etc.).
3. In the Behaviors inspector, add an event (onClick, onMouseOver, onBlur).
4. In the Behaviors inspector, add the action Change Property. The Change Property dialog box will appear (**Figure 41**).
5. In the Change Property dialog box, choose the object whose action you wish to change from the Type of Object drop-down menu (see **Table 12.2**).
6. Dreamweaver may take a moment or two to detect all the named objects on the page, at which point their names (`id=""` or `name=""`) will appear in the Named Object list box. Choose an object by selecting it from the list.
7. The properties you can change are available from the Property drop-down menu (see **Table 12.2**). You may get additional properties by selecting a different browser from the Browser drop-down menu.

8. Repeat steps 5–7 for all the objects you want this Behavior to affect.
9. Click on OK to close the Change Property dialog box.

✔ Tips

- In order to change an object's properties with this Behavior, you must name the object. You can name any object by selecting it and typing a name for it in the Properties inspector. The Name text box is always to the top and left of the Properties inspector.
- You can also change additional properties by clicking on the Enter radio button and typing the property in the text box. There are too many variables here for me to provide any kind of list.
- If the object you're working with is a form field, you can provide a new value for the changed form field by typing it in the Value text box.

Table 12.2

Objects and Properties for Change Property action

OBJECT	PROPERTIES
Layer <div>, <span>, <layer>, <ilayer> (provided those tags have positioning and Z-index elements)	Position (top, left), Z-index, Clipping area, Background color, Background image (NN4 + IE4); Width and height (IE4 only)
Div <div>	Styles, including font family, font size, border width and color, background color and image, and text within the <div> tag (all IE4 only)
Span <span>	Styles, including font family, font size, border width and color, background color and image, and text within the <div> tag (all IE4 only)
Image <img>	Source (NN3, NN4, IE4)
Form <form>	Action (3.0+4.0 browsers)
Checkbox <input type=checkbox>	Status (checked/unchecked) (3.0+4.0 browsers)
Radio button <input type=radio>	Status (checked/unchecked) (3.0+4.0 browsers)
Text box <input type=text>	Value (will appear in text box) (3.0+4.0 browsers)
Text field <textarea>	Value (will appear in text field) (3.0+4.0 browsers)
Password text box <input type=password>	Value (will appear in text box) (3.0+4.0 browsers)
Menu or List <select>	selectedIndex (changes selection within menu, using index numbers for each <option> (3.0 + 4.0 browsers)

Adding New Scripts and Behaviors

If you're a veteran JavaScripter, and you want to set up your own scripts in Dreamweaver, you're more than welcome to. You can type or paste in a script using the Insert Script Object, or you can set up your own actions to use in Dreamweaver Behaviors.

To type in a script:

1. On the Object palette, click on the Insert Script button.

   From the Document window menu bar, select Insert > Script. The Insert Script dialog box will appear (**Figure 42**).

2. Type your script in the Insert Script dialog box, and click on OK. The Insert Script dialog box will close, and the Script element marker will appear in the Document window: .

3. Select the Script marker, if it isn't already selected, and display the Properties inspector, if necessary (**Figure 43**).

4. Select the type of script (JavaScript or VBScript) from the Language drop-down menu. If your script is in another scripting language, type it in the text box.

You can also insert a script from a file on your hard drive.

To insert a script from a text file:

1. Follow steps 1–3, above, but leave the Insert Script dialog box blank.

2. In the Properties inspector, type the source of your script in the Source text box, or click on the folder icon to browse your hard drive for the file.

You can type or edit longer scripts in the script editing window.

Figure 42 You can type a little script in the Insert Script dialog box.

Figure 43 The Properties inspector, displaying Script properties.

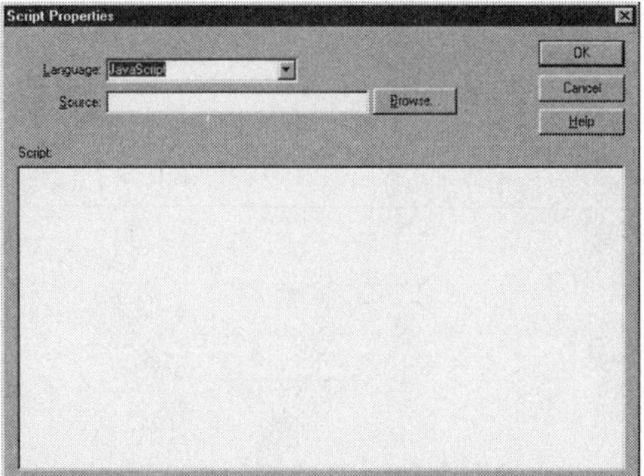

Figure 44 The Script Properties dialog box is like a script editing window, except that it's a dialog box. In other words, you can't switch back and forth between the Script Properties dialog box and, say, the HTML inspector.

To edit a script:

1. View the script properties in the Properties inspector.
2. Click on Edit. The Script Properties dialog box will appear (**Figure 44**).

   When you're finished typing or editing your script, click on OK to return to the Document window.

If you write JavaScript, you can write your own actions and add them to the Behaviors inspector.

To add an action to the Behaviors inspector:

1. If Dreamweaver is running, exit the program.
2. Save the code for the action all by itself in an HTML file (no <html> tags, no <body> tags, and so on.). Name the HTML file something recognizable, following Dreamweaver's suit. The Go to URL action, for instance, is saved in a file called Go To URL.html. (Yes, the spaces are included in the filename, since both Windows 95 and the Mac can understand that.)
3. Drop the new file into the Actions folder:
   - On the PC: C:\Program Files\Macromedia\Dreamweaver\Configuration\Behaviors\Actions
   - On the Mac: file:///Dreamweaver/Configuration/Behaviors/Actions
4. Launch Dreamweaver. The Action will appear on the Add Action menu in the Behaviors inspector.

Drawing Timelines

Figure 1 The magic bus at futurefarmers.com uses a Timeline in a JavaScript pop-up window. This is what it looks like when the page loads.

Figure 2 It moves!

Figure 3 It keeps moving until it's off the screen, and then it starts over.

Figure 4 One click opens a new little window with a new Timeline.

Timelines are a way to add animation to a Web page using JavaScript. As the people at Macromedia are so proud of saying, you don't need to write any code, and Timelines use no ActiveX, Java, or plug-ins.

Timelines use JavaScript to control layers (**Figures 1–4**). A layer can move, resize, appear, or disappear—and what happens when is controlled by a sequence of frames.

These frames are not the same as the frames I discussed in Chapter 8. These are *animation frames*. Just like the frames of footage in a movie, each frame can be slightly different from the last, which creates the illusion of movement over time on a 2-D surface. In this case, of course, the 2-D surface is a Web page projected on a computer screen rather than a film projected on a movie screen.

✔ Tips

- Since Timelines rely on layers in order to work their magic, they can only be viewed in a 4.0 browser.
- If you need information on layers, refer to Chapter 11. For information about Behaviors, turn to Chapter 12.

What Timelines Can Do

Timelines can incorporate three types of objects: layers, images, and Behaviors.

Layer properties that a Timeline can change include the following:

- **Moving** the layer's X+Y coordinates (position on the page or within the parent layer) (**Figure 5**).
- Changing **layer visibility**. You can switch between the three optional states: visible, hidden, or default (**Figure 6**).
- Changing the **stacking order,** or **Z-index** (**Figure 7**).
- Adjusting **layer dimensions** (**Figure 8**).

✔ Tip

- Changes to a layer's dimensions are not supported by Navigator 4.

The only **Image property** that a Timeline can change directly is the image's source. This way, you can perform image rollovers during a Timeline without using additional JavaScript.

Timelines can also call a **Behavior** from a particular frame. You can also use a Behavior to start, stop, or skip to a particular frame within a Timeline.

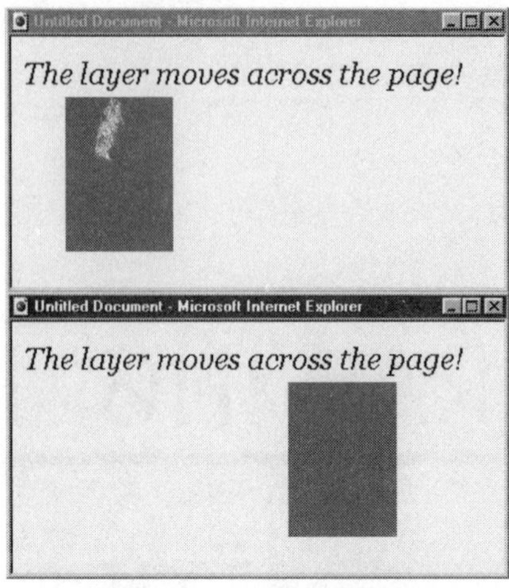

Figure 5 The Timeline moves the layer from left to right.

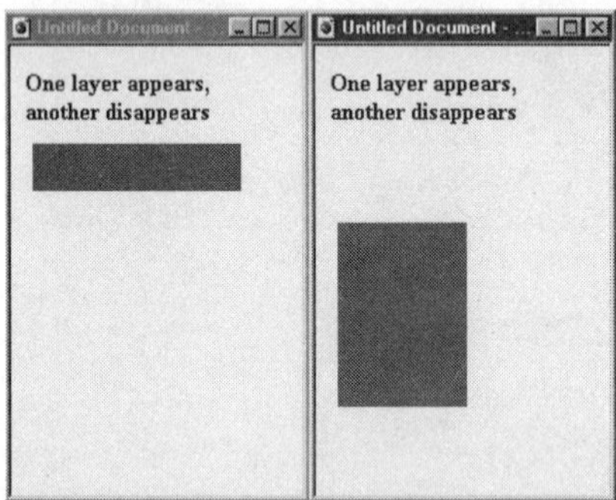

Figure 6 The Timeline shows one layer and hides another.

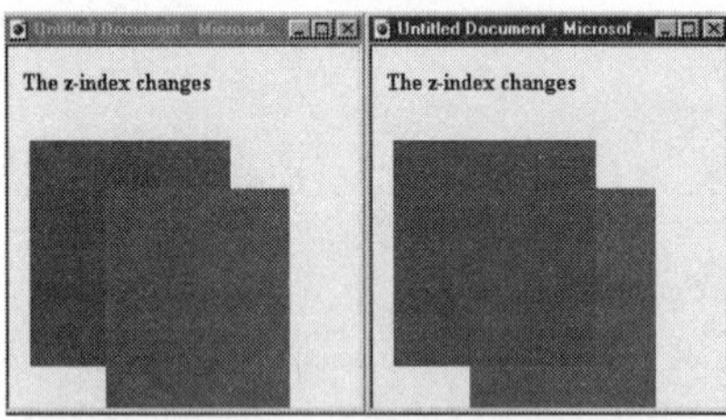

Figure 7 The Timeline changes the Z-index of the layers.

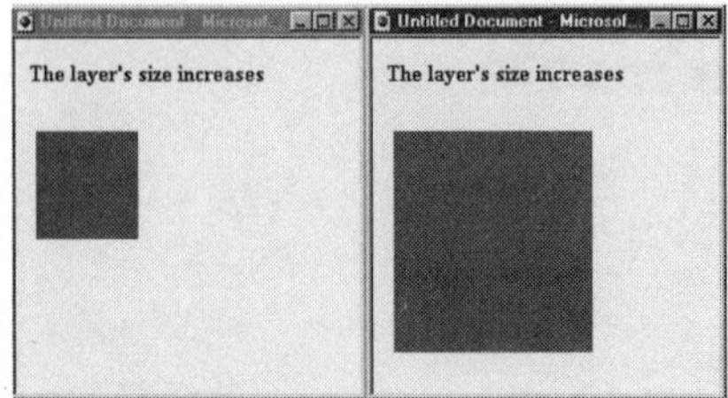

Figure 8 The Timeline increases the size of the layer.

The Timelines Inspector

The Timelines inspector (**Figure 9**) is the tool you use to create and modify Timelines in Dreamweaver.

To view the Timelines inspector:

1. From the Document window menu bar, select Window > Timelines.

   or

   On the Launcher or the Launcher bar, click on the Timeline button.

   or

   Press F9.

In any case, the Timelines inspector will appear.

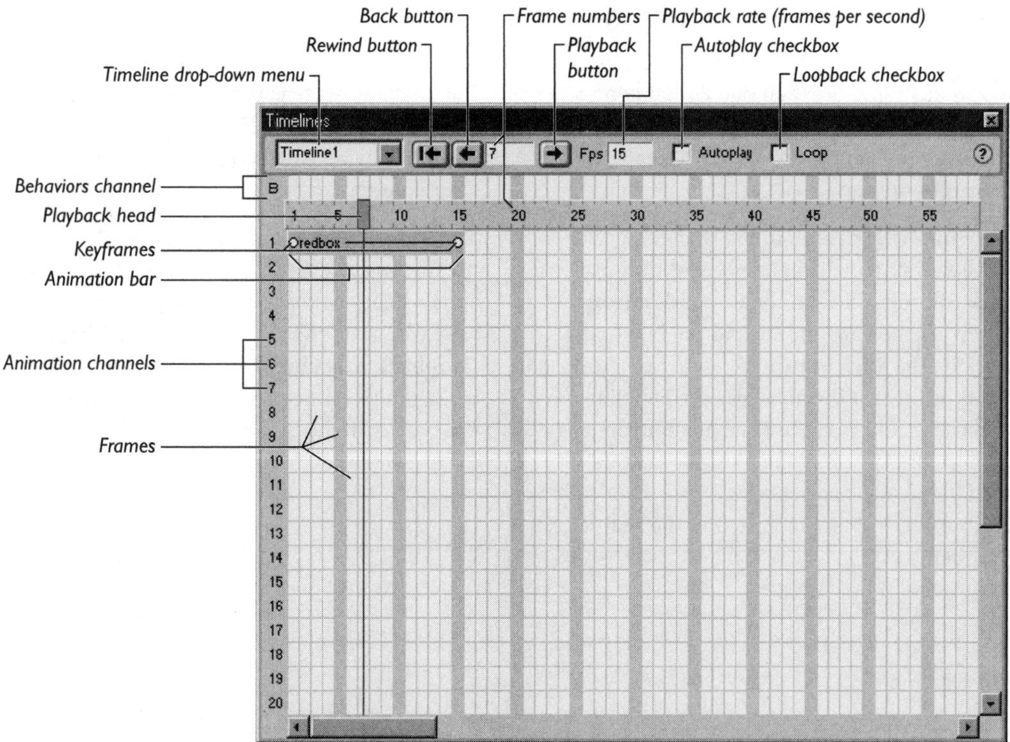

Figure 9 The Timelines inspector

Dissecting the Timelines Inspector

Each part of the Timelines inspector controls a different aspect of the Timelines on the page. Some of these elements won't really make much cognitive sense until you see them in operation, but you can use this page as a reference for what things do. Let's start at the top (**Figure 10**).

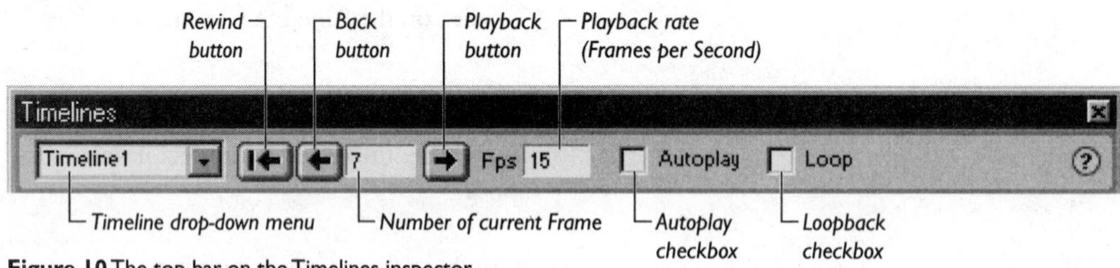

Figure 10 The top bar on the Timelines inspector.

If you include more than one Timeline on a page, you can switch between Timelines by choosing the Timeline from the **Timeline drop-down menu.**

You can play Timelines in the Document window using the Timelines inspector's playback controls. Click on the **Rewind button** to rewind the Timeline back to the beginning. Click on the **Back button** to rewind one frame at a time; hold it down to play the Timeline backwards. Click on the **Playback button** to advance the Timeline one frame at a time; hold it down to play the entire Timeline. The current frame is indicated in the **Frame number** text box.

The **playback rate** is in frames per second (fps). The default playback rate is 15 fps; you can set a higher or lower rate depending on your content.

You can add Behaviors that will control how the document plays. The **Autoplay checkbox** adds a Behavior that will make the Timeline start when the page finishes loading. The **Loopback checkbox** adds a Behavior that will make the Timeline play continuously while the page is in the browser.

Now we move to the part of the Timelines inspector that controls the content (**Figure 11**).

Use the **Behaviors channel** to add Behaviors that will be called from a certain frame in the Timeline.

Each numbered column in the Timeline inspector is a **frame**. Each frame is numbered. The **playback head** (the red bar) shows the advance of the playback. As the playback head passes over each frame, the **frame number** will appear next to the Playback button.

Each numbered row in the Timeline inspector is an **animation channel**. Different objects often occupy different animation channels.

When an object is added to a Timeline, the Timeline inspector displays an **animation bar** in its assigned animation channel. The little bullets at the beginning and end of the Animation bar are **keyframes**. You can add other keyframes to an animation bar to add actions to the Timeline.

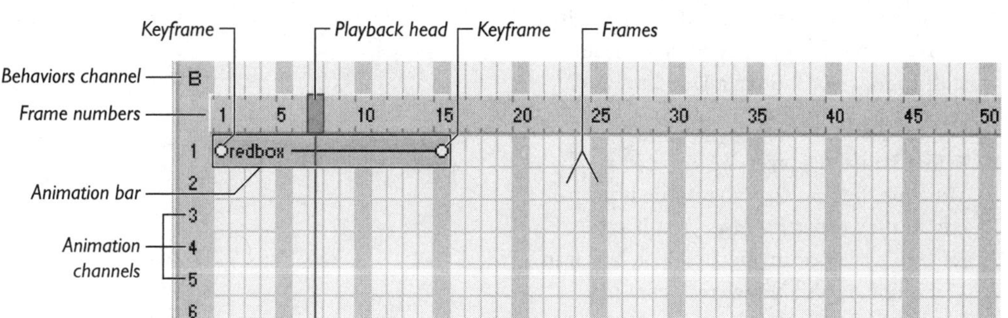

Figure 11 The content area of the Timelines inspector.

Adding a Layer to a Timeline

You create a Timeline by adding an object to it. Once an object is added, Dreamweaver automatically adds the Timeline code to the page.

To add a layer to a Timeline:

1. View the Timelines inspector.
2. Select the layer in the Document window (**Figure 12**).
3. From the Document window menu bar, select Modify > Add Object to Timeline.

   or

   Right-click (hold down the mouse button on a Mac) on the object's animation bar in the Timelines inspector, and select Add Object from the pop-up menu that appears.

A new animation bar will appear in the Timelines inspector (**Figure 13**).

✔ Tips

- The only objects you can add to a Timeline are layers and images. If you want other stuff to move or hide in a Timeline, add the objects to a layer.
- Before you add a layer or image to a Timeline, be sure that you name it properly in the Properties inspector. If you rename a layer or image after you add it to a Timeline, it will be deleted from the Timeline and you'll have to add it again.
- To find out how to add images and Behaviors to a Timeline, see the sections called *To add an image to a Timeline* and *To add a Behavior to a Timeline*.
- You can also drag an object onto the Timeline. Click on the object and drag it to the exact location (channel and frame) where you want it to appear (**Figure 14**).

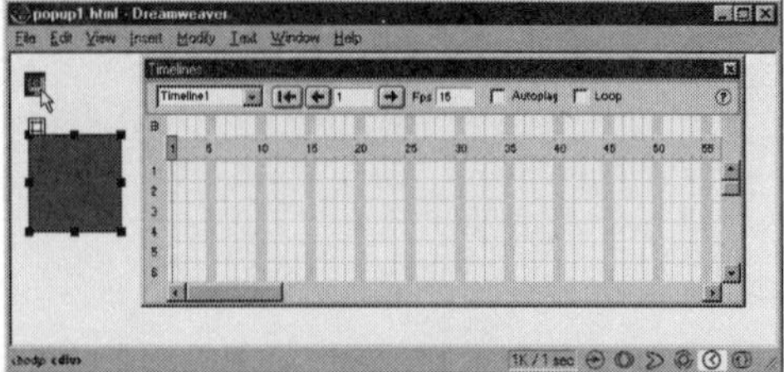

Figure 12 Select the layer in the Document window. Notice that the Timelines inspector doesn't have any objects in it yet.

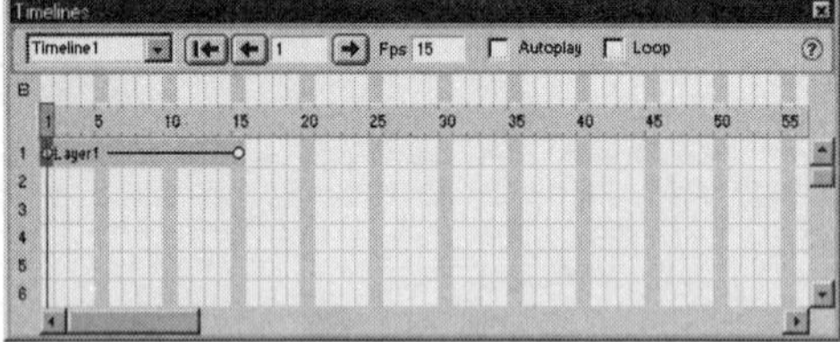

Figure 13 When you add the layer to the Timeline, an animation bar appears in the first available animation channel.

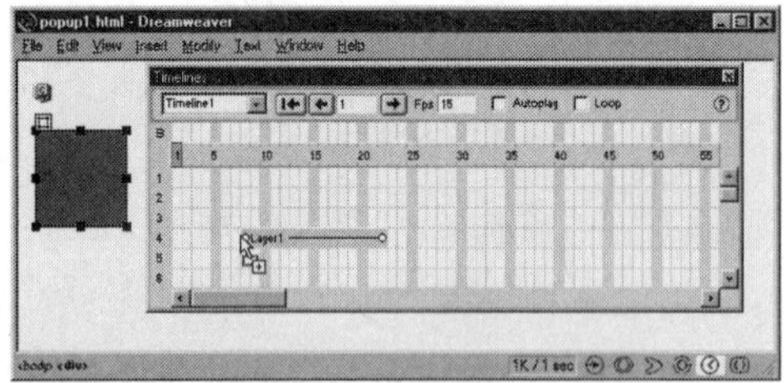

Figure 14 Dragging and dropping a layer into the Timelines inspector—it lands right where you drop it.

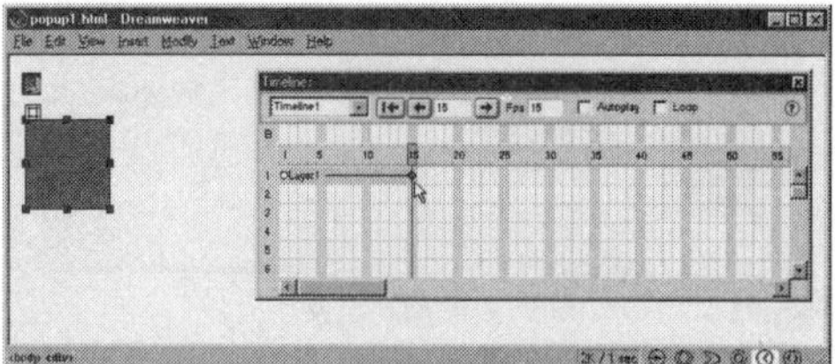

Figure 15 Click on the keyframe bullet at the end of the layer's animation bar to select that frame as well as the layer.

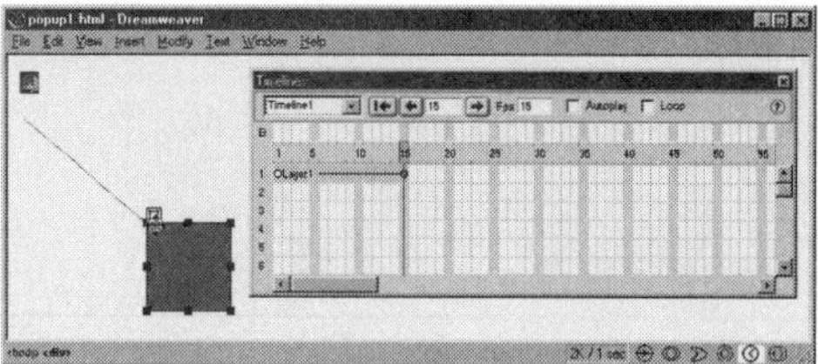

Figure 16 With the end keyframe selected, drag the layer to its new location and let go. The Timelines inspector will record the new position and draw a line from position 1 to position 2.

Setting the Playback Rate

The default playback rate for Dreamweaver Timelines is 15 frames per second. Macromedia advises not to set this rate much faster; the 15 fps rate is based on optimal performance on the average machine. Setting a faster playback rate might not actually make the animation go faster; while it might do so on your local machine, it's also the case that all the images and layers that you're playing with are stored in your memory cache. You can, however, set a lower rate for slower speeds.

Timeline Actions

Timeline actions are briefly described in the section called *What Timelines Can Do*. In this section, I'm going to go over each action, step by step, starting with moving layers. As I go through each action a layer can perform, I'll describe the various modifications you can make to a Timeline.

Moving Layers

The easiest way to start learning Timelines is to move a layer on the page.

To move a layer using a Timeline:

1. Add the layer to the Timeline.
2. In the Timelines inspector, click on the keyframe bullet at the end of the layer's Animation bar (**Figure 15**). The playback head (the red bar) will move to that frame.

   The layer will be selected in the Document window automatically.
3. Click on the layer's selection handle and drag it to the position on the page where you want it to end up.

You'll see a line drawn from the layer's old position to its new position (**Figure 16**). The line connects the top-left corners of the layer in each position. This is the path that the Timeline will follow.

You can watch the layer move in the Document window by playing back the Timeline.

To play back a Timeline:

1. In the Timelines inspector, click on the Rewind button [rewind icon] to move the playback head back to the beginning of the Timeline.
2. Move the Timelines inspector so you can see the area of the Document window that the Timeline takes place in.
3. In the Timelines inspector, click on and hold down the Play button [play icon].

You'll see the layer move across the page (**Figure 17**).

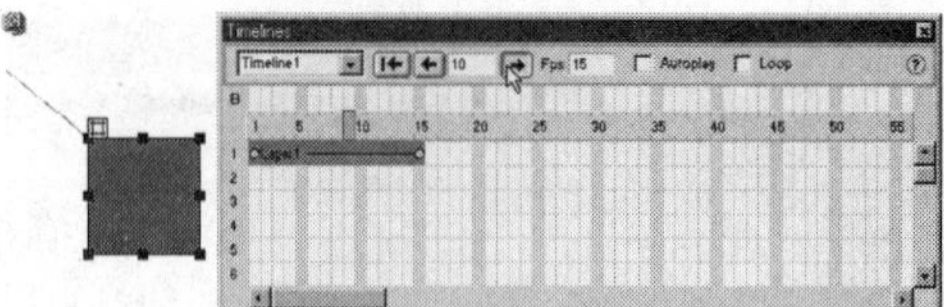

Figure 17 The Timeline in mid-play.

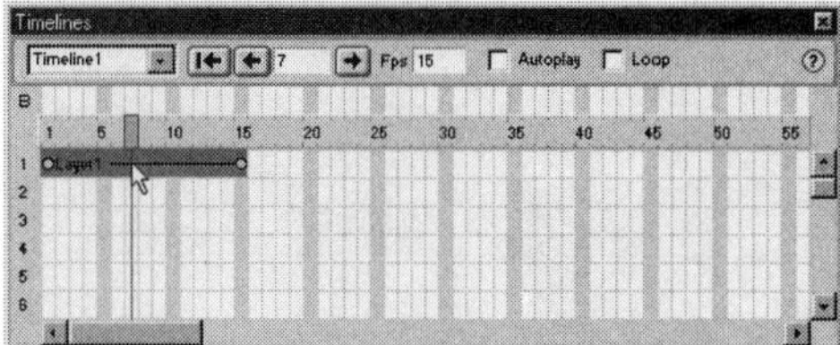

Figure 18 Click at the point on the animation bar where you want to add the new keyframe. The playback head will move, and the number of the frame will be indicated in the frame number text box.

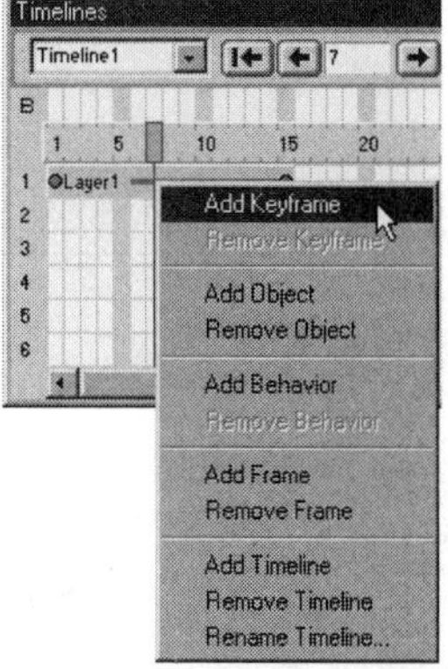

Figure 19 Select Add Keyframe from the pop-up menu.

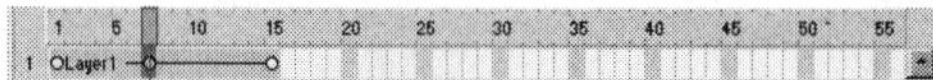

Figure 20 A keyframe bullet will appear on the animation bar.

About Keyframes

The Timeline inspector tracks the movement of a layer from one point to another frame by frame, and it paces the movement of an object so that the frame-to-frame transitions are smooth.

If there are only two points in a Timeline, the line is automatically straight. You can add a third point to a Timeline to make a layer move in an arc, or you can add multiple points to make the layer move wherever you want on the page.

You do this by adding keyframes. A *keyframe* is a point on a Timeline where something happens. Each animation bar in a Timeline automatically has two keyframes: the beginning frame and the end frame.

To add a keyframe:

1. In the Timelines inspector, move the pointer to the place on the animation bar where you want the new action to happen, and click on that point (**Figure 18**). The playback head will automatically move to the new frame.
2. From the Document window menu bar, select Modify > Timeline > Add Keyframe

   or

   Right-click (hold down the mouse button on a Mac) on the object's animation bar in the Timelines inspector, and select Add Keyframe from the pop-up menu that appears (**Figure 19**).

   or

   press F9.

The Timelines inspector will add a keyframe bullet to the animation bar (**Figure 19**).

✔ Tip

- Dreamweaver will automatically add a keyframe to an animation bar if you select an entire animation bar and then modify an attached object while the playback head is on any frame that's not already a keyframe for that object.

To add a new layer position to a keyframe:

1. In the Timelines inspector, click on the new keyframe. The Layer will become selected automatically (**Figure 21**).
2. Move the layer to the position on the page where you want it to be when that keyframe is played (**Figure 22**).

The line drawn between the beginning position on the page and the end position on the page will now arc to fit the third point into the movement line (**Figure 23**).

✔ Tip

- Play back the Timeline now to see how this movement looks.

Now you know how to change a layer's position, play back a Timeline, and add keyframes (and therefore, additional actions) to a Timeline. Let's look at some of the other things Timelines can do.

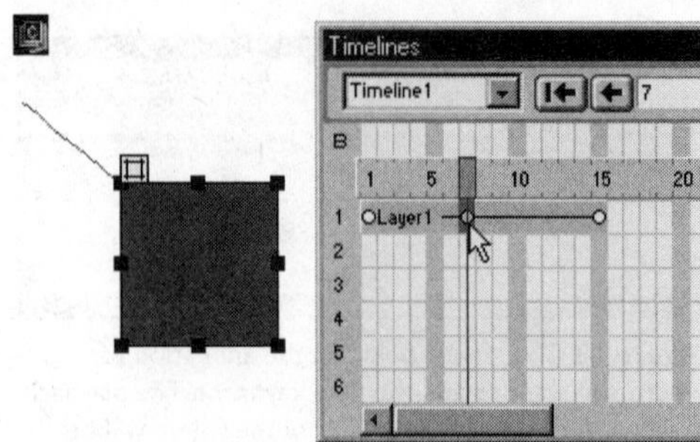

Figure 21 Select the keyframe, and the layer will automatically become selected. If for some reason it doesn't become selected, click on the layer's selection handle.

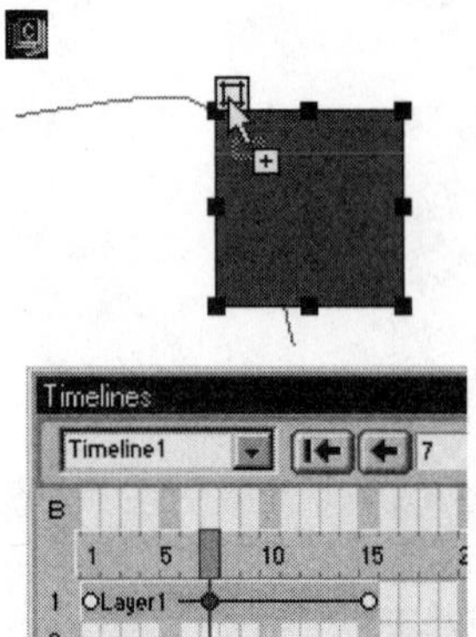

Figure 22 With the keyframe selected in the Timelines inspector, move the layer to its new location.

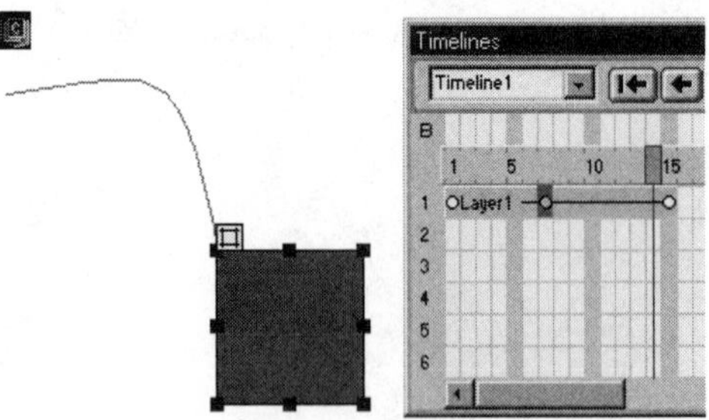

Figure 23 I fast forwarded to near the end of the Timeline so you could see the arc drawn by Dreamweaver between the three keyframes.

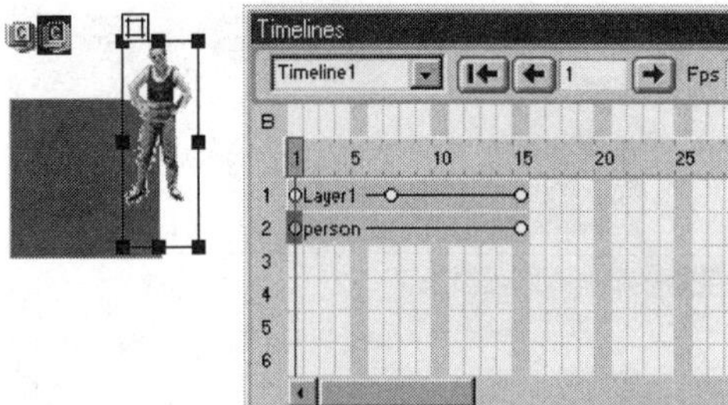

Figure 24 First, I add the new layer to the Timeline.

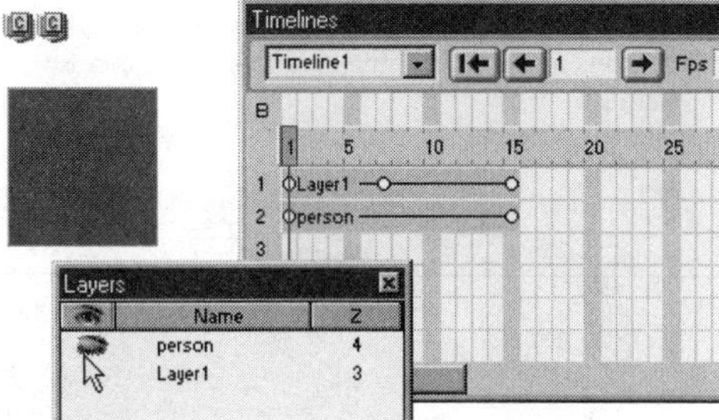

Figure 25 Then, I set its initial visibility to hidden on the first keyframe.

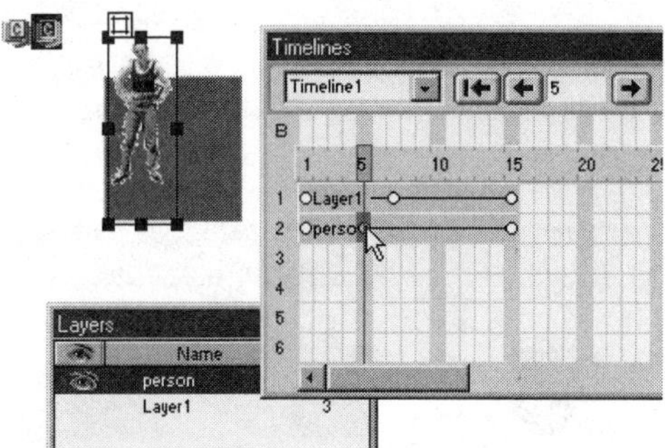

Figure 26 Finally, I added a new keyframe and set the layer's visibility to visible on the fifth keyframe. When the Timeline plays, the second layer will appear while the first layer moves.

Showing and Hiding Layers

You can show or hide a layer in a Timeline by changing its visibility to visible, hidden, or default.

To show or hide a layer during a Timeline:

1. If the layer is not already added to the Timeline, add the layer to the Timeline.
2. Click on the first keyframe on the layer's animation bar (**Figure 24**).
3. Using the Layers inspector or the Properties inspector, set the layer's visibility to the state you want it to be in when the Timeline begins playing (**Figure 25**).
4. On the layer's animation bar, add the keyframe where you want the visibility change to occur.
5. With the proper keyframe selected, change the visibility of the layer (**Figure 26**).
6. If you want the layer to change visibility again at the end of the Timeline, click on the keyframe at the end of the layer's animation bar, and change the layer's visibility.

To change the location of a keyframe:

1. In the Timelines inspector, click on the keyframe you want to move.
2. Hold down the mouse button and drag the keyframe bullet to a different frame.
3. Let go of the mouse button.

Voilà! The keyframe has moved.

✔ Tip

- Images that are in hidden layers are automatically downloaded with the page. This is a good way to preload images for swapping image source. Or skip the source swapping altogether and just show or hide the layers that the new images are in.

Changing the Z-index

As you know, a layer's Z-index is what makes layers so layer-like. You can change the Z-index of layers during a Timeline.

✔ Tips

- Make sure all the layers have the Z-index you want them to have at their beginning keyframe(s) in the Timeline (**Figure 27**).
- Z-index numbers affect the overlap of two or more layers; you can't make a layer hide under an image that isn't in a layer.

To change the Z-index of a layer during a Timeline:

1. In the Timelines inspector, add any keyframes you need to the layer's animation bar.
2. Click on the keyframe that marks the point at which the Z-index will change. The layer will be selected automatically.
3. Using the Layers inspector or the Properties inspector, change the Z-index number of the layer.
4. Play back the Timeline to watch the layer move over or under another layer on the page (**Figure 29**).

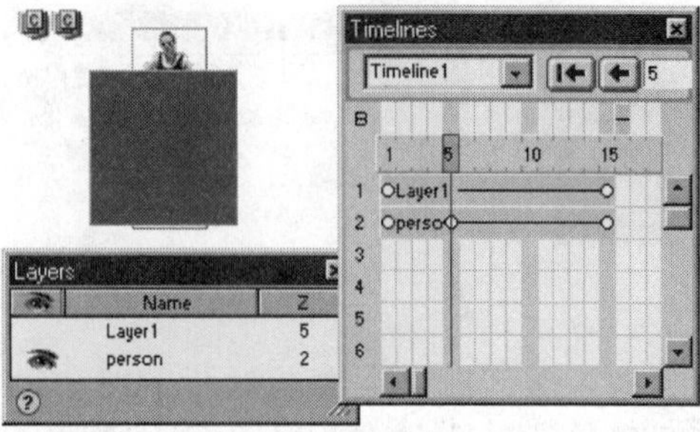

Figure 27 In this variant on the "appearing person and moving square" Timeline, I took out the movement of the box, but in the fifth frame, the person appears. I set the Z-index in the first frame so that the box overlaps the person.

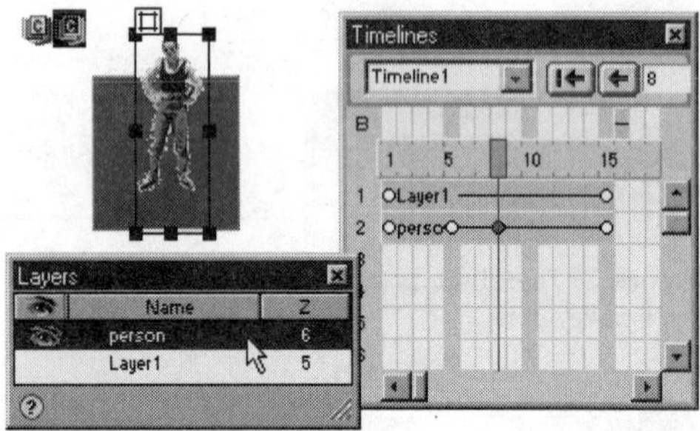

Figure 28 At Frame 8, I changed the Z-index of the person layer so that it would appear on top of the square.

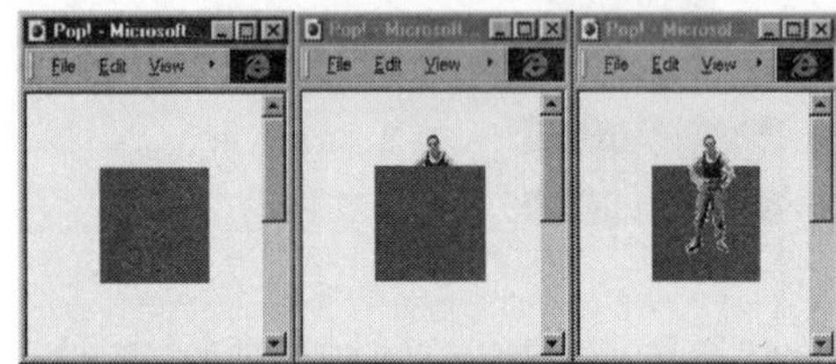

Figure 29 Three frames from a Timeline. In Frame 1, the square is visible. In Frame 5, the person appears, and the box is stacked on top of the person. In Frame 8, the person's Z-index changes so that it's on top of the square.

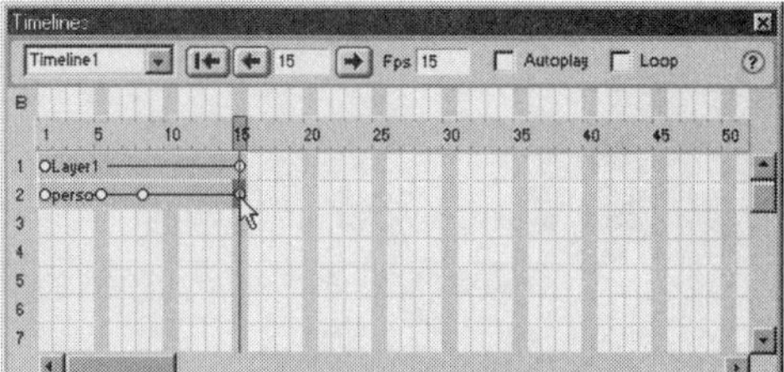

Figure 30 Click on the end keyframe and drag it to a new location.

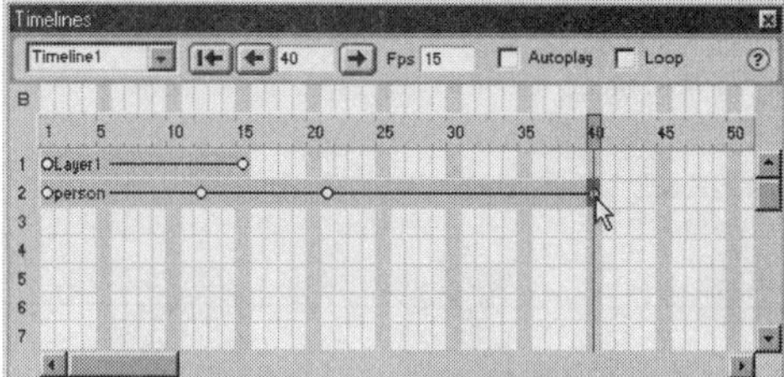

Figure 31 I lengthened the animation bar I selected in Figure 30. Notice how the keyframes in the middle of the animation bar are spaced out over the new length of the animation bar.

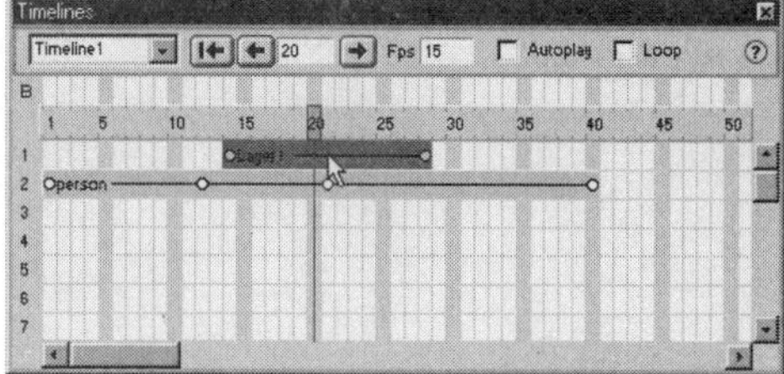

Figure 32 I moved the Layer1 animation bar. It will both start and end later in the Timeline now.

You can change the length and duration of an animation bar if you want a layer to start sooner or end later within the Timeline.

To move the beginning or end of an animation bar:

1. In the Timelines inspector, click on the beginning or ending keyframe on the layer's animation bar (**Figure 30**).
2. Drag the keyframe to a new frame number within the animation channel (**Figure 31**).

   You may notice the other elements in the Timeline moving around as you drag the keyframe.
3. Play the Timeline to see how it looks.
4. Repeat steps 1 and 2 as needed.

Longer Timelines allow for more actions and more gradual movement.

✔ Tips

- If you drag the end keyframe to lengthen the Timeline, any keyframes within the Timeline will be spaced out in proportion to their original position, to preserve the gradual arc of the Timeline (**Figure 31**).
- You can move an entire animation bar. Click on the middle of the bar (not on a keyframe) to select the whole thing, and drag it to a new location (**Figure 32**).
- See the section called *To change the location of a keyframe* earlier in the chapter to find out how to move an individual keyframe.

Changing Layer Dimensions

Besides changing the visibility and Z-index of a layer, you can also use a Timeline to change the dimensions of the layer.

✔ Tips

- Layer size changes only work in Internet Explorer 4, and not in Navigator 4.
- If you want to make a layer shrink in size, you should remember to change the layer's overflow setting to *hidden* or *scroll* in the Properties inspector; otherwise, the shrinking won't have any effect.

To change the dimensions of a layer using a Timeline:

1. In the Timelines inspector, click on the keyframe where you want the size change to occur. The layer will become selected automatically.
2. Change the size of the layer by dragging its handles, or by changing the W(idth) and H(eight) settings in the Properties inspector (**Figure 33**).
3. Play back the Timeline to see how it affects the size change.

Since the Timeline code makes layer properties change gradually rather than abruptly, the size change will begin a few frames before the set keyframe (**Figure 34**).

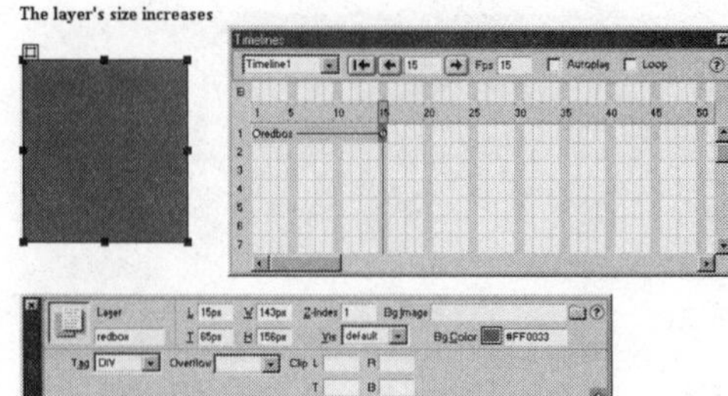

Figure 33 I selected the end keyframe and changed the size of the layer. If I click on each individual frame on the animation bar, the Properties inspector will display what size the layer will be in each succeeding frame leading up to the end frame's dimensions.

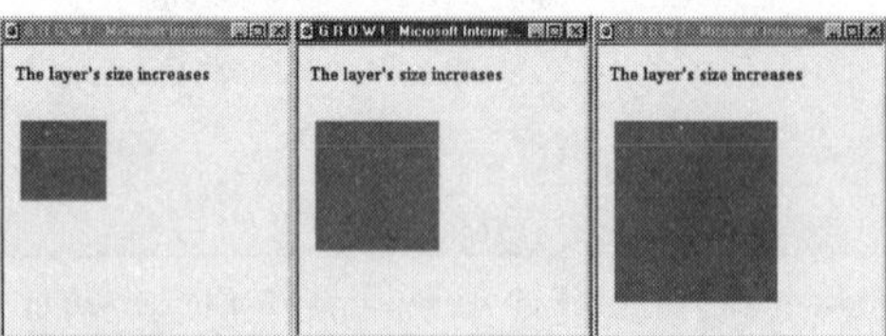

Figure 34 Three windows, showing the progression in size from Frame 1 to Frame 8 to Frame 15. I set two sizes: one in Frame 1, and one in Frame 15. With Dreamweaver Timelines these changes happen gradually; for an abrupt change, make the size change happen in two adjacent frames.

CHANGING LAYER DIMENSIONS

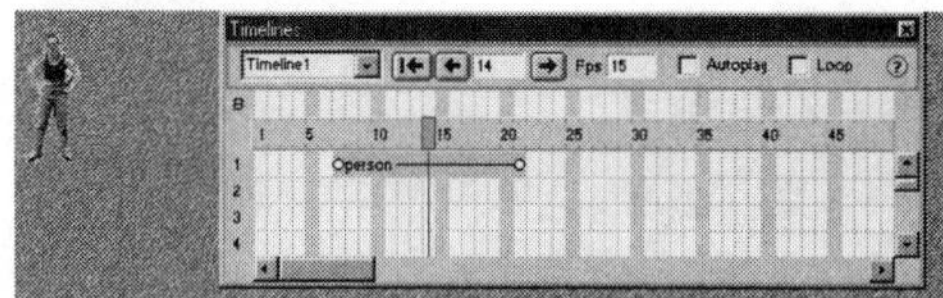

Figure 35 Here I am in the Document window. I've just added the image of the person—this time independent of any layers—to the Timeline.

Adding an Image to a Timeline

You can also add an image to a Timeline, although the only available action for images that are not in layers is swap source.

To add an image to a Timeline:

1. View the Timelines inspector.
2. Select the image in the Document window.
3. From the Document window menu bar, select Modify > Add Object to Timeline.

   or

   Right-click (hold down the mouse button on a Mac) on the object's animation bar in the Timelines inspector, and select Add Object from the pop-up menu that appears.

A new animation bar will appear in the Timelines inspector (**Figure 35**).

✔ Tip

- One way to preload images for source swapping is to place them in a hidden layer on the page.

Changing an image source with a Timeline is similar to using the Swap Image Behavior to create image rollovers, only the rollover will occur as time elapses rather than when triggered by a user event.

To change an image source using a Timeline:

1. Name the image using the Properties inspector.
2. Add the image to the Timeline.
3. Add any keyframes you need to the image's animation bar (**Figure 36**).
4. Click on the keyframe you want to use to change the image's source.
5. In the Properties inspector, change the source of the image to the source of the new image (**Figure 37**).
6. Play back the Timeline to watch the effect (**Figure 38**).

✔ Tip

- If you use Autoplay with a Timeline, and the image changes source on the end keyframe, the image will only roll over for an instant to the new source. You can extend the end of the image's Timeline if you want to use Autoplay with this action.

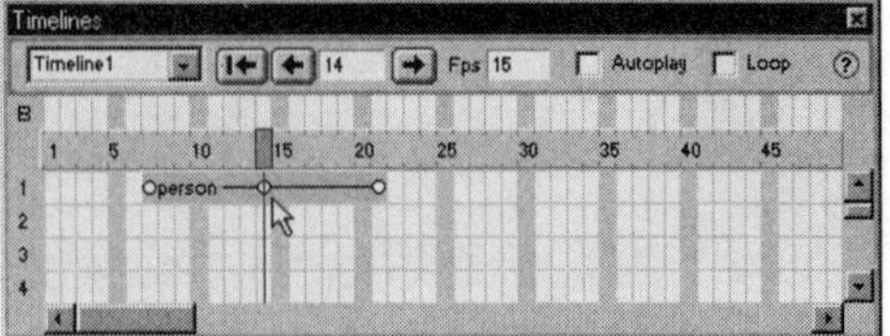

Figure 36 I added a keyframe to the image's animation bar; that's the point at which the source will change.

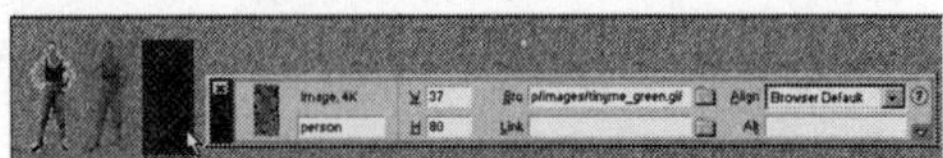

Figure 37 The two images side by side for comparison. With the keyframe selected, change the source in the Properties inspector. The third image, which I selected with the mouse, shows the rectangular borders of the transparent image.

Figure 38 When the Timeline plays the keyframe, the source changes to the second image.

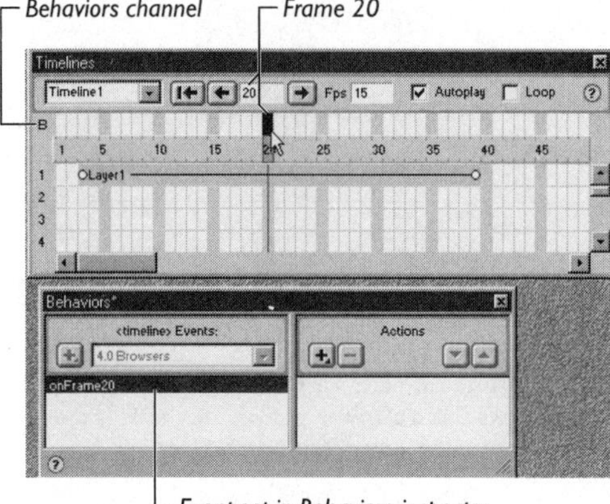

Figure 39 I double-clicked on the intersection of the Behaviors channel and Frame 20, and the Behaviors inspector appeared. The event was preset to onFrame20.

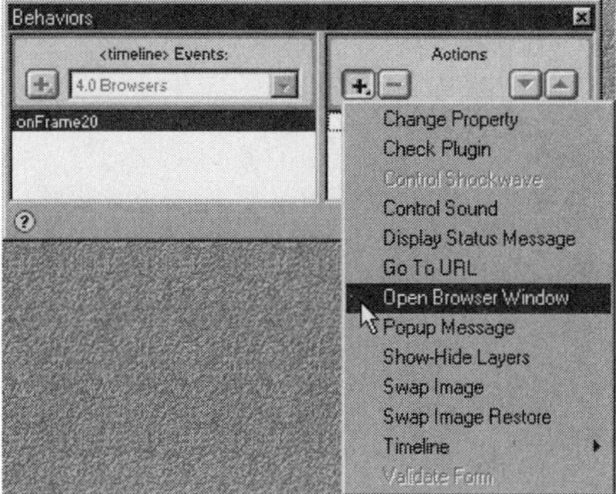

Figure 40 On the Behaviors inspector, click on the Add Action button, and choose an action from the pop-up menu.

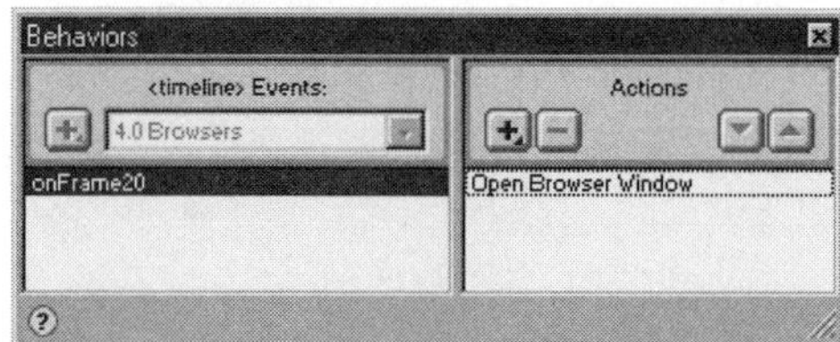

Figure 41 I added the Open Browser Window action to Frame 20 of the Timeline; when the Timeline is played, the window will launch on Frame 20.

Adding a Behavior to a Timeline

All the nifty Behaviors I discussed in Chapter 12 can be added to a Timeline. For instance, you can make the Timeline execute an animation and then load a new page; you can play a sound at a certain frame in a Timeline; or you can use a Timeline to start playing a Shockwave movie at a certain frame.

To add a Behavior to a Timeline frame:

1. In the Timeline inspector, choose the frame that will launch the Behavior, and click on it to move the playback head to that frame.
2. Double-click on the frame number within the Behaviors channel (**Figure 39**). The Behaviors inspector will appear.

   The browser (4.0 browsers) and the event (onFrameNumber) will be preset.
3. In the Actions area of the Behaviors inspector, click on the Add Action button to pop up the menu of available actions (**Figure 40**).
4. Choose the action you want to add. The associated dialog box will appear.
5. Fill out the dialog box and click on OK. The name of the action will appear in the Actions list box (**Figure 41**).

The Behavior will be added to the Timeline. You'll see a little marker at that particular frame in the Behaviors channel.

✔ Tips

- For details about individual JavaScript Behaviors in Dreamweaver, see Chapter 12.
- Like menus? You can also add a Behavior to a particular frame by moving the playback head to that frame and selecting Modify > Add Behavior to Timeline from the Document window menu bar.

Making Timelines Go

Timelines won't start playing in a browser unless another piece of JavaScript tells them to. There are two ways you can make a Timeline start playing, both of which use JavaScript Behaviors.

The Autoplay Behavior is an onLoad Behavior; once the page loads, the animation will begin.

Figure 42 When you check off the Autoplay checkbox, a dialog box will appear informing you that it's going to add the Autoplay behavior. Once you get the point, you can make this dialog box go away by checking the *Don't show me this message again* checkbox.

To make a Timeline play automatically:

1. In the Behaviors inspector, place a checkmark in the Autoplay checkbox. A dialog box will appear (**Figure 42**) letting you know that Dreamweaver will add in the Autoplay code.

Simple, yes?

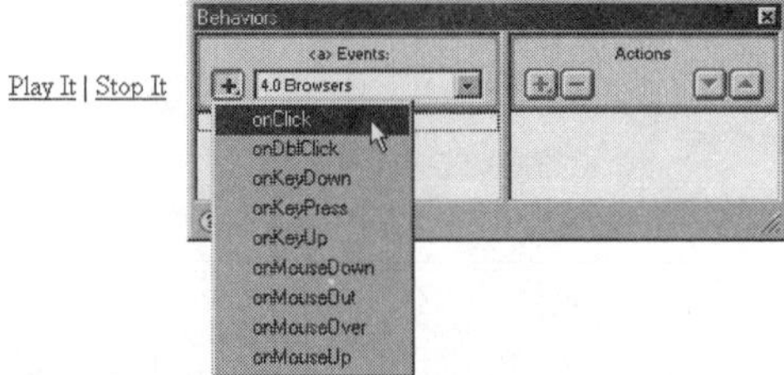

Figure 43 I selected the link called "Play It" and added the onClick event.

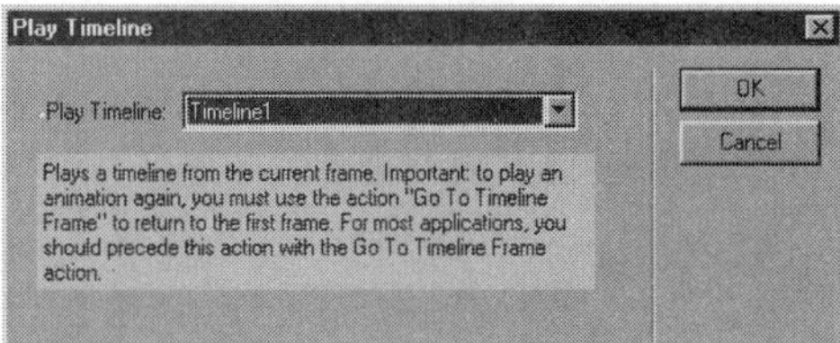

Figure 44 I chose Timeline > Play Timeline from the Add Action menu, and now I can select my Timeline in the Play Timeline dialog box.

You can also make a Behavior call a Timeline; when the user clicks on or mouses over a link or image, the Timeline will play.

To make a Behavior play a Timeline:

1. In the Document window, click on the object you want to use to make the Timeline play (`a`, `img`, form button).
2. In the Behaviors inspector, select 4.0 Browsers from the browser drop-down menu.
3. Click on the Add Event button [+], and add an event (`onClick`, `onMouseOver`) (Figure 43).
4. In the Actions area of the Behaviors inspector, click on the Add Action button [+].
5. From the pop-up menu that appears, select Timeline > Play Timeline. The Play Timeline dialog box will appear (**Figure 44**).
6. If there is more than one Timeline on your page, select the Timeline you want to use from the Play Timeline drop-down menu.
7. Click on OK to close the Play Timeline dialog box.

The event will call the Timeline when the page is loaded in a browser.

You can also make a Behavior stop a Timeline. This is a quite smart thing to do, especially if you're using the Loop function (I'll get to that in a minute). The browser's Stop button will not stop an in-progress Timeline.

To make a Behavior stop a Timeline:

1. In the Document window, click on the object you want to use to make the Timeline stop (`a`, `img`, form button).
2. In the Behaviors inspector, select 4.0 Browsers from the browser drop-down menu.
3. Click on the Add Event button [+], and add an event (`onClick`, `onMouseOver`).
4. In the Actions area of the Behaviors inspector, click on the Add Action button [+].
5. From the pop-up menu that appears, select Timeline > Stop Timeline (**Figure 45**). The Stop Timeline dialog box will appear (**Figure 46**).
6. If there is more than one Timeline on your page, select the Timeline you want to use from the Play Timeline drop-down menu.

   or

   Select ALL TIMELINES from the drop-down menu.
7. Click on OK to close the Stop Timeline dialog box.

✔ Tip

- You cannot make the same link (or image) both play and stop a Timeline. An event that signals both a Play and a Stop event will only advance the Timeline one frame at a time. (If the order is Stop and then Play, it won't stop at all.) I have to admit, though, that this was a great way to get screen captures for this chapter.

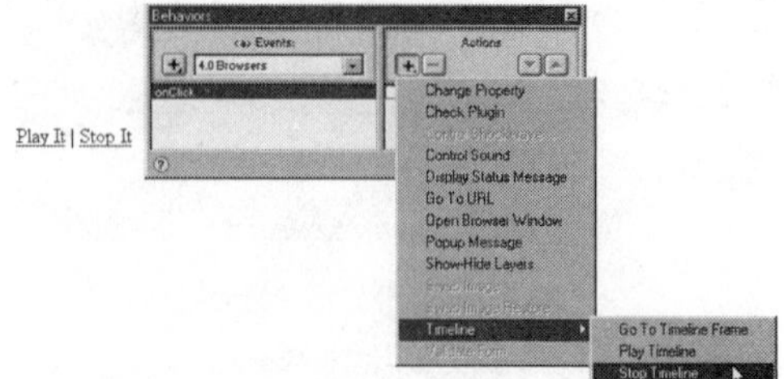

Figure 45 Having selected the Stop It link and the onClick action, I chose Timeline > Stop Timeline from the Add Action menu.

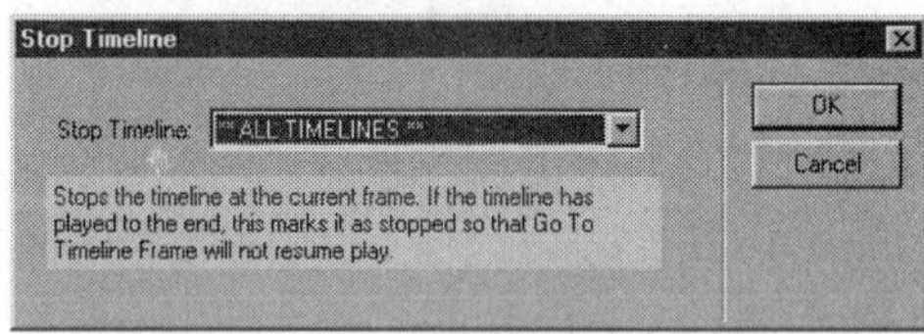

Figure 46 In the Stop Timeline dialog box, I can choose to stop all Timelines or one selected Timeline.

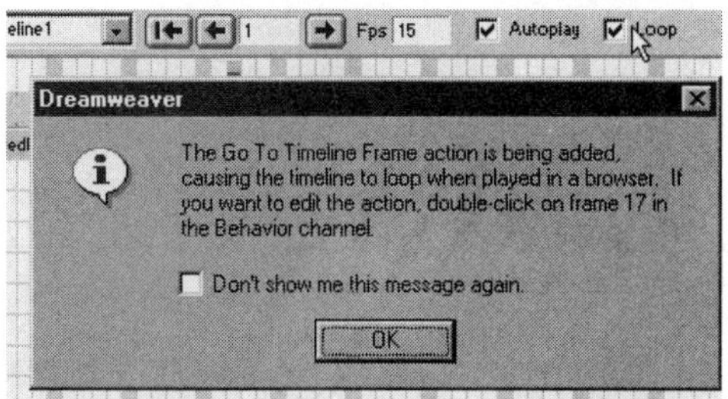

Figure 47 Click on the Loop checkbox, and this friendly dialog box will appear to tell you what's up and to which frame number it's adding the Behavior. To make it go away, click on the *Don't show me this message again* checkbox.

Figure 48 The Behaviors channel in this Timeline has two Behavior markers. The one that follows the last frame is the one to double-click if you want to edit the Loop behavior.

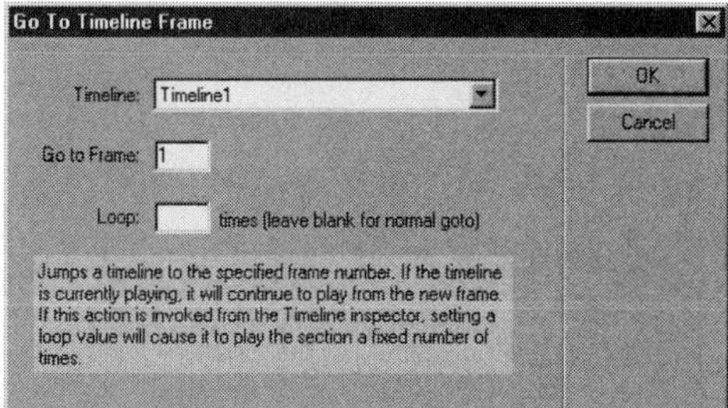

Figure 49 The Go to Timeline Frame dialog box controls the Loop behavior.

Loop and Rewind

Some Timelines are so beautiful, you wish they'd go on forever. (Actually, the first 10 or so Timelines you make will automatically be that beautiful.) You can make a Timeline repeat indefinitely, or a certain number of times, by using the Loop feature.

To add the Loop:

1. In the Timelines inspector, place a checkmark in the Loop checkbox. A dialog box will appear, letting you know that Dreamweaver will add the Go To Frame Behavior code (**Figure 47**).

The Loop Behavior uses an action called Go to Frame. In the case of an automatic loop, the Timeline reaches the end and then goes back to Frame 1.

To modify the Loop:

1. In the Timelines inspector, locate the last frame in the Timeline. You'll see a marker in the Behaviors channel in the frame after that.
2. Double-click on the last Behaviors marker (**Figure 48**). The Behaviors inspector will appear.
3. Double-click on the action Go To Timeline Frame listed in the Actions list box. The Go To Timeline Frame dialog box will appear (**Figure 49**).
4. To make the loop pick up at a frame other than Frame 1, type the frame number in the Go to Frame text box.
5. To make the loop continue for a number of times less than infinity, type a number in the Loop text box.
6. Click on OK to close the Go to Timeline Frame text box.

Preview the Timeline in a 4.0 browser to see if it does what you think it will.

You can also add the Go to Frame Behavior from outside the Timeline. For instance, you can have a "Play Animation" button, a "Stop Animation" button, and a "Go Back to the Part with the Pie" button.

To add a Go to Frame Behavior:

1. In the Document window, click on the object you want to use to make the Timeline jump to a particular frame (a, img, form button).
2. In the Behaviors inspector, select 4.0 Browsers from the browser drop-down menu.
3. Click on the Add Event button, and add an event (onClick, onMouseOver) (**Figure 50**).
4. In the Actions area of the Behaviors inspector, click on the Add Action button.
5. From the pop-up menu that appears, select Timeline > Go to Timeline Frame. The Go to Timeline Frame dialog box will appear (**Figure 51**).
6. If there is more than one Timeline on your page, select the Timeline you want to use from the Timeline drop-down menu.
7. To choose the frame to go to (the frame to rewind or fast forward to), type its number in the Go to Frame text box.

   You cannot set a loop from outside the Timeline.
8. Click on OK to close the Go to Timeline Frame dialog box.

When the user commits the event, the action will cause the Timeline to jump forward or backward to a particular frame.

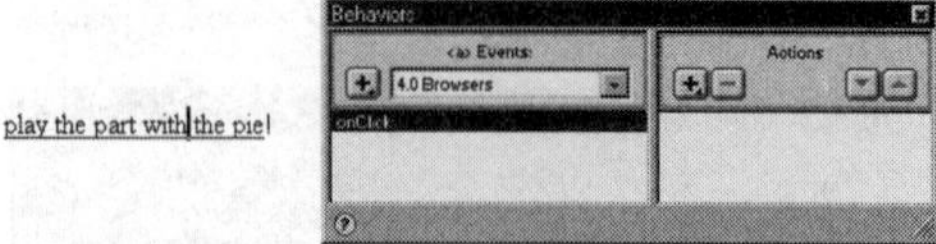

Figure 50 I added the onClick action to the "Play the part with the pie" link.

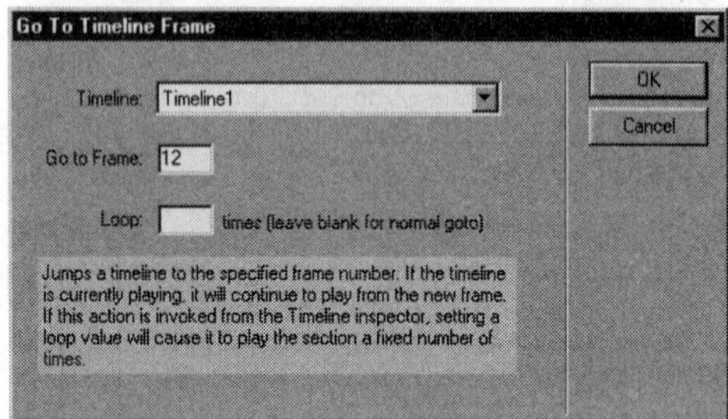

Figure 51 In the Go to Timeline Frame dialog box, I specified Frame 12 to go to.

✔ Tip

- You can add a Go to Timeline Frame action within a Timeline, too—not just at the end of the Timeline. Imagine this: On Frame 8, an image appears. On Frame 14, the Go to Timeline action makes the Timeline jump back to Frame 7. With the number of loops set to 3, the Timeline would go back to Frame 7 three times to make the image pop up before it continued to the end.

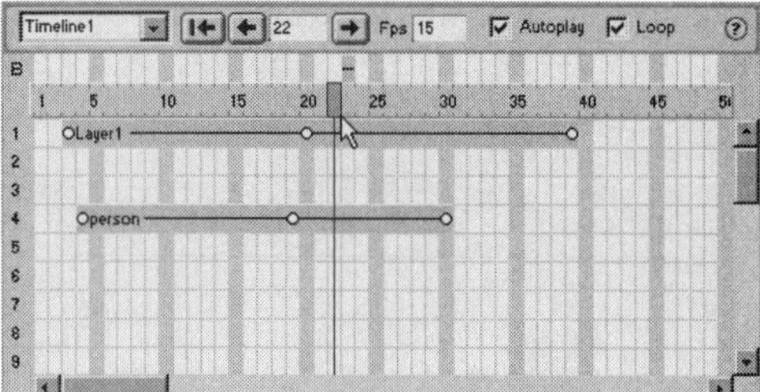

Figure 52 I placed the playback head one frame before a Behavior on my Timeline.

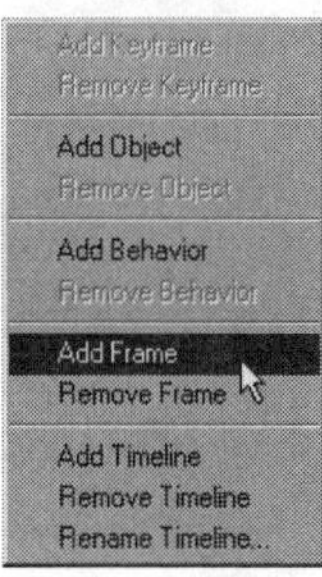

Figure 53 Right-click on the frame, and select Add Frame from the pop-up menu.

Figure 54 A new frame was added between the playback head and the Behavior.

✔ Tips

- Tinkering with the middle of the Timeline by changing the number of frames is easier than moving around all the keyframes, behaviors, and objects.
- Adding and removing frames from the middle of a Timeline will remove any keyframes or Behaviors that reside in those frames.

Adding and Removing Frames

I've already told you how to move the beginning and end of an animation bar, as well as the keyframes. You can also add or remove frames from the middle of a Timeline.

To add frames to a Timeline:

1. In the Timelines inspector, click on a frame to move the playback head to the place in the Timeline where you want to add a frame (**Figure 52**).
2. From the Document window menu bar, select Modify > Timeline > Add Frame.

   or

   Right-click (hold down the mouse button on a Mac) on the object's animation bar in the Timelines inspector, and select Add Frame from the pop-up menu that appears (**Figure 53**).

The frame will be added to the right of the playback head (**Figure 54**).

You can also remove frames from a Timeline if you want to shorten the duration of the animation.

To remove frames from a Timeline:

1. In the Timelines inspector, move the playback head to the place in the Timeline from which you want to remove a frame.
2. From the Document window menu bar, select Modify > Timeline > Remove Frame.

   or

   Right-click (hold down the mouse button on a Mac) on the object's animation bar in the Timelines inspector, and select Remove Frame from the pop-up menu that appears.

The frame the playback head is resting on will be removed.

Using Multiple Timelines

You may want to use more than one Timeline if you want more than one animation to be available on the page. You can use the same objects in different Timelines, which could then be called by Behaviors attached to different links or buttons.

To add an additional Timeline:

1. From the Document window menu bar, select Modify > Timeline > Add Timeline.

The Timeline inspector will reset, hiding the animation bars for the original Timeline; additionally, all the indicators of the Timeline will disappear from the Document window (**Figures 55 and 56**).

To toggle between Timelines:

1. In the Timelines inspector, select the name of the Timeline you want to work with from the Timeline drop-down menu (**Figure 57**).

You can have as many Timelines as you want.

✔ Tip

- Each Timeline should be fairly simple, or your page will take several days to load and will have more opportunities to crash browsers around the world.

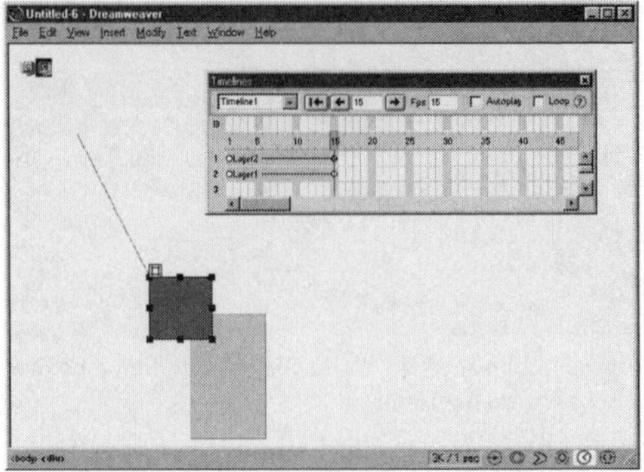

Figure 55 The Before Picture: Here's Timeline 1.

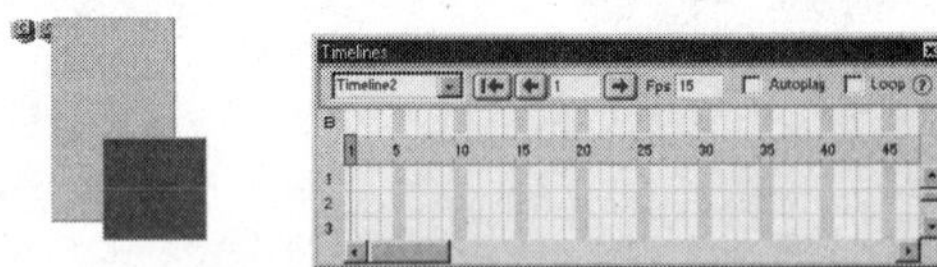

Figure 56 The After Picture: I just added Timeline 2. All traces of Timeline 1 are hidden.

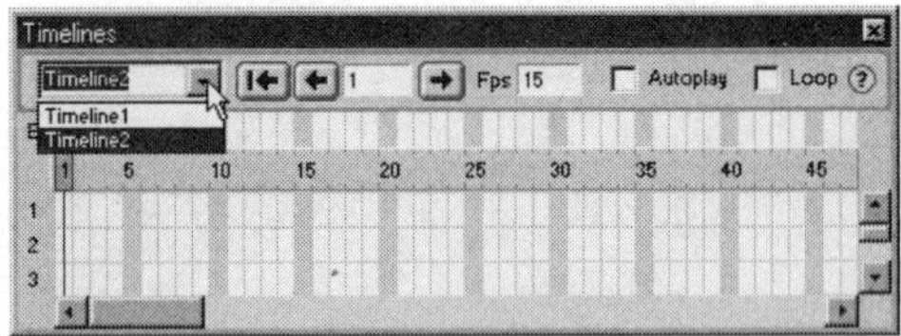

Figure 57 Choose which Timeline to work with from the drop-down menu on the Timelines inspector.

USING MULTIPLE TIMELINES

Figure 58 Type a new name for the Timeline in the Rename Timeline list box.

Tired of "Timeline 1" and Timeline 2"? Rename them.

To rename a Timeline:

1. View the Timeline you want to rename.
2. From the Document window menu bar, select Modify > Timeline > Rename Timeline. The Rename Timeline dialog box will appear (**Figure 58**).
3. Type the new name for your Timeline in the Timeline name text box.
4. Click on OK. The Rename Timeline dialog box will close.

The new name for your Timeline will appear in the Timeline drop-down menu in the Timelines inspector.

Deleting Objects and Timelines

Part of editing Timelines is removing objects from them—and even removing Timelines themselves.

To remove an object from a Timeline:

1. Select the object you want to remove.
2. From the Document window menu bar, select Modify > Timeline > Remove Object (**Figure 59**).

   or

   Right-click (hold down the mouse button on a Mac) on the object's animation bar in the Timelines inspector, and select Remove Object from the pop-up menu that appears.

Either way, the object will be removed from the Timeline.

✔ Tip

- To remove a Behavior from a Timeline, follow the steps above, substituting "Remove Behavior" for "Remove Object."

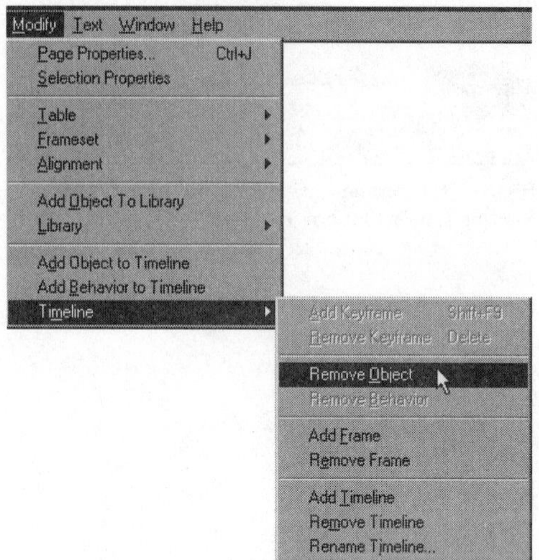

Figure 59 To remove an object, select Modify > Timeline > Remove Object. The Timelines inspector doesn't even need to be open for this.

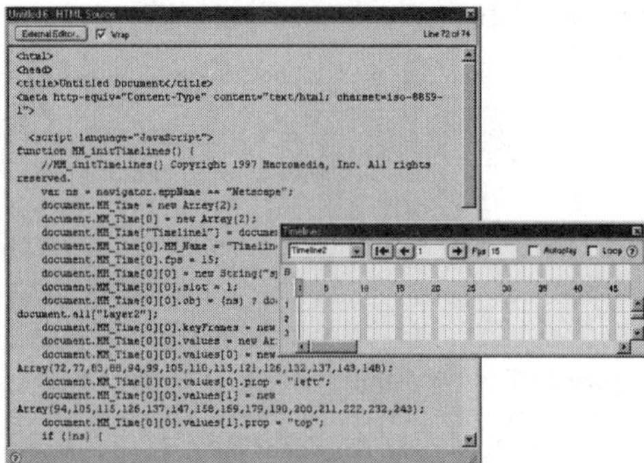

Figure 60 I removed all objects from the Timeline, but as you can see in the HTML inspector, the code for the Timeline is still there.

Even if you remove all the objects from a Timeline, the JavaScript code will still be in the page. You need to "officially" remove a Timeline to remove all traces of the code (**Figure 60**).

To remove a Timeline:

1. Select the Timeline you want to remove.
2. Are you sure you want to remove the whole thing?
3. From the Document window menu bar, select Modify > Timeline > Remove Timeline.

Poof! It's gone.

✔ Tip

- If you have a Timeline with objects and Behaviors already added to it, it might be a good idea to save a version of the document (File > Save As...) so that you don't lose the entire thing. You might decide that you want to use a version of it later on.

Bringing It All Together

Timelines are quite versatile, although my simplistic examples might not do them justice. To wrap up this chapter, I'm going to visually dissect a quasi-useful Timeline I constructed using most of the Timeline's capabilities. Follow the figure captions for **Figures 61–69**.

One note about **Figure 66**: the Map layer doesn't do anything in the second Timeline, but I added it so it would be visible while working. Dreamweaver displays the default image rather than the one that's been swapped in.

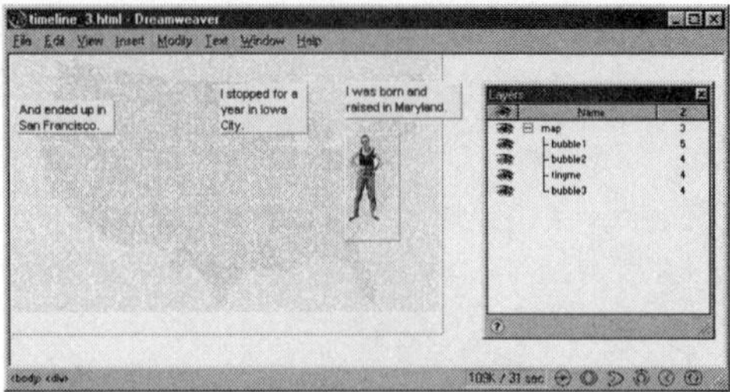

Figure 61 The raw materials. The page contains 5 layers: the map, the person, and three "bubbles." The other layers need to be positioned relative to the map, so they're all nested within the map.

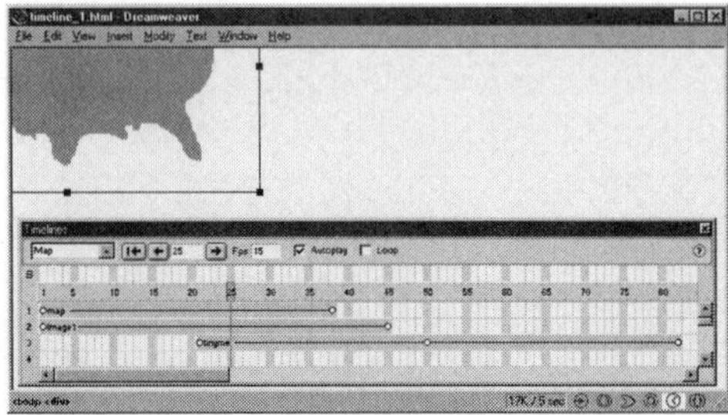

Figure 62 Frame 25 of the first Timeline, called Map. I want the window to begin blank. Then the first map is brought in from off-screen.

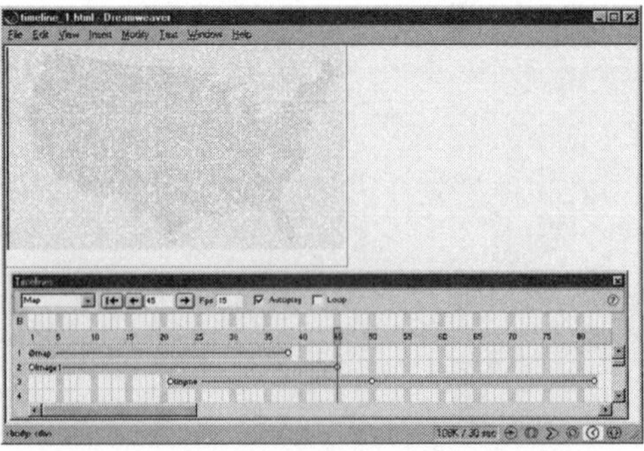

Figure 63 Frame 45 of the Map Timeline. A few frames after the map layer arrives, the image source changes into a different map (on frame 45—I changed the source in the Properties inspector). This map has a larger file size, but the image has been pre-loaded in a layer.

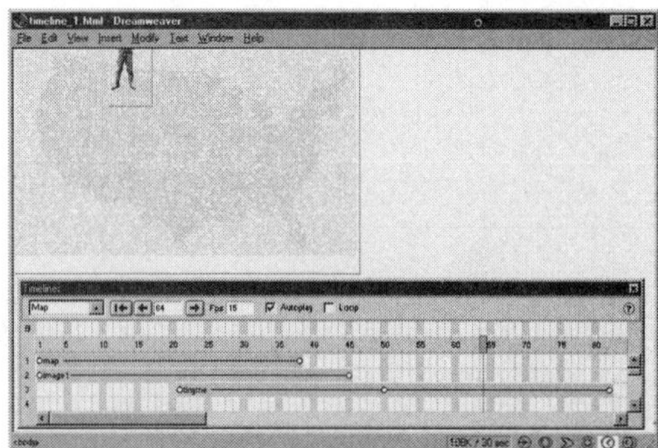

Figure 64 Frame 64 of the Map Timeline. The person layer ("tinyme") begins to arrive from offscreen. Like the map layer, the person was given negative coordinates (L –400px, T –300px) at the start of the Timeline.

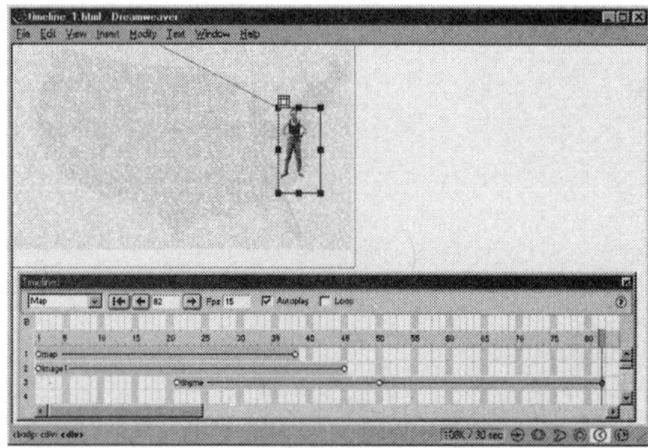

Figure 65 Frame 82 of the Map Timeline. The person has arrived. A few frames later, in Frame 95 (not pictured), a Behavior will play the second Timeline, called Travel.

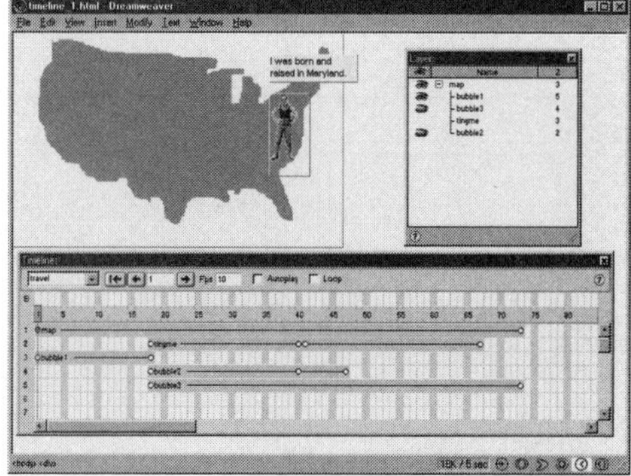

Figure 66 In Frame 1 of the Travel Timeline, the layer "Bubble 1" appears above the person's head.

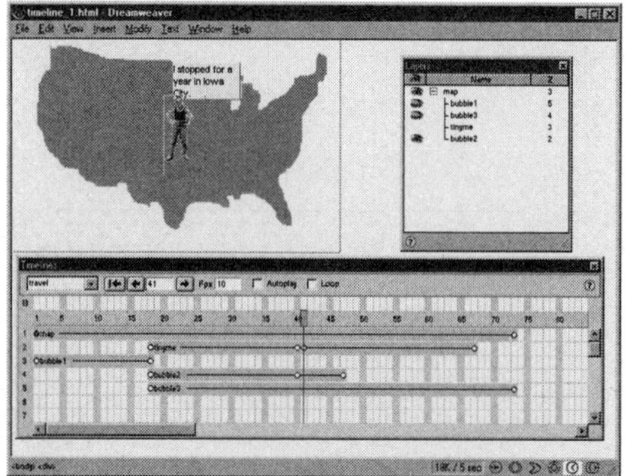

Figure 67 Frame 41 of the Travel Timeline. The person has moved halfway across the country. Bubble 1 is hidden, and Bubble 2 appears. Note that the playback rate is 10 FPS rather than 15; this Timeline moves more slowly.

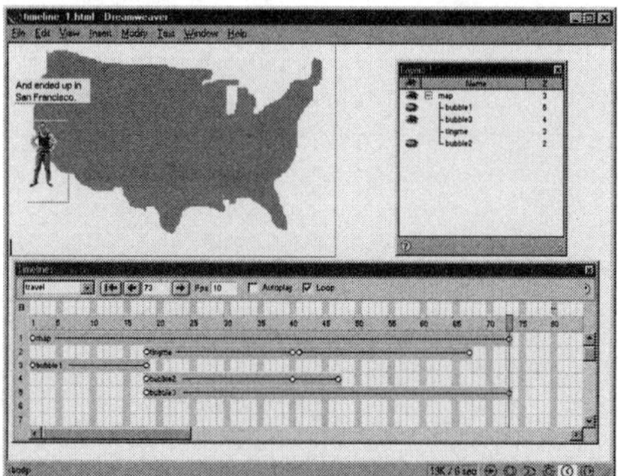

Figure 68 Frame 73 of the Travel Timeline: at the end of the Timeline, the person is all the way across the map. Bubble 2 is hidden, and Bubble 3 appears. I also added a Loop behavior in Frame 80; after a pause, the second Timeline will replay.

Figure 69 The work in action. I created a link to this Timeline in a JavaScript window the same size as the map images.

14

LIBRARIES AND CUSTOM OBJECTS

home | search | help | about | contact | advertise

Copyright © 1997-1998 insecticide9000.com. All rights reserved.
Serial rights for articles revert to authors on publication.
No insects were harmed in the creation of this site.

Figure 1 This page footer, including text, links, and the image and horizontal rule, is perfect fodder for a Dreamweaver Library item. You can insert it onto any new or existing Web page in a matter of seconds. If one of the links changes or the information changes, you can automatically update all pages that use this footer.

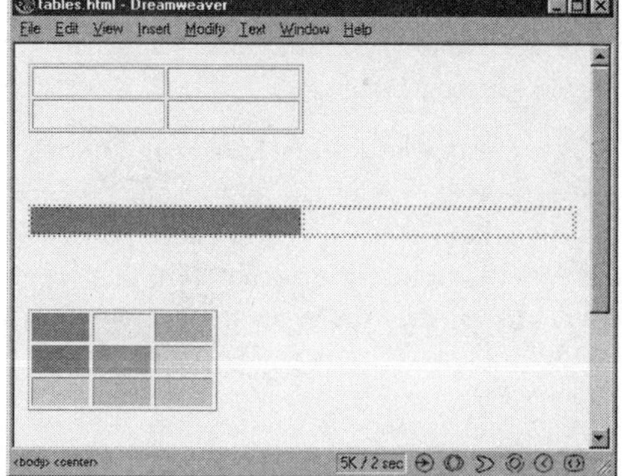

Figure 2 I created these standard tables in Dreamweaver and then turned them into custom objects. Whenever I need a 4x4 cell table, a standard sidebar table that occupies 100 percent of the window, or an obnoxious multicolored miniature table, I can plunk in one of these custom objects without dealing with any dialog boxes or setting Table properties more than once.

Dreamweaver's automation features come into full effect with libraries and custom objects, both of which let you create your own automated HTML widgets that you can plunk onto pages whenever you like.

The Dreamweaver Library is a custom-created storehouse of frequently used items that are updatable (**Figure 1**). Library items operate somewhat like imported style sheets; the HTML for the item is inserted into the page, along with a reference to the Library item's URL. If you change a Library item, you can then update the pages that reference it. (Library items don't update pages automatically, but it's trivial to execute an update.)

Another nifty source of prepackaged widgets is the Object palette. The Object palette consists of buttons that drop a standard chunk of HTML onto a page: a form field, a horizontal rule, or a table. These objects are just pieces of HTML; you can add your own custom objects (**Figure 2**) to the Objects palette, and you can even create your own custom Objects panel.

About Libraries

Libraries are HTML files with the extension .lbi that are stored in a specifically designated Library folder in a local site on your hard drive (**Figure 3**). As part of Dreamweaver's site management tools, the Library folder is stored in the Site root folder of each site you use with Dreamweaver.

If you have more than one local site on your hard drive, each site will use a different Library folder.

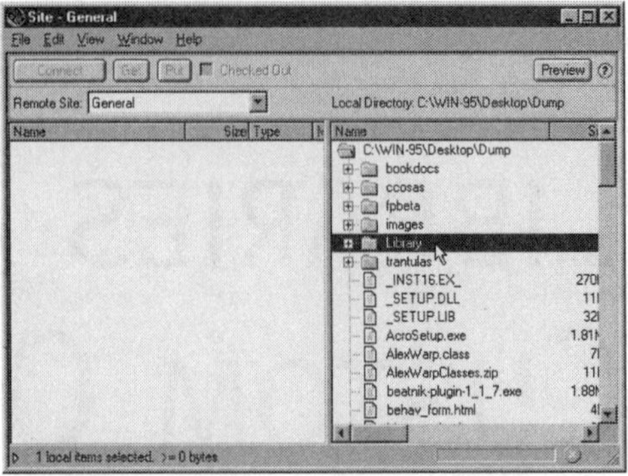

Figure 3: A local site on my hard drive. The Library folder is highlighted.

✔ Tip

- In Dreamweaver, a site is the same as a folder or set of folders. If you designate a folder on your hard drive as a site, Dreamweaver then knows how to code relative paths. Since libraries use site-root relative paths, you need to use them in tandem with Dreamweaver sites. For more on site management, see Chapter 17.

You must save a page in a local site on your hard drive that Dreamweaver knows about before you can use Library items on the page.

So Which Is Which?

Libraries and objects do similar things, so which one do you use for your purposes? Think of it in terms of form and content: libraries are the content, and objects are the form.

Objects are good for inserting standard containers (like tables or layers) that you'll put content in later, or commonly used gizmos like JavaScript buttons or specially sized horizontal rules.

The superpower of libraries is that you can spread them over an entire site and still update them as often as you like. Libraries are best used for inserting content that will change over time.

Today in history:

Born: **Otto von Bismarck** (1755), **Edmond Rostand** (1868), **Sergei Rachmaninoff** (1873), **Lon Chaney** (1883), **Milan Kundera** (1929), **Samuel R Delany** (1942)

Big Day for Baseball Fans: The first official National League baseball game was played today in **1876**. Fifty-five years later, in **1931**, Jackie Mitchell became the first woman to play professional baseball. Then in **1938**, the Baseball Hall of Fame opened in Cooperstown, New York.

Figure 4 This "Today in History" sidebar gets updated every day. Making the whole chunk, including the layer that contains the text, into a Library item means that all you have to do is update the Library item to update the page—you don't even need to *open* the page to update it.

Figure 5 If this navigation bar appears on every page in your site, it would be a pain to replace every instance of it if you added a search function to the site. Make it a Library item, and you can just add a new image and then update every page automatically.

What Library Items Do

Library items can contain HTML and JavaScript. Any items other than text (i.e., images, plug-ins, applets) will not be duplicated in a Library item; the Library item will contain links to those items.

Many big sites use CGI scripts to automatically replace text on page after page of a site, but Library items can accomplish the same thing.

Be sure to double-check the location of relative links and pathnames in Library items if you move any documents that are linked to the library.

Bitchin' Examples

- The footer with copyright info at the bottom of every page in your site (like the one I showed you in **Figure 1**)
- "Daily" updates on pages that aren't otherwise updated (**Figure 4**)
- Navigation bars on sites that are still growing (**Figure 5**)
- Frequently used logo images, contact e-mail addresses, or mastheads

Creating a Library Item

You create a Library item from existing HTML. You might create a page with the sole purpose of adding items to the library from that page, which you might do if you're creating the design and architecture for an entire site. Or you can select part of an existing page to add to the library.

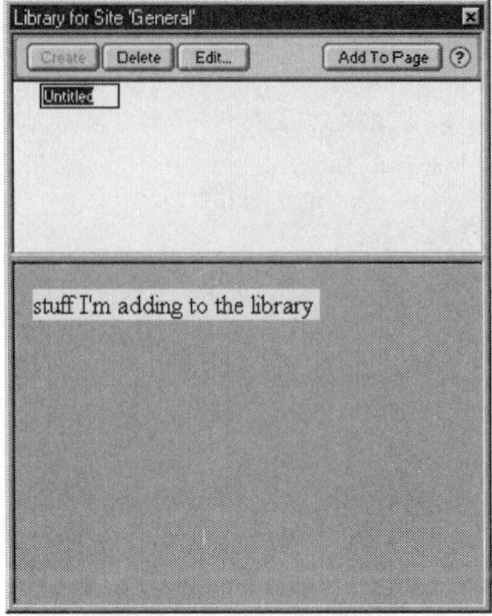

Figure 6 The Library palette. To display the Library palette without adding a new item to it, select Window > Library from the Document window menu bar, or press F6.

home | search | help | about | contact | advertise

Copyright © 1997-1998 insecticide9000.com. All rights reserved.

Serial rights for articles revert to authors on publication.

No insects were harmed in the creation of this site.

Figure 7 The elements you're adding to the library will be highlighted in yellow.

To create a new Library item:

1. Open the page that contains the stuff you want to add to the library.

   If you are working with a new page, save the page in a Dreamweaver Site folder.

2. Select the HTML for the desired objects. (You may want to do this in the HTML inspector.)

3. From the Document window menu bar, select Modify > Add Object to library. The Library palette will appear (**Figure 6**).

   or

   Drag the selection into the Library palette.

   or

   On the Library palette, press the Create button to add the selection to the Library item.

4. Type a name for the Library item in the text box, replacing the word Untitled.

The stuff you selected will be highlighted in the Dreamweaver window with a yellow box (**Figure 7**).

✔ Tips

- Once you designate a selection on a page as a Library item, you will not be able to edit it freely. See the section called *Editing Library Items* for more on this.
- To add the content of a selection to a Library item without replacing the selection with the new Library item, hold down the Ctrl (Command) key while creating the Library item.

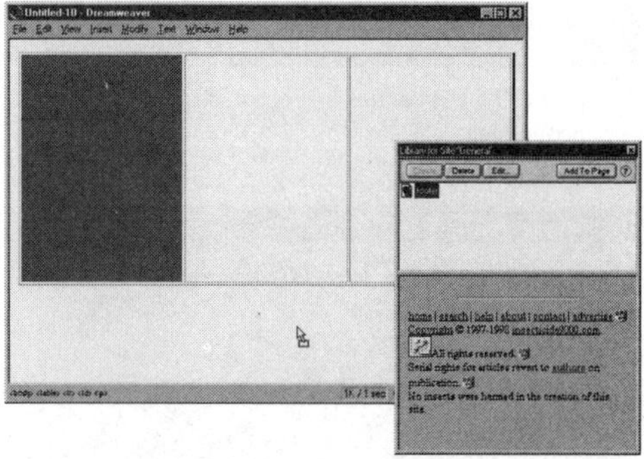

Figure 8 Drag a Library item icon from the Library palette right onto the page. The Library item will be inserted where you drop it.

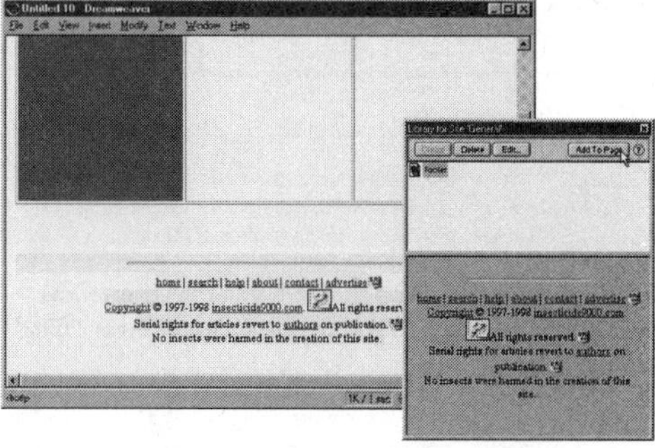

Figure 9 Click on the Add to Page button, and the Library item will appear on the page at the Insertion point.

Figure 10 Click anywhere on a Library item to select the whole thing. Then you can delete it, or cut and paste it elsewhere.

Adding an Existing Library Item to a Page

Now that you've created a Library item, you can add it to other new or existing pages in that site.

To drag a Library item onto a page:

1. The easiest way to add a Library item to a page is to drag the Library item icon from the Library palette to the Document window (**Figure 8**).

To add a Library item at the insertion point:

1. Click to place the insertion point at the place in the Document window where you want the Library item to appear.
2. In the Library palette, click on the icon for the Library item you want to add.
3. Click on the Add to Page button. The Library item will appear at the insertion point (**Figure 9**).

To remove a Library item from a page:

1. Click anywhere on the Library item to select the entire thing (**Figure 10**).
2. Press Backspace or Delete. The Library item will disappear.

✔ Tip

- To add the contents of a Library item without linking it to the Library, hold down the Ctrl (Command) button and drag the Library item onto the page.

Editing Library Items

There are two ways to edit a Library item:

- Make the Library item Editable and then edit it on any page that contains the item (change is local).

  or

- Edit the Library item in its own window (change is global).

To make a Library item editable:

1. In any document that contains the Library item you wish to edit, select the Library item by clicking on it (as we saw in **Figure 10**).
2. View the Properties inspector, if necessary, by selecting Modify > Selection Properties from the Document window menu bar (**Figure 11**).
3. On the Properties inspector, click on Make Item Editable. A dialog box will appear warning you that this will prevent the Library item from being affected by future Library updates.
4. Click on OK to close the dialog box. The item will be de-linked from the Site Library, and you can go ahead and edit it (**Figure 12**).

Making an item editable means that it has the same content as the Library item had, but it is no longer connected to the library.

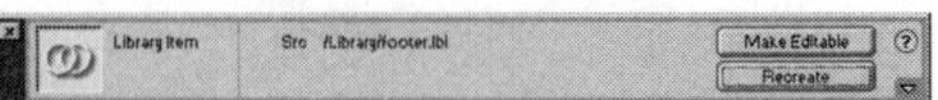

Figure 11 The Properties inspector, displaying Library item properties.

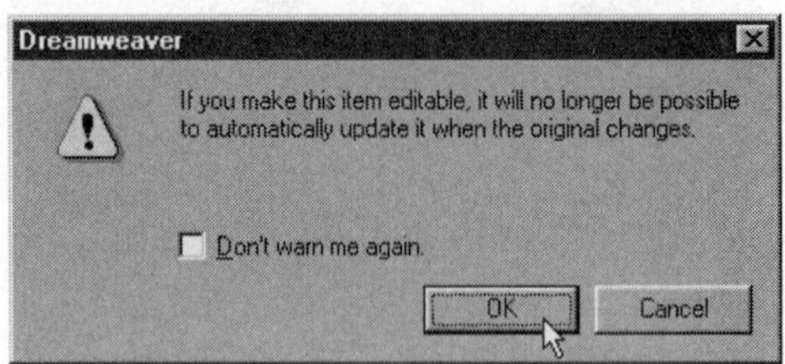

Figure 12 Dreamweaver warns you that the item will no longer be linked to the library. To keep this dialog box from appearing, check off the *Don't warn me again* checkbox.

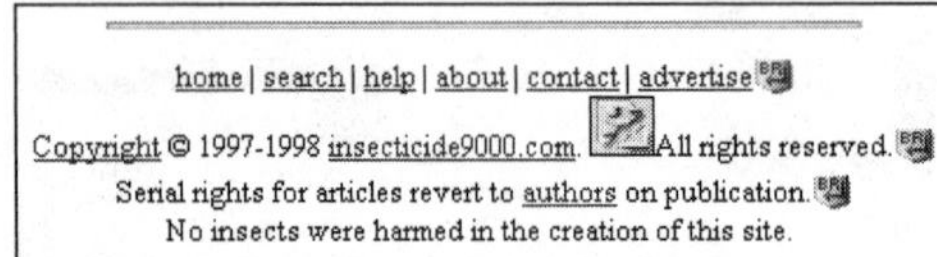

Figure 13 After making the item editable, the yellow highlighting is removed and the item is no longer linked to the library.

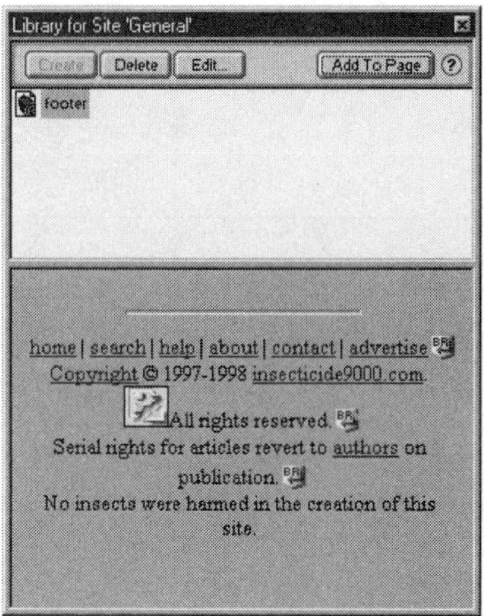

Figure 14 When you select an item in the Library palette, it is displayed in the frame at the bottom of the palette.

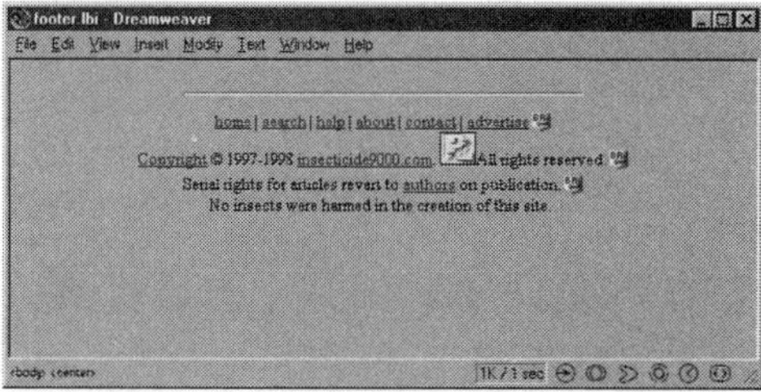

Figure 15: Click on the Library palette's Edit button to open a Library item in its own document window.

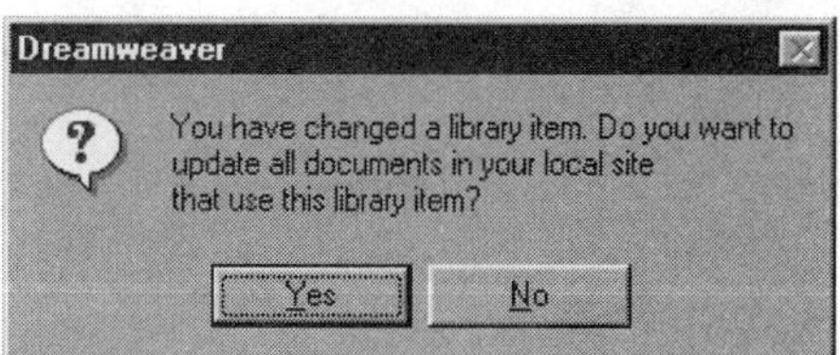

Figure 16 When you save the changes to the Library item, a dialog box will appear asking you if you want to update the entire site.

If you want to edit all instances of a Library item, you need to edit the item in its own window.

To globally edit a Library item:

1. In the Library palette, click on the icon for the item you want to edit. The current version will be displayed in the bottom frame of the Library palette (**Figure 14**).
2. Click on Edit. A new document window will appear that contains only the HTML included in the Library item (**Figure 15**).
3. Make your changes to the Library item.
4. Save the changes to the Library item using File > Save or Ctrl+S (Command+S). A dialog box will appear asking if you want to update all documents in your local site that contain the Library item.
   - To update now, click on Yes.
   - To update later, click on No. (You may want to postpone this until you're finished editing and then update everything at once.)
5. Close the Library item Document window.

✔ Tip

- To find out more about updating pages that use Library items, see the section called *Updating Your Site*, later in this chapter.

Renaming a Library Item

You can rename a Library item after you name it initially, but references to the old name will not be updated. You have to update old references manually in the HTML inspector.

To rename a Library item:

1. In the Library palette, click on the item you want to rename to select it (**Figure 17**).
2. Click on the item name. A box will appear around the name (**Figure 18**).
3. Type the new name in the box and press Enter (Return). A dialog box will appear, warning you that Library items that refer to the old name will not be updated (**Figure 19**).
4. Click on OK to close the dialog box.

The Library item will be renamed, and old references to the item will not link to the newly renamed item. They'll retain their HTML content, but they will no longer be updatable.

✔ Tips

- You can rename a Library item if you want to divorce it on purpose from the pages that reference the item. Then, you can create a new item with the old name, and old references will point to the new item.
- For example, say I have a Library item called Toolbar. I want to completely change the toolbar, but I don't want to get rid of the Library item entirely. I rename the old Toolbar OldToolbar. Then I create a new Library item called Toolbar. The old references will point to the new item.

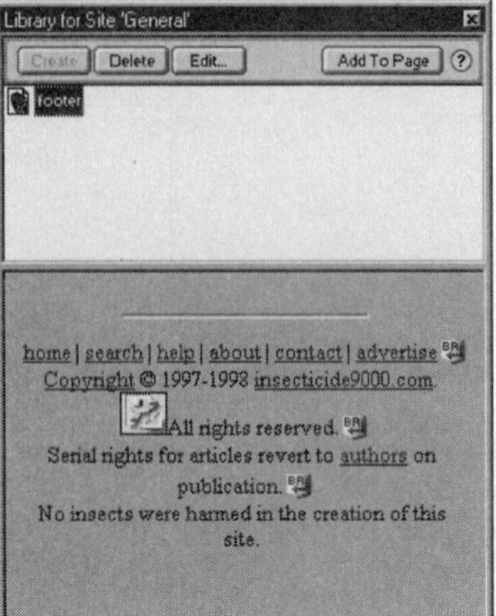

Figure 17 Select the item to rename in the Library palette.

Figure 18 Click inside the name of the item, and then type the new name in the box.

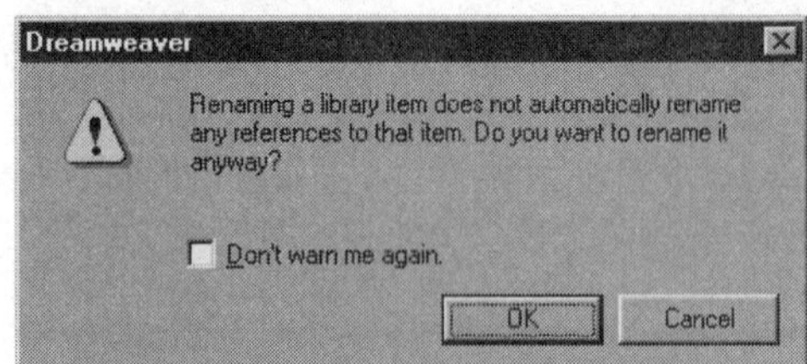

Figure 19 A dialog box warns you that the old references to the item will not be updated. To hide this dialog box forever, select the *Don't warn me again* checkbox.

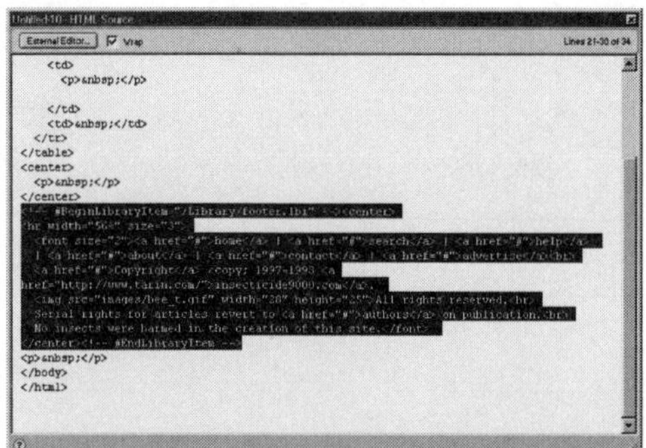

Figure 20 Select the Library item in the Document window, then press F10 to view the HTML inspector, where the code for the Library item will be selected.

If you want to update a reference to point to the new Library item name, you need to work directly with the HTML.

To change Library item references:

1. With the document that refers to the old Library item name in the Document window, click on the Library item in question to select it.
2. Choose Window > HTML from the menu bar. The HTML inspector will appear, with the code for the Library item highlighted (**Figure 20**).
3. The code that refers to the Library item will look something like this:

   ```
   <!-- #BeginLibraryItem "/Library/mailto.lbi" -->
   <center>
   <a href="mailto:me@you.com">mail me some
   money</a>
   </center>
   <!-- #EndLibraryItem -->
   ```

   The `<!--comments-->` indicate the beginning and end of the Library item, so when you update the page, Dreamweaver can locate them.
4. The pathname /Library/mailto.lbi is the name of the file within the Library item. Since I renamed this item mail1, all I have to do is go in and change the pathname from

   /Library/mailto.lbi

   to

   /Library/mail1.lbi

   and then save the changes to the page.

In general, renaming a Library item should be done only when absolutely necessary, especially if you've already used the item a bunch of times.

✔ Tip

- To view the pathname of a Library item, view Library Properties in the Properties inspector.

Deleting a Library Item

Deleting a Library item removes the file from the library, but it doesn't remove any code from any of the pages that use the Item.

To delete a Library item:

1. On the Library palette, select the item you want to delete.
2. Click on the Delete button. Poof! It's gone.

✔ Tip

- Probably the easiest way to remove references to deleted Library items is to select them and then make them editable. That removes references to the .lbi file, but leaves the content intact.

If you delete an item from the Library palette, but it still exists on a Web page, you can re-create it.

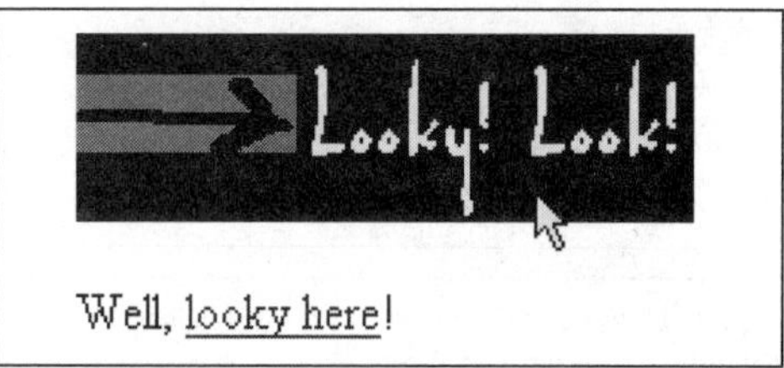

Figure 21 I accidentally edited the "Looky" Library item so that it consisted of the text link on the bottom instead of the selected images. I still have a copy of the old Library item on my page, so I select it.

Figure 22 I click on the Recreate button on the Properties inspector.

Figure 23 A dialog box warns me that I'm about to overwrite the contents of the Library item.

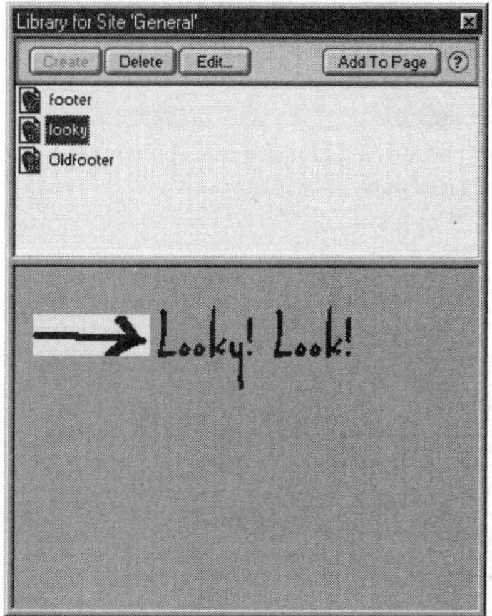

Figure 24 I have successfully rewritten the Looky Library item with the old contents.

Re-creating a Library Item

Besides reinstating deleted Library items, you can use the Recreate function to replace the contents of a Library item with the contents of an edited Library item (or vice versa). This is useful for renamed or mistakenly edited items.

To re-create a Library item:

1. In the Document window, select an edited Library item or an item that was deleted from the Library palette (**Figure 21**).
2. On the Properties inspector, click on the Recreate button (**Figure 22**). If you're overwriting an existing Library item, a dialog box will appear (**Figure 23**).
3. Click on OK. The contents of the selected Library item will overwrite the contents of the existing Library item (**Figure 24**). (In the case of deleted items, the original name will be re-added to the Library palette).

✔ Tip

- You cannot overwrite a Library item with the contents of another Library item. In other words, you can't select the item July and overwrite it with the contents of June.
- The ability to recreate Library items is one reason not to update your site immediately after you edit a Library item. As long as the old Library item content exists on a page somewhere, you can recreate the original.

Updating Your Site

After you edit a Library item, you can update single pages or entire sites that use that item. Then, the next time you upload pages to the site, they'll all have the new content in the place of the old Library content.

To update a single page:

1. Open the page you want to update in the Document window.
2. From the Document window menu bar, select Modify > Update Current Page.
3. A dialog box will appear telling you if any Library items referenced on the page no longer exist (**Figure 25**).
4. Click on OK.

Any updated items will be re-posted to the page in their new form (**Figure 26**).

To update an entire site:

1. From the Document window menu bar, select Modify > Library > Update Entire Site. The Update Site dialog box will appear (**Figure 27**).
2. If there is more than one local site on your hard drive, choose the name of your site from the Update Site drop-down menu.
3. Click on Start. Dreamweaver will scan all the HTML files in the current site for references to Library items.
4. When the update process is complete, a log file will appear in the Log box showing you how many files were scanned, which files were updated, and which Library files, if any, are missing from the Library folder (**Figure 28**).
5. When you're done, click on Close to return to the Document window.

Figure 25 When you update a site using Libraries, this dialog box appears if you've deleted a Library item referenced on an updated page.

Figure 26: After I re-created the "Looky" item, I updated the page, and now both items reflect the changes. (I'm not going to keep both of them there.)

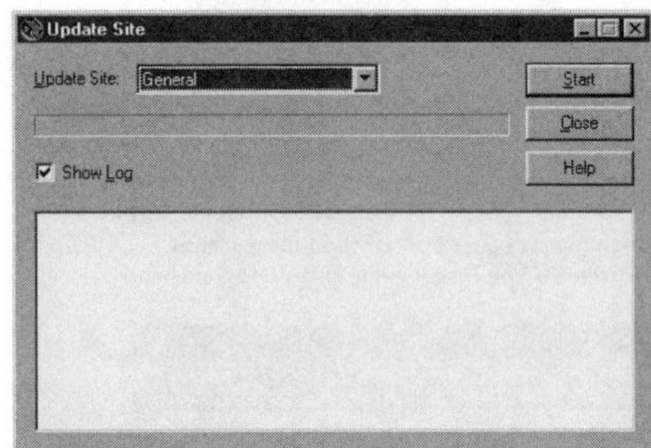

Figure 27 The Update Site dialog box. You don't need to have any pages open to update your site.

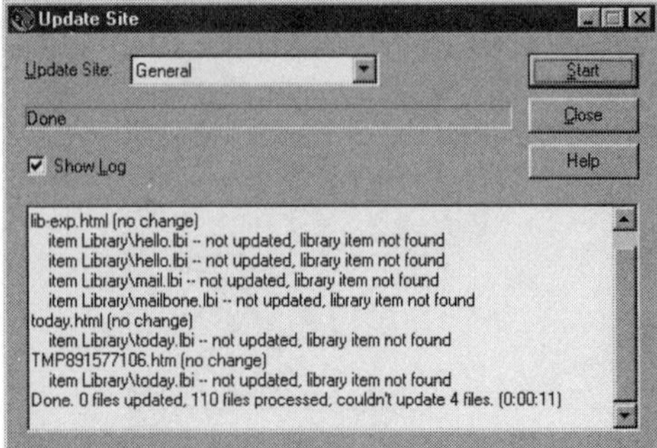

Figure 28 After the update is complete, a log file will display letting you know if any Library items were missing, along with other useful data.

Figure 29 Our old friend the Objects palette. In this part of the chapter, we'll find out how to add objects to it.

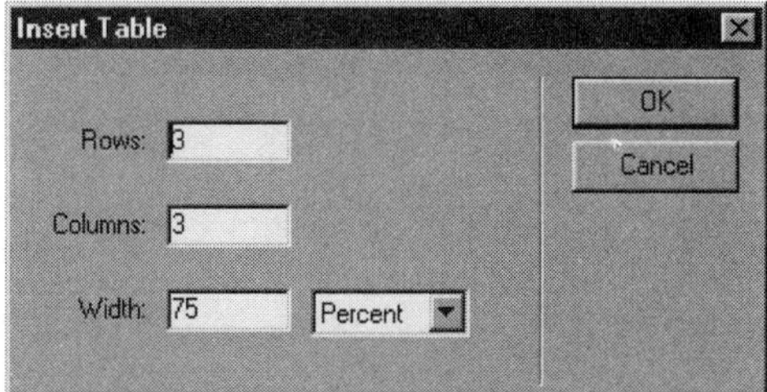

Figure 30 The Insert Table dialog box is called by a Dreamweaver object file that takes user input before inserting the object.

Custom Objects

Object files, which are added using the Objects palette or the Insert menu, are simple HTML files that contain just snippets of HTML rather than entire documents.

Once you create an object file, you add it to the Dreamweaver interface by referencing it in the InsertMenu file and adding an image to the Objects palette (**Figure 29**).

Dreamweaver's pre-installed objects all use JavaScript to insert objects. Some objects, such as Images and Tables, include enough JavaScript to create dialog boxes that you use to define the object before it's inserted (**Figure 30**). Others, such as Horizontal Rules and Line Breaks, include a single function, called the objectTag() function, that inserts the code onto the page.

For instance, the HTML for the Line Break object is as follows:

```
function objectTag() {
return "<BR>";
}
```

You could accomplish the same thing by creating an HTML document which consisted of a single <BR> tag.

Modifying Dreamweaver Objects

Besides creating new custom objects, you can modify existing Dreamweaver objects. This involves modifying the HTML and/or the JavaScript that controls the insertion of each object—yet another good way to pick up some JavaScript fluency. (In particular, check out the JavaScript form tools used to create dialog boxes like the one in **Figure 30**.)

In some instances, this is simple; for instance, you could edit the <br> object so that it became <br=clear>.

Before you start fooling around with the JavaScript, though, I recommend that you save a copy of the original object in a different folder, so you can restore it if you need to. There's nothing wrong with writing a JavaScript function that crashes the program every time you use it, as long as you can fix it later.

The first, and most important part of creating a custom object is creating the object file itself.

To create an object file:

1. Using Dreamweaver, another HTML editor, or a text editor, create a new, blank file.
2. Type or paste in the code for the object you want to create.
3. If the program automatically includes tags such as <html> and <body>, be sure to delete them (**Figure 31**).
4. Save the file as an HTML file (.htm or .html) in the Dreamweaver Objects directory:
   - Windows: C:\Program Files\Macromedia\Dreamweaver\Configuration\Objects\[Object Folder Name]
   - Macintosh: Dreamweaver/Configuration/Objects/[folder name]
5. Quit and restart Dreamweaver.

Now you need to add the Object to the Insert menu and the Object palette.

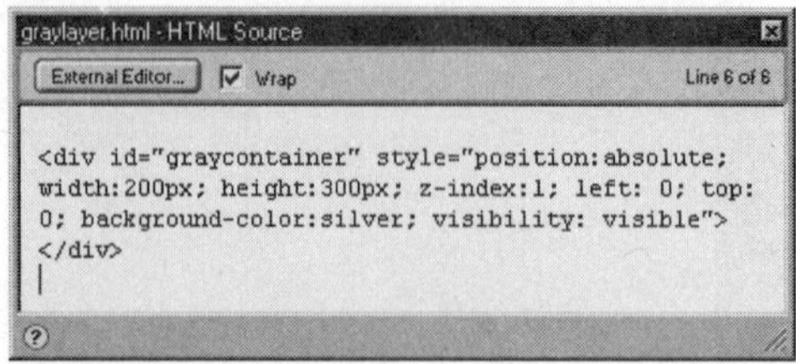

Figure 31 A normal HTML file includes <html>, <head>, and <body> tags. I deleted them here to create an object file with only the tags for the layer.

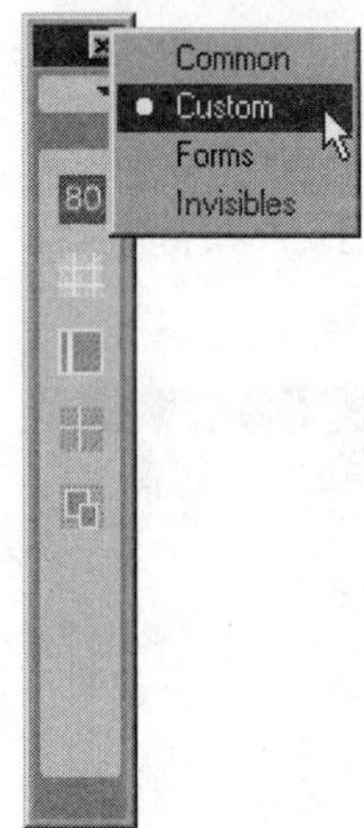

Figure 32 I created a Custom panel in the Objects palette.

Custom Object Panels

The Object palette contains three panels: Common, Forms, and Invisibles. These panels correspond to folders within the Dreamweaver Objects folder. To create your own custom panel in the Objects palette, just create a new folder within the Objects folder. **Figure 32** shows the Custom panel of the Objects palette, which I added by creating a folder called Custom in the Objects folder to hold my custom objects.

Figure 33 I created a 16-pixel by 16-pixel image.

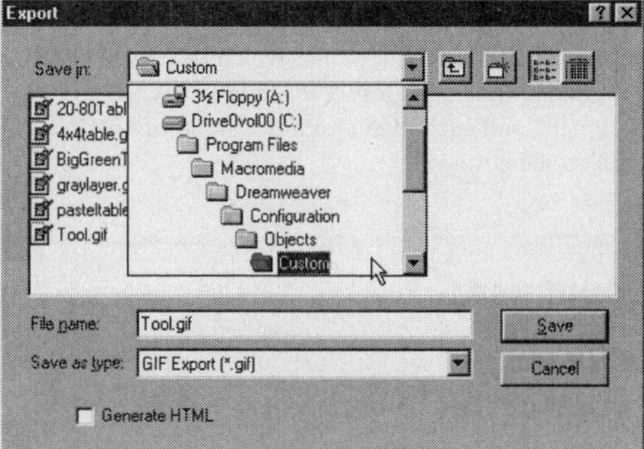

Figure 34 I saved the image in my Custom folder within the Objects folder.

Figure 35 Now the image is on the Objects palette. Dreamweaver automatically shows the Object file's filename as a tooltip.

You add the new object to the Object palette by creating a 16-pixel by 16-pixel image with the same name as the object file. For instance, if the object file is named GrayLayer.html, the GIF should be named GrayLayer.gif.

You save this image in the Object folder.

Adding the new object to the Object palette:

1. Create the 16-pixel by 16-pixel GIF image (**Figure 33**).
2. Name it the same thing as the Object file, and save it in the proper Objects folder (**Figure 34**).
3. Quit and Restart Dreamweaver.
4. View the Objects palette (Window > Objects) (**Figure 35**).
5. Click on the image to make sure it does what you want it to.

Don't Do Images?

Not a big image person? Try creating a 16-pixel by 16-pixel GIF that consists of a color and a letter: W.

Another solution is to take an existing image from the object folder and invert or colorize it using an image editor: .

I recommend using Jasc Paint Shop Pro or Macromedia Fireworks.

Each Dreamweaver object is represented in the Insert menu by a line of code in the InsertMenu HTML file (**Figure 36**).

✔ Tips

- Each individual item is a list item **<li>** in a bulleted list **<ul>**.
- Menu dividers are represented by a dashed line:
  - ----------
- Submenus are created by nesting **<ul>** tags.

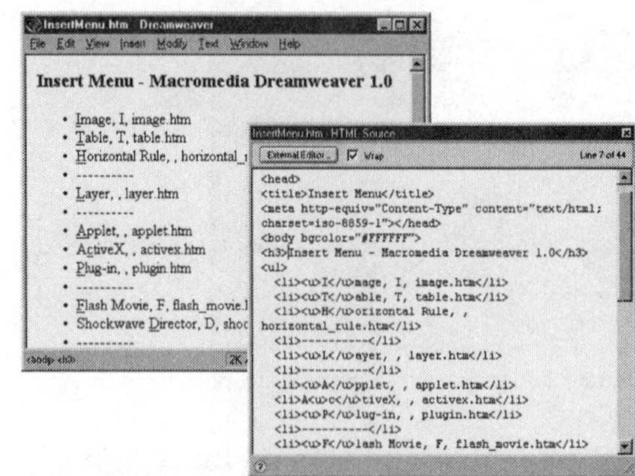

Figure 36 The InsertMenu file, which resides in the Object folder. The Insert menu is an HTML document, and each menu item is a list item <li> in a bulleted list <ul>.

Creating Alt-Key Commands

To create Ctrl+Alt selections (Command+Option), do the following; Underline the letter character you want to use for the Alt-key command, and type that same letter where the blank commas go:

```
<li>Big <u>G</u>reen Table, G, big_green.html</li>
```

or

- **Big Green Table, G, big_green.html**

In this example, the Ctrl+Alt+G (Command+Option+G) command will insert the Big Green Table. Additionally, when Windows users select the Insert menu with the Alt key, they can press the G key to insert the Big Green Table.

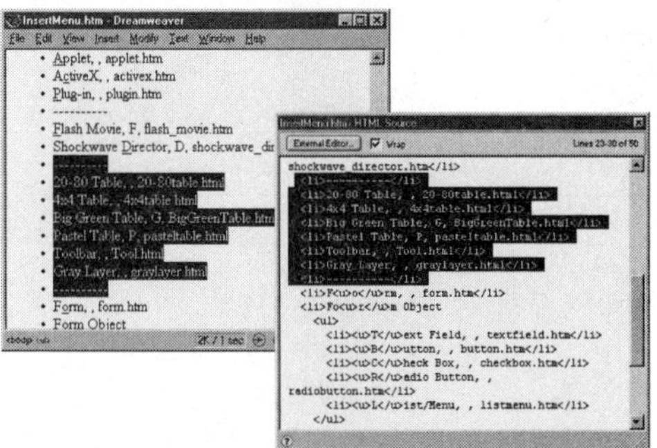

Figure 37 I added a line in the Insert menu for each of my custom objects. Note that the filenames are case sensitive.

Figure 38 The Insert menu now has my objects on it.

To add the new object to the Insert menu:

1. Using Dreamweaver, another HTML editor, or a text editor, open the InsertMenu.htm (InsertMenu.html) file located inside the Dreamweaver Objects folder (**Figure 36**).
2. Locate the menu line where you wish to add the new item.
3. Add a list item for each object you wish to add (**Figure 37**). In Dreamweaver, you can add the lines in either the Document window or the HTML inspector. If you use the Document window, omit the <li> tags.

   You must use the following format:

   - <li>Name of Object, , nameoffile.html</li> (in the HTML inspector)

   or

   - **Name of Object, , nameoffile.html** (in the Document window)

   Note the blank space between the two commas. You can substitute a letter for an Alt-menu selection (see the sidebar).
4. Save and close the file.
5. Close and restart Dreamweaver.
6. Look at the Insert menu to make sure your object is there (**Figure 38**), and select the new item to see if it works the way you expect.

Plug-ins and Active Content

15

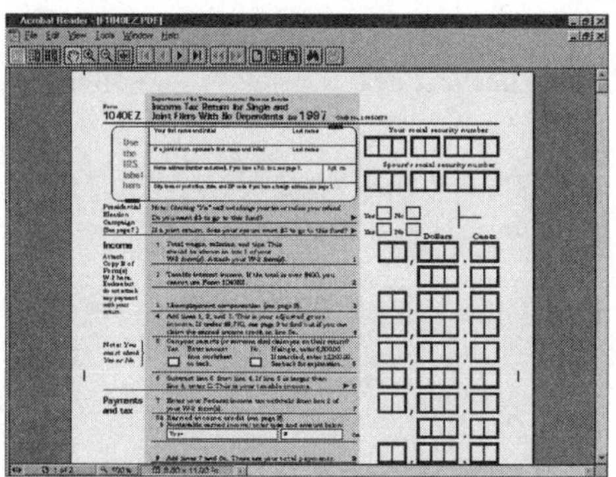

Figure 1 Netscape Navigator 1.1 could simplify downloads by automatically launching helper apps such as Adobe Acrobat as soon as the download was complete. Navigator 4 goes as far as being able to open and edit Microsoft Word files in the browser window.

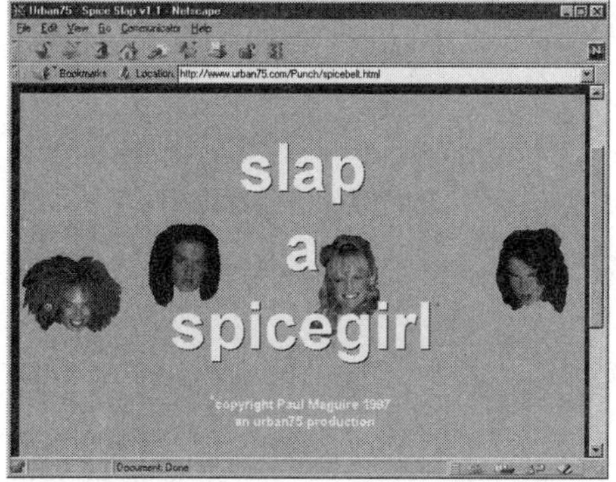

Figure 2 Plug-ins such as Shockwave turned the Web into a multimedia experience. Without Shockwave, online gaming wouldn't be nearly as cool. And I wouldn't be able to slap Spice Girls at http://www.urban75.com/Punch/spicebelt.html.

Before Mosaic, any file that wasn't text or HTML had to be downloaded and saved to open later with a separate application. When Mosaic hit the scene, some images could be viewed inline, but other forms of media were still "save and play." (Many computers back then weren't true multitaskers and most people didn't do a lot of simultaneous audio, much less video.)

Netscape Navigator 1.1 could automatically launch helper applications to play these downloaded files. Audio started becoming part of the life of the Web, and programs like Adobe Acrobat came onto the scene (**Figure 1**).

Navigator 2 went a step further and forever changed the face of the Web. Plug-ins could play or view darned near any type of file you could think of. Now, not only could you view Shockwave movies inline (**Figure 2**), but music could be embedded invisibly into Web pages, and RealAudio could even play these files while they downloaded. Netscape 2 also introduced Java and VRML capabilities to the mainstream world.

Microsoft's answer to plug-ins was ActiveX, a scripting language that used Visual Basic and OLE technology to duplicate the plug-in idea and take it a step further.

Dreamweaver makes it easy to insert the code for these multimedia objects onto your pages. Dreamweaver tries to be as cross-platform as possible about these doo-dads.

✔ Tip

- You can insert any of these objects using the Objects palette (Window > Objects) and you can modify them using the Properties inspector (Window > Properties or Modify > Selection Properties). I'm just refreshing your memory, in case you'd forgotten.

Using Sound Files

Sound files come in more flavors than ice cream (see the sidebar *Sound File Types*). Not all browsers support all sound files, but any browser that supports plug-ins or ActiveX (Navigator or Explorer versions 2 or later) should be able to play most sound files. Navigator 3's preinstalled LiveAudio plug-in plays every common sound file type.

There are two ways to add a sound file to your page. One way is to link to the sound file, so that the user downloads and plays it when they click on a link. The other way is to embed the sound file so that it begins to load when the page loads, and a plug-in will play it automatically when the sound file finishes loading.

The Sound of Downloads

When linking to sound files, it's a good idea to let your users know what they're in for. Unless the sound is very small, it's good practice to indicate the file type and file size of sound files so that users know whether to download them. For instance, some older Mac browsers don't support .WAV files, and some older PC browsers don't support .AIFF files. And any user on a 14.4 kbps modem wants advance notice before they start downloading a 100K+ sound file.

A line like this near the link should do the trick:

They Killed Kenny! (10K .WAV)

or even better:

They Killed Kenny! (10K .WAV, 9K .AIFF)

Figure 3 Type the location of the sound file in the Properties inspector's Link text box.

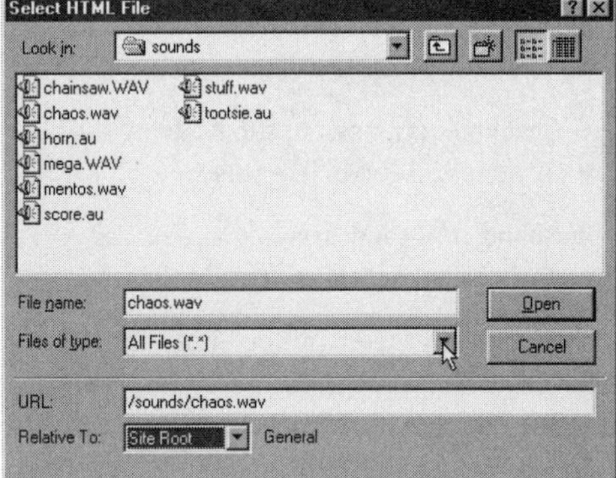

Figure 4 Select the file from your computer. Be sure to choose All File Types from the Files of Type drop-down menu.

Figure 5 A standard Netscape audio controller for playing downloaded links

Linking to a sound file is similar to linking to any other sort of file.

To link to a sound file:

1. In the Document window, select the text or image that you want to make into the link.
2. In the Properties inspector, type the path-name for the sound file in the Link text box (**Figure 3**).

   or

   Click on the folder icon, and use the Open dialog box to choose a sound file from your computer (**Figure 4**). Be sure to select *.* All File Types from the *Files of Type* drop-down menu.
3. Press Enter (Return). The selection will be linked to the sound file.

When the user clicks on the link, they'll download the sound file (**Figure 5**).

When the user clicks on the link on your page, one of three things will happen:

- An external program, or "Helper App," will launch to play the sound file; or
- The browser itself will play the sound file using its own capabilities or those of a plug-in; or
- If the browser doesn't support or recognize the file type, an error will occur. Sometimes a dialog box will open that says "Unrecognized file type," and sometimes the browser will open the file as if it were text.

Embedding a sound file is similar to linking to an image. It's unfortunate that Dreamweaver doesn't directly support the use of embedded sounds without JavaScript, but writing the line of code is simple enough.

To embed a sound file:

1. View the document you want to attach the sound file to in the Document window.
2. Click to place the insertion point at the place in the document where you want the sound controller to appear. For invisible sound files, you can place the file anywhere, although at the top or bottom of the document is usually more convenient.
3. View the HTML source for the page in the HTML inspector by selecting Window > HTML from the Document window menu bar (or by pressing F9).
4. For a sound file with no controls showing, type the following line of code:

   ```
   <embed src="sounds/yoursound.wav"
   controller=FALSE autoplay=TRUE loop=TRUE>
   ```

   Where *sounds/yoursound.wav* is the pathname of the sound file.
5. Save your changes to the page.
6. Preview the page in a browser to make sure it works.

✔ Tip

- You can embed a sound file with or without the use of a plug-in. Since Dreamweaver's Insert > Plug-in feature doesn't include all the stuff you need for embedding sounds in a page, I'm going to discuss embedded sound and plug-ins as if they were two different entities.

Explorer's <bgsound> Tag

Versions of Internet Explorer before 4.0 do not support embedded sound files. Explorer uses a proprietary tag called <bgsound>. You can use the <embed> and <bgsound> tags on the same page.

A <bgsound> tag goes in the body of the document and looks like this:

```
<bgsound src="sounds/mysound.wav"
loop="infinite" autoplay="true" volume=0>
```

The loop parameter can be either infinite or a number. Volume can be 0 (full) to −10,000 (lowest). There are no user controls to display with the <bgsound> tag.

Sound File Parameters

Embedding a sound requires a plug-in, which is no sweat for browsers that support such things. If you want to use Dreamweaver to insert these parameters into a sound plug-in file (rather than typing them into the code), see the section called *Extra Parameters*, later in this chapter.

Here's the skinny on the different parameters you can use with sound files:

src="" (required)

The source of the file.

name=""

Name the embedded file if you want to call it from a script. If you use the name value, you must also include the mastersound attribute (no value).

controller=true|false

Determines whether the controller has buttons or not.

controls=console|smallconsole

(Required for visible controllers.)

(Other options available for use with JavaScript. See this book's Web site for details.)

hidden=true|false

Determines whether the controller is visible.

autoplay=true|false

Determines whether the sound begins playing as soon as it loads. If autoplay=false, then controller should be set to true.

volume=0%–100%

Percent of system volume used.

loop=true|false|n

Determines whether the sound will loop continuously. A setting of loop=3 would make the file loop three times.

height and width (required)

Determines the height and width of the controller. For console: height=60 width=144. For smallconsole: height=15 width=144.

A standard audio controller (**Figures 6** and **7**) would have the following settings:

```
<embed src="sounds/yoursound.wav"
height="60" width="144" controller="TRUE" con-
trols="CONSOLE" autostart="FALSE"
loop="TRUE"></embed>
```

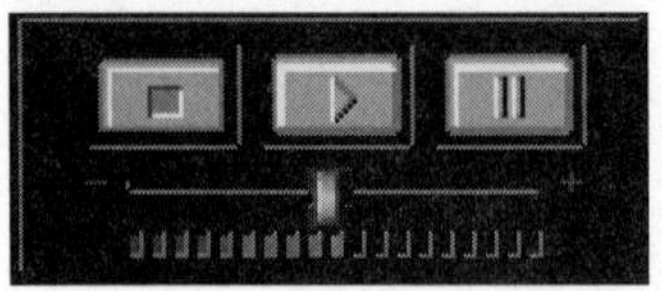

Figure 6 The standard Netscape LiveAudio sound controller, embedded in a page. LiveAudio plays .AIFF, .AU, .MID, and .WAV files, among others.

Figure 7 The same controller in Explorer. Note that it ignores the given dimensions.

✔ Tips

- If the source for the sound file isn't correct, the console will not show up in Navigator.
- Quotation marks are not essential for anything but SRC, but Dreamweaver prefers them.

Sound File Types

.AIFF: Macintosh Audio format.

.AU: Sun Audio format.

.DCR: Shockwave audio (also used for Shockwave movies). Requires Shockwave plug-in.

.LA, .LAM, .LMA: Netscape streaming audio. Handled automatically by Netscape 4 and over.

.MID, .MIDI: MIDI electronic music format. Requires plug-in in Netscape 2.0.

.MOD, .RMF: Beatnik audio format. Requires Beatnik plug-in. (Note: once Beatnik is installed, it will also handle .AIFF, .AU, .MID, and .WAV by default.)

.MOV: QuickTime audio (also used for QuickTime movies). Requires QuickTime plug-in.

.RAM, .RPM: RealAudio (also used for RealVideo). Requires RealAudio or RealPlayer plug-in.

.WAV: Windows Audio.

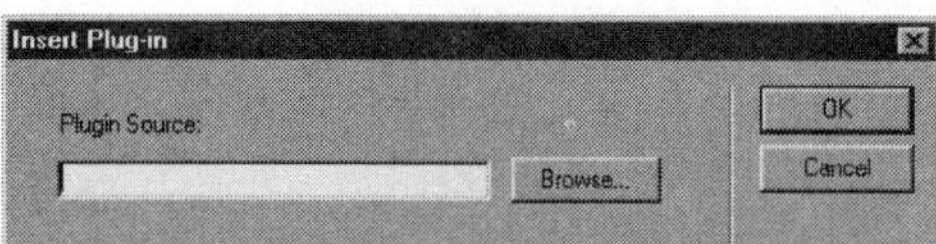

Figure 8 Type the pathname of the plug-in file in the Insert Plug-in dialog box, or click on Browse to choose a file from your computer.

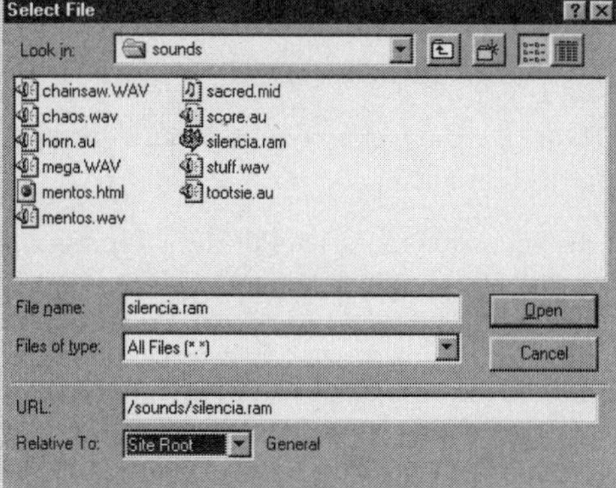

Figure 9 Browse for the plug-in files on your computer. Remember that you're looking for the media file to be played, not the plug-in component (dll) that plays it.

Netscape Plug-ins

Netscape plug-ins work in Netscape 2 or later. Many plug-ins can be set either to run inline or to launch a helper app. They can also be set to play different qualities of content depending on the computer or modem speed. The RealPlayer is a good example of both of these traits.

There are some ActiveX equivalents to Netscape plug-ins; see the section on ActiveX and the documentation for the specific plug-in.

To insert a Netscape plug-in:

1. In the Document window, click to place the insertion point at the place on the page where you want the plug-in to appear.
2. From the Document window menu bar, select Insert > Plug-in.

   or

   Click on the Insert Plug-in button on the Objects palette.
3. Either way, the Insert Plug-in dialog box will appear (**Figure 8**).
4. In the Plug-in Source text box, type the pathname of the Plug-in file.

   or

   Click on Browse and use the Select File dialog box to locate the Plug-in file on your computer (**Figure 9**). When you locate the file, click on Open.
5. When the pathname of the Plug-in appears in the Plug-in Source text box, click on OK. The dialog box will close and a plug-in placeholder will appear in the Document window: .

✔ Tip

- You can use the Behavior called Check Plug-in to determine whether a user has a particular plug-in installed. See Chapter 12 for more details.

After you insert the placeholder, you can set additional properties for the plug-in.

To set Plug-in properties:

1. Select the Plug-in Placeholder in the Document window. The Properties inspector will display Plug-in properties (**Figure 10**).
2. Change any properties in the Properties inspector, and click on the Apply button.
3. To set Extra Parameters, click on the Parameters button. (See the section called Extra Parameters, later in this chapter.)

✔ Tip

- If you change the source for the plug-in by clicking on the folder icon, you'll need to select the appropriate file type, or **All Files**, from the *Files of Type* drop-down menu.

Figure 10 The Properties inspector, displaying plug-in properties.

Plug-in Properties

Properties you can set for Netscape plug-ins include the following:

Name the plug-in by typing a name for it in the text box.

Set dimensions for the plug-in by typing the **W**(idth) and **H**(eight) in the associated text boxes.

Change the **Source** by typing it in the Src text box. Click on the Folder icon to browse for the file on your computer.

If a user doesn't have the plug-in installed, they can be directed to an installation page. Type the URL for this page in the **Plg URL** text box.

Set the **alignment** of the plug-in on the page by selecting an alignment from the Align drop-down menu. These alignment options are the same as for images. (I discuss image alignment in Chapter 5.)

To provide an **alternate image** for browsers without plug-in capabilities, type the Image source in the Alt text box. Click on the Folder icon to browse for the image on your computer.

V space and H space denote an amount of space around the plug-in. **Border** describes a visible border around the plug-in. (I discuss these options further with regard to images in Chapter 5.) The units for these options are in pixels. Type a number without units in the appropriate text box.

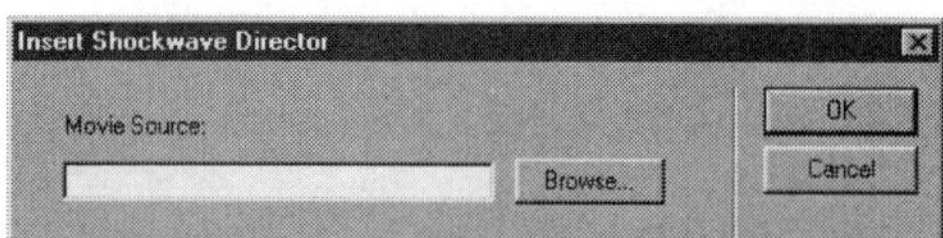

Figure 11 The Insert Shockwave dialog box. The Insert Flash dialog box looks just like it.

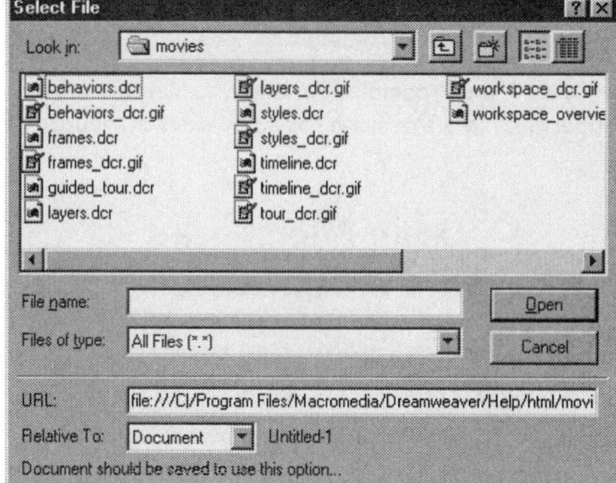

Figure 12 Choose a .DCR or .DIR file (Director) or a .SWF file (Flash) from your computer.

Shockwave and Flash

Shockwave and Shockwave Flash are Netscape plug-ins, but you get more up-front ability to set their attributes by using the Insert > Shockwave and Insert > Flash tools. Director, Flash, and Dreamweaver are all made by Macromedia, after all, and integration of the three is one of Dreamweaver's big selling points.

To insert a Shockwave or Flash file:

1. In the Document window, click to place the insertion point at the place on the page where you want the Shockwave or Flash movie to appear.
2. From the Document window menu bar, select Insert > Shockwave Director or Insert > Flash Movie.

   or

   Click on the Insert Shockwave or Insert Flash button on the Object palette.
3. A dialog box will appear: Insert Flash or Insert Shockwave (**Figure 11**).
4. Type the pathname of the file in the Movie Source text box.

   or

   Click on Browse, and use the Select File dialog box to locate the file from your computer (**Figure 12**). Click on Open when you find the file.
5. When the filename of the movie appears in the Movie Source text box, click on OK. The dialog box will close and an icon will appear in the Document window: .

✔ Tip

- Behaviors for detecting whether a browser has Shockwave installed and for inserting Shockwave controls are discussed in Chapter 12.

Once you've gone through the motions of inserting a Shockwave or Flash file, you can change the properties.

To set Shockwave properties:

1. Select the Shockwave or Flash Placeholder in the Document window. The Properties inspector will display Shockwave properties (**Figure 13**) or Flash properties (**Figure 14**).
2. Change any properties in the Properties inspector, and click on the Apply button.
3. To set extra parameters, click on the Parameters button. (See the section called *Extra Parameters*, later in this chapter.)

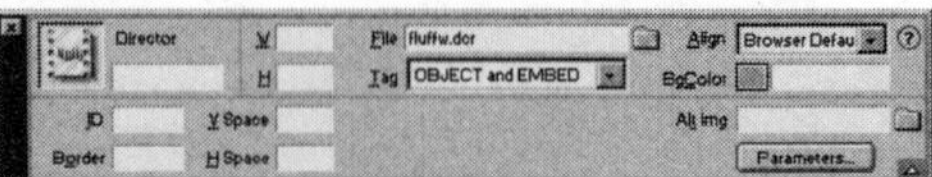

Figure 13 The Properties inspector, displaying Shockwave for Director properties.

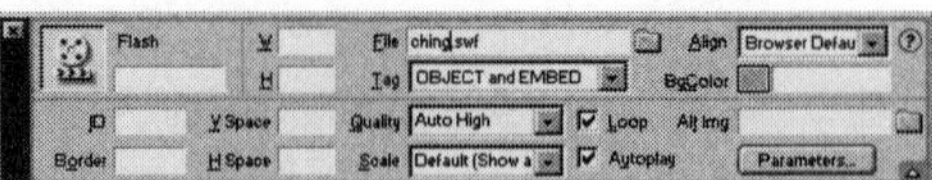

Figure 14 The Properties inspector, displaying Flash properties. Note that Flash has a few extra attributes.

Using Aftershock with Dreamweaver

Aftershock is an HTML tool used with Director and Flash to create HTML files using Shockwave. You can open files created with Aftershock and edit them in Dreamweaver. You can also select the relevant HTML and paste it into other Dreamweaver documents.

If you want to edit Aftershock object files that have been inserted into Dreamweaver HTML documents, view them in the Properties inspector and click on Launch Aftershock. Edit the Aftershock file, close the program, and accept the This File has Been Edited dialog box. For more on using Dreamweaver with external editors, see Appendix B.

Shockwave and Flash Properties

Properties you can set for Shockwave for Director and Shockwave Flash include the following:

Name the plug-in by typing a name for it in the text box.

Set dimensions for the Shockwave movie by typing the **W**(idth) and **H**(eight) in the associated text boxes.

Change the **Source** by typing it in the File text box. Click on the Folder icon to browse for the file on your computer.

Set the **Tag** by selecting it from the Tag drop-down menu. The `<object>` tag is used by Internet Explorer, and the `<embed>` tag is used by Netscape Navigator. By default, Dreamweaver inserts code for both tags so the object shows up in both browsers. If you're making browser-dependent pages, choose the appropriate tag.

Set the **alignment** of the movie file on the page by selecting an alignment from the Align drop-down menu. These alignment options are the same as those for images. (I discuss image alignment in Chapter 5.)

To set the **background color** that will fill the dimensions before the movie loads and after it finishes playing, type a hex code for the color in the Bgcolor text box, or click on the Color button to choose a color. (I discuss choosing colors in the most detail in Chapter 2.)

ID sets the ID parameter for the Shockwave ActiveX control.

V space and **H space** denote an amount of space around the plug-in. **Border** describes a visible border around the plug-in. (I discuss these options further with regard to images in Chapter 5.) The units for these options are in pixels. Type a number without units in the appropriate text box.

To provide an **alternate image** for browsers without plug-in capabilities, type the Image source in the Alt text box. Click on the Folder icon to browse for the image on your computer.

Additional Flash Properties:

Quality sets the quality of Flash movies according to processor speed. Anti-aliasing is used to smooth the appearance of frame-to-frame playback in Flash, and that requires a fast machine. *Low* turns off anti-aliasing in favor of playback speed. *High* turns on anti-aliasing in favor of appearance. *Autohigh* starts out using anti-aliasing and turns it off if the machine's performance isn't keeping up. *Autolow* starts off without anti-aliasing and turns it on if possible.

Scale is used if the H and W settings are different from the original movie size. *Default (Show All)* scales the movie using its original aspect ratio and may fill in the blanks using borders. *No borders* makes these borders invisible. *Exact fit* abandons the original aspect ratio to make the movie fit the dimensions. You can also set the H and W values to % instead of pixels to scale the Flash movie to the window size.

Autoplay causes the Flash movie to begin playing as soon as it loads. **Loop** makes the Flash movie loop as long as the page is in view.

Java Applets

Java is an object-oriented programming language based on C++ and developed by Sun Microsystems. The goal of Java is to be as cross-platform as possible. Currently, most Java applets (little applications) are run inline inside a Web browser, although standalone programs—and even operating systems—have been written for Java.

Java applets run on Netscape 2 or later for PCs and Power PCs, Netscape 2.2 or later for the Mac, and Internet Explorer 3 or later.

To insert a Java applet:

1. In the Document window, click to place the insertion point at the place on the page where you want the Java applet to appear.
2. From the Document window menu bar, select Insert > Applet.

   or

   Click on the Insert Applet button on the Objects palette.

   Either way, the Insert Applet dialog box will appear (**Figure 15**).
3. In the Java Class Source text box, type the pathname of the Java applet.

   or

   Click on Browse and use the Select File dialog box to locate the applet on your computer (**Figure 16**). When you locate the source file, click on Open.
4. When the pathname of the applet appears in the Java Class Source text box, click OK. The dialog box closes and a placeholder appears in the window.

✔ Tip

- Some applets run on your computer; others must be on a Web server, depending on how many additional classes they require to run.

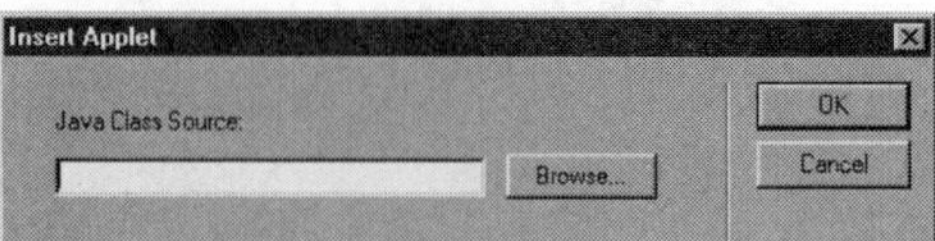

Figure 15 Type the source for the Java class file (the applet) in the Java Class Source text box.

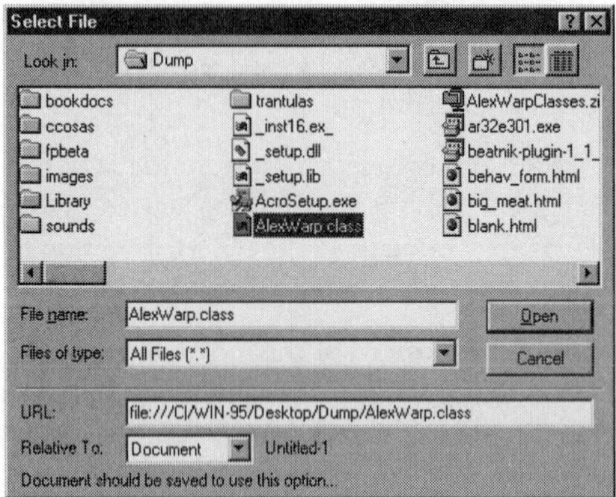

Figure 16 Select the class file from your computer. The file will probably have the .class extension.

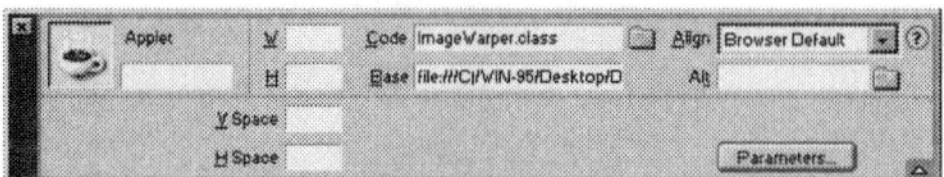

Figure 17 The Properties inspector, displaying Applet properties

After you insert the placeholder, you can set additional properties for the Applet.

To set Applet properties:

1. Select the Plug-in Placeholder in the Document window. The Properties inspector will display Applet properties (**Figure 17**).
2. Change any properties in the Properties inspector, and click on the Apply button.
3. To set extra parameters, click on the Parameters button. (See the section called *Extra Parameters*, later in this chapter.)

Applet Properties

Properties you can set for Java Applets include the following:

Name the applet by typing a name for it in the text box.

Set dimensions for the applet by typing the **W**(idth) and **H**(eight) in the associated text boxes.

Change the Source by typing it in the **Code** text box. Click on the Folder icon to browse for the .class file on your computer. When you set the source for an applet, the **Base** text box is automatically filled in. This indicates the home directory for the applet.

Set the **alignment** of the applet on the page by selecting an alignment from the Align drop-down menu. These alignment options are the same as for images. (I discuss image alignment in Chapter 5.)

V space and **H space** denote an amount of space around the plug-in. (I discuss these options further in regard to images in Chapter 5.) The units for these options are in pixels. Type a number (without units) in the appropriate text box.

To provide an **alternate image** for browsers without Java capabilities, type the Image source in the Alt text box. Click on the Folder icon to browse for the image on your computer.

ActiveX

ActiveX is a proprietary language written by Microsoft for use in Internet Explorer 3 or later. An ActiveX control can act like a plug-in and invisibly play multimedia content, or it can act like Java or JavaScript and serve as a miniature program that runs inside the Internet Explorer Web browser.

There is a plug-in for Netscape 4 that plays some ActiveX controls, but support is not built into the program and the plug-in should not be counted on to work. Dreamweaver tries to be as cross-platform as possible about this; you can insert an ActiveX Control and specify the Netscape plug-in equivalent, and Dreamweaver will write code for both programs simultaneously.

To insert an ActiveX control:

1. In the Document window, click to place the insertion point at the place on the page where you want the ActiveX control to appear.
2. From the Document window menu bar, select Insert > ActiveX.

   or

   Click on the Insert ActiveX button on the Objects palette.
3. Either way, an ActiveX placeholder will appear in the Document window at the insertion point.

✔ Tips

- You can use JavaScript to have the browser go to one URL if the browser is ActiveX capable and to a different URL if it's not. See the section in Chapter 12 called *Check Plugin*, and use the ActiveX checkbox.
- Macromedia recommends that you refer to the documentation for the ActiveX control to determine the requisite IDs and parameters needed.

ActiveX Properties

Properties you can set for ActiveX controls include the following:

Name the control by typing a name for it in the text box.

Set dimensions for the control by typing the **W**(idth) and **H**(eight) in the associated text boxes.

Set the **Class ID** for the control by selecting it from the drop-down menu or typing it in the Class ID text box. (See Step 3 in the section called *To set ActiveX properties* for information about Shockwave and ActiveX.) If you change your mind about the selected ID, select the text and press Delete. Clicking on the Minus button will permanently remove the ID from the list of options.

If the class is not on the list, type the URL from which Explorer can download the ActiveX control in the **Base** text box.

To set up the Netscape equivalent of the control using the `<embed>` tag, place a checkmark in the **Embed** checkbox. Once you've selected this option, the **Src** (source) text box will become available. Type the URL for the plug-in file source in the Src text box.

Data sets the source for a data file used by some ActiveX controls.

ID sets the ActiveX ID parameter. This optional number can be used to pass information from control to control; it can also be used for security purposes.

Set the **alignment** of the control on the page by selecting an alignment from the Align drop-down menu. These alignment options are the same as for images. (I discuss image alignment in Chapter 5.)

To provide an alternate image for browsers without ActiveX capabilities, type the Image source in the Alt text box. Click on the Folder icon to browse for the image on your computer.

V space and **H space** denote an amount of space around the plug-in. **Border** describes a visible border around the plug-in. (I discuss these options further in regard to images in Chapter 5.) The units for these options are in pixels. Type a number without units in the appropriate text box.

After you set up the placeholder, you can set additional properties for the ActiveX control.

To set ActiveX properties:

1. Select the ActiveX placeholder in the Document window. The Properties inspector will display ActiveX properties (**Figure 18**).
2. Change any properties in the Properties inspector, and click on the Apply button.
3. Control IDs for RealPlayer, Shockwave, and Shockwave Flash are pre-installed. If you select Shockwave or Shockwave Flash, the placeholder will change from ActiveX to Shockwave, since Dreamweaver automatically writes ActiveX code for those programs.
4. To set extra parameters, click on the Parameters button. (See the section called *Extra Parameters*, later in this chapter.)

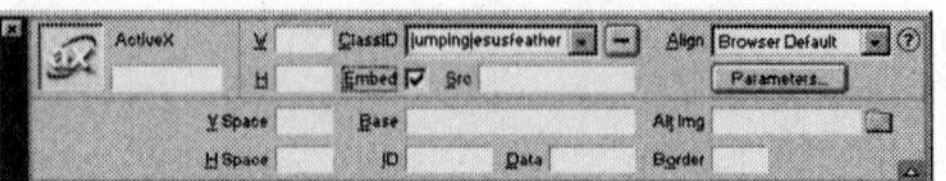

Figure 18 The Properties inspector, displaying ActiveX properties.

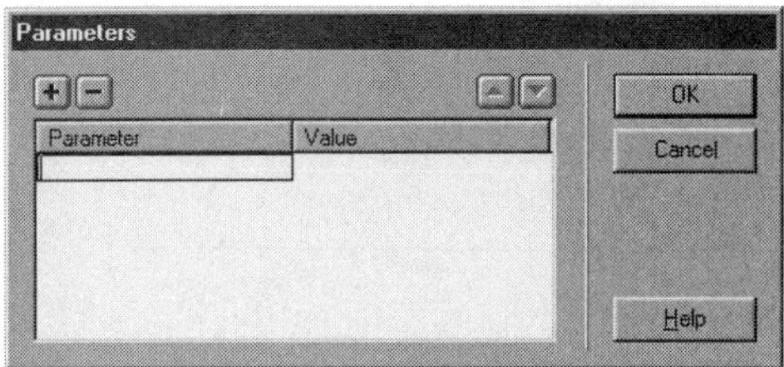

Figure 19 Add any extra attributes for your multimedia files in the parameters dialog box.

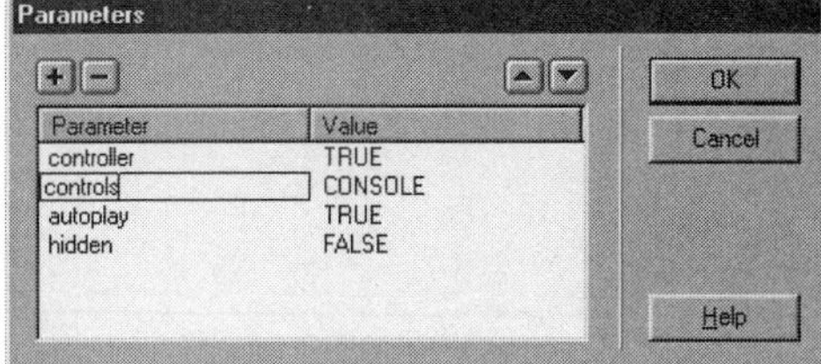

Figure 20 These are the parameters for an embedded sound file. I find it more expedient to type the parameters in the HTML inspector and then proof them in the Parameters dialog box.

Extra Parameters

Some multimedia objects require other parameters for optimal performance. These parameters may be indicated in the documentation for the language or program you're using. Of course, if it's an applet or object you wrote yourself, you'll know all about it already. (See the sections on sound for details about embedded sound parameters.)

To set additional object parameters:

1. In the Document window, select the placeholder for the object. The Properties inspector will display the object's properties.
2. On the Properties inspector, click on the Parameters button. The Parameters dialog box will appear (**Figure 19**).
3. Click on the Plus button. The Parameter text field will become available.
4. Type the name of the parameter in the Parameter text field (such as **loop**).
5. Press the Tab key. The Value text field will become available.
6. Type the value of the parameter in the Value text field (such as **TRUE**).
7. Repeat steps 3–6 for any additional parameters.
8. When you're all set, click on OK to close the dialog box and return to the Document window.

Figure 20 shows the Parameters dialog box displaying parameters for an embedded sound file.

To remove a parameter:

1. Follow steps 1 and 2 in the preceding list to open the Parameters dialog box.
2. Click on the name of the parameter you want to delete.
3. Click on the Minus button. The parameter will be deleted.

✔ Tip

- You can change the operation order of parameters by clicking on the name of the parameter in question and clicking on the up or down arrow buttons to move the parameter through the list.

16

Managing Your Web Sites

Sometimes half the battle of creating a Web site is figuring out where all the files are. If they're scattered all over your hard drive, you need to locate them, check all the relative links, upload the files, and then check all the relative links again.

Dreamweaver's file management tools don't preclude having to check your links, but they do make things easier to administer.

Dreamweaver's Sites window is a full-fledged FTP client that lets you upload and download files, move stuff from directory to directory, and view files in the Document window or in a browser with a click or two.

In the Sites window, you designate a directory on your computer or local network as a local site. This folder becomes the site root folder, and Dreamweaver uses its location to code site-root relative links.

Once you create a local site, you can connect to a remote server—the place where your Web site will be live. As you move files back and forth from place to place, Dreamweaver makes sure that the directory structure of the two versions of the site mirror one another. Dreamweaver doesn't make automatic updates, and if you delete or add a file in one location, it doesn't change the counterpart automatically. But it is nice to have an FTP client and an HTML editor so closely linked.

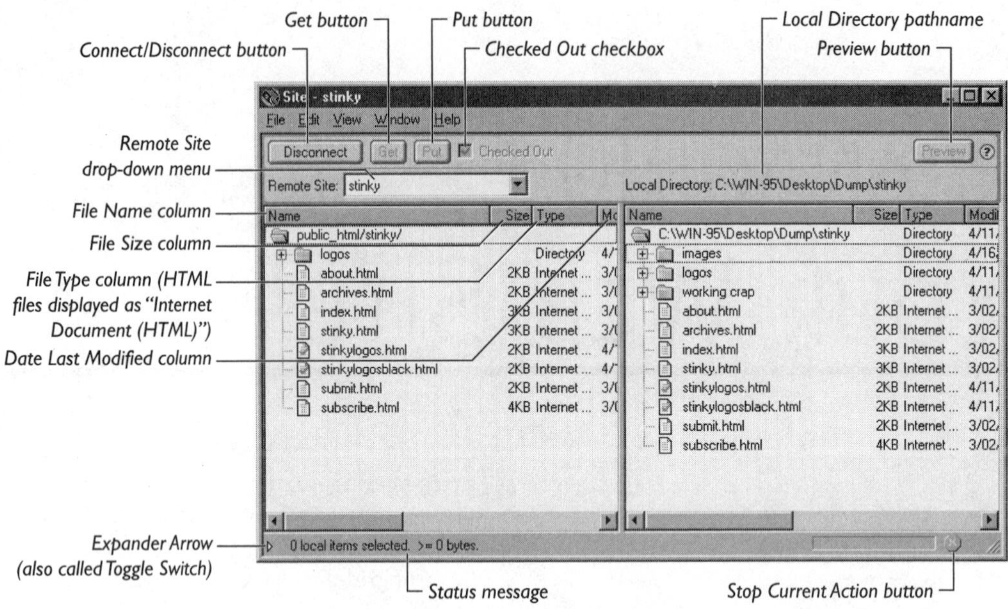

Figure 1 The Sites window is a combination file management tool and FTP client.

The Sites Window

Managing files in local and remote sites takes place in the Sites window (**Figure 1**).

To view the Sites window:

1. From the Document window menu bar, select Window > Sites.

   or

   Press F5.

Either way, the Sites window will appear (**Figure 1**).

When you first view the Sites window, it will be empty. Before you can begin working with a local site, you must set up a site on your computer.

✔ Tips

- All the column headings are also buttons; click on any one of them to sort the directory contents by that criteria.
- You can drag the borders between the column buttons to make the column wider or thinner.

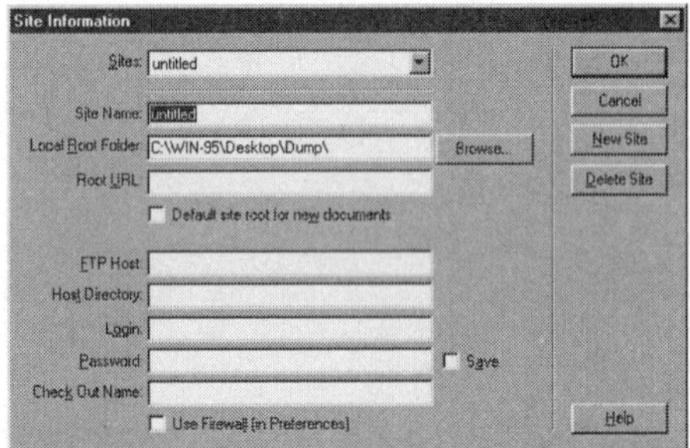

Figure 2 Set up local sites and connection information for their remote equivalents in the Site Information dialog box.

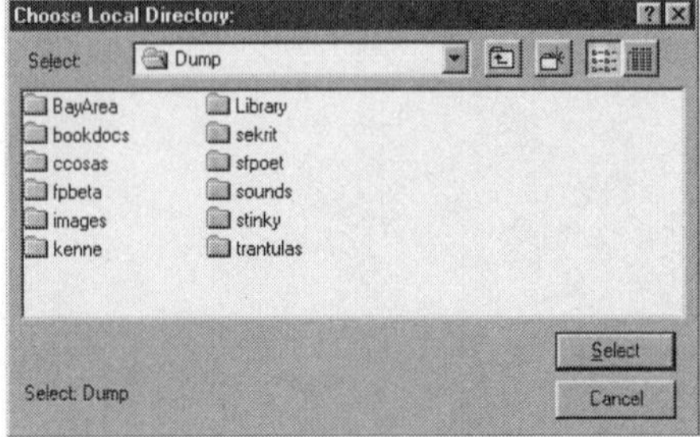

Figure 3 Use the Choose Local Directory dialog box to select a folder to designate as the site root for your new local site.

It's All Relative

You've probably noticed by now that Dreamweaver is picky about coding relative paths. When you insert an image or a link to a local file on a page in Dreamweaver, a dialog box appears notifying you that the link will use a file:/// path until you save the site. At the point at which you save the site, Dreamweaver converts these file:/// paths into relative paths.

When you create a local site in Dreamweaver, it codes site-root relative paths based on the directory structure of the local sites. Take this example: your local site root is C:\HTML. The current page is in C:\HTML\Bubba, and your images folder for the project is C:\HTML\Images\Current. When you save the page, Dreamweaver will make a site-root relative link like this one:

```
<img src="../images/current/bubba.gif">
```

Using local sites in Dreamweaver is easier than hand-coding site-root relative links. I designate each project folder on my computer as a separate local site. Then, when I upload it to the Web server, everything is intact.

You can choose to have Dreamweaver update all relative links when you perform a Save As. You set this option in the Preferences. Press Ctrl+U (Command+U) to view the Preferences dialog box, and click on General to bring that panel to the front. Select the *Correct Relative Links on Save As* checkbox, and then click on OK to close the Preferences dialog box.

Setting Up a Local Site

You can base a local site on the contents of an existing Web site (one that's already online), or you can set up a local site before any version of it exists online.

Before you do either, you need to designate a local site root directory.

To designate a new local site root:

1. From the Sites window menu bar, select File > Open Site > Edit Sites

   or

   From the Remote Site drop-down menu, select Edit Sites.

   Either way, the Site Information dialog box will appear (**Figure 2**).

2. If necessary, click on New Site to create a new, untitled site in the Site Information dialog box.

3. Type the pathname of the local site root folder in the Site Root Folder text box

   or

   Click on Browse to open the Choose Local Directory dialog box (**Figure 3**).

4. You can select an existing folder or create a new one;
   - To select an existing folder, click on its icon, click on Open, and then click on Select to close the Choose Local Directory dialog box and return to the Site Information window.
   - To create a new folder, click on the New Folder button and type a name for the new folder. Then double click on its icon to select it and return to the Site Information window.

5. Type a name for the site in the Site Name text box.

6. You can close the Site information dialog box (Click on OK), or leave it open to set up Remote Site information.

Remote site information (**Figure 4**) allows you to connect to an existing Web site. Skip this part if you haven't set up a local site yet.

To set up remote site information:

1. With the Site Information dialog box open,

   Create a new local site, as described in the preceding section

   or

   Select an existing local site by choosing its name in the Site Information dialog box.

2. In the FTP host text box, type the alphanumeric address for the Web server (e.g., ftp.site.com or www.site.com).

3. In the Host Directory text box, type the name of the initial root directory for the site (e.g., public_html or html/public/personal).

4. In the Login text box, type the user name for the ftp or www account.

5. In the Password text box, type the password for the ftp or www account.

6. To save the username and password, place a checkmark in the Save checkbox.

7. To specify a checkout name, type it in the Check Out Name text box (see the section called *Checking In and Checking Out*, later in this chapter, to find out what this does).

8. When both the local and remote site information are filled out, click on OK to close the Site information dialog box. You'll return to the Site window, where you'll see your local site displayed.

A new local site may or may not have any documents in it when you create it. You can create a local site based on an existing folder that's chock full of docs, or you can create a blank folder and download part or all of an existing site into it.

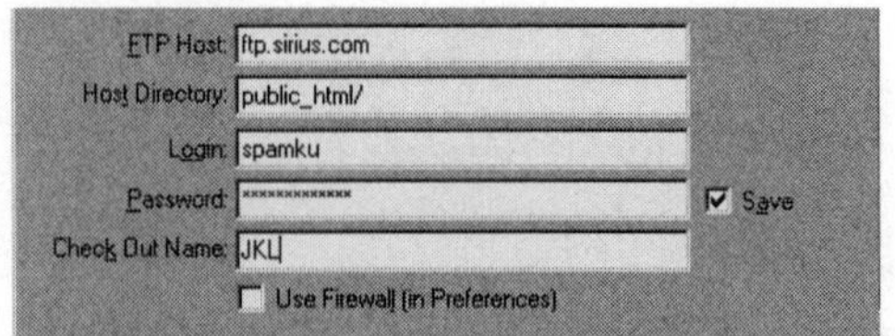

Figure 4 The remote site information area of the Site Information dialog box.

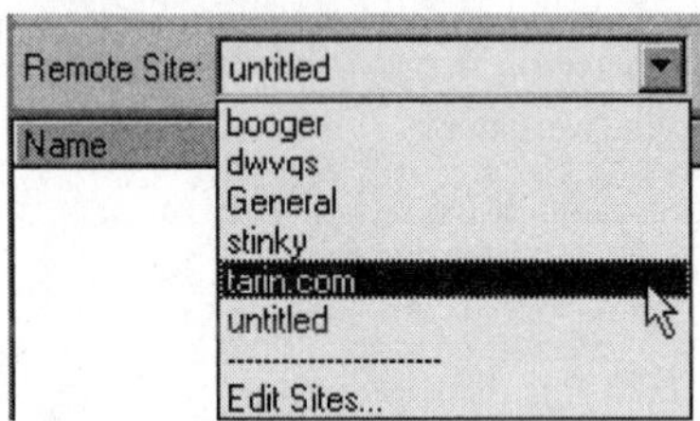

Figure 5 I have several different local sites set up for different projects in progress.

✔ Tips

- You can create as many local sites as you want. I have different local sites for different parts of my main remote site (**Figure 5**).
- To designate a particular local site as the default site root folder for new files, place a checkmark in the *Default site root folder for new documents* checkbox. Only one site can be designated as such.

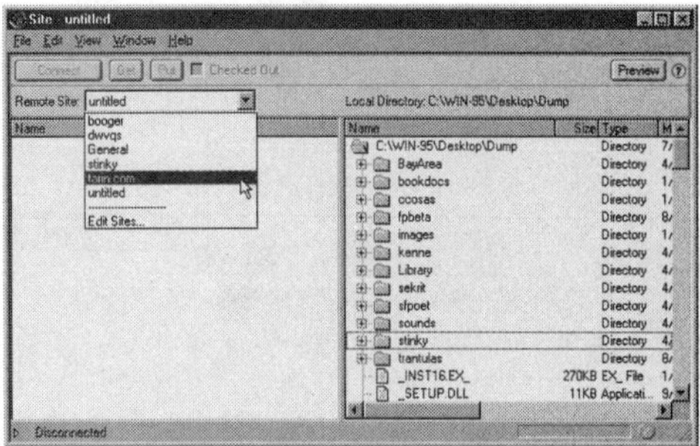

Figure 6 Choose the site you want to connect to from the Remote Site drop-down menu.

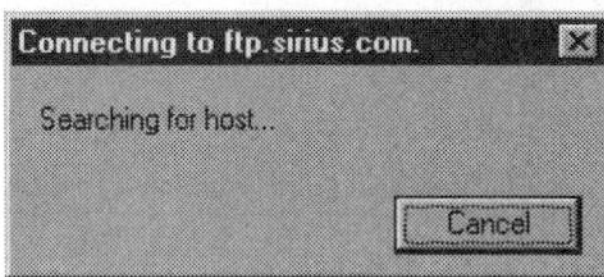

Figure 7 A series of dialog boxes will briefly appear while Dreamweaver connects to the remote site.

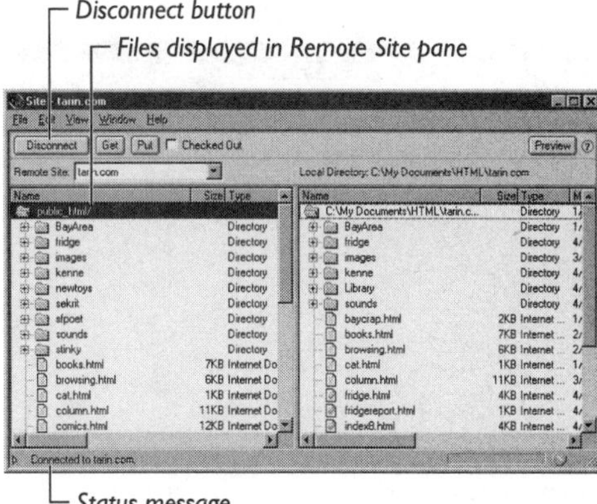

Figure 8 You'll know you're connected when Dreamweaver says so. The status message will say "Connected to [site name]" and the Connect button will be a Disconnect button. Oh, yeah, and the files will be displayed in the Remote Site pane of the Sites window. (They do stay in view after you've disconnected, however.)

✔ Tip

- If you don't move a file for a period of 30 minutes, Dreamweaver will disconnect for you. To change this, see the section called *Site FTP Preferences*, later in this chapter.

Connecting to a Remote Site

Before you can download an existing remote site or upload to it, you need to connect to it.

To connect to a remote site:

1. Set up a remote site profile, as described in the preceding section.
2. In the Sites window, select the site you want to connect to from the Remote Site drop-down menu (**Figure 6**).
3. Click on Connect. Dreamweaver will use the FTP Host, User Name, and Password information you gave it to connect to the remote Web server.
4. A Connecting to [host name] dialog box will appear while Dreamweaver contacts the Web server (**Figure 7**).
5. When you've successfully connected to the remote server, the words "Connected to [site name]" will appear in the status bar of the Sites window, and the Connect button will change to a Disconnect button (**Figure 8**).

After you've finished getting and putting files, you can disconnect from the remote site.

To disconnect from a remote site:

1. In the Sites window, make sure there aren't any files being transferred by checking in the status bar. If the window is idle, the status line should read "Connected to [site name].
2. Click on Disconnect. The status line will read "Disconnected" and the Disconnect button will again read Connect.

Editing and Deleting Local Sites

You can edit a local site if the information changes, or delete a local site that you're no longer using.

To edit a local site:

1. From either the Document or the Sites window menu bar, select File > Open Sites > Edit Sites (**Figure 9**)

   or

   In the Sites window, select Edit Sites from the Remote Site drop-down menu.

   Either way, the Site Information dialog box will appear.

2. In the dialog box, select the name of the site you want to edit from the Sites drop-down menu (**Figure 10**). The dialog box will display the information about that site.

3. Make any necessary changes to the information in the dialog box.

4. When you're done, click on OK to return to the Sites window.

To delete a site:

1. Follow Steps 1 and 2, above, to display the Site Information for the site you want to delete.

2. Click on Delete Site.

Dreamweaver will remove the site from the listing of local sites in the Sites window, but it will not delete any files or folders on any remote or local site.

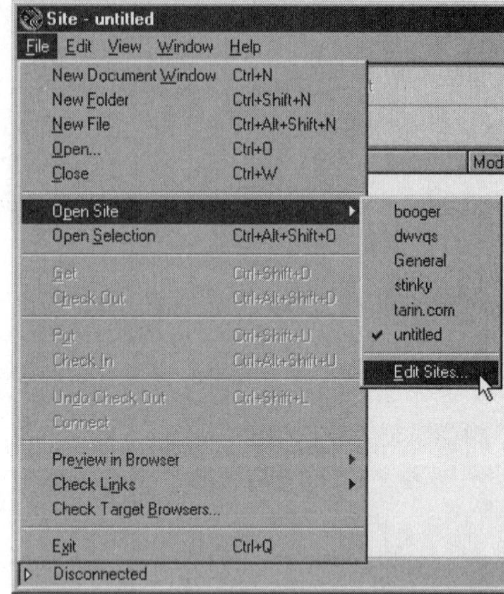

Figure 9 Select File > Open Site > Edit Sites from the Sites window menu bar.

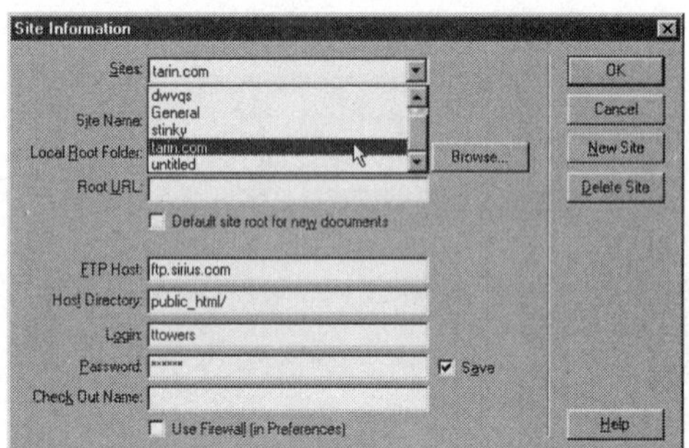

Figure 10 Select the name of the site to edit from the Sites drop-down menu.

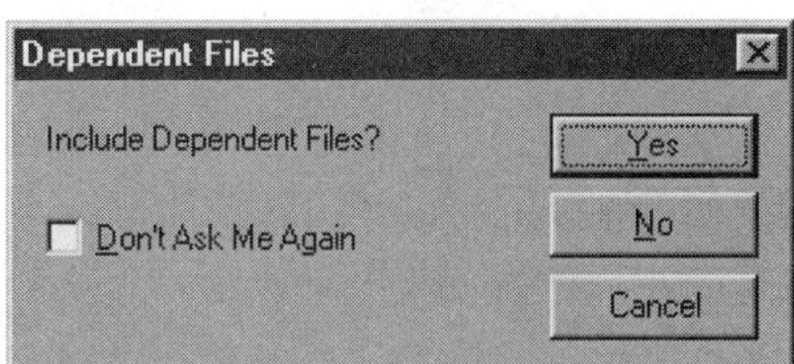

Figure 11 The dependent files dialog box can automatically get or put images or other files attached to the page.

Getting and Putting

Now you're ready to download (Get) and upload (Put) stuff to and from your local and remote sites.

To download files from a remote site:

1. Connect to the remote site as described in the preceding section.
2. In the Sites window, select the file(s) or folder(s) you want to download.
3. Click on Get. The Dependent Files dialog box will appear (**Figure 11**). Click on Yes or No (see *About Dependent Files*, next page).
4. The progress of the download will appear in the status bar of the Sites window while the files are being retrieved.

If the files are in a directory on the remote site that doesn't yet exist on the local site, the directory will be created on the local site.

Selecting Newer Files

If you want to retrieve a whole bunch of files from a remote site, or put up a lot of stuff from the local site, how can you be sure you're not overwriting more recent files?

Dreamweaver can automatically select a batch of newer files in a directory or entire site.

1. Select the proper local site and connect to the associated remote site.
2. From the Sites window menu bar, select View > Select Newer Local or View > Select Newer Remote, depending on in which pane you want the newest files to be highlighted.

   or

   Right-click on a file in either the remote or local site and, from the pop-up menu that appears, choose Select Newer. This will compare the entire site.
3. Dreamweaver will retrieve the directory information from the remote site and compare the dates with the local files. You can watch the progress of this in the status bar.
4. When the comparison is complete, the files that are newer than the ones on the other site will be highlighted.

With these files selected, you can get or put the entire batch of newer documents.

To upload files to a remote site:

1. Connect to the remote site as described in the preceding section.
2. In the Sites window, select the file(s) or folder(s) you want to upload to the remote site.
3. Click on Put. The Dependent Files dialog box will appear (**Figure 11**). Click on Yes or No (see *About Dependent Files*, this page).
4. The progress of the upload will appear in the status bar of the Sites window while the files are being sent to the remote server.

If the files are in a directory on the local site that doesn't yet exist on the remote site, the directory will be created on the remote site.

✔ Tips

- A handy shortcut: right-click on a file and select Get or Put from the pop-up menu that appears.
- To stop the current transfer, click on the Stop Current Task button, or press Esc (Command+. (period) on the Mac).

About Dependent Files

When you get or put a file in the Sites window, the Dependent Files dialog box will appear, asking you if you want to include dependent files (**Figure 11**).

Dependent files include images, sound files, plug-ins, and other objects the page links to. Dependent files also include all the files in a frameset.

This feature can be really convenient; you can click on the frameset document and then click on Yes in the Dependent Files dialog box, and all the files and images in the frameset will be uploaded to the site.

On the other hand, if you do most of your dealing in single documents, you may find this feature annoying. Just place a check-mark in the Don't Ask Me Again checkbox and you won't see the dialog box again.

To set preferences for dependent files, see the section called *Site FTP Preferences*, at the end of this chapter.

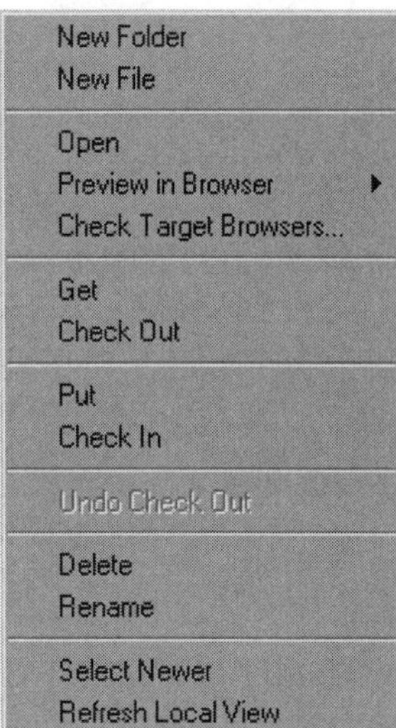

Figure 12 Lots of good shortcuts are available on this handy pop-up menu. Just right-click on a file or folder in the Sites menu. (Mac users with one mouse button: hold down the mouse button for a second or two until the menu appears.)

✔ Tip

- If the file is on the remote server when you open or preview it, a read-only version will be transferred to the local site.

Site Window Tips & Shortcuts

You can perform a lot of common Dreamweaver file tasks with a couple clicks.

To open a file (2 clicks):

1. In the Sites window, view the local or remote site the file resides in.
2. Double-click on it. The file will open in the Document window.

To preview a file (1 click):

1. In the Sites window, view the local or remote site the file resides in.
2. Right-click on the file. From the pop-up menu that appears (**Figure 12**), choose Preview in Browser > [Browser name].

   or

   Click on the Preview button

The file will open in the selected browser. (See Chapter 16.)

To perform a target browser check (1 click):

1. In the Sites window, view the local site the file resides in.
2. Right-click on the file. From the pop-up menu that appears (**Figure 12**), choose Check Target Browsers. The Check Target Browsers dialog box will appear. (See Appendix C on the Web site.)

To delete a file or folder (2 clicks):

1. In the Sites window, view the local or remote site the file or folder resides in.
2. Right-click on the file. From the pop-up menu that appears (**Figure 12**), choose Delete. A dialog box will appear to confirm your choice; click on OK to delete the file.

You can also use the Sites window like a file manager to move files around.

To create a new folder:

1. In the Sites window, click on the area where you want the new directory to appear.
2. From the Sites window menu bar, select File > New Folder. A new folder will appear in the local or remote site.

✔ Tip

- Folders on local and remote sites that contain files will be indicated by a + next to the folder. To display the contents of the folder, double-click on it (**Figure 13**).

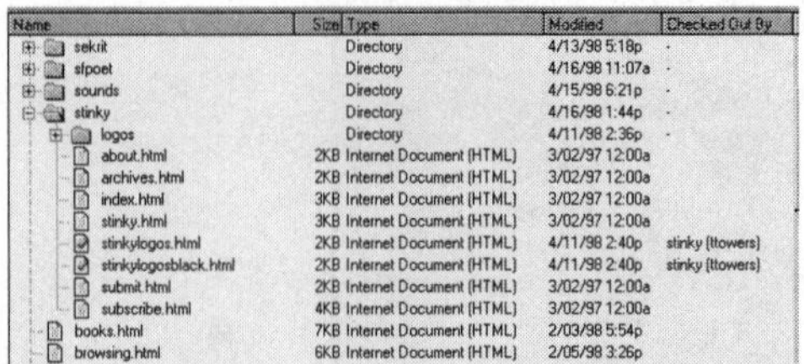

Figure 13 Folders with hidden contents have a plus sign to the left of them. Folders with their contents displayed have the files indented under them. To open or close a folder, double-click on it.

To move files from folder to folder:

1. View the file(s) you want to move, by displaying their directory information, if necessary.

   To select multiple files, hold down the Ctrl (Command) key while clicking. To select a contiguous batch of files, hold down the Shift key while clicking.
2. Click on the selected file(s) or folder(s), hold down the mouse button, and drag them to a new location.

✔ Tip

- If you drag a file or folder from a local directory to a remote directory (or vice versa), Dreamweaver will commence a Get or Put action automatically.

Figure 14 You can refresh the local or remote site directory info by using the View menu.

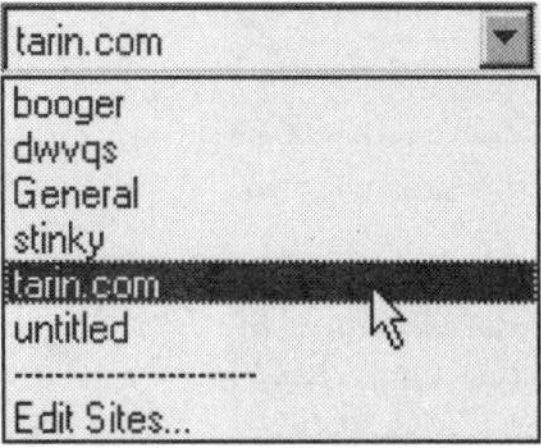

Figure 15 Select a site from the Remote Site drop-down menu.

If you move files around on your local site using a local file management program, or if you move them around on the remote site using a different FTP program, the Sites window might not accurately reflect what's where. You can refresh the view—just like reloading a page in a browser window.

To refresh the Sites window:

1. From the Sites window menu bar, select View > Refresh Local (Shift+F5) (**Figure 14**) or View > Refresh Remote (Alt+F5 (Option+F5)).

Dreamweaver will check the displayed directory info against the actual directory info and display the actual info.

When you're working with more than one local site, you'll want to toggle between sites. This is simple.

To toggle between local sites:

1. In the sites window, select the name of the site you want to display from the Remote Site drop-down menu (Figure 15).

The Sites window will display the information for the site you selected.

✔ Tip

- If you are connected to a remote site when you switch sites in the Sites window, Dreamweaver will automatically disconnect you from the remote site, even if the two local sites are on the same server. Just reconnect to establish contact with the server again.

There are three different site views you can use when working with the Sites window: Local, Remote, or Both. The default view is Both.

To change the Sites View:

1. From the Sites window menu bar, select View > Show Local; View > Show Remote; or View > Show Both.

The window will expand or contract into the view option you selected (**Figures 16** and **17**).

✔ Tips

- You can also expand or contract the window by clicking on the expander arrow in the lower left of the Sites Window (**Figure 17**).
- Drag the lower-right corner of the sites window to change the window size. Drag the frame border between the two window panes to adjust the space given to each.
- To hide floating windows that may cover the Sites window, press F4. Press F4 again to show only the windows open before.

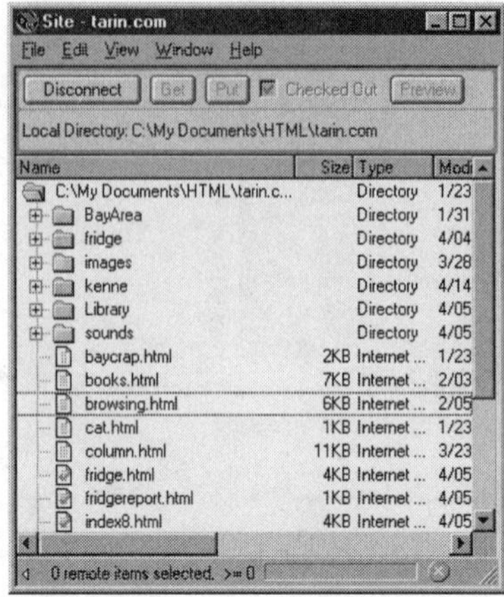

Figure 16 Local view in the Sites window.

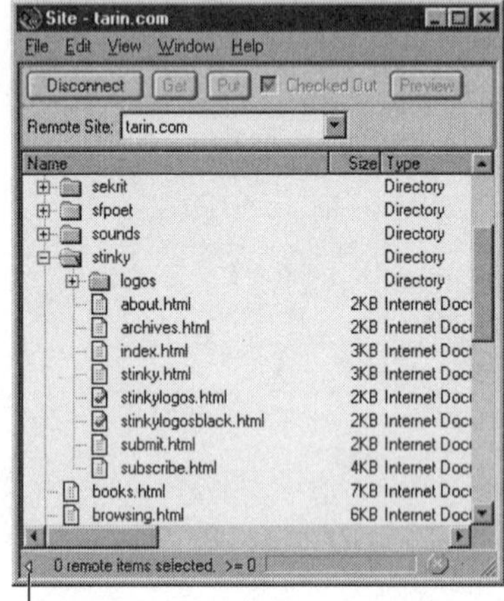

Figure 17 Remote view in the Sites window. Click on the expander arrow to expand the site; click on the same spot to contract it from "Both" view.

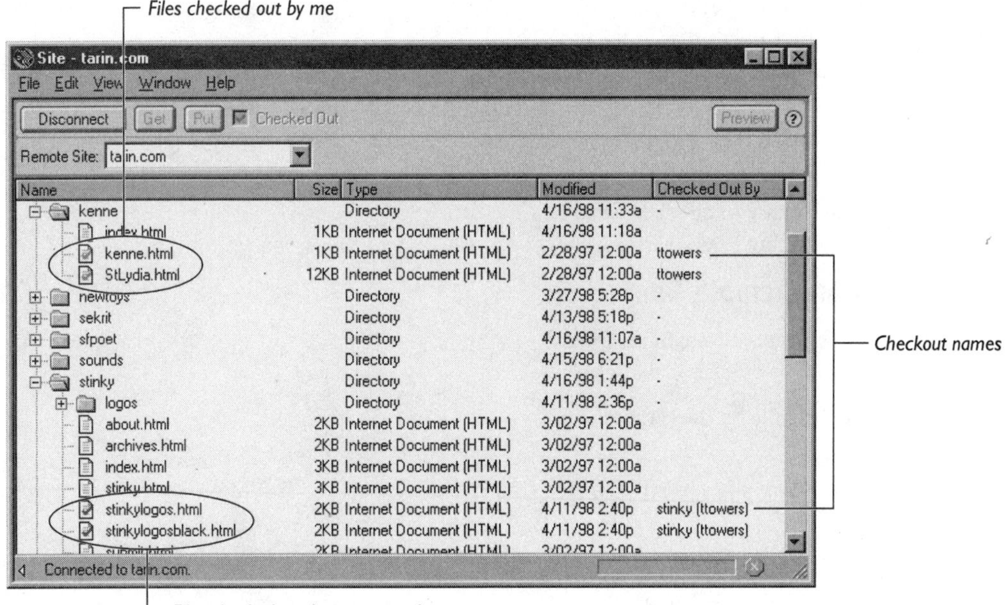

Figure 18: The circled files have been checked out; you can see the checkout names in the Checked Out By column.

Checking In and Checking Out

If several people are collaborating on a site, it might be helpful to know who put which file where, and when they did it. (If there's only one or two of you, you should already know the answer.)

Checking out a file marks the file with a green checkmark, assigns your username to that file, and locks it in the Dreamweaver Sites window. Other team members who use Dreamweaver will not be able to overwrite locked files (files checked out by another person). These files can be overwritten by any other FTP client, however.

Files other people have checked out are marked in the Sites window with a red checkmark and with the person's checkout name in the remote server pane (**Figure 18**).

Checking in a file unlocks it on the remote server, but makes it read-only on your local site, so that you don't accidentally edit a checked-in file.

Think of it like a library book: When you check out a book, no one else can read it until you return it. When you check it back in, anyone can access it but you.

To check out one remote file:

1. Connect to the appropriate site in the Sites window.
2. Double-click on the file on the remote server.
3. Respond to the Dependent Files dialog box.

The file will open in a Document window, and it will be copied to the local site.

You may have to refresh the local site view to see the file (or its folder, if that was freshly created, too).

About .LCK Files

When you check out a file using Dreamweaver, a lock is placed on the file that's only effective in the Dreamweaver Sites window. This lock is a text file with the .LCK extension. .LCK files are invisible in the Dreamweaver Sites window, but you can see them using a different FTP client (**Figure 19**).

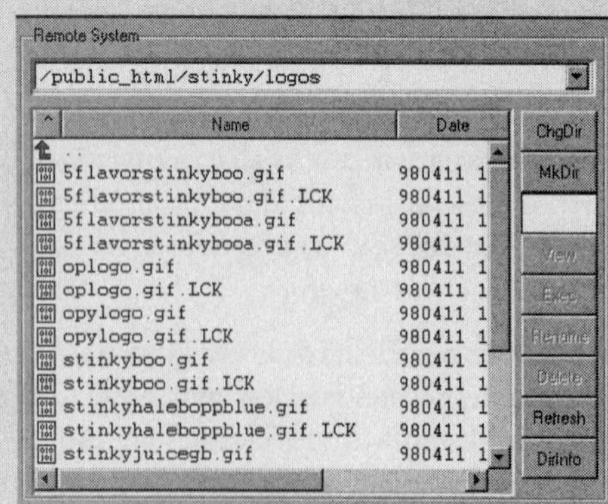

Figure 19: You can see the .LCK files if you examine the site with another FTP client (not Dreamweaver).

An .LCK file contains the username of the person who checked it out. Dreamweaver documentation says that this file also includes the date and time of the checkout, or a "message" that says someone else is working on the file, but none of the .LCK files I examined included information other than the checkout name.

You can see the date and time of a .LCK file in most FTP clients in the date and time column. The .LCK files I examined were only 7 bytes each (there are 1000 bytes in 1 Kilobyte), so they aren't going to make you run out of server space any time soon.

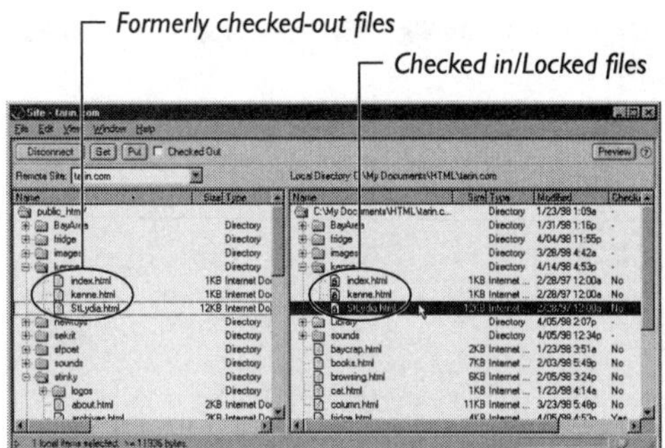

Figure 20 The formerly checked out files have the checkmarks removed, and the checked in files are locked.

✔ Tip

- When a file is checked out, a checkmark will appear in the Checked Out checkbox when the file is selected. You can automatically check out a file by selecting it and then clicking on this checkbox.

To check out more than one file:

1. Connect to the appropriate site in the Sites window.
2. Select the files or folders you want to check out in the remote site.
3. From the Document window menu bar, select File > Check Out (File > Sites Window > Check Out on the Mac).
4. Respond to the Dependent Files dialog box.

The files will be transferred to the local site, but they will not automatically open in the Document window. The files will get a green checkmark and a .LCK file on the remote server.

To undo a file checkout:

1. After checking out the files, select File > Undo Check Out (File > Sites Window > Undo Check Out) from the Sites window menu bar.
2. You may see a dialog box that warns you that you're about to replace the local file with the remote one. Click on Yes to continue or No to cancel.

To check in files:

1. Connect to the appropriate site in the Sites window.
2. Select the files or folders you want to check in in the local site.
3. From the Document window menu bar, select File > Check In (File > Sites Window > Check In on the Mac).
4. Respond to the Dependent Files dialog.

The file will appear with a locked icon on the local site. The Checked Out status and the .LCK file will be removed from the remote server (**Figure 20**).

Site FTP Preferences

You can change a variety of preferences for the Sites window, including the timeout limit, whether the dependent files dialog box shows up, and whether or not to use check in and check out.

To change Site FTP preferences:

1. From the Sites window menu bar, select Edit > Preferences. The Preferences dialog box will appear, with the Site FTP panel at the front (**Figure 21**).
2. The check in/check out functions are enabled by default. To disable this option, deselect the checkbox marked *Enable File Check In/Check Out*. Deselecting this option turns the next option off automatically.
3. When working with check in and check out, you may or may not want to *Check out files when opening* by default. Deselect this option to turn it off.
4. The Dependent Files dialog box (Figure 22) will appear whenever you get, put, check in, or check out a file. You can turn the dialog off by checking the Don't Ask Me Again box on the dialog box. To turn the dialog off, or to reinstate it, select or deselect the *Show Dependent Files*... check-boxes.
5. By default, Dreamweaver will disconnect after 30 minutes of idling. To change this number, type it in the *minutes* text box. To turn off automatic timeouts (for instance, if you have a direct connection to the Internet), deselect the *Disconnect After*... checkbox.
6. When you're satisfied, click on OK to save the changes to the preferences and close Preferences dialog box. You'll return to the Sites window.

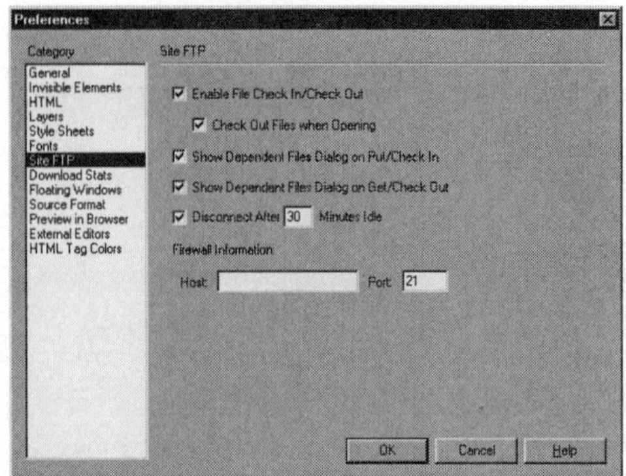

Figure 21: The Preferences dialog box, displaying Site FTP Preferences.

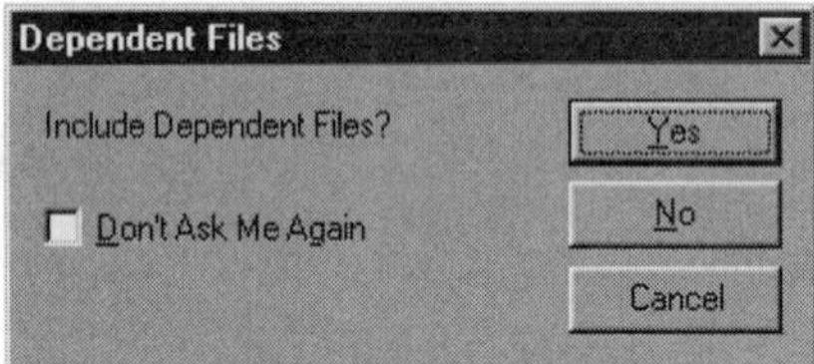

Figure 22: Our old pal the Dependent Files dialog box.

Burn, Burn, Burn—A Wall of Fire

A firewall is a piece of security software that sits on the server and prevents outsiders and people without privileges from so much as viewing the stuff on all or part of a server. If your server uses a firewall, you need to set up your Remote Site Information in Dreamweaver to get around it. You set this up in the Preferences for Dreamweaver. Press Ctrl+J to view the Preferences dialog box, and click on Site FTP to view that panel of the dialog box. Enter the hostname of the proxy server in the Host text box, and if the server uses an FTP port other than 21, enter that in the Port text box.

For any sites that use the proxy server, check off the Use Firewall checkbox in the Site Information dialog box.

Making a Mirror Site

A *mirror site* is a more-or-less exact copy of an existing site that resides on a different server. Mirror sites are used for three main reasons: testing; providing faster access to different physical locations; and spreading the pain of downloads around to more than one site.

For instance, big, popular sites like TUCOWS, WebMuseum, and the Internet Movie Database have mirror sites positioned around the world so that everyone who uses the site can have speedier access.

Setting up a mirror site is easy using the Sites window.

1. If you don't have a local copy of the original site, Site 1, create one. You can download an entire site by selecting everything in the remote site window and "Get"ting it into the local site folder.
2. Disconnect from the remote site.
3. Change the site information for the local site so that the Web server and username correspond to the Web server at Site 2.
4. Connect to Site 2.
5. Put the contents of the local site onto the Site 2 Web server.

Now you have three copies of the site: One local, one on Site 1, and one on Site 2.

INDEX

C

D

E

F

G

H

I

J

K

L

Q

R

S

T

U

V

W

Z